HOW TO GET A

JOB

IN

Chicago

Robert Sanborn and Susan Schwartz

The Insider's
Guide Series

SURREY BOOKS
CHICAGO

HOW TO GET A JOB IN CHICAGO

Published by Surrey Books, Inc., 230 E. Ohio St., Suite 120, Chicago, IL 60611.

This book is manufactured in the United States of America.

7th Edition. 1 2 3 4 5

Library of Congress Cataloging-in-Publication data:
Sanborn, Robert, 1959-
    How to get a job in Chicago—7th ed./ Robert Sanborn and Susan Schwartz.
        p. cm.
    Rev. ed. of: How to get a job in Chicago/Thomas M. Camden, Susan Schwartz. 6th
ed. c1995.
    Includes bibliographical references and index.
    ISBN 0-940625-99-7
    1. Job hunting—Illinois—Chicago—Directories. 2. Job vacancies—Illinois—
Chicago—Directories. 3. Business enterprises—Illinois—Chicago—Directories.
4. Vocational guidance—Illinois—Chicago—Directories. I. Schwartz, Susan.
II. Camden, Thomas M., 1938-1995. How to get a job in Chicago. III. Title.
HF5382.75.U62C43   1997   96-39377
650.14'09773'4—dc21   CIP

AVAILABLE TITLES IN THIS SERIES—$16.95
How To Get a Job in Atlanta
How To Get a Job in Chicago
How To Get a Job in The New York Metropolitan Area
How To Get a Job in The San Francisco Bay Area
How To Get a Job in Seattle/Portland
How To Get a Job in Southern California

Single copies may be ordered directly from the publisher. Send check or money order for book price plus $4.00 for first book and $1.50 for each additional book to cover insurance, shipping, and handling to Surrey Books at the above address. For quantity discounts, please contact the publisher.

Editorial production by Bookcrafters, Inc., Chicago.
Cover and book design by Joan Sommers Design, Chicago.
Illustrations by Mona Daly.
Typesetting by On Track Graphics, Inc., Chicago.
"How To Get a Job Series" is distributed to the trade by Publishers Group West.

Acknowledgments

Robert Sanborn wishes to thank his personal support system: Ellen Sanborn and Virginia Elisabet, wife and daughter respectively. Susan Schwartz would like to acknowledge the contributions of Northwestern University Career Services Director William J. Banis, Managing Editor Gene DeRoin, researchers Lauren Mistretta and Kim Lila, and typesetter Sheila Donohue of On Track.

We also wish to acknowledge the seminal contributions of Thomas M. Camden, Editor Emeritus.

NAMES AND ADDRESSES CAN CHANGE

The authors and editors have made every effort to supply you with the most useful, up-to-date information available to help you find the job you want. Each name, address, and phone number has been verified by our staff of fact checkers. But offices move and people change jobs, so we urge you to check before you write or visit. And if you think we should include information on companies, organizations, or people that we've missed, please let us know.

The publisher, authors, and editors make no guarantee that the employers listed in this book have jobs available

DROP US A LINE

Among the new features in this edition are "Dear Dr. Bob" letters—short notes from job seekers or workers like yourself, recounting their experiences. For this feature to be a success, we need your input. So if you have any interesting stories to share with your fellow job hunters, write to us in care of Surrey Books. We cannot guarantee publication, and letters will not be returned. Send your letters to:

Dear Dr. Bob, Job Hunting Stories
c/o Surrey Books
230 E. Ohio St., Suite 120
Chicago, IL 60611

JOB HUNTING?

These books, covering 6 major markets, can help you achieve a successful career

HOW... to get the job you want: Each book gives you more than 1,500 major employers, numbers to call, and people to contact.

WHERE... to get the job you want: How to research the local job market and meet the people who hire.

PLUS... how to use the World Wide Web, local networks and professional organizations; how to choose a career; advice on employment services; how to sell yourself in the interview; writing power resumes and cover letters; hundreds of names and numbers, many available nowhere else!

Contents

So You Want To Get a Job in Chicago

You've decided to get a job in one of the great cities of the world. Chicago is a vibrant metropolitan area with a dynamic, broad, and deep economy that offers countless possibilities for the focused job seeker. In fact, the Chicago job market is so large and diversified that you may not know how to make sense of it. This book will help you get started and give you vital information to help you find the job you're looking for.

How This Book Can Help

There are, of course, other books about finding jobs and about aspects of the job search such as resume writing and interviewing. This book is a little different. We have taken an approach that will make your Chicago job search easier and, hopefully, successful.

How is this book any different from the rest? First, we are local. This book focuses on the Chicago area. We have inside information on the job market and things unique to the job search in the city, suburbs, and adjacent areas. Second, this book combines job-search information from the World Wide Web with conventional information on how to conduct a job search. Once you have access to the Internet, you will see how your search for a career can be made easier with a wealth of information at your fingertips. Finally, this Insider's Guide is coauthored by an expert on the local job market and a national career guru; the information you'll get is cutting edge and proven effective. This book is designed to help you find *and land* the best job for you.

1

Before You Arrive

Preparation is a key to any job search, and this is especially true if you are relocating from another city to the Chicago area. If you're from out of town, you'll want to learn as much about the area as possible. This will help ease the transition to your new home and allow you to concentrate on your job search. This chapter will give you a head start on learning about the region and its job market.

Much of this chapter is devoted to surveying the vast array of media sources that can help you gain a better knowledge of the area. But for some readers, the first step in the job search might be to figure out their best career options. In other words, you might need to revisit the old "what do I want to do when I grow up?" question. Choosing a career direction early on will help you focus on which industries to target. Chapter 2 will help you get that part of your search behind you.

The Chicago Area Job Search

As unique as the area is, it is no different from any other place in the world when it comes down to finding a job. It takes work and perseverance. Chapter 4 outlines the ten steps toward seeking and securing a job. From networking to interviewing, all steps in the process are important. Chapter 5 highlights one of the most important and proven activities of the search for a career: networking. Chapter 6 will help you get your resume in shape, and Chapter 7 gets you ready to give that prospective employer the "killer" interview. Chapter 8 will help if you are looking for a summer or temporary job. And Chapter 10 is our exclusive listing of major employers in the Chicago area, complete with addresses, phone numbers, and brief descriptions where available.

Going to a new city to look for a job is much different from being a tourist. You'll face not only the challenges of getting to know a new place but you'll face the task of carving a niche for yourself as well. Getting a head start on researching the city and employers will make your search much easier.

Using Local Newspapers

Learning more about Chicago and all it has to offer should be one of the more interesting and enjoyable parts of your preparation. There are a number of local publications that can help you learn more about the city and, of course, provide insight into the local job market.

Local newspapers are an excellent place to begin. As you start your job search, it is important to read the want ads for more than job vacancies. The classified ads can give you an idea of who the key employers are in your field and which ones are growing.

MAJOR NEWSPAPERS IN THE CHICAGO AREA

Chicago Tribune
435 N. Michigan Ave.
Chicago, IL 60611
(800) TRIBUNE
http://www.chicago.tribune.com/
AOL: Tribune
The *Tribune* is a highly respected source of business information and publishes a business section in its daily and Sunday papers. The Sunday paper includes a huge classified ad section with opportunities for entry-level to experienced professionals in a wide range of fields. The *Tribune's* Web site provides an index on news, business, sports, and entertainment. Most importantly for job seekers, the *Chicago Tribune's* extensive employment listings can be searched with its easy-to-use database browser on-line. The *Tribune's* Web site also includes information on top employers, job fairs, and articles on employment. In addition, the *Tribune's* Web site has a real estate section that is very useful for those looking for housing.

Each year, the *Tribune* publishes special sections that cover business, education, etc. Be sure to review the *Tribune's* annual review of "Chicago's Top 100 Companies," usually published each June.

Chicago Sun-Times
401 N. Wabash Ave.
Chicago, IL 60611
(800) 945-5000
http://www.suntimes.com/

Daily Herald
Paddock Publications Inc.
155 E. Algonquin Road
P.O. Box 280
Arlington Heights, IL 60006
(847) 566-0781

Pioneer Press Newspapers
3701 W. Lake Ave.
Glenview, IL 60023
(847) 486-9200
http://www.pioneerlocal.com/
Pioneer Press publishes 48 local community newspapers for the towns and villages surrounding Chicago. These community newspapers can be viewed on-line by accessing Pioneer Press's Web site at the above address. Although job vacancy listings in these publications generally are limited, the community newspapers can provide relocating job seekers with valuable lifestyle, networking, and real estate information.

Crain's Chicago Business
Crain Communications
740 N. Rush St.
Chicago, IL 60611-9791
(312) 649-5200; Fax (312) 649-7832
This weekly paper covers only business news about Chicago or national news as it affects the Chicago business community. Recruitment and classified ads are also included. *Crain's* is a "must read" to keep current with local business affairs.

　　Crain's Chicago Business annually publishes its "Top Business Lists" that rank a variety of categories. Its lists give job seekers an excellent view of the diversity of Chicago's economy and employment possibilities. *Crain's Chicago Business* is available on-line by contacting Chicago Online at (312) 222- 4256 or America Online at (800) 617-8989 for connecting software.

The Wall Street Journal
1 S. Wacker Drive, 21st floor
Chicago, IL 60606
(312) 750-4000
The *Journal* is the nation's leading newspaper for news about the business community. The paper also publishes yearly special reports on careers and small business. The *Journal* also publishes the *National Business Employment Weekly,* which includes the classified ad sections of the paper's four regional editions. The jobs here are generally targeted to mid- to upper-level senior managers. Editorials about the business community are also included as well as articles on the job-search process, resume writing, interviewing, networking, changing jobs, relocating, and entrepreneurial options.

SUBURBAN AND COMMUNITY PAPERS

There are many outstanding community newspapers in the Chicago area. All carry want ads and stories and items about local businesses and business people that will give you more input for your job search. For a complete list of all the community newspapers published in Chicago and suburbs, see *Illinois Media,* available at the Chicago Public Library's Business Information Center, 400 S. State St., 4th floor.

Chicago Citizen Group
412 E. 87th St.
Chicago, IL 60619
(773) 487-7700
Chain of weekly papers serving south suburban neighborhoods.

Chicago Suburban Times Newspaper
1000 Executive Way
Des Plaines, IL 60018
(847) 824-1111
Chain of papers serving north and northwest communities.

Chicago Tribune
DuPage Bureau
908 N. Elm St.
Hinsdale, IL 60521
(630) 850-2960
Publishes local section inserted into the *Chicago Tribune.*

Daily Herald
Paddock Publications
P.O. Box 280
Arlington Heights, IL 60006
(847) 870-3450
Daily paper, covering national news and northwest suburban news.

Daily Southtown Economist
5959 S. Harlem Ave.
Chicago, IL 60638
(773) 586-8800
Daily paper, covering national news
and south suburban news.

Extra Publications
3918 W. North Ave.
Chicago, IL 60647
(773) 252-3534
Large chain of weekly papers serving
North Side and South Side
neighborhoods.

Lakeland Publishers
P.O. Box 268, 30 S. Whitney St.
Grayslake, IL 60030
(847) 223-8161
Chain of papers serving far north
suburbs.

**Leader Newspapers and Post
Newspapers**
6010 W. Belmont Ave.

Chicago, IL 60634-5195
(773) 283-7900
Large chain of weekly papers, covering
city and suburban neighborhoods.

Lerner Newspapers
8135 River Drive
Morton Grove, IL 60053
(847) 966-5555
Large chain of weekly papers, covering
city neighborhoods and suburbs.

The News Sun
100 W. Madison Ave.
Waukegan, IL 60085
(847) 336-7000
The voice of far northern Illinois;
published daily.

Star Publications
1526 Otto Blvd.
Chicago Heights, IL 60411
(847) 755-6161
Chain of weekly papers, covering
south suburban neighborhoods.

Local Feature Magazines and Newspapers

The following periodicals do not necessarily cover business news but can be valuable sources of information about Chicago itself, information you need to be a
well-informed Chicagoan.

Chicago Life
P.O. Box 11311
Chicago, IL 60611-0311
Lifestyle magazine emphasizing fit-
ness, finance, real estate, trends, fash-
ion, health, and book reviews.

Chicago Magazine
414 N. Orleans, Suite 800
Chicago, IL 60610
(312) 222-8999
Goings-on about town, restaurants,
lectures and seminars, theater, sports,
movies, intriguing articles about the
city's neighborhoods and people,
occasional business exposes, and a
quarterly listing of social and service

organizations, arts, community,
career, political, and other special-
interest groups.

Chicago Weekend Newspaper
Citizen Corp.
412 E. 87th St.
Chicago, IL 60619
(773) 487-7700
Weekly; local features, news, sports.

Inside Chicago
2501 W. Peterson Ave.
Chicago, IL 60659
(773) 784-0800
Covers business, trends, local news,
fashion, and lifestyle.

Key—This Week In Chicago
904 W. Blackhawk St.
Chicago, IL 60622
(312) 943-0838
Another free weekly, listing local happenings; also distributed through hotels.

New City
711 S. Dearborn St., #807
Chicago, IL 60605
(312) 663-4685

Nightlines Weekly
3059 N. Southport
Chicago, IL 60657
(773) 871-7610
Chicago area calendar and entertainment guide for the gay/lesbian community.

North Shore Magazine
874 Green Bay Road
Winnetka, IL 60093
(847) 441-7892
Monthly guide to business, events, and activities of interest to those living in the North Shore suburbs (and to those who aspire to live there).

Outlines
3059 N. Southport
Chicago, IL 60657
(773) 871-7610
Monthly news magazine; local, national, and international news.

The Reader
11 E. Illinois St.
Chicago, IL 60611
(773) 828-0350
This formerly "underground" urban newspaper can be spotted even in the hands of middle-aged suburbanites these days. For the city's most complete entertainment listings, apartments to rent, interesting classifieds, and frequently innovative reporting, pick up this free tabloid on Thursday afternoon at record stores and selected downtown and neighborhood locations. To locate your nearest distributor, call the Reader office.

Today's Chicago Woman
233 E. Ontario St.
Chicago, IL 60611
(312) 951-7600
Monthly magazine of features and events for Chicago women.

Where Magazine
1165 N. Clark St., Suite 302
Chicago, IL 60610
(312) 642-1896
Distributed through hotel lobbies, this weekly provides theater, restaurant, entertainment, and trade show listings of value not only to conventioneers but to the savvy job hunter as well.

The Big Picture: Business Magazines and Newspapers

The general business climate affects the local job market, no matter what career field you are in. You should keep abreast of changing trends in the economy, both regional and national. The following publications can help.

Business Week
1221 Avenue of the Americas
New York, NY 10020
(212) 997-1221

Published weekly, this magazine will keep you informed as to key happenings in the business world. Special issues include: Industry Outlook (24 key industries; January), Corporate Scoreboard (ranks companies in selected industries; March), Hot Growth Companies/Best Small Companies (May), and Best Business Schools (October).

Forbes
60 5th Ave.
New York, NY 10011
(212) 620-2200
Publishes 26 issues/year. Special issues include: The Annual Report on American Industry (January), Top 500 U.S. Companies (April), International 500 (July), 800 Top U.S. Corporate Executives (personal and compensation information; May), 200 Best Small U.S. Companies (November), and 400 Largest Private Companies in the U.S. (December).

Fortune
Time-Life Building
1271 Avenue of the Americas
New York, NY 10020-1301
(212) 586-1212
http://www.uophx.edu/lrc2.html#Business
Publishes 27 issues/year. Special issues include: 18-Month Economic Forecast (January and July), America's Most Admired Corporations (February), U.S. Business Hall of Fame (profiles selected business leaders; March), Fortune 500: Largest U.S. Industrial Corporations (April), Service 500 (June), Global 500: U.S. and Foreign Corporations (July), Fastest Growing 100 Public Companies (October), Pacific Rim Survey (October), and Best Cities for Business (November). *Fortune*'s various lists and key articles are available on-line at the above Web address.

Inc.
38 Commercial Wharf
Boston, MA 02110
(617) 248-8000
Published monthly. Special issues include: Best Cities for Starting a Business (April), 100 Fastest Growing Public Companies (May), and 500 Fastest Growing Private Companies (October).

Investor's Business Daily
19 W. 44th St.
New York, NY 10036
(212) 626-7676
National daily paper focusing on marketplace trends with intensive coverage of business and technology. Features include career management and effective job strategies. The "Leaders and Success" column profiles successful people and their keys to achievement.

Money
Time-Life Building
1271 Avenue of the Americas
New York, NY 10020-1301
(212) 522-1212
Published monthly. Annual September issue (Best Places to Live) is especially insightful for those thinking of relocating.

Working Woman
342 Madison Ave.
New York, NY 10173-0008
(212) 309-9800
This monthly publication is a great resource for professional women. Special issues include: Salary Survey (January), Top 50 Women in Business (May), Top 25 Careers for Women (July), and Ten Women to Watch (November).

The Internet

The last time this publication was produced, the World Wide Web was just getting started. Since then, the Web has exploded as a phenomenon and as a vital information research resource. One of the key features of this book is the inclusion of numerous World Wide Web (WWW) addresses to help you learn about the local area and jump-start your job search. If you have never used cyberspace or the WWW, don't worry. In most cases it's as simple as point and click. Surfing the Internet is an excellent way to stay up-to-date on career opportunities and techniques. The Internet provides access to volumes of information and numerous contacts, all without leaving your desk.

To get started you'll need a computer, modem, and software to give you Internet access. You'll probably find it most convenient to have your own computer, but if you don't, fear not. Friends, universities, libraries, public schools, and cybercafes can provide you access to the Internet so you can join the millions now "on-line."

The "information superhighway" is really a worldwide link-up of computers and computer networks. All WWW addresses start with the letters http:// Following this will usually be a long string of characters—often words or abbreviations—with no spaces in between. When you type that "address" into the Web browser on your computer (Netscape, Mosaic, or something similar), you will be linked with the organization listed.

There are many articles and books about the Web and how to access it. We will let you explore those on your own. However, we would like to give you an idea of the type of information the Web addresses provide. For example, there are places to get career counseling, learn about careers, post your resume, find information on companies, and view the types of positions they have open. You should note the cost of each Internet-access service (America Online, Prodigy, or others) and other charges before signing up for any service. In addition, there are career services on the Net that will offer you some free service with hopes that you will buy others. Keep in mind that many of the best sites and homepages are free.

Let's get you started with some WWW addresses that can provide information about Chicago, its attractions and institutions, lifestyle, potential employers, and the local job search. When you access any Web site, you can save its address on your computer by creating a "bookmark" with your Web browser. Bookmarks are saved in a file so you don't have to rekey addresses every time you want to visit a site. It is a good idea to create bookmarks when you find a useful site just in case you forget to write down a site address.

Cybertip
If you don't know the Web address of an organization, type http://www.name-of-organization.com. For example, if you wanted to access Motorola's homepage but don't have their address, typing http://www.motorola.com will connect you.

CYBERINFO ABOUT THE CHICAGO AREA

Chicago's Internet community is very active. Job seekers have many on-line resources available to help them learn about Chicago and to research employment possibilities. Many sites have links to each other so you can "cyber loop" around the city! Remember to create bookmarks as you go along.

If you need access to the Internet in the Chicago area, visit these two sites.

Chicago Area Internet Providers
http://www.mcs.com/~wsmith/providers.html
Contact and service information for connecting with the Internet.

NetChicago
http://www.ais.net/netchicago/resources.html
A guide to Chicago Internet resources.

Here are our recommended sites to get you started exploring Chicago.

Chicago Mosaic
http://www.ci.chi.il.us/
Chicago's official Web site is a good place to begin your community research.

Citynet Guide to Chicago
http://www.city.net/countries/united_states/illinois/chicago/
Contains wide-ranging information about Chicago, including businesses, gov-

ernment, area attractions, city guides, education, events, lodging, entertainment, museums, media, restaurant, sports, transportation, and tourism. A great site to get a feel for the city as well as to research career possibilities.

WorksMart Directory of City Services
http://www.ci.chi.il.us/worksmart/
Provides both alphabetical and categorical listings of Chicago city departments, including finance and administration, city development, community services (including employment and training), public safety, regulatory agencies, and public infrastructure. This is a key resource for anyone interested in public service and municipal government.

Chicago Public Library Site
http://cpl.lib.uic.edu/cpl.html
A robust site, full of information about Chicago's history and its public libraries. Facts about the city, frequently requested telephone numbers, and the Chicago Public Library Catalog are listed. Links are provided to the State of Illinois, colleges and universities, public schools, apartment guides, hotels, events, and resources. For new Internet users, there is even information about the Internet. This site is worth browsing.

Metroscope
http://isotropic.com/metro/chicago.html
A very rich site with information/links to cultural attractions, businesses, colleges, media, financial institutions, professional services, and much more. Another must-see site!

Chicago!
http://tezcat.com/web/chicago.html
Provides general information about the city, entertainment, music, art, religion, libraries, politics, museums, and universities.

Chicago Information System
http://reagan.eecs.uic.edu/
Covers demographics and statistics on population, income, housing, and other social indicators. It also links to government, education, tourism, and event sites.

Centerstage Chicago
http://centerstage.net/chicago/
Gives extensive coverage to restaurants, music, clubs, and record stores.

State of Illinois Site
http://www.state.il.us/
Covers state agencies (including employment services), educational institutions, tourism, libraries, museums, legislative information, and the capitol complex.

Illinois Department of Employment Security
http://il.jobsearch.org/
Allows users to search for jobs on-line and to locate regional employment

offices. The serious job seeker should use this site regularly to make sure that job opportunities are not missed.

You are probably starting to get the idea of what these sites have to offer. Here are a few more sites providing general information about the Chicago area. Many more are interspersed throughout this book.

Illinois Library and Information Network (ILLINET)
http://www.library.sos.state.il.us/

North Suburban Library System (NSLS)
http://www.nsls/us.org

Cook County Clerk's Office
http://www.cookctyclerk.com/
Directory of elected city and county officials.

Chicago NewCity
http://suba.com:80/~newcity/
News and arts weekly.

Blues in Chicago
http://nightscape.com/chicago/blues/
Information about blues clubs and performers.

Chicago Sports
http://cpl.lib.uic.edu/004chicago/chisports.html

Online A to Z Chicago
http://a2z.com/
Information on Chicago neighborhoods and real estate.

Here's another option. You can gain access to the Internet through the local coffee house. A list of cybercafes can be found on the World Wide Web at: http://www.easynet.co.uk/pages/cafe/ccafe.html.

Chicago's cybercafe scene is changing fast. Check the above Web site for the latest listings. If you're in the neighborhood, you might want to visit **The Interactive Bean** on Belmont Ave. or **Screenz** on Clark St.

Other Chicago Internet resources include these:

Chicago Online Apartment Guide
http://www.tezcat.com/~ermiller/shelters.html

Chicago Transit Authority
http://transitchicago.com/
Fairs, schedules, and maps for getting around the city; useful for interviews.

Chicago Metra Schedule
http://www.metrarail.com/
Information for commuting in and out of the city for interviews.

Chicago Area Bookstores
http://nuinfo.nwu.edu/ev-chi/bookstores/index/html

CYBERRESOURCES FOR YOUR JOB SEARCH

Try a few of these sites on the World Wide Web to get an overview of the job search and how the Internet might help. Many of these sites will give you a multitude of other links to continue honing your job-hunt skills.

http://www.cs.purdue.edu/homes/swlodin/jobs.html
Provides a comprehensive list of major job sites including:

United States Dept. of Labor
http://www.dol.gov/
The latest jobs news and issues.

America's Employers
http://americasemployers.com/
A good site for managers and professionals to explore employment opportunities, career information, and corporate information.

America's Help Wanted
http://helpwanted.com/

America's Job Bank
http://www.ajb.dni.us
An increasingly large collection of actual jobs posted at state Job Service offices nationwide. Over 100,000 jobs were available in a recent week.

Business Job Finder (Ohio State University College of Business)
http://www.cob.ohio-state.edu/dept/fin/osujobs.htm
A well-organized and comprehensive collection of accounting, finance, and consulting career resources on the Internet.

Career Action Center
http://www.GATENET.com/cac/
A good page with links to other career-related resources.

The Career Channel
http://riceinfo.rice.edu:80/projects/careers/
A lot of links to other career sites, as well as material on all aspects of careers and the job search, from Rice University's Career Center.

Career Catapult
http://www.jobweb.org
An excellent page, with links to almost all other good career-related Internet resources, run by the National Association of Colleges and Employers.

Career Magazine
http://www.careermag.com/careermag/
Internet links and career information.

Career Mosaic
http://www.careermosaic.com/cm/
Includes information on hot companies, new products and technology, benefits and employee programs, and sites and lifestyles around the world.

CareerNet (Career Resource Center)
http://www.careers.org
Thousands of job, employer, and career-reference Web links. Also maintains a growing database, including employers, professional associations, government jobs, educational resources, career counselors, self-employment resources, career events, and more.

Career Path
http://www.careerpath.com
Chicago Tribune (and five other major dailies) classifieds, but no display ads.

Employment Opportunities and Job Resources (Margaret Riley)
http://www.wpi.edu/~mfriley/jobguide.html
One of the most highly respected collections of career resource links, with extensive advice on using the Internet's resources in the career-search process.

Interactive Employment Network
http://www.espan.com
Provides current resources for the job seeker, salary guides, advice from career specialists, and job listings (mostly in technical fields).

Job Center
http://www.jobcenter.com/home.html

JobHunt (Dane Spearing at Stanford University)
http://rescomp.stanford.edu/jobs.html
A well-organized list of major Internet career-resource links.

Job Listings Available via Dial-Up on BBSs (Harold Lemon)
http://rescomp.stanford.edu/jobs-bbs.html
A very large list of BBS systems nationwide, available by "dial-up" modem with no Internet connection.

Job Web
http://www.jobweb.com
Run by the National Association of Colleges and Employers. Contains advice and information for recent college graduates.

Monster Board, The
http://www.monster.com/home.html
Visit this site and you'll understand its name!

NationJob Online
http://www.nationjob.com/

Online Career Center
http://www.occ.com
A highly respected Internet jobs resource. OCC is a nonprofit employer association, providing a database, job and resume files, company information and profiles, and on-line search software for both employers and applicants.

Rensselaer Polytechnic Institute (Career Resource Homepage)
http://www.rpi.edu/dept/cdc
An excellent collection of career resource links maintained by the R.P.I. Career Development Center.

This address will link you to Web sites of Fortune 500 companies:
http://www.cs.utexas.edu/users/paris/corporate.real.html

Here are two special resources that can be used in support of your job search:

The BigBook
http://www.bigbook.com/
Contains 11 million businesses in its database. Your search can bring up a company, its address, telephone number, business category, and a map to find it. A great site to help you get to your interview!

The Switchboard
http://switchboard.com
A database of 90 million names, addresses, and telephone numbers compiled from White Page directories from across the U.S.

RECOMMENDED BOOKS FOR THE ON-LINE JOB SEARCH

Gonyea, James C. *The On-line Job Search Companion.* McGraw-Hill, New York, NY, 1994. A complete guide to hundreds of career-planning and job-hunting resources available via your computer.

Hahn, Harley, and Rick Stout. *The Internet Yellow Pages.* Osborne McGraw-Hill, Berkeley, CA, 1994. Provides listing of where to search for ads or post your resume.

Kennedy, Joyce Lain, and Thomas J. Morrow. *Electronic Resume Revolution.* John Wiley & Sons, New York, NY, 1994. Provides resume information and resources via the Internet.

Kennedy, Joyce Lain. *Hook Up, Get Hired!* John Wiley & Sons, New York, NY, 1995. Provides job-search information via the Internet.

Rittner, Don. *The Whole Earth On-line Almanac: Info from A to Z.* Brady Publishing, New York, NY, 1993. Describes bulletin boards and on-line services along with phone numbers.

Using Chambers of Commerce

Most chambers of commerce publish material that is helpful to newcomers or anyone who wants to be better informed about a community, and the Chicagoland Chamber of Commerce is no exception. They provide brochures and maps available free or for a nominal charge and provide much of what you'll want to know about area businesses, city services, transportation, public schools, utilities, and entertainment. Additionally, they publish lists of professional organizations and other networking options within the area as well as directories and publications pertaining to Chicago.

The Chicagoland Chamber of Commerce
1 IBM Place, Suite 2800
Chicago, IL 60611
(312) 494-6700; Fax: (312) 494-0196
The Chamber produces a monthly newsletter, *Buyer's Guide and Membership Directory*, and a *Major Employers Guide*. Their relocation kit is well worth the investment; it gives the out-of-town job seeker a great overview of lifestyle and business information.

Other local chambers of commerce and their telephone numbers include these:
Greater North Michigan Ave. Association (312) 642-3570
Greater State Street Council (312) 782-9160
Oak Brook Association of Commerce and Industry (630) 572-0616
Chicago Southland Chamber of Commerce of Southern Suburbs (312) 957-6950
Lake County Economic Development Corp. (847) 360-6350

Employment Projections to 2005

The Chicago area economy and job market are microcosms of the national economy and job market. Local trends tend to mirror broader national trends. So, where are the jobs? What are the trends? We'll start with a national overview, then present information for the State of Illinois.

The U.S. Department of Labor (DOL) forecasts employment trends regularly and publishes many resources. We recommend that you use the *Occupational Outlook Handbook* to obtain specific information on occupations that interest you. It is updated every two years by DOL. Here are forecasts from the 1996-97 edition:

During the 1994-2005 period, employment nationally is expected to increase by 17.7 million, or 14%. Services and retail will account for 16.2 million of the new jobs. Business, health, and education will account for 70% of the growth, or 9.2 million of the 13.6 million service sector jobs. Health care will account for 20% of the total growth. Temporary agencies are expected to add 1.3 million jobs to the economy during this period. In sum, service-producing industries will account for most new jobs, while the goods-producing sector will decline. Manufacturing is expected to lose 1.3 million jobs nationally.

In addition to employment growth, replacement hiring will continue to increase as the workforce ages and as people leave jobs. Replacement hiring will account for 29.4 million job openings between 1994-2005. Between growth and replacement hiring, employment changes will vary widely by occupation. *Occupations having the largest numerical increase in employment nationally (from highest demand to lower demand) are these:*

cashiers
janitors
retail sales
hospitality workers (waiters,
   waitresses)
registered nurses
general managers and executives
systems analysts
home health aids
guards
nursing aids, orderlies, attendants
secondary teachers

marketing and sales supervisors
teachers aids and assistants
receptionists and information
   clerks
truck drivers
secretaries, except legal and
   medical
clerical supervisors and managers
child care workers
maintenance workers
elementary teachers

These occupations will account for half of all job growth during 1994-2005.

Occupations projected to grow the fastest nationally (in descending order) are:

personal, home care, and health
   care aids
systems analysts
computer engineers
physical therapy assistants
electronic systems workers
occupational therapy aids
physical therapists
residential counselors
human service workers

manicurists
medical assistants
paralegals
medical records technicians
special education teachers
recreation attendants
correction officers
operations research analysts
guards

The fastest growing occupations nationally will be concentrated in health care and computer technology and, generally, will require the most education and training.

The Illinois Department of Employment Security (IDES) also produces similar analyses and projections. Between 1992 to 2005, employment in Illinois is expected to grow 17.96% from 5,755,022 to 6,788,749. Average annual openings during this period are expected to be 211,160 positions. White collar occupational projections for Illinois are listed below.

Illinois Occupations	Percent Change (1992 to 2005)	Annual Openings
Administrators and managers (all)	20.34	21,526
Advertising and marketing managers	33.57	1,528
Clerical, office administration workers	9.55	29,099
Computer programmers	19.31	1,066
Computer science, math	62.60	3,102
Engineering technicians	13.97	1,663
Engineers, architects, surveyors	30.86	3,552
Financial managers	22.74	1,248
Food service, lodging managers	36.11	1,225
Food and beverage workers	30.47	21,588
Health diagnostic and treatment	26.28	7,365
Health technicians	26.17	3,515
Health service workers	40.26	3,421
Lawyers and judges	18.08	1,295
Management support	27.73	7,234
Marketing and sales	19.00	28,307
Protective services	27.99	5,810
Salespersons	19.07	8,016
Social and religious workers	27.09	2,023
Supervisors	20.20	3,011
Teachers, librarians, counselors	19.73	9,407
Writers, artists, and entertainers	16.43	2,587

Selected State of Illinois employment projections by industry between 1992 to 2005 are presented below.

Industry	Projected Change
All industries	18.63%
Communication and utilities	1.65%
Construction	27.93%
Finance/insurance/real estate	19.63%
Commodity and security brokers	34.57%
Insurance carriers	20.14%
Insurance agents and brokers	33.15%
Real estate	18.98%
Holdings and investments	29.94%
Manufacturing	4.09%
Durable goods	3.60%
Electric equipment	11.42%
Furniture	9.31%
Wood products	13.14%
Nondurable goods	4.77%
Printing and publishing	5.77%
Plastics and rubber	22.12%
Services	29.94%
Amusements and recreation	62.25%
Business services	50.53%
Education	16.23%
Health	28.29%
Hotels/lodging	27.10%
Legal	22.57%
Membership organizations	18.09%
Motion pictures	23.80%
Social services	58.59%
Government	8.39%
Federal	- 4.41%
State	11.74%
Local	10.38%
Trade	17.11%
Retail	7.30%
Building materials	27.58%
General merchandise	16.75%
Food stores	13.93%
Furniture	28.14%
Eating and drinking establishments	32.97%
Wholesale	20.94%
Transportation	20.15%

The Chicago area labor force comprises approximately 3.5 million workers employed by nearly 160,000 establishments. At the time this publication goes to press, the unemployment rates in the Chicago area are: 5.5% in Cook County; 3.4% in Du Page County; and 4.0% in Lake County.

As you review our lists of employers in Chapter 10, you will see that Chicago has great depth in finance and financial management businesses—commercial, investment and savings banks, brokers and traders, insurance and diversified holding companies. Health care and related businesses also abound in the region. Despite the national decline in manufacturing employment, Chicago's manufacturing base remains quite substantial and diversified.

However, Chicago's employment growth will mirror the national trends in technology and services. Chicago has some of the nation's leading high-technology firms, doing cutting edge work in a variety of areas. Likewise, business service firms are numerous and growing. The large and varied list of consulting firms and other professional service organizations that operate in Chicago is impressive.

But, if you're not into finance, health care, consulting, or high-tech, don't despair! Chicago also has great strength in hospitality, retail, transportation, education, and research, plus all the other employment sectors that enable a vibrant metro area to work—government services, law enforcement, construction, social services, and media.

Chicagoans do more than work! When it comes time to play, our arts, entertainment, cultural, and sports organizations give the people of Chicago lots of options, and may give you the career opportunity you seek. Whatever your career interests and skills, we believe that Chicago offers the job seeker countless possibilities for employment. Our hope is that this book provides you with a springboard to action and a stepping stone to success.

To help get your job search underway and to stimulate your thinking about employment possibilities, here's a list of the Chicago area's fastest growing firms, derived from local media reports and our own research. Be sure to check out the more extensive employer listings in Chapter 10.

Chicago's Fastest Growing Firms

Abbott Laboratories
1 Abbott Park Road
Abbott Park, IL 60064
(847) 937-6100
Diversified health care products and services.

Alberto-Culver Co.
2525 Armitage Ave.
Melrose Park, IL 60160
(708) 450-3000
Food and personal care products.

AMCOL International Corp. (formerly American Colloid Company)
1500 W. Shure
Arlington Heights, IL 60004
(847) 394-8730
Minerals, absorbent polymers, and environmental services.

Andrew Corp.
10500 W. 153rd St.
Orland Park, IL 60462
(708) 349-3300
Communications systems and equipment.

Aon Corp.
123 N. Wacker Drive
Chicago, IL 60606
(312) 701-3000
Insurance and consulting services.

Artra Group
500 Central Ave.
Northfield, IL 60093
(847) 441-6650
Packaging manufacturer.

Circuit Systems
2350 E. Lunt Ave.
Elk Grove Village, IL 60007
(847) 439-1999
Printed circuit boards.

Donnelley, R.R., & Sons Co.
77 W. Wacker Drive
Chicago, IL 60606
(312) 326-8000
Major print and digital media products, systems, and services.

Federal Signal Corp.
1451 W. 22nd St.
Oak Brook, IL 60521
(630) 954-2000
Safety, sign, tool, and vehicle products.

Fruit of the Loom
233 S. Wacker Drive, Suite 5000
Chicago, IL 60606
(312) 876-1724
Apparel company.

Gallagher, Arthur J., & Co.
2 Pierce Place
Itasca, IL 60143
(847) 773-3800
Insurance brokerage and risk management.

GATX Corp.
500 W. Monroe St.
Chicago, IL 60661
(312) 621-6200
Holding company in transportation and storage.

General Binding Corp.
1 GBC Plaza
Northbrook, IL 60062
(847) 272-3700
Business machines and supplies.

Grainger, W.W., Inc.
5500 W. Howard St.
Skokie, IL 60077
(847) 982-9000
Maintenance, repair, and operating supplies distributor.

HA-LO Industries
5980 Touhy Ave.
Niles, IL 60714
(847) 647-2300
Logoed trophies, caps, jackets, and other promotional products.

HealthCare Compare Corp.
3200 Highland Ave.
Downers Grove, IL 60515
(630) 241-7900
Health care utilization and cost management services.

Helene Curtis Industries
325 N. Wells St.
Chicago, IL 60610
(312) 661-0222
Cosmetics.

Household International
2700 Sanders Road
Prospect Heights, IL 60070
(847) 564-5000
Consumer finance and credit services.

Idex Corp.
630 Dundee Road, Suite 400
Northbrook, IL 60062
(847) 498-7070
Fluid handling and industrial
products.

Illinois Tool Works
3600 W. Lake Ave.
Glenview, IL 60025
(847) 724-7500
Manufacturer of engineered products
and systems.

Information Resources
150 N. Clinton St.
Chicago, IL 60661
(312) 726-1221
Consumer-packaging-goods consulting and software.

Intercargo Corp.
1450 American Lane, 20th floor
Schaumburg, IL 60173
(847) 517-2990
Insurance holding company.

Insurance Auto Auctions
1270 W. Northwest Highway
Palatine, IL 60067
(847) 705-9550
Buys and sells wrecked or stolen cars
from insurance companies.

Juno Lighting
2001 S. Mount Prospect Road
Des Plaines, IL 60017
(847) 827-9880
Lighting equipment.

Mercury Finance Co.
40 Skokie Blvd.
Northbrook, IL 60062

(847) 564-3720
Automobile financing for dealers.

Methode Electronics
7444 W. Wilson Ave.
Chicago, IL 60656
(312) 867-9600
Electrical control equipment.

MFRI
7720 Lehigh Ave.
Niles, IL 60714
(847) 966-1000
Industrial pollution control
equipment.

MicroEnergy
350 Randy Road
Carol Stream, IL 60188
(630) 653-5900

Middleby Corp.
1400 Toastmaster Road
Elgin, IL 60120
(847) 741-3300
Commercial food service equipment.

Molex Inc.
2222 Wellington Court
Lisle, IL 60532
(630) 969-4550
Extensive line of high-tech electronic
products.

Motorola Inc.
1303 E. Algonquin Road
Schaumburg, IL 60196
(847) 576-5000
Diversified high-tech electronics
and communications products
and systems.

MYR Group
2550 W. Golf Road, Suite 200
Rolling Meadows, IL 60008
(847) 290-1891
Power line, mechanical, and electrical
construction.

Oil-Dri Corp. of America
410 N. Michigan Ave.
Chicago, IL 60611
(312) 321-1515
Sorbent products.

Quixote Corp.
1 E. Wacker Drive
Chicago, IL 60601
(312) 467-6755
Highway crash cushions and CD-ROM manufacturing.

Safety-Kleen Corp.
777 Big Timber Road
Elgin, IL 60123
(847) 697-8460
Environmental recycling of fluids.

Schawk Inc.
1695 River Road
Des Plaines, IL 60018
(847) 827-9494
Prepress and filtration equipment.

Scotsman Industries
775 Corporate Woods Pkwy.
Vernon Hills, IL 60061
(847) 215-4500
Refrigeration technologies and products.

ServiceMaster L.P.
1 ServiceMaster Way
Downers Grove, IL 60515
(630) 964-1300
Diversified consumer and business services.

Spiegel Inc.
3500 Lacey Road
Downers Grove, IL 60515
(630) 986-8800
Apparel, furnishings, and merchandise distributor/marketer.

System Software Associates
500 W. Madison St.
Chicago, IL 60661
(312) 641-2900
Business information systems.

Telephone & Data Systems
30 N. LaSalle St.
Chicago, IL 60602
(312) 630-1900
Telecommunications company.

Tellabs Inc.
4951 Indiana Ave.
Lisle, IL 60532
(630) 969-8800
Voice, data, and network systems.

Tootsie Roll Industries
7401 S. Cicero Ave.
Chicago, IL 60629
(773) 838-3400
Candy manufacturer.

Trans Leasing International
3000 Dundee Road
Northbrook, IL 60062
(847) 272-1000
Leaser of medical and office equipment.

U.S. Cellular Corp.
8410 W. Bryn Mawr, Suite 700
Chicago, IL 60631
(773) 399-8900
Cellular telecommunications.

United Stationers
2200 E. Golf Road
Des Plaines, IL 60016
(847) 699-5000
Distributor of business products.

Varlen Corp.
55 Shuman Blvd.
Naperville, IL 60566
(630) 420-0400
Transformation and laboratory products.

Walgreen Co.
200 Wilmot Road
Deerfield, IL 60015
(847) 940-2500
Retail drug store chain.

WMX Technologies
3003 Butterfield Road
Oak Brook, IL 60521
(630) 572-8800
Environmental services.

Woodhead Industries
2150 E. Lake-Cook Road, Suite 400
Buffalo Grove, IL 60089
(847) 465-8300
Electrical power equipment.

Wrigley, Wm., Jr. Co.
401 N. Michigan Ave.
Chicago, IL 60611
(312) 644-2121
Producer of chewing gum.

Choosing a Career

Choosing a career or making a decision about which direction you wish to take in the world of jobs is certainly important, but it also can be one of the most difficult processes we go through in life. Ever since we learned to speak as two-year-olds, aunts, uncles, and other assorted adults have asked us, "What do you want to be when you grow up?" Now we ask ourselves that same question. So how do we choose that career, anyhow?

The first step in choosing a career is to learn who you are and what you want. In other words, start with self-assessment. We've outlined a few tools for you to use in assessing yourself and your abilities. It is important to remember that it is very difficult to get a job if you do not know what you want to do. Self-assessment will enable you to start with a goal in mind. After you figure out who you are, it is much easier to find a compatible career.

A Few Facts about Career Decision Making

According to a recent Gallup poll, most people don't have goals when starting to think about the job search. No real planning goes into what is arguably the most important decision of their lives. The poll shows that:

- 59% of us work in an area or career in which we never planned to work.
- 29% of us are influenced by another person to go into a career. It's like the advice given to Dustin Hoffman in *The Graduate*. Someone says, "Plastics—that's where you should be. Try working in plastics." So we consider plastics.
- 18% of us fall into jobs by chance. You're looking for a job in banking and someone mentions that they know of a job in consulting. Sure you're willing to look at it. Next thing you know, you're a consultant.
- 12% of us took the job because it was available. You're walking by the local GAP store and see a "management trainee" sign. You take it!

This same Gallup poll indicated that we fail to properly assess ourselves and our career options. If we had to do it over, the poll indicates, 65% of the American public would get additional information on career options early on. Other polls show that up to 80% of the working public is dissatisfied with one or more aspects of their career and have seriously considered changing.

All of these facts and figures certainly bode poorly for those who jump into a career haphazardly. And, conversely, the statistics bode well for those who delve into a little career exploration before taking the plunge. This is especially true in light of the fact that the average American emigrates through seven to ten jobs and three to four careers in a lifetime. Thus, we will probably need to assess ourselves more than once as our own life changes with the changing job market. Self-assessment is a tool we will use throughout our professional lives.

Strategies in Self-Exploration

Practically everyone wants a job that provides personal satisfaction, growth, good salary and benefits, a certain level of prestige, and a desirable location. But unless you have a more specific idea of the kind of work you want, you probably won't find it. You wouldn't take off on your big annual vacation without some kind of destination in mind. Given that your job will take up much more of your time than your vacation, a little planning is certainly in order.

There are several strategies that can help you learn who you are. Among them are talking with friends and family, self-assessing, and getting help from a career professional.

Friends and family sometimes know you better than you think. They can also provide great support throughout the job search. Try the self-assessment exercises in this chapter, then discuss your results with those who know you best. They may have some insight that you overlooked. However, it is important to follow your own desires and not the dreams of family and friends when choosing a career.

Everyone can benefit from a thorough self-appraisal. The insight gained from self-appraisal is valuable not only in deciding on a career but also in articulating this knowledge in the resume and interviewing process. Perhaps you want to be a little more scientific in your appraisal of yourself. Try career testing. Professionals in vocational planning have literally dozens of tests at their disposal designed to assess personality and aptitude for particular careers.

Getting Started with Self-Assessment

What follows is a list of highly personal questions designed to provide you with insights you may never have considered and to help you answer the Big Question, "What do I want to do?"

To get the most from this exercise, write out your answers. This will take some time, but it will force you to give each question careful thought. The more effort you put into this exercise, the better prepared you'll be for the tough questions you'll be asked in any job interview. The exercise also can be the basis for constructing a winning resume—a subject we'll discuss in more detail in Chapter 6.

QUESTIONS ABOUT ME

Here are some questions to get you started. The answers will indicate what kind of person you are. Be honest. Take as much time as necessary.

1. Describe yourself in less than 500 words. Address these questions: Do you prefer to spend time alone or with other people? How well disciplined are you? Are you quick-tempered? Easygoing? Do you prefer to give orders or take orders? Do you tend to take a conventional, practical approach to problems? Or are you imaginative and experimental? How sensitive are you to others?
2. What accomplishment are you most proud of?
3. What are the most important things you wish to accomplish?
4. What role does your job play in those achievements?
5. Why do you (or don't you) want your career to be the most important thing in your life?
6. What impact do you have on other people?
7. Describe the kind of person others think you are.
8. What role does money play in your standard of values?
9. What do you enjoy most/dislike most?
10. What do you want your life to be like in 5 years?
11. What are your main interests?

What Job Attributes Do You Value Most?

After answering the above questions, it is important to match the job attributes you value to your career. Job burnout usually happens when people are in jobs that don't allow them to do and get the activities and rewards they want. But job satisfaction will occur if a person follows his or her motivations into a career. The following ranking will assist you in beginning to match the job attributes you value with careers that are in step with them.

Rank the following in order of importance to you:

- Leadership
- Creativity
- High Salary
- Helping Others
- Job Security
- Competition
- Taking Risk
- Variety
- Physical Activity
- Self-development
- Recognition
- Working with My Mind
- Prestige
- Independence

Once you've ranked the above, you should begin to get an idea of what's important to you. Compare your priorities to those of the workplace in your potential career/job. Values of the workplace can be determined in several ways. One method is to interview current employees of the company. Another is to research the company through articles and publications to determine its values and beliefs.

QUESTIONS ABOUT MY JOBS

Questions about your jobs can also help in your self-assessment.

1. Describe *in detail* each job you have had. Begin with your most recent employment and work back toward graduation. Include your title, company name, responsibilities, salary, achievements and successes, failures, and reason for leaving. If you're a recent college graduate and have little or no career-related work experience, you may find it helpful to consider your collegiate experience, both curricular and extracurricular, as your work history for questions 1, 2, 3, 7, 8, 9, and 10.
2. What would you change in your past, if you could?
3. In your career thus far, what responsibilities have you enjoyed most? Least? Why?
4. How hard are you prepared to work?
5. What jobs would allow you to use your talents and interests?
6. What have your subordinates thought about you as a boss? As a person?
7. What have your superiors thought about you as an employee? As a person?
8. If you have been fired from any job, what was the reason?
9. Does your work make you happy? Should it?
10. What do you want to achieve by the time you retire?

Answering these questions will help clarify who you are, what you want, and what you realistically have to offer. They should also reveal what you don't want and what you can't do. It's important to evaluate any objective you're considering in light of your answers to these questions. If a prospective employer knew nothing about you except your answers to these questions, would he think your career objectives were realistic?

One way to match who you are with a specific career is to refer to the *Dictionary of Occupational Titles (DOT)*. The *DOT* is an encyclopedia of careers, covering hundreds of occupations and industries. For the computer buff, *The Perfect Career* by James Gonyea (3444 Dundee Rd., Northbrook, IL 60062) has a database of over 600 occupations for IBM and compatibles.

Professional Testing

As mentioned earlier, professionals in career counseling (see list below) have literally dozens of tests at their disposal designed to assess personality and aptitude for particular careers. Here are a few of the most commonly used career tests.

Strong Interest Inventory
This test looks at a person's interests to see if they parallel the interests of people already employed in specific occupations. It is used chiefly as an aid in making academic choices and career decisions. It continues to be one of the most researched and highly respected counseling tools in use.

Myers-Briggs Type Indicator
This test is based on Carl Jung's theory of perception and judgment and is a widely used measure of personality dispositions and preferences. Used in career counseling, it helps to identify compatible work settings, relate career opportunities and demands to preferences in perception and judgment, and gain insight into personality dimensions, all of which provide the opportunity for greater decision-making ability.

16 PF (Personality Factor) Questionnaire
This test measures 32 personality traits of a normal adult personality along 16 dimensions. Used frequently in counseling, the computerized printout and narrative report show how personality traits may fit into various career fields.

Career Counseling

Although the terms are often used synonymously, there is a difference between a career counselor and consultant. Most professionals use the title "counselor" if they have an advanced degree in psychology, counseling, social work, or marriage, family, and child counseling and are licensed by the state.

In Illinois, however, licensed counselors are required to possess only a bachelor's degree, while licensed clinical counselors must possess at least a master's degree. If you seek assistance, we recommend that you consult with career counselors who have earned at least a master's degree in counseling, are licensed clinical counselors or psychologists, if in private practice, and preferably are National Certified Career Counselors. Career counseling is a professional specialty requiring advanced graduate training. While many people can assist you in acquiring career and employment information, assessment and testing require professional qualifications and training.

Need a list of certified counselors?

The National Board for Certified Counselors provides a list of professional "certified career counselors" in local areas. Certification requires a master's degree in counseling, three years of supervised counseling experience, and successful passage of a National Board qualifying examination. For further information call (800) 398-5389 or send a self-addressed 55-cent return envelope to:

The National Board for Certified Counselors
599 Stevenson Ave.
Alexandria, VA 22304

Also check out the *Journal of Career Planning and Development,* which has articles on career counseling.

Professionals who are not licensed often call themselves "career consultants." This field attracts people from a variety of backgrounds, education, and levels of competency. It's important, then, to talk to others who have used a given service before committing yourself.

Because most career counseling and consulting firms are private, for-profit businesses with high overhead costs, they usually charge more for testing than local colleges or social service agencies, which are listed later in this chapter.

What can you expect from a career counselor? For one thing, counselors offer an objective viewpoint. One licensed professional career counselor puts it this way: "You may not be able to discuss everything with family, friends, and especially coworkers if you happen still to be working. A trained professional can serve as a sounding board and offer strategies and information that you can't get elsewhere. We can essentially help a person become more resourceful."

This particular career counselor usually spends four sessions with individuals who want to establish a sense of direction for their careers. Here's what sessions cover:

- Exploring problems that have blocked progress and considering solutions.
- Establishing career objectives and determining strengths and areas to work on.
- Writing a career plan that outlines a strategy to achieve goals.
- Preparing an ongoing, self-directed plan to explore career goals.

"A counselor should help people develop methods and a framework on which to base continual exploration about what they want from a career, even after they are employed," our counselor friend says. All too often people look for "quick fixes" in order to get back to work, she says. "In haste, they may not take time to reflect on where their career is going, to make sure they look for a job that will be challenging and satisfying."

CAREER COUNSELORS AND CONSULTANTS IN THE CHICAGO AREA

What follows are a few counselors and consultants who may be able to help you in your job search. Keep in mind, though, that a listing in this book does not constitute an endorsement of any consulting firm or testing service. Before embarking on a lengthy or expensive series of tests, try to get the opinion of one or more persons who have already used the service you're considering.

American Personnel Consultants
300 W. Washington St., Suite 601
Chicago, IL 60606
(312) 263-6463
Supplies comprehensive testing in 12- to 15-hour period. Ph.D. supplies a written report. Vocational analysis.

American Psychological Laboratories
300 W. Washington St.
Chicago, IL 60606
(312) 726-3570

Aptitude Consultants
180 W. Washington Blvd., Suite 1200
Chicago, IL 60602
(312) 332-7449
Two-day program; Ph.D. business psychologists administer battery of standardized tests; counseling.

Jack Arbit, Ph.D.
Testing and Career Counseling
233 E. Erie St.
Chicago, IL 60611
(312) 266-3411

Associated Certified Psychologists
625 N. Michigan Ave.
Chicago, IL 60611
(312) 266-0566

Ball Foundation/ Career Vision
800 Roosevelt Road, Suite 120, Building C
Glen Ellyn, IL 60137
(847) 469-6270
Interview with counselor; personality, interest, and aptitude assessment; standardized tests, career recommendations, follow-up sessions for one year. Fees for individual and group testing.

Career Directions
3701 Algonquin Road, Suite 700
Rolling Meadows, IL 60008
(847) 870-1290

Second Location:
25 E. Washington St., Suite 1500
Chicago, IL 60602
Vocational testing, workshops, seminars, individual counseling.

Career Express
151 E. Wacker Drive
Chicago, IL 60601
(312) 616-0500
Specializes in job search, practice interview sessions, resume writing, and a Job
Hunter Data Base. It also houses computer stations and over 400 books.

Career Strategies
1150 Willmette Ave.
Willmette, IL 60091
(847) 251-1661
Produces one of the best newsletters in the nation on employment trends and
job-search strategies.

Career Success Services
3166 S. River Road, Suite 27
Des Plaines, IL 60018
(847) 298-8383
Individualized consulting, career analysis, goal setting. Also resume writing,
interviewing skills, and time management techniques.

Challenger, Gray & Christmas
150 S. Wacker Drive
Chicago, IL 60606
(312) 332-5790
Large national firm specializing in outplacement.

Drake Beam Morin
1011 E. Touhy Ave.
Des Plaines, IL 60018
(847) 299-2286
One of the nation's largest career counseling and outplacement firms.

Educational Counseling Service
28 E. Jackson, Room 808
Chicago, IL 60604
(312) 427-2777
Vocational testing; counseling; each case handled individually. Open 8 a.m.
until noon.

Friedland & Marcus
300 W. Washington St., Suite 1106
Chicago, IL 60606
(312) 641-3050
One-day program tailor-made for each candidate includes testing, 3 follow-up

counseling sessions, and a resume. Also cover letters, development counseling, and motivational training.

Gerald Greene, Ph.D.
500 N. Michigan Ave., Suite 542
Chicago, IL 60611
(312) 266-1456
Vocational testing, career counseling, and therapy. Fee varies.

Hay Group
205 N. Michigan Ave., Suite 4000
Chicago, IL 60601
(312) 819-2100

David Helfand, Ed.D.
250 Ridge Ave., #3E
Evanston, IL 60202
(800) 649-2433
Vocational counseling, testing and interpretation. Resume and interviewing help.

Arlene Hirsch
Career and Job Search Counseling
850 N. State St.
Chicago, IL 60610
(312) 642-1535

Human Research & Data
800 E. Northwest Highway
Palatine, IL 60067
(847) 358-8222
Preliminary interview, vocational testing, follow-up report by registered psychologists; also specific counseling with no testing.

Human Resource Developers
126 W. Delaware Place
Chicago, IL 60610
(312) 644-1920
Vocational testing, counseling.

Jewish Vocational Services
1 S. Franklin St.
Chicago, IL
(312) 346-6700

Johnson O'Connor Research Foundation
161 E. Erie St., Room 204
Chicago, IL 60611
(312) 787-9141
Day-and-a-half session: aptitude tests, counseling, career direction, and follow-up session.

Operation Able Career Center
180 N. Wabash Ave.
Chicago, IL 60601
(312) 782-3335

Chuck Pistorio, Ph.D.
Licensed Clinical Psychologist
(773) 794-2951 (answering service)

Psychological Consultation Services
1103 Westgate St., Suite 200
Oak Park, IL 60302
(708) 386-1761
Ph.D.s administer vocational tests, supply counseling.

Diane G. Wilson, M.A.
Career Development
111 N. Wabash Ave.
Chicago, IL 60602
(312) 201-1142
Individual and corporate testing.

To check out a particular practitioner, you can contact the following:

http://www.igc.apc.org/bbb/
This is the homepage of the Better Business Bureau. It offers a geographic directory of offices, list of publications, reliability reports on businesses, scam alerts, and more. Following are phone numbers of consumer-protection offices in the area:

Better Business Bureau of Chicago and Northern Illinois
211 Wacker Drive
Chicago, IL 60606
(312) 346-3313; Inquiries: (312) 444-1188; Tel-tips: (312) 444-1194

Consumer Protection Division
Illinois Attorney Generals Office
100 W. Randolph, 12th floor
Chicago, IL 60601
(312) 814-3580

Career Assistance at Colleges and Universities

Students often don't realize how much help is available through college and university career and placement centers. Career and placement centers provide assistance in choosing a program of study as well as career testing to current students. After graduation, many colleges and universities continue to work with alumni through their career centers. Check with your school and others to find out what's available and who is eligible for assistance.

While most colleges and universities don't permit the general public to use their counseling and placement services, some will offer programs to the public for a fee. The extent of assistance varies from campus to campus.

Some colleges and universities offer non-credit and credit courses as well as special lectures and seminars to help individuals prepare for the job hunt and explore options in the work world. In recent years, schools also have offered more practical courses that are designed to help individuals acquire job skills or brush up on ones they already have.

Try on a career with an internship

Internships are more popular today than ever before—with both new grads and seasoned workers interested in changing careers. It's a form of on-the-job training that lets both you and your employer determine your potential in a specific work environment.

If you're about to graduate, check the career services office at your college, where lists of available internships usually abound. If you're already in the workforce, get in touch with the same office at the college you attended or try the career offices in nearby colleges. When applying, be sure to stress what you can offer an organization and express your enthusiasm for the field.

For more information, look into these resources:

America's Top 100 Internships, Mark Oldman and Samer
   Hamadeh (Princeton Review).
Internships 1997 (Peterson's Guides, Princeton, NJ).
Internships Leading to Careers (The Graduate Group,
   West Hartford, CT).
Job Finder series, Daniel Lauber (Planning/Communications
   Publishers, River Forest, IL).
National Association for Interpretation (Ft. Collins, CO), call
   (303) 491-6784 for free Dial-an-Intern service.

National Directory of Internships (National Society for Experiential Education, Raleigh, NC).

Non-profit organizations are a particularly good bet for internships and were among the first organizations to go on-line. Here are two highly recommended Web sites to explore the world of non-profit organizations:

Meta-Index for Nonprofit Organizations
http://www.duke.edu/~ptavern/pete.met-index.html

NonProfit Organizations
http://www.ai.mit.edu/people/ellens/non-nopic.html

AREA COLLEGES OFFERING CAREER GUIDANCE TO THE PUBLIC

The International Association of Counseling Centers accredits college and university counseling centers and provides regional referrals. Contact them at 101 S. Whiting St., Suite 211, Alexandria, VA 22304, (703) 823-9840 for further information.

College of DuPage
Instructional Center, Room 2010
425 22nd St.
Glen Ellyn, IL 60137
(630) 858-2800
Career counseling and testing for residents of Du Page County.

College of Lake County
19351 W. Washington St.
Grayslake, IL 60030
(847) 223-7200
Interest and aptitude testing for residents of Lake County; help with job search.

Elgin Community College
1700 Spartan Drive
Elgin, IL 60120
(847) 697-1000, ext. 7390
Career counseling, vocational testing. Fees.

Harper College
1375 Wolf Road
Prospect Heights, IL 60070
(847) 459-8233
The Career Transition Center offers group workshops including tests, job listings, resume help, and job search strategy. Fees vary.

Harper College Social Services
1200 W. Algonquin Road
Palatine, IL 60067
(847) 397-3000, ext. 6220

Institute for Psychological Services
Educational, Career and Industrial Assessment
Illinois Institute of Technology
3300 S. Federal
Chicago, IL 60616
(773) 565-3514

Moraine Valley Community College
10900 S. 88th Ave.
Palos Hills, IL 60465
(708) 974-5721
Vocational testing, career counseling, seminars. Fees.

Morton College
3801 S. Central Ave.
Cicero, IL 60650
(708) 656-8000
Vocational testing, career counseling. Fees.

Oakton Community College
Career Counseling Services
1600 E. Golf Road
Des Plaines, IL 60016-1268
(847) 635-1600
Fees vary.

Prairie State College
202 S. Halsted St.
Chicago Heights, IL 60411
(708) 756-3110
Computerized career guidance system, career counseling.

South Suburban College
15800 S. State St.
South Holland, IL 60473
(708) 596-2000
Career counseling.

Triton College
Office of Career Planning and Placement, S-122
2000 5th Ave.
River Grove, IL 60171
(708) 456-0300, ext. 671

Vocational testing; career counseling. Computerized job notification service available. Fee varies.

University of Illinois at Chicago
Office of Applied Psychological Services
1007 W. Harrison St.
Chicago, IL 60607
(312) 996-2540
Vocational testing and counseling. Fees vary.

Waubonsee Community College
Rt. 47 at Harter Road
Sugar Grove, IL 60554
(630) 466-4811
Vocational testing, career counseling, job listings. Fees vary.

Be sure to check with other public community colleges near you. Most provide some type of career guidance services. In addition, your alma mater may be able to request reciprocal services at Chicago area colleges and universities. Schools offering reciprocal privileges usually limit services to nongraduates and charge fees.

Cybertips for career testing and counseling

Try this site to determine your Myers-Briggs (MBTI) type and to get more information on your MBTI personality type:
http://sunsite.unc.edu/jembin/mb.pl

For more information on personality types try:
http://www.yahoo.com/Science/Psychology/Personality/

Career Action Center (http://WWW.GATENET.COM/cac/) offers extensive services in interest and skills testing, test interpretation, and career counseling.

America On-Line and eWorld both provide career information and on-line career counseling services.

Social Service Agencies

Unlike independent career counselors and consultants, social service agencies are not-for-profit. They offer a wide range of services, from counseling and vocational training to job placement and follow-up—and their services are either low cost or free. Keep in mind, though, that a listing in this book does not constitute an endorsement of any agency.

Chicago Urban League
4510 S. Michigan Ave.
Chicago, IL 60653
(773) 285-5800

Greek American Community Services
3940 Pulaski Road
Chicago, IL 60641
(773) 545-0303

Japanese American Citizens League
5414 N. Clark St.
Chicago, IL 60640
(773) 728-7170

Korean American Association of Chicago
5914 N. Lincoln Ave.
Chicago, IL 60659
(773) 878-1900

Midwest Women's Center
828 S. Wabash Ave.
Chicago, IL 60605
(312) 922-8530

South East Asia Center
1128 W. Ainslie
Chicago, IL 60640
(773) 989-6927

Women Employed
22 W. Monroe St.
Chicago, IL 60603
(312) 782-3902

YMCA Training Alliance
18 S. Michigan Ave., Suite 608
Chicago, IL 60653
(312) 580-1911

YWCA
180 N. Wabash Ave.
Chicago, IL 60601
(312) 372-6600

In addition, we recommend that you contact the Community Information and Referral Service of the Chicago United Way Crusade of Mercy at (312) 876-0010 or (800) 564-5733 for possible referrals to other social service agencies. Trained consultants link callers with service providers. Chicago has hundreds of social service agencies, and United Way consultants can help you find the best options.

Career Change: Reality Bites

One morning you wake up, put on your $200 sunglasses, and head to work in your new Lexus. When you get to the office the doors are locked. To your surprise a sign on the door says "Filed for Bankruptcy." At this point you are probably saying, "I must be dreaming." Well, in today's work world, downsizing, mergers, and cost-cutting are all real—and sometimes reality bites!

Dramatic setbacks can often be your best opportunity for considering a career change. However, most people changing careers tend to believe they lack the skills for another career field. Maybe and maybe not. Self-assessment, defining your aptitudes and values, and possibly vocational testing can assist you in deciding on a career change.

There are three main reasons why people change careers:

1. A desire for a better fit among occupation, interests, and values is the primary reason that managers and professionals change careers. People want more career satisfaction and are usually willing to change careers to get it. Those who were coerced into that first career either by parents, misguided ambition, or lack of career information are highly likely to be dissatisfied. In time, they seek change.

2. Job loss. People that are laid off or fired make up a significant portion of those deciding to change careers rather than just replace the job that was lost. Appropriately, it is these people who may experience depression in their search because they feel they have been forced into the change.

3. A smaller group of career changers comprise those who at mid-career decide to turn a passion or hobby into an occupation.

The ability to transfer your skills is crucial in a career change. Many people feel their experience is only relevant to the previous job. In reality, most skills may be applied to a wide variety of jobs. Below are a number of commonly transferable skills. How many do you have?

administering	operating
analyzing	organizing
assisting	persuading
calculating	planning
creating	problem-solving
distributing	recommending
editing	researching
gathering	speaking
instructing	supervising
monitoring	trouble-shooting
motivating	writing

From customer service to fund-raising

After working for a year in customer service for a large retail chain, Sharon decided to make a career change when the company was faced with financial difficulties and had to downsize. Having been a music major in college, Sharon was not sure if she had acquired enough useful job skills to transfer into a new career. She became interested in a fund-raising job at a local university when one of her business contacts mentioned an opening in the development office.

"I volunteered for the annual tele-fund-raising campaign at the university to find out if I could handle development activities. I discovered that I really enjoyed the work. Best of all, many of my skills from my previous job, especially in communication, writing, and computer literacy, were well suited for it. I interviewed for the job and got it, with the additional help of a recommendation from my business contact."

Starting Your Own Business

Perhaps your self-assessment results lead you away from employment altogether and toward starting your own business. If so, a wealth of information is provided through the **U.S. Small Business Administration** (SBA) which provides free information on a variety of topics, including loan programs, tax preparation, government contracts, and management techniques. Although simple questions can be answered by telephone, you'll learn more by dropping by one of the offices to meet with staff members or volunteers from **SCORE** (**Service Corps of Retired Executives**). Their offices are located at:

SBA-SCORE Regional Office
500 W. Madison, Suite 1250
Chicago, IL 60661
(312) 353-7224
http://www.sbaonline.sba.gov/business_management/score.html
SCORE is a federally funded organization of retired executives who volunteer their time and expertise to assist small business owners. They, in turn, receive support and advice from **ACE** (**Active Corps of Executives**).

SCORE—Greater O'Hare
1050 Busse Highway
Bensenville, IL 60106
(847) 350-2944

SCORE—Northbrook Chamber of Commerce
2002 Walters Ave.
Northbrook, IL 60062(847) 498-5555

Small Business Centers

The Small Business Administration also supports university small business development centers staffed by full-time professional consultants. One-on-one counseling is available to focus on business plan development.

SCORE—Chicago State University
95th and King Drive
Chicago, IL 60628
(773) 995-3944

SCORE—Governors State University
University Park, IL 60466
(847) 534-8399

You can also contact the Small Business Administration Web site at:
http://www.sbaonline.sba.gov

The following organizations offer continuing education courses, seminars, workshops, and/or counseling designed to keep the small business owner informed of educational, economic, and research trends and developments.

City Colleges of Chicago
226 W. Jackson Blvd.
Chicago, IL 60606
(312) 641-0808

Cook County Cooperative Extension Service
25 E. Washington St., Suite 707
Chicago, IL 60602
(312) 201-0909

DePaul School for New Learning
243 S. Wabash
Chicago, IL 60604
(312) 362-8001

Harper College
1200 W. Algonquin Road
Palatine, IL 60067
(847) 397-3000

Industrial Engineering College of Chicago
14 N. Sagamon

Chicago, IL 60607
(312) 563-1115

Lakeview Learning Center
3310 N. Clark St.
Chicago, IL 60657
(773) 907-4400

Mundelein College of Loyola University
820 N. Sheridan Road
Chicago, IL 60611
(312) 915-6501

National Lewis University
Main Campus
2840 Sheridan Road
Evanston, IL 60201
(847) 256-5150

Northwestern University College
612 Weiboldt Hall
339 E. Chicago Ave.
Chicago, IL 60611
(312) 503-6950

One-to-One Learning Center
778 Frontage Road, Suite 108
Northfield, IL 60093
(847) 501-3300

South Suburban College
15800 S. State St.
South Holland, IL 60473
(708) 596-2000

Career and Business Resources for Women and Minorities

The following resources for women, minorities, and immigrants may also be of help. Refer to the networking organizations listed in Chapter 5 for additional support groups and information.

WOMEN'S WEB SITES

http://www.sbaonline.sba.gov/womeninbusiness/
The SBA's homepage for women in business. Links are provided to the National Women's Business Council and other related sites.

http://www.intac.com/~kgs/bbpw/meta.html
Lists sites related to businesswomen's issues and organizations, employment, and more.

http://www.igc.apc.org/womensnet/
Links you to services and resources for women.

http://www.web-search.com/women.html
WebSearch, the Business of Women maintains an on-line database of women-owned businesses. Firms have brief descriptions and hyperlinks are provided to other Web sites where available.

The following selection of organizations provides assistance specific to women-owned and minority-owned businesses:

American Women's Economic Development Corp.
71 Vanderbilt Ave.
New York, NY 10169
(212) 692-9100
(800) 222-AWED
http://www.sbaonline.sba.gov/business_management/score.html
Offers courses for all levels of business development and provides support services to help women sharpen their business skills. Counseling by business experts is available in person or by phone, and a special hotline service answers urgent questions. Financial aid is available.

Women, Inc.
125 Park Ave., 8th floor
New York, NY 10017
(212) 479-2366

(800) 930-3993 (membership information)
A national non-profit organization designed to help improve the working environment for women business owners and those interested in starting a small business. A loan program is available for start-up and expanding businesses. Membership fee includes a business plan kit, discounts on business services, and special events and conferences.

Each of the following organizations provides some level of career and/or employment assistance. You should evaluate the appropriateness of any agency's services for you.

American Indian Economic Development
4753 N. Broadway, #1126
Chicago, IL 60640
(773) 784-0808

Hispanic Alliance for Career Enhancement
2000 S. Michigan Ave., #1210
Chicago, IL 60604
(312) 435-0498

Institute for Latino Progress
2570 S. Blue Island
Chicago, IL 60608
(773) 890-0055

National Organization for Women
53 W. Jackson Blvd., Room 924
Chicago, IL 60604
(312) 922-0025

Women Employed Institute
22 W. Monroe, Suite 1400
Chicago, IL 60603
(312) 782-3902
Career development counseling and workshops, employment advocacy and consulting.

Women's Self Employment Project
166 W. Washington St., Suite 730
Chicago, IL 60602
(312) 606-8255
Entrepreneurial, business, and technical consulting for women.

Great Books to Help You Figure Out Your Career

People who are entering the job market for the first time, those who have been working for one company for many years, and those who are considering a career change can usually use a little more help than we have supplied here, and certainly the more help the better. To get that little extra boost, we can refer you to some excellent books. If you have access to college resources, be sure to take advantage of the career libraries as well as the counseling and career planning services that are available on most campuses.

CAREER STRATEGY BOOKS

Baldwin, Eleanor. *300 Ways to Get a Better Job.* Holbrook, MA: Adams Publishing, 1991.

Beatty, Richard H. *Get the Right Job in 60 Days or Less.* New York: John Wiley & Sons, 1991.

Bolles, Richard N. *The Three Boxes of Life and How to Get Out of Them.* Berkeley, CA: Ten Speed Press, 1981.

Bolles, Richard N. *What Color Is Your Parachute?* Berkeley, CA: Ten Speed Press. The bible for job hunters and career changers, this book is revised every year and is widely regarded as one of the most useful and creative manuals on the market.

Clawson, James G., et al. *Self Assessment and Career Development.* Englewood Cliffs, NJ: Prentice-Hall, 1991. A very thorough guide with self-assessment worksheets and a good bibliography.

Dubin, Judith A., and Melonie R. Keveles. *Fired for Success.* New York: Warner Books, 1990.

Harkavy, Michael. *One Hundred One Careers: A Guide to the Fastest Growing Opportunities.* New York: John Wiley & Sons, 1990.

Jackson, Tom. *Guerrilla Tactics in the Job Market.* New York: Bantam Books, 1991. Filled with unconventional but effective suggestions.

Krannich, Ronald L. *Change Your Job, Change Your Life: High Impact Strategies for Finding Great Jobs in the 90's.* Manassas, VA: Impact Publications, 1994.

Levinson, Harry. *Designing and Managing Your Career.* Boston: Harvard University Press, 1989.

Morin, William J., and James C. Colvena. *Parting Company: How to Survive the Loss of a Job and Find Another Successfully.* San Diego, CA: HBJ, 1991.

Munschauer, John L. *Jobs for English Majors and Other Smart People.* Princeton, NJ: Peterson's Guides, 1991.

Petras, Kathryn and Ross. *The Only Job Hunting Guide You'll Ever Need.* New York: Fireside, 1995.

Roper, David H. *Getting The Job You Want . . . Now!* New York: Warner Books, 1994.

Washington, Tom. *Complete Book to Effective Job Finding.* Bellevue, WA: Mount Vernon Press, 1992.

Weinstein, Bob. *Resumes Don't Get Jobs: The Realities and Myths of Job Hunting.* New York: McGraw-Hill, 1993.

Yate, Martin. *Knock 'Em Dead.* Holbrook, MA: Adams Publishing, 1995.

If you're **still in college or have recently graduated,** the following books will be of particular interest:

Briggs, James I. *The Berkeley Guide to Employment for New College Graduates.* Berkeley, CA: Ten Speed Press, 1984.

Holton, Ed. *The M.B.A.'s Guide to Career Planning.* Princeton, NJ: Peterson's Guides, 1989.

La Fevre, John L. *How You Really Get Hired: The Inside Story from a College Recruiter.* New York: Prentice-Hall, 1993.

Richardson, Bradley G. *Jobsmarts for Twentysomethings.* New York: Vintage Books, 1995.

Steele, John, and Marilyn Morgan. *Career Planning & Development for College Students and Recent Graduates.* Lincolnwood, IL: National Textbook Co., 1991.

Tener, Elizabeth. *Smith College Guide: How to Find and Manage Your First Job.* New York: Plume, 1991.

For those involved in a **mid-life career change,** here are some books that might prove helpful:

Anderson, Nancy. *Work With Passion: How to Do What You Love for a Living.* Rafeal, CA: New World Library, 1995.

Birsner, E. Patricia. *The Forty-Plus Job Hunting Guide: Official Handbook of the 40-Plus Club.* New York: Facts on File, 1990.

Byron, William J. *Finding Work Without Losing Heart: Bouncing Back from Mid-Career Job Loss.* Holbrook, MA: Adams Publishing, 1995.

Helfand, David. *Career Change: Everything You Need to Know to Meet New Challenges and Take Control of Your Life.* Lincolnwood, IL: VGM Career Horizons, 1994.

Holloway, Diane, and Nancy Bishop. *Before You Say "I Quit": A Guide to Making Successful Job Transitions.* New York: Collier Books, 1990.

Logue, Charles H. *Outplace Yourself: Secrets of an Executive Outplacement Counselor.* Holbrook, MA: Adams Publishing, 1995.

Stevens, Paul. *Beating Job Burnout: How to Turn Your Work into Your Passion.* Lincolnwood, IL: VGM Career Horizons, 1995.

For workers who are **nearing retirement age** or have already reached it, here are some books that might be useful:

Kerr, Judy. *The Senior Citizen's Guide to Starting a Part-Time, Home-Based Business.* New York: Pilot Industries, 1992.

Morgan, John S. *Getting a Job After Fifty.* Blue Ridge Summit, PA: TAB Books, 1990.

Ray, Samuel. *Job Hunting After 50: Strategies for Success.* New York: John Wiley & Sons, 1991.

Strasser, Stephen, and John Sena. *Transitions: Successful Strategies from Mid-Career to Retirement.* Hawthorne, NJ: Career Press, 1990.

And for people with **disabilities**, these titles could prove helpful:

Pocket Guide to Federal Help for Individuals with Disabilities. Clearinghouse on the Handicapped, Washington, DC: U.S. Department of Education, 1989. Discusses the many types of federal help for disabled job seekers. Useful and concise, only $1.

Rabbi, Rami, and Diane Croft. *Take Charge: A Strategic Guide for Blind Job Seekers.* Boston: National Braille Press, 1990.

Human Care Services Directory of Metropolitan Chicago for the United Way/Crusade of Mercy. Available from:
Morgan Rand
1800 Bayberry Road
800 Mason Mill Business Park
Huntington Valley, PA 19006
(800) 388-1197

For **women and minority groups** in the workforce, these titles will be of interest:

Berryman, Sue E. *Routes Into the Mainstream: Career Choices of Women & Minorities.* Columbus, OH: Continuing Educational Training Employment, 1988.

Betz, Nancy E., and Louise Fitzgerald. *The Career Psychology of Women.* Orlando: Academic Press, 1987.

Lunnenborg, Patricia. *Women Changing Work.* New York: Bergin & Garvey Publishers, 1990.

Nivens, Beatrice. *The Black Woman's Career Guide.* New York: Anchor Books, 1987.

Thompson, Charlotte E. *Single Solutions—An Essential Guide for the Single Career Woman.* Brookline Village, MA: Branden Publishing, 1990.

If I Can't Find a Job, Should I Go Back to School?

" **I**'m having a real hard time finding a job. Maybe I'll just go back to school." The rationale seems logical: more schooling equals better job. The facts, however, don't always show the "more schooling" route to be the best one, as we will discuss below. Sometimes, however, getting another degree or a bit more education can make the difference between a job and a great career.

When To Go Back to School

Admittedly, additional education can enhance your marketability. But as you weigh the pros and cons of committing time and money to the classroom, you should never consider additional education a panacea for all of your career woes.

A myth people want to believe is that an advanced degree, a different degree, or even a bit more education will automatically translate into a better job. People considering law school or an MBA frequently fall prey to this myth. The reality is that the job market is very tight, especially for lawyers, and employers are resistant to hire people who may have entered a particular field on a whim and don't have any real long-term commitment to the profession. It is less risky for employers to hire someone with a proven track record than someone with a new advanced degree. Those pursuing graduate work in the liberal arts, not wishing to teach, are also in for a big surprise when they realize that they often end up in the same predicament they were in upon graduating with a B.A.: undecided upon a career and having very few options.

Despite the negatives, though, there are several good reasons for returning to school for additional education. These include:

47

To Acquire Additional Skills
If you find that your skills are not keeping pace with the demands of your career, you may consider returning to school. Learning accounting, computer systems, or a foreign language, for example, may be the boost your career needs.

To Prepare for a Career Change.
Frequently, job changers will realize that they want to leave their current field altogether. If after talking with a career counselor, assessing your goals, and weighing your options, you decide that a career change is the right choice, additional education—a different degree—may be a requirement.

To Advance in Your Career.
For certain fields, such as investment banking, an MBA is necessary to advance. In other fields, the standards for additional education may be more subtle. Another degree or merely additional course work toward a degree may translate into a salary increase or consideration for a promotion.

Some people may be intimidated at the thought of acquiring additional education because they associate it with spent time and money. In reality, professional education can take many forms and carry a wide range of price tags. Other options to graduate school with varying cost-benefit trade-offs include community college courses, evening classes at a university, professional training for certification, or even executive education programs offered by many business schools. The bottom line is that when you consider additional education, do not limit your thinking only to formal degree programs at a university.

Tips on Considering Additional Schooling

There are many issues to consider before returning to school. First, determine how an additional degree or professional training will fit into your long-term goals. As you prepare to invest money, time, and energy on education, it is essential to know how you will benefit one year, five years, or even ten years later. Additionally, in order to select your best educational alternative, you must be able to articulate what benefit it will offer your career.

Second, many graduate schools require work experience before you can apply. For example, top business schools require two years of work experience. Thus, it is important to be familiar with the requirements of your proposed field of study.

Third, ask yourself whether you've really done your homework when weighing alternatives. Your watchword should be research. If you are changing career fields, avoid any post-degree surprises by researching the market, employment trends, and major employers. When evaluating professional training programs, be sure you have researched the schools to know who is offering accredited and respected courses. Make your decisions based on facts and figures and not on the suggestions of well-meaning friends and family members—and certainly not on the advice of admission representatives from graduate schools.

Finally, the biggest obstacle to returning for more education may be yourself. Saying that you're too old, you don't want to invest the money, or you don't want to take time off from your current job may merely be excuses to justify your refusal to take the plunge. Alternatively, you may have valid reasons for staying put for the time being. Be honest with yourself; only you can decide.

Law school at sixty—you're never too old!

One of our favorite stories is about a man who decided at the age of 60 to go to law school. "That will take three years," his friends and family moaned. "You'll be 63!" "So what?" Ed replied. "If I don't go to law school, in three years I'll still be 63." In Ed's way of thinking, he couldn't put three years to better use than to accomplish a lifelong goal.

In considering additional education, ask yourself, "If I do not choose to pursue additional education now, will I be satisfied with my career progress in a year?... five years?" This may be the best measure of how you might benefit from additional education.

Education and Income

Most of us have heard of the guy down the street who flunked out of college or failed to complete high school and is now a millionaire. *Forbes* magazine listed Bill Gates, a Harvard dropout, the founder of Microsoft computers, as the world's richest individual in 1995. Howard Hughes flunked out of Rice University and still managed to gain genius status and amass an empire. The fact is that there are many such success stories among the not-so-educated.

What we don't hear are stories about the many failures. According to the Bureau of the Census, when salaries of all working people over the age of 25 were examined, on average those with the most education had the highest annual incomes. People who failed to enter high school averaged a salary of $15,223 a year. These figures include those with large amounts of experience. Those with less than a high school diploma but with some high school education increased on average to $18,012 per year, and high school graduates earned $23,410 per year.

In terms of income, even some college education is better than none. Americans who have completed some college average incomes of $27,705. Those completing a bachelor's or four-year degree earn an average of $35,900 per year, some $12,000 higher per year than the high school graduate.

Finally, there are those that strive for more than a bachelor's degree. For those who complete graduate, professional, or other college work beyond the bachelor's, the extra education will garner them an average of $43,032 per year. This will, of course, vary with the type of graduate study pursued. Law or medical school will almost certainly give you a higher income than one year of graduate study in a less marketable area.

Dear Dr. Bob

I recently heard that a doctor who is a general practitioner makes on average $117,000 a year and that internal medicine specialists make $181,000 a year. Should I change careers to become a doctor? Signed, Curious Career Changer

Dear Curious Career Changer
Certainly, becoming a doctor can seem like a wonderful choice. The drama of the emergency room, a good salary, knowing that you're making a difference in people's lives. However, you should consider the hard work, high cost, and many years it takes to become a doctor. Since there are three times as many applicants as there are slots for med school, I recommend exploring all your options in the medical field.

First, make sure that the health field is the field you are most interested in, then look into all the options. Options such as medical physics, physicians' assistants, pharmacy, and occupational and physical therapy are a few alternatives in the health field that may be a good fit and more time and cost effective for you.

However, don't do anything drastic! Being in medicine isn't exactly what you see on TV. You ought to talk to a few real health professionals or a career counselor before leaping into anything.

Getting Organized for Graduate School

If you decide that graduate or professional school is definitely what you need in your life and you've weighed the pros and cons, then get ready for the graduate school application process, which can be "The Nightmare on Elm Street." However, organization can make your life much easier and good preparation can eventually land you in the school of your choice. Here are some tips to help you:

- Request application materials around September of the year prior to the year you want to enroll.
- Know each school's application timeline (exam results, application due date, etc.).
- Establish a time frame for yourself, setting goals to complete tests and prepare paperwork and other relevant information well before the actual due date.
- Take practice tests, and learn what to expect on the tests, how answers are scored, whether you lose points for wrong answers, and so on.
- Take the actual tests.
- Forward exam results to selected schools.
- Get transcripts from schools attended.
- Obtain letters of recommendation.
- Write essays.
- Use certified mail, U.P.S., FedEx, or a courier service to deliver materials to schools. This insures receipt of the materials by the school.
- Visit schools you are interested in attending, if possible.

Preparing for graduate school admissions tests

Graduate schools, law schools, and medical schools all require test scores before admitting anyone. The standardized tests include the GMAT (Graduate Management Admission Test), LSAT (Law School Admission Test), and MCAT (Medical College Admission Test). Prep courses can help ready you for these tests. Such courses help familiarize you with the contents of the tests and question types. They also offer strategies of test taking to help you improve your scores. Below are two services that provide test preparation courses.

Kaplan Education Center
188 W. Randolph
Chicago, IL 60601
(312) 346-9346 or (800) K.P.-TEST

Princeton Review
(800) 2-REVIEW

Selecting a Graduate School

Selecting a graduate school requires much consideration before committing money and two to three years of your life. The task of making the best selection in a graduate school is one that will have a significant impact on subsequent job placement, starting salary, and career potential. Here are some criteria to help in evaluating potential graduate schools: the school's reputation, both academically and among the employment community, curriculum, specialization(s), geographic location, department size, selectivity of admissions, faculty reputations and areas of expertise, and level of financial aid/support for students.

CYBERTIPS ON GRADUATE SCHOOLS

The Career Channel
http//:riceinfo.rice.edu:80/projects/careers/
Provides information on graduate school application deadlines; rankings of top professional, medical, and graduate schools; test prep courses; and test examples.

CollegeNET Page for Chicago
http://www.collegenet.com:80/cn/geograph/ny.html
Find information about colleges and universities in Chicago, including Web addresses.

Other good graduate school information links include:

National Association of Graduate and Professional Students
gopher://accgopher.georgetown.edu/11gopher_root%3a%5bnagps%5d

Graduate & Professional Schools from the University of Virginia
http://minerva.acc.virginia.edu/~career/grdsch.html

JOBTRAK
http://www.jobtrak.com/gradschool_docs/gradschool.html
Offers advice on grad school: applying, testing, and financing; also has links to grad school sites by topic.

Peterson's Guide to Graduate and Professional Study
http://www.petersons.com:8080/gsector.html
Links to over 1,500 universities on the Net that offer grad programs; arranged by geography.

Educational Testing Service
http://hub.terc.edu/ra/ets.html
Provides test dates.

The Best Graduate Programs for Your Success

There are many resources to help you select graduate programs such as *Peterson's Guides* and *Barron's Guide, Gorman's, Business Week's* annual "Best B Schools" edition and the follow-up book, and *U.S. News and World Reports'* issue on best graduate schools. All of these give some type of information on graduate schools.

We encourage you to look at all these sources. However, we have compiled a list, along with Web addresses, of programs from around the country that consistently show up at the top of national rankings. Additional lists outline programs in the professional, trade, and continuing studies areas available in this city and its environs.

The WWW addresses for business and law schools listed below will provide information on each university listed, its faculty and students, admission requirements, financial assistance, and general information about its graduate school. Entries are listed alphabetically and are not intended to imply any ranking.

TOP BUSINESS SCHOOLS

Harvard University
http://www.hbs.harvard.edu/

Massachusetts Institute of Technology (Sloan)
http://www-sloan.mit.edu/

Northwestern University Kellogg Graduate School of Management
http://www.nwu.edu/graduate/

Stanford University
http://www-gsb.stanford.edu/home.html

University of Chicago
http://uchicago.edu:80/

University of Pennsylvania (Wharton)
http://www.wharton.upeen.edu/

TOP LAW SCHOOLS

Columbia University (NY)
http://www.janus.columbia.edu/

Harvard University
http://www.harvard.edu/

Northwestern University School of Law
http://www.nwu.edu/

Stanford University
http://www-leland.stanford.edu/group/

University of California at Berkeley
gopher://law164.law.berkeley.edu:70/1

University of Chicago
http://www.uchicago.edu:80/

Yale University
http://www.yale.edu/

GRADUATE SCHOOLS IN THE CHICAGO AREA

Below is a partial list of universities in the Chicago area. Most of the following have graduate programs that are nationally ranked and/or highly regarded in their field. Be sure to obtain graduate school catalogs from your targeted institutions, examine their program offerings, talk with working professionals in your field of interest about the various schools' reputations, and schedule an appointment with graduate program directors to compare program requirements.

Chicago College of Osteopathic Medicine
555 31st Ave.
Downers Grove, IL
(630) 971-6080

Chicago State University
95th St. at King Drive
Chicago, IL 60628
(773) 995-2000

Columbia College
600 S. Michigan Ave.
Chicago, IL 60605-1997
(312) 663-1600

DePaul University
1 E. Jackson Blvd.
Chicago, IL 60604-2287
(312) 362-8000

Illinois Institute of Technology
IIT Center
Chicago, IL 60616
(312) 567-3000

Keller Graduate School of Management
10 S. Riverside Plaza
Chicago, IL 60606
(312) 454-0880

Loyola University Chicago
820 N. Michigan Ave.
Chicago, IL 60611-2196
(312) 915-6000

John Marshall Law School
315 S. Plymouth Court
Chicago, IL 60604
(312) 427-2737

McCormick Theological Seminary
5555 S. Woodlawn Ave.
Chicago, IL 60637
(773) 947-6300

National-Louis University
2840 Sheridan Road
Evanston, IL 60201-1730
(847) 475-1100

Northeastern Illinois University
5500 N. St. Louis Ave.
Chicago, IL 60625-4699
(773) 583-4050

Northwestern University
633 Clark St.
Evanston, IL 60208
(847) 491-3741

Roosevelt University
430 S. Michigan Ave.
Chicago, IL 60605-1394
(312) 341-3500

School of the Art Institute of Chicago
37 S. Wabash
Chicago, IL 60603-3103
(312) 899-5100

University of Chicago
5801 Ellis Ave.
Chicago, IL 60637-1513
(773) 702-1234

University of Illinois at Chicago
1140 S. Paulina
Chicago, IL 60680
(312) 996-7000

Vocational Schools in the Chicago Area

If you want to try a new career such as chef, real estate agent, or medical assistant, vocational schools can provide the skills necessary. Below are a few resources for vocational schools in the Chicago area.

If you need to update your skills, such as computing or accounting, you may want to consider an apprenticeship program. An apprenticeship program is less costly than a full-time program and may provide just the current skills you need.

Many professionals opt to take short courses in specific technology to stay abreast of their field. Some fields, such as nursing, require a certain amount of course work each year to maintain a license. And for all of us, education is a personally enriching lifelong process. Whatever the reason, there are many good continuing education classes being offered. Below are a few schools providing continuing education courses.

DeVry Institute of Technology
3300 N. Campbell Ave.
Chicago, IL 60618-5994
(773) 929-8500
Four-year college. Awards Associate and Bachelor's degrees. Proprietary.
Enrollment: 2,858

DeVry Institute of Technology
1221 N. Swift Road
Addison, IL 60101-6106
(847) 953-1300
Four-year college. Awards Associate and Bachelor's degrees. Proprietary.
Enrollment: 2,871

Harrington Institute of Interior Design
410 S. Michigan Ave.
Chicago, IL 60605-1496
(312) 939-4975
Four-year college. Awards Associate and Bachelor's degrees. Proprietary.
Enrollment: 293

International Academy of Merchandising & Design, Ltd.
1 N. State St.
Chicago, IL 60602-9736
(312) 541-3910
Four-year college. Awards Associate and Bachelor's degrees. Proprietary.
Enrollment: 662

Kendall College
2408 Orrington Ave.
Evanston, IL 60201-2899
(847) 866-1300

Four-year college. Awards Associate and Bachelor's degrees. Independent religious. Enrollment: 508

Ray College of Design
350 N. Orleans
Chicago, IL 60654
(312) 280-3500
Four-year college. Awards Associate and Bachelor's degrees. Proprietary. Enrollment: 610

West Suburban College of Nursing
Erie at Austin
Oak Park, IL 60302
(708) 383-3901
Four-year college. Awards Associate and Bachelor's degrees. Independent nonprofit. Enrollment: 241

On-line Education

No need to pack those bags or leave your job and friends to head off for school. Today's technology brings the teachers, ideas, books, and dialogue to the student electronically. The advantages are that correspondence study is dependable, low cost, and can be done anywhere. Still it is important to check out what credits, degree, or credentials you may receive. Additionally, consider all costs associated with on-line education and don't forget to inquire about financial aid.

Although on-line education is convenient, some people may not do well outside a typical classroom environment where you see the teacher and take part in dialogue. Think about the kind of study environment that works best for you. It is also important to note that the field of on-line education is constantly changing, and new possibilities certainly will pop up after the publication of this book.

If you would like to learn more about on-line or long-distance learning programs, the following books can assist you:

The Electronic University: A Guide to Long-distance Learning Programs. Princeton, NJ: Peterson's Guides, 1993.

Peterson's Guide to Independent Study. Princeton, NJ: Peterson's Guides, 1992.

Did you know that you can also take courses offered by certified teachers and professional experts on-line? Typical courses offered include: History, English, Sociology, Languages, Math, Science, the Arts, and Computer Science. However, no college credit or certificates are awarded for these courses. For further information contact **The Electronic University Network** (Sarah Blackmun, Director of Instruction, 1977 Colestin Road, Hornbrook, CA 96044, (415) 221-7061). This network consists of organizations that work with groups of colleges to provide long-distance learning programs.

The 10-Step Job Search

Almost everything can be broken down into steps. The job search is no different. If you take the process one step at a time and follow our basic rules, you are more likely to find a job. As you begin, it is important to remember that you are in control, and in the end it is you who must land the job. To get there you need to be proactive; companies will not come looking for you. Rather, you have to search out the companies, the jobs, and the people that are in a position to hire.

The 10-Step Job Search

1. Know Thyself—Where Are You Going?
2. Research the Job Market.
3. Organize Your Search.
4. Network.
5. Persistence and Follow-Up.
6. Prepare Your Resume.
7. Mail Your Resume.
8. Use Your Career Resources.
9. The Killer Interview.
10. Make Sure This Is the Job for You.

Step 1: Know Thyself—Where Are You Going?

Hopefully, Chapter 2 has set you on the right path to choosing a career. To get somewhere you need to decide where it is you are going, what you want to do, and what you are capable of doing. Other items to assess include the characteristics of your ideal work environment, the type of experience you wish to gain from the job, and how much money you intend to make. To a large extent, your happiness with your job coincides with how closely it meets your needs and motivates you.

Once you've answered these questions you will be able to articulate why you are interviewing for a particular position and why you are right for that position.

Step 2: Research the Job Market

The alarm clock rings, and you slowly get out of bed and head downstairs for your morning jolt of java along with the want ads from the daily paper. Tempted to read the comics, you resist the urge and resume your job search with the want ads. After all, this is how people find jobs. Wrong! According to *Forbes* magazine, only about 10 percent of professional and technical people find their jobs through want ads.

Your best bet is *not* to send a resume to every ad in the paper. Instead, try to identify who's hiring and where the opportunities may be. How do you learn these things? Research.

Libraries

Libraries provide vast amounts of resources for job searching, ranging from company information (ranking, annual sales, product information, number of employees, who's running the show) to resume writing guides, business newspapers and magazines, salary statistics, and, of course, directories such as *Standard and Poor's Register of Corporations, Directors, and Executives.* To save precious time in your research, the reference desk is invaluable in locating materials for your job search.

Local university and community college libraries may also offer resources for job seekers. Many local schools have reference libraries that are well equipped with career resource information and job directories that you can use even if you are not an alumnus. Some libraries also offer vocational testing and career guidance, often in conjunction with the school's career planning office.

The **Chicago Public Library's Business Information Center** (400 S. State St., 4th floor) carries many major business directories for conducting job market research. Its Computer-Assisted Reference Center at (312) 747-4470 is one of the most valuable services offered by the Chicago Public Library. For very little money, you can find out if there are recent articles about a particular company. Tell the researcher/librarian you want to know the latest news on XYZ Corp. The computer can search out anything that has recently appeared in print.

In addition to on-line databases, major public libraries and university libraries have CD-ROM collections that can be very helpful to the job seeker. In particular, *ABI Inform* and *Lexus/Nexus* are very useful for researching business and industry organizations. For education, use the *ERIC* database to research current topics. These CD-ROM collections incorporate articles from the major periodicals and professional journals in their respective fields. CD-ROM collections vary by library, so be sure to consult with a reference librarian or the head of the automated reference department to check on what is available.

Just about any type of information can be accessed by computer today. Journals, occupational outlooks, professional magazines, and business and financial information are easy to access. It's also easy to tap into news groups providing information on job openings in a particular field, discussions of the job market in a specific area, and workplace and employment-related issues. Also see "Cyberresources for Your Job Search" in Chapter 1 and a list for company homepages and corporate data in Chapter 7. For a longer list of Internet job resources, see the section on "Internet Job Listings" farther on in this chapter.

CYBER RESEARCH AT CHICAGO AREA LIBRARIES, PUBLIC SCHOOLS, OR FROM HOME

Many public colleges and universities permit citizens to use their facilities at no charge or for a modest patron's fee. But libraries have been leaders in using new information technologies; reference librarians, in particular, are usually experts in conducting electronic information searches. If you are new to conducting electronic research, it would be valuable to spend a little time in a major library, attend an orientation session, consult with a reference librarian, and check out their computer access. Libraries often enable patrons to access the Internet in their computer labs.

If you cannot access the Internet through a library or college, contact the adult/continuing education division of your local public school district. Most high schools now have computer labs for students that may be available to citizens.

Finally, if all else fails and you have a home computer with a high-speed modem, contact a local Internet provider. Prices have fallen dramatically as more competitors have jumped into this growing market. You may now be able to get local access for as little as $20-25 per month. Here are two Chicago sites that may help you locate providers:

NetChicago
http://www.ais.net/netchicago/resource.html
A guide to Chicago Internet resources.

Chicago Area Internet Providers
http://www.mcs.com/~wsmith/providers.html
Provides contact and service information.

As you surf the Web for career information, you may have to experiment with times. Depending on use at any given time, the Internet can become very congested and slow to respond to your requests. Regardless, the Internet search is still more efficient than physically traveling to information sites.

Chicago Public Library
http://cpl.lib.uic.edu/cpl.html
Has many branches throughout the city, with a complete site directory available at their Web address. Also included is their on-line library catalog. The main branch is the Harold Washington Library Center, 400 S. State St., Chicago, IL 60605, (312) 747-4999. Check their Web directory for a branch near you.

The Business Information Center of the Chicago Public Library (400 S. State St., 4th floor, (312) 269-2814) is an invaluable source of career information. It systematically collects, files, and displays current career reference materials for easy access, including books, government documents, pamphlets, and directories. Most of the titles mentioned in this book can be found in the Business Information Center. Reference librarians are helpful and well-informed, if somewhat overworked. The Business Information Center is open Monday through Thursday from 9 a.m. to 7 p.m.; Friday 9 a.m. to 6 p.m.; Saturday 9 a.m. to 5 p.m.

Evanston Public Library
http://www.evanston.lib.il.us/library/library.html
1403 Orrington Ave.
Evanston, IL 60201
(847) 866-0300
Has computers with Internet access available for public use.

Illinois Library and Information Network
http://www.library.sosstate.il.us/

Libraries on the Web (compiled by University of Washington)
http://weber.u.washington.edu/~tdowling/libweb/usa.html
An extensive list of national and international library Web sites.

North Suburban Library System
http://www.nsls/us.org
You may want to call the following libraries to check your eligibility for service:

University of Illinois at Chicago Library
801 S. Morgan
Chicago, IL 60607
(312) 996-2716

Harold Washington College Library
30 E. Lake St.
Chicago, IL 60601
(312) 553-5600

Williams Library for Northeastern Illinois University
5500 N. St. Louis Ave.
Chicago, IL 60625
(773) 794-2615

RECOMMENDED READING

Dixon, Pam, and Sylvia Tiersten. *Be Your Own Headhunter Online.* New York: Random House, 1995.

Kennedy, Joyce Lain. *Hook Up, Get Hired! The Internet Job Search Revolution.* New York: John Wiley & Sons, 1995.

Directories

Directories provide you with corporate structures, company financial figures, company rankings, best companies to work for, best places to live, who's making what salary, and top careers. When you're beginning your homework, whether you're researching an entire industry or a specific company, there are five major directories with which you should be familiar.

OUR FIVE FAVORITE DIRECTORIES

Sorkins' Directory of Business and Government (Chicago Edition), is an annual 17-volume set that covers industry, services, education, nonprofit, and government organizations. It provides company profiles and indices by products, services, location, and individuals' names. This may be the most comprehensive directory available on Chicago-area organizations. *Sorkins'* developed their own classification codes that provide better differentiation among organization types than the Standard Industrial Classification (S.I.C.) codes. The set is published by Sorkins' Directories Inc., P.O. Box 4249, Chesterfield, MO 63006, (800) 758-3228. Highly recommended!

The Directory of Corporate Affiliations (National Register Publishing, New Providence, NJ) is an organized business reference tool covering public and private businesses in the U.S. and throughout the world. This six-volume directory allows the user to examine the parent company and all subsidiaries of the parent company, categorized by geographic area or S.I.C. (Standard Industrial Classification) codes that identify the company's product or service. If you want to know the corporate reporting structure, the company's subsidiaries, or the company's banking, legal, or outside service firms, this is the directory to use.

Standard and Poor's Register of Corporations, Directors, and Executives (Standard and Poor's Publishing, 25 Broadway, New York, NY 10004) is billed as the "foremost guide to the business community and the executives who run it." This three-volume directory lists more than 50,000 corporations and 70,000 officers, directors, trustees, and other bigwigs.

Each business is assigned an S.I.C. number. Listings are indexed by geographic area and also by S.I.C. number, so it's easy to find all the companies in a local area that produce, say, industrial inorganic chemicals.

You can also look up a particular company to verify its correct address and phone number, its chief officers (that is, the people you might want to contact for an interview), its products, and, in many cases, its annual sales and number of employees. If you have an appointment with the president of XYZ Corporation, you can consult *Standard and Poor's* to find out where he or she was born and went to college—information that's sure to come in handy in an employment interview. Supplements are published in April, July, and October.

Ward's Business Directory of U.S. Private and Public Companies (Gale Research Inc., New York, NY) is the leading source for hard-to-find information on private companies. This six-volume publication lists more than 142,000 companies in alphabetic, geographic, and industry arrangements. It also provides rankings and analyses of the industry activity of leading companies. If you want to determine parent/subsidiary relationships, merger and acquisition positions, or general information on private and public companies, this is the directory to use.

The Million Dollar Directory (Dun & Bradstreet, 3 Century Drive, Parsippany, NJ 07054) is a three-volume listing of approximately 160,000 U.S. businesses with a net worth of more than half a million dollars. Listings appear alphabetically, geographically, and by product classification and include key personnel. Professional and consulting organizations such as hospitals and engineering services, credit agencies, and financial institutions other than banks and trust companies are not generally included.

So much for our favorite directories. The following listings contain more than 40 additional directories and guides that may come in handy. Many of these, as well as other directories, are available at area libraries.

NATIONAL/REGIONAL DIRECTORIES

Bacon's Magazine Directory
Bacon's Newspaper Directory
Bacon's Radio Directory
Bacon's TV/Cable Directory
(Bacon's Publishing Co., 332 S. Michigan Ave., Chicago, IL 60604.)
Each volume covers thousands of sources in the U.S. and Canada. Organized geographically.

Career Guide: Dun's Employment Opportunities Directory
(Dun and Bradstreet, 3 Century Drive, Parsippany, NJ 07054.)
Employment information on companies with at least 1,000 employees, including hiring practices and disciplines hired geographically.

Chicago Apparel Center Directory
(Directory Publications, 470 Merchandise Mart, Chicago, IL 60654.)
Lists apparel retailers and wholesalers and Chicago area fashion events; published yearly.

Chicago Banks Directory
(Law Bulletin Publishing Co., 415 N. State St., Chicago, IL 60610.)
Banking institutions in Chicago and Cook County, including names of officers.

Chicago and Cook County Marketing Directory
(Manufacturer's News, Inc., 4 E. Huron St., Chicago, IL 60611.)
Profiles of manufacturers and service businesses in Chicagoland area.

Chicago Creative Directory
(333 N. Michigan Ave., Chicago, IL 60601, $40.)
People and firms in the fields of photography, illustration, film, printing services, audio/visual, and music production; talent agencies, media reps, and firms that service the media industry.

Chicago Mercantile Exchange Membership List
(Chicago Mercantile Exchange, 30 S. Wacker Drive, Chicago, IL 60606, $6.)
National listing of Mercantile Exchange traders; their firms and addresses.

Chicago Purchaser Roster Issue
(Purchasing Management Association of Chicago, 201 N. Wells St., Suite 618, Chicago, IL 60606.)
Annual listing of personal members and their firms.

Chicago Talent Handbook
(Swift Publishing Co., 445 W. Fullerton Ave., Chicago, IL 60614.)
Guide to modeling, acting, voice, trade show, and runway work
in Chicago.

Chicago Talent Sourcebook
(Alexander Communications, Inc., 212 W. Superior St., Chicago, IL 60610, $50.)
Names and numbers of Chicago firms in advertising, photography, illustration;
audio/visual, film, and tape production; music and
printing services.

Chicagoland Chamber of Commerce Buyer's Guide and Membership Directory
(1 IBM Plaza, Suite 2800, Chicago, IL 60601.)

Directory of Chicago Fashion and Apparel Manufacturers
(Apparel Industry Board, Apparel Center, Suite 1346, 350 N. Orleans St.,
Chicago, IL 60654.)
Lists manufacturers, includes label names produced by the manufacturer.

Directory of Community Organizations in Chicago
(Institute of Urban Life, 1 E. Superior St., Chicago, IL 60611.)

Consultants and Consulting Organizations Directory
(Gale Research Co., 835 Penobscot Bldg., Detroit, MI 48226.)
Descriptions of 20,000 firms and individuals involved in consulting, indexed
geographically.

Corporate Technology Directory
(Corporate Technology Information Services, 1 Market St., Wellesley Hills, MA
02181.)
Profiles of high-technology corporations, indexed by company names, geography, technology, and product.

Directories in Print, 13th edition
(Gale Research Co., 835 Penobscot Bldg., Detroit MI 48226-4094.)
This is a directory of directories. It is an annotated guide to over 14,000 directories published worldwide, including business, industry, professional, scientific,
entertainment, recreation, and cultural listings. Includes electronic databases.

Directory of Public Interest Law Centers
(Alliance for Justice, 1601 Connecticut Ave., N.W., Suite 601, Washington, DC
20506.)
About 200 non-profit groups that provide legal assistance and referral for
under-represented interests in courts and agencies. Arranged geographically.

Dun and Bradstreet State Sales Guide
(Dun and Bradstreet, 430 Mountain Road, New Providence, NJ 07974.)
Covers all businesses in each state that are included in Dun and Bradstreet's
Reference Book.

Encyclopedia of Associations: National Organizations of the U.S.
(Gale Research Co., 835 Penobscot Bldg., Detroit, MI 48226.)
Multi-volume compendium of trade, cultural, and community organizations
across the U.S.

Encyclopedia of Business Information Sources
(Gale Research Co., 835 Penobscot Bldg., Detroit, MI 48226.)
Lists each industry's encyclopedia, handbooks, indexes, almanacs, yearbooks, trade associations, periodicals, directories, computer databases, research centers, and statistical sources.

Environmental Engineering Selection Guide
(American Academy of Environmental Engineers, 130 Holiday Court, Suite 100, Annapolis, MD 21401.)
A directory of engineering firms and educational institutions employing Board Certified Specialists.

First Chicago Guide
(Scholl Communications Inc., P.O. Box 560, Deerfield, IL 60015.)
Describes major publicly held corporations and financial institutions headquartered in Illinois, indexed by S.I.C. codes and ranked by sales or revenue.

Fortune Double 500 Directory
(Time, Inc., Rockefeller Bldg., Rockefeller Center, New York, NY 10020.)
Lists the 500 largest and the 500 second-largest industrial corporations, along with the 500 largest commercial banks, utilities, life insurance companies, diversified financial companies, retailers, transportation companies, and diversified services.

Grocery Commercial Food Industry Directory
(GroCom Group, Inc., P.O. Box 10378, Clearwater, FL 34617.)
Profiles 2,500 manufacturers, wholesalers, brokers, distributors, and other suppliers of food and beverage products and food-industry-related products.

Harbinger File
(Harbinger Communications , 50 Rustic Lane, Santa Cruz, CA 95060.)
Directory of government agencies, companies, citizen's groups, and governmental education programs concerned with energy and environmental issues.

Hollywood Reporter Studio Blue Book Directory
(Hollywood Reporter, 5055 Wilshire Blvd., Los Angeles, CA 90036.)
Thousands of listings of major studios, record and production companies, actors, etc.

Hoover's Guide to the Top Chicago Area Companies
(The Reference Press, 6448 Highway 290 E., Suite E-104, Austin, TX 78723.)

Human Care Services Directory of Metropolitan Chicago
(United Way/Crusade of Mercy/Community Renewal Society, 560 W. Lake St., Chicago, IL 60606.)
Profiles the agencies of Chicago that help people in all areas; useful client descriptions.

Illinois Blue Book
(Illinois Secretary of State, State House, Room 213, Springfield, IL 62756, free.)
Descriptions of state departments and agencies; Chicago city government; key
personnel.

Illinois Foundation Directory
(Foundation Data Center, 401 Kenmar Circle, Minnetonka, MN 55343, $625.)
Describes 2,000 active and inactive foundations; major contributors; financial
data; indexed geographically.

Illinois Manufacturers Directory
(Manufacturers News, Inc., 4 E. Huron St., Chicago, IL 60611, $125.)
Describes all manufacturing companies located in Illinois; key personnel; cross-
referenced and indexed geographically.

Illinois Media
(Midwest Newsclip, Inc., 213 W. Institute Place, Chicago, IL 60610.)
Lists daily and weekly newspapers, radio and TV stations in Illinois,
and key personnel.

Illinois Services Directory
(Manufacturers News, Inc., 4 E. Huron St., Chicago, IL 60611, $135.)
Describes all wholesalers, jobbers, contractors, retailers, services located in
Illinois; key personnel; cross-referenced and indexed geographically.

Illinois Solar Energy Directory
(Illinois Department of Energy and Natural Resources, 325 W. Adams,
Springfield, IL 62706, free.)
Lists distributors and manufacturers of solar equipment; consultants; associa-
tions.

Job Seeker's Guide to Private and Public Companies
(Gale Research Co., 835 Penobscot Bldg., Detroit, MI 48226.)
Lists over 15,000 firms, including products and services, size, human resource
contacts, and application procedures.

Literary Marketplace
(R.R. Bowker, 245 W. 17th St., New York, NY 10011.)
Lists virtually every U.S. and Canadian book publisher. Includes editorial ser-
vices, agents, printers, and professional associations.

Membership Directory
(International Advertising Association, 342 Madison Ave., New York, NY
10017.)
Covers 3,200 member advertisers, advertising agencies, media, and other firms
involved in advertising. Arranged geographically and by function or service.

National Directory of Minority-Owned Business Firms
(Business Research Services, 4201 Connecticut Ave., N.W., Washington, DC 20008.)
Lists company name, size, description, and address.

National Directory of Women-Owned Business Firms
(Business Research Services, 4201 Connecticut Ave., N.W., Washington, DC 20008.)
Lists company name, size, description, and address.

Occupational Outlook Handbook
(U.S. Bureau of Labor, 200 Constitutional Ave., N.W., Washington, DC 20210.)
Describes what people do in their jobs, training and education needed, earnings, working conditions, and employment outlook.

O'Dwyer's Directory of Public Relations Firms
(J.R. O'Dwyer & Co., 271 Madison Ave., New York, NY 10016.)
Describes 2,200 public relations firms in the U.S., their key personnel, local offices, and accounts; indexed geographically.

Peterson's Job Opportunities for Engineering, Science, and Computer Graduates
(Peterson's Guides, 202 Carnegie Center, P.O. Box 2123, Princeton, NJ 08543-2123.)
Lists specific companies within these industries.

Publicity Club of Chicago Membership Guide
(Publicity Club of Chicago, 435 N. Michigan Ave., Chicago, IL 60611.)
Lists individuals and firms in media and public relations.

Recording Industry Sourcebook
(Mix Publications, 6400 Hollis St., Suite 10, Emeryville, CA 94608.)
National directory of the recording industry, including record labels, production agencies, and industry associations.

Sheldon's Retail Directory
(Phelon, Sheldon & Marsar, 15 Industrial Ave., Fairview, NJ 07022.)
Directory of the largest department stores, women's specialty stores, chain stores, and resident buying offices. Geographical listings plus alphabetical index.

Ward's Business Directory of U.S. Private and Public Companies
(Gale Research Co., 835 Penobscot Bldg., Detroit, MI 48226.)
Covers nearly 85,000 privately owned companies, representing all industries.

Don't overlook the burbs
When looking for a job in the Chicago area, be sure not to neglect the surrounding suburbs. The communities around Chicago have enjoyed unprecedented growth in the past

several years as many large companies expand into the suburbs and new companies base their headquarters there, taking advantage of large tracts of available land and lower taxes.

Electronics giant Motorola is based in northwest suburban Schaumburg. Amoco has a huge research faciltiy located in west suburban Naperville. Sears moved its headquarters from the Sears Tower downtown to Hoffman Estates. Baxter pharmaceuticals is based in the northern suburb of Deerfield.

Jack Romine, President of the Naperville Chamber of Commerce, says that city adds 1,000-2,000 new jobs every year.

"We get all types, from scientists and engineers at the Amoco Research Center to people who wash dishes and clean rooms."

Romine says large companies that move to the suburbs and employ thousands of people, such as Amoco, AT&T, and Chrysler, spur the initial growth that leads to secondary jobs in retail, services, and construction

"We also see the formation of new businesses because of the downsizing of large companies," Romine says. "People take employee buy-outs and then get into an entrepreneurial spirit. They start a restaurant or begin consulting in the field they've worked in all their lives, and eventually offer more jobs to other people."

Trade Magazines

Every industry or service business has its trade press—that is, editors, reporters, and photographers whose job it is to cover an industry or trade. You should become familiar with the magazines of the industries or professions that interest you, especially if you're in the interviewing stage of your job search. Your prospective employers are reading the industry trade magazines; you should be, too.

Trade magazines are published for a specific business or professional audience; they are usually expensive and available by subscription only. Many of the magazines we've listed here are available at the Chicago Public Library's Business Information Center, 400 S. State St., 4th floor. For those that are not to be found at the library, call the magazine's editorial or sales office and ask if you can come over to look at the latest issue.

The following magazines have editorial offices in metropolitan Chicago, reporting Chicago area news about the people and businesses in their industry. Most carry local want ads and personnel changes. For a complete listing of the trade press, consult the *Ayer Directory of Publications, Gale Directory of Publications,* and/or *Broadcast Media* at the Library's Business Information Center.

AAII Journal
American Association of Individual
Investors
625 N. Michigan Ave., Suite 1900
Chicago, IL 60611
(312) 280-0170

ABA Banking Journal
175 W. Jackson Blvd., Suite A1927
Chicago, IL 60604
(312) 427-2729

ABA Journal
American Bar Association
750 N. Lake Shore Drive
Chicago, IL 60611
(312) 988-6018

ADA News
American Dental Association
211 E. Chicago Ave.
Chicago, IL 60611
(312) 440-2780

Advertising Age
740 N. Rush St.
Chicago, IL 60611-2590
(312) 649-5200

Adweek/Midwest
435 N. Michigan Ave., Suite 819
Chicago, IL 60611
(312) 467-6500

American Banker
53 W. Jackson #230
Chicago, IL 60604
(312) 663-6380

American Metal Market
Fairchild Publications
190 N. State St.
Chicago, IL 60603
(312) 609-0900

American Printer
29 N. Wacker Drive
Chicago, IL 60606
(312) 726-2802

Appliance/New Product Digest
Dana Chase Publications
1110 Jorie Blvd.
Oak Brook, IL 60522-9019
(630) 990-3484

Appraiser News
Appraisal Institute
875 N. Michigan Ave., Suite 2400
Chicago, IL 60611-1980
(312) 335-4100

Architectural Record
4546 N. Leavitt
Chicago, IL 60625
(312) 616-3324

Assembly
Hitchcock Publications
191 S. Gary Ave.
Carol Stream, IL 60188
(630) 462-2339

Automobile Law Reports-Insurance Cases
Commerce Clearing House
4025 W. Peterson Ave.
Chicago, IL 60646
(773) 583-8500

Automotive Electronics Newsletter
Irving Cloud Publishing Co.
417 N. Hough St.
Barrington, IL 60010
(847) 382-3405

Automotive News
740 N. Rush St.
Chicago, IL 60611
(312) 649-5200

Back Stage Shoot
205 W. Randolph Ave.
Chicago, IL 60606
(312) 236-9102

Bank Management
Bank Administration Institute
2550 W. Golf Road
Rolling Meadows, IL 60008
(847) 228-6200

Bank Marketing Magazine
309 W. Washington St.
Chicago, IL 60606
(312) 782-1442

Bank Network News
Barlo Communications Corp.
118 S. Clinton St., Suite 450
Chicago, IL 60606
(312) 648-0261

Barron's National Business &
Financial Weekly
1 S. Wacker Drive, #2100
Chicago, IL 60606-4614
(312) 750-4125

Billboard Magazine
205 W. Randolph, Suite 920
Chicago, IL 60606
(312) 236-9818

Brewing Industry News
P.O. Box 27037
Riverdale, IL 60627
(708) 841-1639

Building Design & Construction
Cahners Publishing Co.
1350 E. Touhy Ave.
Des Plaines, IL 60018
(847) 635-8800

Building Supply Home Centers
Cahners Publishing Co.
1350 E. Touhy Ave.
Des Plaines, IL 60018
(847) 635-8800

Business Insurance
740 N. Rush St.
Chicago, IL 60611
(312) 649-5275

Business Marketing
740 N. Rush St.
Chicago, IL 60611
(312) 649-5260

CBA
Chicago Bar Association
321 Plymouth Court
Chicago, IL 60604-3997
(312) 554-2000

Chicago Advertising and Media
KB Communications
1412 N. Halsted St.
Chicago, IL 60622
(312) 944-0100

Chicago Business Review
1407-B N. Wells
Chicago, IL 60610
(312) 944-1900

The Chicago Computer Guide
120 W. Madison #1218
Chicago, IL 60602
(312) 332-0419

Chicago Computing
912 Chicago Ave.
Evanston, IL 60202
(847) 328-7270

The Chicago Daily Law Bulletin
415 N. State St.
Chicago, IL 60610
(312) 644-7800

Chicago Film and Video News
2600 W. Peterson Ave.
Chicago, IL 60659
(773) 465-7246

Chicago Lawyer
415 N. State St.
Chicago, IL 60610
(312) 644-7800

Chicago Medicine
515 N. Dearborn St.
Chicago, IL 60610
(312) 670-2550

Chicago Purchaser
201 N. Wells St., Suite 618
Chicago, IL 60606
(312) 782-1940

Chicago Union Teacher
Chicago Teachers Union
222 Merchandise Mart Plaza, #400
Chicago, IL 60654
(312) 329-9100

Commercial Investment Real Estate Journal
Commercial Investment Real Estate Institute
430 N. Michigan Ave.
Chicago, IL 60611-4092
(312) 321-4460

Common Market Reports
Commerce Clearing House
4025 W. Peterson Ave.
Chicago, IL 60646
(773) 583-8500

Communications News
233 N. Michigan Ave., 24th floor
Chicago, IL 60601
(312) 938-2300

The Compleat Lawyer
Family Advocate
750 N. Lake Shore Drive
Chicago, IL 60611
(312) 988-6056

Computerized Investing
625 N. Michigan Ave.
Chicago, IL 60611
(312) 280-0170

Concrete Construction Magazine
426 S. Westgate
Addison, IL 60101
(630) 543-0870
Construction equipment.

Consulting Specifying Engineer
Cahners Publishing Co.
1350 E. Touhy Ave.
Des Plaines, IL 60018
(847) 635-8800

Contractor
Cahners Publishing Co.

1350 E. Touhy Ave.
Des Plaines, IL 60018
(847) 635-8800

Control Engineering
Cahners Publishing Co.
1350 E. Touhy Ave.
Des Plaines, IL 60018
(847) 635-8800

Corporate Risk Management
250 S. Wacker, Suite 1150
Chicago, IL 60606
(312) 977-0859

Curriculum Review
407 S. Dearborn St.
Chicago, IL 60605
(312) 922-8245

Daily News Record
Fairchild Publications
190 N. State St.
Chicago, IL 60603
(312) 609-0900

Datamation Magazine
Cahners Publishing Co.
1350 E. Touhy Ave.
Des Plaines, IL 60018
(847) 635-8800

Dateline
Publicity Club of Chicago
1163 Shermer Road
Northbrook, IL 60062
(847) 564-8180

The Dental Assistant
Journal of the American Dental Assistants Association
919 N. Michigan Ave., Suite 3400
Chicago, IL 60611
(312) 664-3327

Die Casting Engineer
Triton College Campus
2000 N. 5th Ave.
River Grove, IL 60171
(708) 452-0700

Discovery
111 E. Wacker Drive, #1700
Chicago, IL 60601
(312) 565-1200
Travel magazine.

Dodge Construction News
2 Prudential Plaza
180 N. Stetson Ave., Suite 910
Chicago, IL 60601
(312) 616-3282

Dollars and Sense
National Publication Sales Agency
1610 E. 79th St.
Chicago, IL 60649
(773) 375-6800

Editor & Publisher
8 S. Michigan Ave., Suite 1601
Chicago, IL 60611
(312) 641-0041

Electric Light & Power
Pen Well Publishing Co.
1250 S. Grove Ave., Suite 302
Barrington, IL 60010
(847) 382-2450

Electronic Media
Crain Communications
740 N. Rush St.
Chicago, IL 60611
(312) 649-5200

Electronic Packaging & Production
Cahners Publishing Co.
1350 E. Touhy Ave.
Des Plaines, IL 60018
(847) 635-8800

Employee Benefit Plan Review
Charles D. Spencer & Associates
250 S. Wacker Drive, Suite 600
Chicago, IL 60606-5834
(312) 993-7900

Environmental Watch
430 N. Michigan Ave.
Chicago, IL 60611-4088
(312) 329-8559

Fancy Food
208 W. Huron St.
Chicago, IL 60610
(312) 670-0800

Filmfax
P.O. Box 1900
Evanston, IL 60204
(847) 866-7155

Fleet Equipment
7300 N. Cicero
Lincolnwood, IL 60646
(847) 674-7300

Food Business
301 E. Erie
Chicago, IL 60611
(312) 644-2020

Food Industry News
2702 W. Touhy
Chicago, IL 60645
(773) 743-4200

Food Processing
301 E. Erie
Chicago, IL 60611
(312) 644-2020

Food Service Equipment Specialist
Cahners Publishing Co.
1350 E. Touhy Ave.
Des Plaines, IL 60018
(847) 635-8800

Food Technology
221 N. LaSalle
Chicago, IL 60601
(312) 782-8424

Footwear News
Fairchild Publications
190 N. State St.
Chicago, IL 60603
(312) 609-0900

Forum
Illinois Credit Union League
1807 Diehl Road
Naperville, IL 60566
(630) 983-3400

Futures
The Magazine of Commodities &
Options
250 S. Wacker Drive, Suite 1150
Chicago, IL 60606
(312) 977-0999

Graphic Arts Product News
800 W. Huron
Chicago, IL 60622
(312) 726-2802

Grocery Distribution Magazine
455 S. Frontage St., Suite 116
Burr Ridge, IL 60521
(630) 986-8767

Grocery Marketing
8750 W. Bryn Mawr
Chicago, IL 60631-3508
(773) 693-3200

Health Care Strategic Management
770 N. LaSalle #701
Chicago, IL 60610
(312) 943-3200

Health Facilities Management
211 E. Chicago Ave.
Chicago, IL 60611
(312) 440-6800

Health Industry Today
770 N. LaSalle #701
Chicago, IL 60610
(312) 943-3200

Healthcare Executive
840 N. Lake Shore Drive
Chicago, IL 60611
(312) 943-0544

Healthcare Financial Management
2 Westbrook Corporate
Center, #700
Westchester, IL 60154
(708) 531-9600

Heat Treating
Fairchild Publications

190 N. State St.
Chicago, IL 60603
(312) 609-0900

Highway & Heavy Construction Products
Cahner's Publishing Co.
1350 E. Touhy Ave.
Des Plaines, IL 60018
(847) 635-8800

Home Center Magazine
Vance Publishing Co.
400 Knightsbridge Pkwy.
Lincolnshire, IL 60069
(847) 634-2600

Home Furnishing Daily (HFI)
Fairchild Publications
190 N. State St.
Chicago, IL 60603
(312) 609-0900

Hospital Materials Management
770 N. LaSalle #701
Chicago, IL 60610
(312) 943-3200

Hospitals
American Hospital Publishing
737 N. Michigan Ave.
Chicago, IL 60611
(312) 440-6800

Hotels
Cahner's Publishing Co.
1350 E. Touhy Ave.
Des Plaines, IL 60018
(847) 635-8800

The Illinois Banker
111 N. Canal St.
Chicago, IL 60606
(312) 876-9900

Illinois Banknews
111 N. Canal St.
Chicago, IL 60606
(312) 876-9900

Illinois Bar Journal
424 S. 2nd St.
Springfield, IL 62701
(800) 252-8908

Illinois Entertainer
2250 E. Devon, Suite 150
Des Plaines, IL 60018
(847) 298-9333

Illinois Legal Time
420 W. Grand Ave.
Chicago, IL 60610-4036
(312) 644-4378

Illinois Medicine
Illinois State Medical Society
20 N. Michigan Ave.
Chicago, IL 60602
(312) 782-1654

Illinois Reporter
Illinois League of Savings Institutions
220 E. Adams St.
Springfield, IL 62701
(217) 552-5575

Illinois Truck News
Illinois Trucking Association
2000 N. 5th Ave.
River Grove, IL 60171
(708) 452-3500

Industry Week
2 Illinois Center
233 N. Michigan Ave., Suite 1300
Chicago, IL 60601
(312) 861-0880

Inland Architect
10 W. Hubbard St.
P.O. Box 10394
Chicago, IL 60610
(312) 321-0583

Inside Data Processing Management
Association
505 Busse Highway
Park Ridge, IL 60068
(847) 693-5070

Instant & Small Commercial Printer
P.O. Box 368
Northbrook, IL 60065
(847) 564-5940

Iron Age
Fairchild Publications
190 N. State St.
Chicago, IL 60603
(312) 609-0900

JAMA (Journal of the Amer. Medical
Assn.)
515 N. State St., 10th floor
Chicago, IL 60610
(312) 464-2446

Jobber Topics Reports
Irving Cloud Publishing Co.
417 N. Hough St.
Barrington, IL 60010
(847) 382-3405

Laboratory Medicine
2100 W. Harrison
Chicago, IL 60612
(312) 738-1336

Lodging Hospitality
2 Illinois Center
233 N. Michigan Ave., Suite 1300
Chicago, IL 60601
(312) 861-0880

Maintenance Technology
Applied Technology Publications
1300 S. Grove Ave., Suite 205
Barrington, IL 60010
(847) 382-8100

Manufacturing Systems
Hitchcock Publications
191 S. Gary Ave.
Carol Stream, IL 60188
(630) 462-2339

Marketing News
American Marketing Association
250 S. Wacker Drive, Suite 200
Chicago, IL 60606-5819
(312) 993-9517

Masonry Construction
426 S. Westgate
Addison, IL 60101
(630) 543-0870

Metal Center News
Fairchild Publications
190 N. State St.
Chicago, IL 60603
(312) 609-0900

Metro Chicago Office Guide
415 N. State St.
Chicago, IL 60610
(312) 644-7800

Metro Chicago Real Estate Guide
415 N. State St.
Chicago, IL 60610
(312) 644-7800

Midwest Automotive News
2900 W. Peterson Ave.
Chicago, IL 60659
(773) 764-1640

Modern Health Care
Crain Communications
740 N. Rush St.
Chicago, IL 60611
(312) 649-5200

Modern Salon
Vance Publishing Co.
400 Knightsbridge Pkwy.
Lincolnshire, IL 60069
(847) 634-2600

Modern Steel Construction
1 E. Wacker Drive
Chicago, IL 60610
(312) 644-7800

Money Maker
5705 Lincoln
Chicago, IL 60659
(773) 275-3590

Motor Service
950 Lee St.

Des Plaines, IL 60616
(847) 296-0770

NASCI News
Woodfield Financial Center
1450 E. American Lane, Suite 140
Schaumburg, IL 60173
(847) 517-7110

National Paralegal Reporter
104 Wilmot Road, #201
Deerfield, IL 60015
(847) 940-8800

National Petroleum News
950 Lee St.
Des Plaines, IL 60016
(847) 296-0770

National Real Estate Investor
307 N. Michigan Ave., #803
Chicago, IL 60601
(312) 726-7266

National Underwriter
20 N. Wacker Drive, Room 1725
Chicago, IL 60606
(312) 922-2704

Nuclear News
555 N. Kensington Ave.
LaGrange Park, IL 60525
(708) 352-6611

Office Products Dealer
Hitchcock Publications
191 S. Gary Ave.
Carol Stream, IL 60188
(630) 462-2339

Packaging Magazine
Cahners Publishing Co.
1350 E. Touhy Ave.
Des Plaines, IL 60018
(847) 635-8800

Paperboard Packaging
233 N. Michigan Ave., 24th floor
Chicago, IL 60601
(312) 938-2345

Pensions & Investments
Crain Communications
740 N. Rush St.
Chicago, IL 60611
(312) 649-5407

PIMA
Paper Industry Management
Association
2400 E. Oakton St.
Arlington Heights, IL 60005
(847) 956-0250

Plan & Print
611 E. Butterfield Road #104
Lombard, IL 60148
(630) 852-3055

Plant Engineering
Cahners Publishing Co.
1350 E. Touhy Ave.
Des Plaines, IL 60018
(847) 635-8800

Plant Services
301 E. Erie St.
Chicago, IL 60611
(312) 644-2020

Pollution Engineering
Cahners Publishing Co.
1350 E. Touhy Ave.
Des Plaines, IL 60018
(847) 635-8800

Power Engineering
Pen Well Publishing Co.
1250 S. Grove St., Suite 302
Barrington, IL 60010
(847) 382-2450

PR/Chicago
30 N. Michigan #508
Chicago, IL 60602
(312) 372-7744

Practicing Architect
1245 S. Highland Ave.
Lombard, IL 60148
(630) 932-4622

Printing News Midwest-PN/M
800 W. Huron
Chicago, IL 60622
(312) 226-5600

Professional Builder
Cahners Publishing Co.
1350 E. Touhy Ave.
Des Plaines, IL 60018
(847) 635-8800

Quality
Hitchcock Publications
191 S. Gary Ave.
Carol Stream, IL 60188
(630) 462-2339

Real Estate News
2600 W. Peterson, Suite 100
Chicago, IL 60659
(773) 465-5151

Realty & Building
311 W. Superior St., Suite 316
Chicago, IL 60610
(312) 944-1204

Research & Development
Cahners Publishing Co.
1350 E. Touhy Ave.
Des Plaines, IL 60018
(847) 635-8800

Restaurant Hospitality
1030 State St.
Chicago, IL 60601
(312) 861-0880

Restaurants and Institutions
Cahners Publishing Co.
1350 E. Touhy Ave.
Des Plaines, IL 60018
(847) 635-8800

Road King
23060 Cicero Ave.
Richton Park, IL 60471
(708) 481-9240

Savings Institutions
U.S. League of Savings Institutions
111 E. Wacker Drive
Chicago, IL 60601
(312) 644-3100

Screen Magazine
720 N. Wabash
Chicago, IL 60611
(312) 664-5236

Security
Cahners Publishing Co.
1350 E. Touhy Ave.
Des Plaines, IL 60018
(847) 635-8800

Security Distributing & Marketing
Cahners Publishing Co.
1350 E. Touhy Ave.
Des Plaines, IL 60018
(847) 635-8800

Semiconductor International
Cahners Publishing Co.
1350 E. Touhy Ave.
Des Plaines, IL 60018
(847) 635-8800

Sporting Goods Business
6160 N. Cicero, Suite 122
Chicago, IL 60646
(773) 545-0700

Student Lawyer
750 N. Lake Shore Drive
Chicago, IL 60611
(312) 988-6048

Super Automotive Service
Irving Cloud Publishing Co.
417 N. Hough St.
Barrington, IL 60010
(847) 382-3405

Supermarket News
Fairchild Publications
190 N. State St.
Chicago, IL 60603
(312) 609-0900

Supply House Times
Cahners Publishing Co.
1350 E. Touhy Ave.
Des Plaines, IL 60018
(847) 635-8800

Systems 3X/400
950 Lee St.
Des Plaines, IL 60016
(847) 296-0770

Telephone Engineering & Management
233 N. Michigan Ave., 24th floor
Chicago, IL 60601
(312) 938-2378

Top Shelf: Barkeeping At Its Best
P.O. Box 306
Grayslake, IL 60030
(847) 223-1363

Tours & Resorts
World Publishing Co.
900 Grove St., 4th floor
Evanston, IL 60201-4370
(847) 491-6440

U.S. Glass, Metal, & Glazing Magazine
560 Oakwood Ave., Suite 202
Lake Forest, IL 60045-1906
(847) 295-2900

Water Engineering and Management
380 Northwest Highway
Des Plaines, IL 60016
(847) 298-6622

Water and Wastes Digest
380 Northwest Highway
Des Plaines, IL 60016
(847) 298-6622

Women's Wear Daily
Fairchild Publications
190 N. State St.
Chicago, IL 60603
(312) 609-0900

Wood & Wood Products
Vance Publishing Co.
400 Knightsbridge Pkwy.
Lincolnshire, IL 60069
(847) 634-2600

Worldwide Travel Planner
7842 N. Lincoln Ave.
Skokie, IL 60077
(847) 676-1900

Job Listings

Cover all your bases and respond to promising job advertisements in your field. The following resources contain only job listings and job-related information and advice.

AA/EEO Affirmative Action Register
8356 Olive Blvd.
St. Louis, MO 63132
(314) 991-1335
Academic, professional, and administrative jobs for women, minorities, veterans, and people with disabilities. Monthly magazine consists totally of job listings.

Black Employment & Education
2625 Piedmont Road 56-282
Atlanta, GA 30324
(404) 469-5891
Magazine lists career opportunities nationwide. Your resume may be placed on their database for employer access.

Career Pilot
Future Aviation Professionals of America
4959 Massachusetts Blvd.
Atlanta, GA 30337
(409) 997-8097
Monthly magazine outlines employment opportunities for career pilots.

Community Jobs
30 Irving Place, 9th floor
New York, NY 10003
(212) 485-1001
Monthly nationwide listings of jobs with community organizations and advocacy groups.

Contract Engineer Weekly
CE Publications
P.O. Box 97000
Kirkland, WA 98083
(206) 823-2222
Weekly magazine of job opportunities for contract engineers.

Federal Jobs Digest
Breakthrough Publications
310 N. Highland Ave.
Ossining, NY 10562
Civil service job listings (semi-monthly).

International Employment Hotline
Cantrell Corp.
P.O. Box 3030
Oakton, VA 22124
(703) 620-1972
Monthly listing of overseas jobs. Features current job openings &
helpful advice.

National and Federal Legal Employment Report
Federal Reports
1010 Vermont Ave., N.W.
Washington, DC 20005
(202) 393-3311
Monthly in-depth listings of attorney and law-related jobs in federal government and with other public and private employers throughout the U.S.

Opportunities In Non-profit Organizations
ACCESS: Networking in the Public Interest
50 Beacon St.
Boston, MA 02108
(212) 475-1001
Monthly listings of community jobs around the country, organized by type of
non-profit.

Publishing Program News
5835 S. Kimbark Ave.
Chicago, IL 60637, Room 207
(773) 702-1724
Monthly listings of jobs in publishing from the University of Chicago, 12 issues,
$10.

Voice-Based Job Hotlines

"Let your fingers do the walking!" Just dial any one of the numerous telephone
job banks and listen to the taped recordings that describe available positions and
how to apply. Many are available at no charge other than what you might spend
for the telephone call. Some company-oriented job information lines include:

City of Chicago: (312) 744-1369

Commonwealth Edison Co.: (312) 838-4218 and (847) 816-5596

DePaul University: (312) 362-6803

Federal Job Information Center: (312) 353-6192

First Chicago Corporation/NBD Bank: (312) 407-JOBS

Harris Bank: (312) 461-6900

Library Job Line of Illinois: (312) 828-0930

Prudential Insurance: (800) 778-8326

Quaker Oats Company: (312) 222-7744

Internet: Best bet for job listings

Telephone-based job lines are being converted to job listings on the Internet. You will find more Internet-based job listings today than telephone-based services. For example, most corporations and colleges now post their job vacancies on their Web homepages. Electronic recruiting is less expensive than most other types of advertising and employers increasingly are taking advantage of the new technology.

Internet Job Listings

Use the Net as another source of job listings. Below are a few places to begin.

American Employment Weekly
http://branch.com/aew/aew.html
Contains help-wanted ads, ranging from data processing to medical positions from over 50 leading newspapers.

America's Job Bank
http://www.ajb.dni.us/
A federal program that may eventually include the jobs posted with state unemployment offices (Job Service, Employment Security, etc.) nationwide.

Career Channel
http://riceinfo.rice.edu:80/projects/careers/
Rice University lists jobs, links, and a wealth of other job-search information.

Career Connections
http://www.employmentedge.com/employment.edge/
Specializes in professional career placement throughout the U.S.

Career Magazine
http://www.careermag.com/careermag/
A comprehensive resource that includes job-opening database, employer profiles, articles, and news to assist in the career search and career forums.

CareerNet
http://www.careers.org/
A good source, with links to many other job-listing organizations.

CareerPath
http://www.careerpath.com
Lists the *Chicago Tribune, New York Times,* and four other major dailies' classifieds, but no display ads.

CareerWeb
http://www.cweb.com/
Job seekers can browse worldwide career opportunities, including the *Wall Street Journal National Business Employment Weekly.*

Contract Employment Weekly
http://www.ceweekly
Furnishes job openings throughout U.S. and overseas.

Easynet Job-Centre
http://www.easynet.co.uk/
Here you can peruse the jobs on offer, and look for people to employ.

Employment Opportunities and Resume Postings-EINet
http://galaxy.einet.net/
A guide to worldwide information and services.

Entry Level Job Seeker Assistant
http://www.utsi.edu:70/students
Ideal for people who have never held a full-time, permanent job in their field or who have less than a year of non-academic experience.

E-Span
http://www.espan.com/
Provides a searchable database of high-tech job openings as well as a wide variety of resources for the job seeker.

Help Wanted
http://www.webcom.com/
On-line employment services.

JobCenter
http://www.jobcenter.com
Matches job searcher's skills with employer's needs.

Job Junction
http://www.iquest.net/iq/jobjunction
Contains career information, reference material, and on-line job database.

JobWeb
http://www.jobweb.org
Operated by the National Association of Colleges and Employers. Primarily targeted at college students, JobWeb offers career planning and employment information, job-search articles, and job listings.

Monster Board
http://www.monster.com/
Companies around the country list jobs along with employer profiles. Search for jobs by location, industry, company, and discipline.

Online Career Center
http://www.occ.com/
Includes job listings from over 300 U.S. companies. Browse by job title, company name, or geographic region.

PursuitNet Jobs
http://www.tiac.net/users/job
Job-search service matches skills and desires with compatible jobs in the U.S.

Recruiters Online Network
http://www.onramp.net
Recruiters, employment agencies, search firms, and employment professionals share business opportunities and job postings.

Today's Classifieds
http://www.nando.net/classads/
Internet users can search classifieds by career field.

JOB LINKS SPECIFIC TO THE CHICAGO AREA

Private Sector Jobs from Illinois Department of Employment Security (IDES)
http://www.careers.org/html/s-il.htm or
http://il.jobsearch.org/
Search jobs posted at IDES Service Centers. Updated weekly. Details about the job listings are available through the local IDES Service Centers at no charge. Simply provide the listed job order number to receive a referral.

Federal Jobs in Chicago
http://www.careers.org/text/il.txt
Jobs with the federal government in Chicago, updated several times per week.

FedWorld Information Network
http://www.fedworld.gov/index.html
Federal job openings.

Chicago Tribune Employment Advertisements
http://www.careerpath.com/

College and University Job Listings
Your college or university may be affiliated with JOBTRAK, an Internet job listing service for higher education. Access to JOBTRAK is limited to students and alumni of partnership schools and is not available to the general public. If you're an alum of a partnership school, you will need to obtain a password to access job listings targeted to your alma mater. Contact your school's career service office to check on your eligibility and service fees.

Most schools charge a modest alumni access fee for basic service, e.g., $30-50 for 3-6 months access. You can also list your resume with JOBTRAK. Remember, employers who use JOBTRAK want to target students and alumni of specific schools, not the general public. JOBTRAK links employers who have specific openings with candidates from specific schools.

Beyond job listings, JOBTRAK provides a wealth of information on job finding, education, job fairs, and other career-related topics. Check it out at:
http://www.jobtrak.com/

Small Companies

Today's job market has changed. Big business is no longer the biggest employer. Today, 80% of new jobs created in the United States are by small and medium-sized firms that are four or five years old.

Small and medium-sized businesses, those that employ less than 500 people, are good bets for employment opportunities. These companies are expected to expand. Small businesses employ 48% of the American workforce. Two-thirds of all first jobs come from these growing businesses. The big boys of business may still provide better benefits and pay to their employees, but they only manage to provide 11% of the jobs sought by first-time job seekers.

Searching for jobs with small businesses is not, however, as easy as the traditional job search at the large corporation. Small business is less likely to advertise for a position, use an agency, or post a listing at a local college. They generally use the networking method of knowing someone who knows someone. Thus, you may need to be creative when searching out small companies. Use your resources, such as Chambers of Commerce and Small Business Centers (see Chapter 2) to help you in your search.

RECOMMENDED READING

Colton, Kitty, and Michele Fetterolf. *1995: A Job Seeker's Guide to America's 2000 Little-known, Fastest-Growing High-Tech Companies.* Princeton, NJ: Peterson's Guides, 1994.

Step 3: Organize Your Search

The most difficult part of any job search is getting started. The next most difficult is staying organized. Preparing a resume, sending it out, scheduling interviews, and returning phone calls is enough to cause anyone to grab for the extra-strength aspirin! Organize your job search and you'll have fewer headaches.

Don't Get Caught Without Your Daily Planner

Have you ever noticed how many people carry around those little black "Daily Planners"? In this case, what's good for the crowd is also good for you, the job searcher. You need to keep a written record of every person you contact in your job search and the results of each contact. This will prevent a job lead from falling through the cracks. It may even come in handy for future job searches.

Your Daily Planner should serve as a way of organizing your efforts for greatest efficiency. Much of your job search will be spent developing your network of contacts. Still, you should allocate a portion of each week for doing research on companies that interest you and for pursuing other means of contacting employers.

As you go through your contacts and begin to research the job market, you'll begin to identify certain employers in whom you're interested. Keep a list of them. For each one that looks promising, start a file that contains articles on the company, its annual report, product brochures, company profile, and any other interesting information. Every so often, check your "potential companies" list against your planner to insure that you stay in contact with them.

Step 4: Network

While Chapter 5 will give you the essentials of networking and a list of networking resources, it is important to remember that it's "who you know" that gets you ahead in the job search. Professional organizations are a great source for networking and gleaning vital information about employment. Get involved in organizations in your field of interest to keep abreast of opportunities as they become available. And don't forget to stay abreast of the business world in general through business magazines and newspapers (see Chapter 1 for listings).

If you are just starting your network, use the information interview (see Chapter 5) to find out more about a particular career field and to acquaint yourself with professionals in that field. People like to hire individuals they know, so the more potential employers you meet, the better your odds for landing a job.

Dear Dr. Bob

Is there job-search etiquette I should know about?—Proper Etiquette Job Searcher

Dear Proper Etiquette Job Searcher
As everywhere else, there exists proper etiquette in the job search. For example, the telephone is a wonderful tool by which an assertive job seeker can make contact with employers and follow-up on job applications and leads. However, reminding the employer of your interest in a position is not tantamount to badgering him or her into interviewing you. Follow every letter you mail with a phone call, but allow ample time for the employer to receive and review your credentials. One to two weeks is the usual rule of thumb.

Manic Monday mornings are a particularly unpleasant time for employers to receive phone calls. A better time is between 10 a.m. and 2 p.m. Tuesdays, Wednesdays, or Thursdays. And always check to see if you have called at a convenient time.

The fax machine can be a dangerous beast and should be used cautiously by the job searcher. Certainly it does offer instant communication with an employer. But unsolicited faxes are annoying to employers. Not only does it tie up the fax line and use expensive paper but it is likely that the hiring authority will not even see it. However, my advice is to fax only when requested to do so by a hiring authority.

Finally, treat the potential employer with the utmost respect. Be sure to keep meetings at the time you both agreed on. Follow up with a thank-you letter, reiterating your qualifications and thanking your host for his time. Try to keep everyone in your network informed of your status in the job search.

Step 5: Persistence and Follow-Up

Persistence is one of the key strategies in the job search. Whether you are pursuing job leads, sending out resumes, scheduling interviews, or contacting a hiring authority, you need to be persistent. The passive job searcher relies upon the want ads as his or her only source of job leads. The persistent job searcher is proactive, using resources such as networking groups, newspapers, professional organizations, and directories. The passive job searcher will accept "no" without questioning or pursuing the hiring authority. The persistent job searcher will make a few more calls. Being persistent can help you accomplish the ultimate goal— landing the job.

Persistence is also a state of mind. It's important to remain enthusiastic, to keep going, and to make calls. It is only too easy for the job searcher to lose energy and conveniently forget to make those important follow-up calls. Remember you most likely are just one of many applicants for a job, and persistence is the key to success. Plenty of rejection will probably come your way. It is up to you to keep going and put rejection behind you.

Follow-up all promising contacts with calls and letters. Whether you're networking or actually talking with someone in a position to hire you, it is important to stay in touch with whomever can assist you in your job search. If someone takes the time to give you a lead, it is only proper for you to inform the individual of the outcome.

Follow-up resumes with a phone call to ensure that your resume was received. It is impossible to get an interview if your resume got lost in the mail. Likewise, a thank-you note after an interview will keep your name foremost with the interviewer and less likely to be lost in the shuffle.

Our "silent" president speaks

"Nothing in this world can take the place of persistence. Talent will not; nothing is more common than unsuccessful men with great talent.
Genius will not; unrewarded genius is almost a proverb.
Education will not; the world is full of educated derelicts.
Persistence and determination alone are omnipotent."
—Calvin Coolidge

Step 6: Prepare Your Resume

Writing a good resume and a cover letter to accompany it is important in marketing yourself and lining up interviews. Chapter 6 goes into detail on resume writing. It is important to remember that this step can be crucial to your other steps.

Remember that most resumes get about 20 seconds of the employer's time. Therefore, it is vital to keep the resume to one page and skimmable enough to grab the reader's attention. The following guidelines should help you develop a well-written resume:

- Tailor your resume to the potential job as much as possible.
- Information should be easy to skim and locate.
- Length should be one page and no more than two.
- Proofread your final version; then have someone else proofread it.
- The overall appearance should be professional.
- Printing should be done on a laser printer.

A cover letter should always accompany your resume. The purpose of the cover letter is to persuade the employer to read your resume and invite you for an interview. The cover letter should be sent to a specific person. It should be brief but provide enough information to entice the employer. The following information should be in the cover letter:

- The first paragraph should identify who you are, whether you were referred by someone, and what your objective is.
- The second paragraph is your chance to sell yourself. It should tell the employer why you are good for the company and what you can offer. Use facts and figures to describe your qualifications.
- The last paragraph is where you request an interview and state how you will follow up with the employer.

The cover letter and the resume are often the first impression the employer will have of you. Do your best in preparing them!

Step 7: Mail Your Resume

When sending your resume out, the Personnel Department is probably not your best target since their job is to screen out rather than welcome applicants. Understand that Personnel or Human Resources can help your career once you're in the company. However, your best initial target is the decision-maker who is the "hiring authority."

Mass Mailing

A common job-search technique is to research a list of companies and send off as many resumes and cover letters as possible. Then you wait for your hard work and many dollars in postage to pay off with a call back and an interview. Sometimes mass mailings work, but mostly they don't. We recommend the targeted mailing technique.

Targeted Mailing

A targeted mailing is one that focuses only on companies with jobs you know you are qualified for and in which you have names of specific hiring authorities. Most importantly, in a targeted mailing you must be prepared to follow-up with phone calls.

In doing your research about prospective companies you have come up with the names of many that you are interested in working for. Prioritize these companies and target the top 15—those you are most interested in. Send these a resume and carefully written cover letter directed to the individual who can help or hire you. Follow-up with a phone call. When you take a company off your list, add a new one.

Various directories and networking contacts will help you come up with names of individuals who could be in a position to help or hire you. Or a phone call to the company can sometimes secure the name of the right person to mail to. Never be afraid to mail letters to more than one person at a firm, especially at some of the larger companies, where the more people who see your resume and are in a position to do something about it, the better.

A targeted mailing cannot work without follow-up phone calls. Let the employer know you will be calling so that the resume remains on his or her desk, and make sure you call within 10 to 14 days after you send the letter.

Although we make this sound easy, contacting the hiring authority could require talking with two or three people in order to determine who the decision-maker is. It could take many phone calls and much follow-up, but don't get discouraged. The important thing is to get your resume in front of the right person and away from the resume graveyard.

Treat the secretaries/assistants with all the respect possible since they are essentially gatekeepers. They often have the power to grant or deny you access to a hiring authority. Getting off on the right foot with the secretary enhances your chances of talking directly with the more influential person. Treating the secretary/assistant as a professional is crucial since he or she often knows everything going on in the office and can give you access to the boss.

Step 8: Use Your Career Resources

Finding a good job is difficult and today the traditional job search is insufficient. You need to use every resource available, including employment agencies, executive search firms, social service agencies, government agencies, career consultants, college career centers, career fairs, and, of course, the Internet. Let's examine these resources one by one.

Employment Agencies and Search Firms

Your first impulse may be to turn the job hunt over to a professional employment service. However, if you're a recent college graduate or offer no special or high-demand skills, employment agencies can be less than helpful. Those that specialize in temporary jobs are even less likely to lead you to your dream job. We recommend taking charge of your own job search since you know yourself and your goals better than anyone else. If you do decide to use employment services, become familiar with their operations and limitations. This will save you a lot of time, effort, and possibly money.

Employment agencies act as intermediaries in the job market between buyers (companies with jobs open) and sellers (people who want jobs). Agencies are paid either by the employer or the worker for placing people. Find out the total cost beforehand and how the fee is handled.

Employment agencies seldom place a candidate in a job that pays more than $50,000 a year. Most employment agencies concentrate on support jobs rather than middle or upper-management positions. A company will do a job search on their own or utilize an executive search firm to fill top management positions. However, if you are in the secretary/assistant field, it may be worth your while to look at employment agencies. To many companies, it's worth the agency fee to avoid the hassle of prescreening dozens, if not hundreds, of applicants.

If you decide to use an agency, be sure it's a reputable firm. Ask people in your field to recommend a quality agency, and consult the Better Business Bureau or one of the consumer services departments listed below to see if there have been any complaints about the agency you're considering. Most important, read the contract thoroughly, including all the fine print, before signing anything. Remember, the agency is loyal to its source of income—usually the company. Also remember that if a company has to pay a fee to hire you, you may be at a disadvantage over other candidates not using an agency. Finally, the job-search strategies an agency provides are all outlined in this book and you can implement most of them yourself.

A listing in this book does not constitute an endorsement of any agencies or firms. Before using a service, try to get the opinion of one or more people who have already used the service you're considering. You can also contact the following:

Better Business Bureau of Chicago
211 Wacker Drive
Chicago, IL 60606
(312) 346-3313
http://www.igc.apc.org/bbb/
This is the homepage of the Better Business Bureau. It offers a geographic directory of offices, list of publications, reliability reports on businesses, scam alerts, and more.

City of Chicago Consumer Services Office
(312) 744-4091

City of Chicago Office of Consumer Complaints
(312) 744-9400

Governor's Office of Consumer Services
(312) 814-3580

Chicago is home to more than 300 employment agencies, executive search firms, and temp agencies. Let's start with executive search firms.

SELECTED CHICAGO AREA EXECUTIVE SEARCH FIRMS

Executive search firms are paid by companies to locate people with specific qualifications to meet a precisely defined employment need. Most reputable executive search firms belong to an organization called the Association of Executive Recruiting Consultants (AEC). A search firm never works on a contingency basis. Only employment agencies do that. Because the company has to pay a large fee, they may opt to forgo using an executive search firm during hard times.

Yet, if you choose to use an executive search firm, as specialists who know the market they can be very helpful in providing advice and leads. Keep in mind that you are only useful to the search firm if there is an assignment that matches your background and qualifications exactly.

Dear Dr. Bob
I have recently graduated and was considering using an executive search firm to simplify my job search. What do you recommend?—Recently Confused Graduate

Dear Recently Confused Graduate
Unless you are middle to upper-management, the search

firm will not be interested in helping you. Since the search firm looks for candidates with highly developed skills in a particular area, your experience may seem inadequate compared to the candidate with 15 years of work history. For the present time, try the techniques in this book to land a job on your own.

Below is a list of selected local executive search firms.

Allerton Heneghan & O'Neill
70 W. Madison St., Suite 2015
Chicago, IL 60602
(312) 263-1075

Paul Ray Berndtson
10 Riverside Plaza, Suite 720
Chicago, IL 60606
(312) 876-0730

Boyden
180 N. Stetson Ave., Suite 5050
Chicago, IL 60601
(312) 565-1300

Callan Associates Ltd.
1550 Spring Road
Oak Brook, IL 60521
(708) 832-7080

Chestnut Hill International
2345 Waukegan Road, Suite 165
Deerfield, IL 60015
(847) 940-9690

DHR International
10 S. Riverside Plaza, Suite 1650
Chicago, IL 60606
(312) 782-1581

Dieckmann & Associates Ltd.
2 Prudential Plaza, Suite 5555
Chicago, IL 60601
(312) 819-5900

Egon Zehnder International
1 First National Plaza, Suite 3300
Chicago, IL 60603
(312) 782-4500

Heidrick Partners
20 N. Wacker Drive, Suite 2850

Chicago, IL 60606
(312) 845-9700

Heidrick & Struggles
125 S. Wacker Drive, Suite 2800
Chicago, IL 60606
(312) 372-8811

A.T. Kearney Executive Search
222 W. Adams St.
Chicago, IL 60606
(312) 648-0111

Kennedy & Co.
20 N. Wacker Drive, Suite 2507
Chicago, IL 60606
(312) 372-0099

Kensington International
1420 Kensington Road, Suite 114
Oak Bridge, IL 60521
(708) 571-0123

Korn/Ferry International
120 S. Riverside Plaza, Suite 918
Chicago, IL 60606
(312) 726-1841

Lamalie Amrop International
123 N. Wacker Drive, Suite 950
Chicago, IL 60606
(312) 782-3113

Lynch Miller Moore Partners
10 S. Wacker Drive, Suite 2935
Chicago, IL 60606
(312) 876-1505

McFeely Wackerle Shulman
20 N. Wacker Drive, Suite 3110
Chicago, IL 60606
(312) 641-2977

Nordeman Grimm
150 N. Michigan Ave., Suite 3610
Chicago, IL 60601
(312) 332-0088

Russell Reynolds Associates
200 S. Wacker Drive, Suite 3600
Chicago, IL 60606
(312) 993-9696

Shepherd Bueschel & Provus
401 N. Michigan Ave., Suite 3020
Chicago, IL 60611
(312) 832-3020

John Sibbald Associates
8725 W. Higgins Road
Chicago, IL 60631
(773) 693-0575

Slayton International
181 W. Madison St., Suite 4510
Chicago, IL 60602
(312) 456-0080

Spencer Stuart
401 N. Michigan Ave., Suite 3400
Chicago, IL 60611
(312) 822-0080

Ward Howell International
300 S. Wacker Drive, Suite 2940
Chicago, IL 60606
(312) 236-2211

Witt/Kieffer Ford Hadelman & Lloyd
2015 Spring Road, Suite 510
Oak Brook, IL 60521
(630) 990-1370

SELECTED CHICAGO AREA EMPLOYMENT AGENCIES FOR PROFESSIONALS AND MANAGERS

Abbott Smith Associates
1308 N. Astor St.
Chicago, IL 60610
(312) 664-1976

Accountants On Call
200 N. LaSalle St., Suite 2830
Chicago, IL 60601
(312) 782-7788

Advanced Search Group
1910 Highland, Suite 106
Lombard, IL 60148
(708) 620-8778

American Resources Corp.
833 N. Orleans St., 1st floor
Chicago, IL 60610
(312) 587-9000

Banner Personnel Service
122 S. Michigan Ave., Suite 1510
Chicago, IL 60603
(312) 704-6000

Barrett Partners
100 N. LaSalle, Suite 1420

Chicago, IL 60602
(312) 443-8877

John Bell & Associates
20 N. Wacker Drive, Suite 2507
Chicago, IL 60606
(312) 346-7677

Briant Associates
200 N. Wacker Drive, Suite 1529
Chicago, IL 60606
(312) 629-4670

Bryant Associates
20 N. Wacker Drive, Suite 2507
Chicago, IL 60606
(312) 346-7445

Business Systems of America
150 N. Wacker, Suite 2970
Chicago, IL 60606
(312) 849-9222
Specialty: PC Technical support.

The Calkins Group
303 W. Madison St., Suite 2650
Chicago, IL 60606
(312) 346-3033

Chicago Legal Search, Ltd.
33 N. Dearborn St., Suite 2302
Chicago, IL 60202-3109
(312) 251-2580

Compusearch of Chicago-Downtown
2 N. Riverside Plaza, Suite 1815
Chicago, IL 60606-2701
(312) 648-1800

Consultants to Executive Management Co., Ltd.
2 First National Plaza, Suite 610
Chicago, IL 60603
(312) 855-1500

Creative Financial Staffing
1 Mid America Plaza
P.O. Box 3697
Oak Brook, IL 60522-3697
(630) 586-5200

Dunhill of Chicago
68 E. Wacker Drive, 12th floor
Chicago, IL 60601
(312) 346-0933

Flex Execs Management Solution
16350 S. 105th Court
Orland Park, IL 60462
(708) 460-8500

Godfrey Personnel
300 W. Adams, Suite 612
Chicago, IL 60606
(312) 236-4455

Hedlund Corp.
1 IBM Plaza, Suite 2618
Chicago, IL 60611
(312) 755-1400

Hinman & Company
2040 N. Mohawk St.
Chicago, IL 60614
(312) 951-8010

Jacobson Associates
150 N. Wacker Drive, Suite 1120
Chicago, IL 60606
(312) 726-1578

The Jefferson Group
900 W. Grace, Suite 3
Chicago, IL 60613
(773) 935-9052

Major, Hagen & Africa
35 E. Wacker Drive, Suite 2150
Chicago, IL 60601
(312) 372-1010

Management As Needed
2625 Butterfield Road, Suite 203N
Oak Brook, IL 60521
(630) 573-0910

Juan Menefee & Associates
503 S. Oak Park Ave., Suite 206
Oak Park, IL 60304
(708) 848-7722

Mengel & McDonald, Ltd.
650 N. Dearborn, Suite 750
Chicago, IL 60610
(312) 266-0581

Gregory Michaels & Associates
8410 W. Bryn Mawr Ave., Suite 400
Chicago, IL 60631
(773) 380-1333

John R. O'Connor & Associates
111 W. Jackson Blvd., Suite 1300
Chicago, IL 60604
(312) 939-1392

Paladin Companies
875 N. Michigan, Suite 3218
Chicago, IL 60611
(312) 654-2600

Protemp Temporaries
150 N. Wacker Drive, Suite 1020
Chicago, IL 60606
(312) 346-4300

Sales & Management Search
10 S. Riverside Plaza, Suite 1424
Chicago, IL 60606
(312) 930-1111

Search Dynamics
9420 W. Foster Ave., Suite 200
Chicago, IL 60656-1006
(773) 992-3900

D. W. Simpson & Company
625 N. Michigan Ave., 12th floor
Chicago, IL 60611
(312) 654-5220

Smith Hanley Associates
200 W. Madison, Suite 480
Chicago, IL 60606
(312) 629-2400

Source Edp
150 S. Wacker Drive, Suite 400
Chicago, IL 60606
(312) 372-1900

Source Finance
150 S. Wacker Drive, Suite 400
Chicago, IL 60606
(312) 346-7000

Stone Enterprises, Ltd.
645 N. Michigan, Suite 800
Chicago, IL 60611
(312) 836-0470

Stone Management Corp.
208 S. LaSalle, Suite 1601

Chicago, IL 60604
(312) 236-0800

Technical Search
450 E. Devon, Suite 100
Itasca, IL 60143
(630) 775-0700

Tesar Reynes
500 N. Michigan Ave., Suite 1300
Chicago, IL 60611
(312) 661-0700

Trilogy Enterprises
1919 Midwest Road, Suite 108
Oak Brook, IL 60521
(630) 268-0900

White, Roberts & Stratton
100 W. Chestnut St., Suite 2910
Chicago, IL 60610
(312) 944-5554

Winston, Rooney & Green
201 N. Wells St., Suite 1410
Chicago, IL 60606
(312) 201-9777

Zenner Kleiman Consultants
75 E. Wacker Drive, floor 3000
Chicago, IL 60601
(312) 849-3800

Social Service Agencies

Unlike professional employment agencies, career consultants (see farther on), and executive search firms, social service agencies are not-for-profit. They offer a wide range of services, from counseling and vocational testing to job placement and follow-up—and their services are either low cost or free.

There are hundreds of social service agencies in Chicago. To help you find the services, fees, and client qualifications that meet your specific needs, consult the *HumanCare Services Directory of Metropolitan Chicago*, a United Way/Crusade of Mercy publication, available from Morgan-Rand, Inc., 1800 Bayberry Road, Huntington Valley, PA 19006, (800) 388-1197. The directory is indexed by topic as well as agency name. Address, phone, qualification requirements, and description of services offered are listed. This book is particularly useful for finding programs for people with disabilities, hearing or sight impairments, veterans, immigrants, displaced homemakers, and others with specific needs. Chicago area social service agencies are listed with full contact information and brief descriptions of their services.

Most nongovernment social service agencies are affiliated with the United Way/Crusade of Mercy of Metropolitan Chicago, 560 W. Lake St., Chicago, IL 60661, (312) 876-1808. The United Way/Crusade of Mercy operates a community information and referral service from 8:30 a.m. to 5:00 p.m. For information or referrals, call (312) 876-0010 or (800) 564-5733. Trained consultants link people who need assistance with service providers. In addition, the United Way/Crusade of Mercy operates a social services library at the above location that is available to the public on an appointment basis by calling (312) 906-2345. The United Way/Crusade of Mercy with its library is the best single source of information on social service agencies in Chicago.

Government Agencies

Whether your passion is photography or journalism or finance, don't rule out a job in the public sector. City, state, and federal job listings cover nearly as many fields as the private sector. Visit the following Internet sites to check out local possibilities.

FedWorld Information Network
http://www.fedworld.gov/index.html
This site is a major gateway to federal government information and resources, including job openings. You can connect to more than 10,000 library files, order government information products, search abstracts of government reports, access government Web servers, and search through a database of U.S. government job openings.

State of Illinois Directory
http://www.state.il.us/
This is the Internet gateway to state agencies, educational institutions, libraries, museums, legislative information, and the state capital.

Cook County Clerk's Office
http://www.cookctyclerk.com/
Posts a directory of elected officials.

City of Chicago Directory
http://www.ci.chi.il.us/worksmart
This is the definitive electronic guide to the municipal government of Chicago. It provides both alphabetical and categorical listings of all city departments, including the employment office. You can even conduct a keyword search to locate information. All public officials are also listed...just in case your uncle knows someone who knows someone!

If you want a hard-copy reference, check this out:

Key to Government in Chicago and Suburban Cook County
Citizens Information Service of Illinois
332 S. Michigan Ave.
Chicago, IL 60604
(312) 939-INFO

State Job Service

The Illinois Department of Employment Security (IDES) is a state-run agency that screens applicants and tries to fill positions for jobs in the private sector. The agency has offices throughout Chicagoland and you can visit any of them to view the available openings, which change daily. All IDES offices and telephone numbers are listed on their Web site. Better yet, visit IDES at their interactive Web site http://il.jobsearch.org/

Since the job market constantly churns, we recommend that you search their database of current job openings weekly. If you don't have access to the Internet, call one of these regional IDES offices to locate the facility closest to you:

3710 N. Kedzie, 2nd floor
Chicago, IL 60618
(773) 604-4448

8630 S. Pulaski Ave.
Chicago, IL 60652
(773) 838-5707

1572 Maple Ave.
Evanston, IL 60201
(847) 864-3530

Career Consultants

Career consultants vary greatly in the kind and quality of the services they provide. Some may offer a single service, such as vocational testing or preparing resumes. Others coach every aspect of the job search and stay with you until you accept an offer. The fees vary just as broadly and range from $100 to several thousand dollars. You, not your potential employer, pay the fee.

A qualified career consultant can be an asset to your job search. But no consultant can get you a job. A consultant can help you focus on an objective, develop a resume, teach you to research the job market, decide on a strategy, and provide interviewing techniques. But in the end, the consultant can't interview for you. You are responsible.

The only time you should consider a consultant is after you've exhausted all the other resources we've suggested here and still feel you need expert and personalized help with one or more aspects of the job search. The key to choosing a career consultant is knowing what you need and verifying that the consultant can provide it.

Check references. A reputable firm will gladly provide them. Check the Better Business Bureau and get referrals from friends who have used a consultant. Before signing anything, ask to meet the consultant who will actually provide the services you want. What are their credentials? How long have they been practicing? What does the consultant promise? What is required from you? How long can you use the consultant's services? Be sure to shop around before selecting a consultant. Refer to Chapter 2 for a list of possible counselors.

College and University Career Resources

If you are in college and are not acquainted with your school's career center, make a point to stop by and check out the services available. Colleges and universities usually provide services to their alumni and members of the local community also.

There is more to a college career center than just job postings. It's a great resource for building your network, researching the job market, and seeking counseling to establish a career strategy. And most colleges and universities also offer services such as vocational testing and interpretation and the use of the resource library to their alumni and/or the public.

In addition, contact your alma mater's alumni association for a list of alumni in the Chicago area who are working in your occupation or industry. Most alumni associations and career centers sponsor alumni career advising networks with the express purpose of linking students and alumni job seekers to professionals in specific geographical areas and occupations. Also, check if your alumni association has a Chicago area chapter. If so, send in your membership dues and contact your local alumni representative! Alumni are usually terrific networking resources for the savvy job seeker.

Career Fairs

Another job-search resource that can help is the ubiquitous career fair. Career fairs are the shopping malls for job searchers. Employers line up to market their companies and job opportunities. Job searchers browse the aisles, often stopping when a particularly glitzy brochure or big company name catches their eye. And like the shopping mall, employers want to sell, sell, sell their opportunities while job searchers want to snatch up great deals.

Career fairs are a job shopper's delight. The large number of employers in one place makes it easy to research many companies. Additionally, career fairs afford the job searcher a chance to meet face to face with company representatives, often an advantage for people who make a better impression in person than on paper. Finally, at some career fairs candidates can actually interview for jobs with prospective employers during the event.

Career fairs are most often advertised in the classified section of the newspaper. Professional associations will also frequently receive announcements. Colleges and universities often sponsor career fairs and post announcements of these and other events. Some coordinators of career fairs will even put up billboards and advertise on television.

As more and more employers rely on career fairs to meet qualified applicants, the savvy job searcher must be comfortable attending these events. These few tips will help you more effectively use a career fair.

- Prior to the fair, get a list of the companies attending in order to begin researching potential employers. Knowing what a company does allows you to use the precious few minutes you will have with a company representative to sell yourself rather than ask basic questions about the company's products.

- Plan a strategy. Use your research to prioritize the companies you want to talk with. Sequence the companies according to which companies you must, without a doubt, talk with before the end of the fair.
- Arrive early the day of the fair in order to scope out the facilities and meet with company representatives before lines get too long. Familiarize yourself with the location of employers, the flow of traffic, and the layout of the building.
- Avoid wasting time in long lines to talk to big-name employers, even if they have great company give-away goodies. Smaller employers and their representatives will have less traffic, which means that you may be able to spend more time talking with him or her and making a positive impression.
- Take the initiative in approaching employers. Prepare a short two-to-three minute "infomercial" about yourself so that you can quickly acquaint employers with your background. Have a list of questions ready so you don't have to squirm while trying to decide what to say.
- Bring lots of resumes and be prepared to leave them with any employer who interests you. Before leaving the career fair, revisit your favorite employers and leave your resume with them again to make sure your name does not get lost in the pile.

The shopping mall was created as a convenience to vendors who want lots of consumers and consumers who want lots of vendors in one easy place; the career fair provides the same convenience to job searchers and employers. A successful strategy will help you avoid lost time and hopefully get you inside the company for a proper interview later.

CAREER FAIR ORGANIZATIONS

There is no one-stop-shopping list or single source of information on job and career fairs in the Chicago area. However, here are some suggestions:

http://www.espan.com/js/jobfair.html
Lists career fairs geographically.

The business section and/or the employment classified section in the Sunday edition of the *Chicago Tribune* usually lists upcoming job fairs. Check out their Web site at:
http://www.chicago.tribune.com

The Lendman Group, located in Virginia Beach, VA at (804) 473-2450, is a major national organizer of career fairs and has been in business for more than 30 years. They hold Technical Fairs, which include computer and engineering positions, and Sales and Retail Management fairs each year in the Chicago metropolitan area. While most organizers charge between $2 and $20, entrance here is free.

Step 9: The Killer Interview

The killer interview consists of three parts: preparation, success during the inter-view, and follow-up. We'll highlight key aspects of this process. However, Chapter 7 discusses the interview in greater detail.

Preparation

Before any interview, you need to prepare and practice in order to do the best job possible in selling yourself to the employer. Follow this procedure for best results:

- Identify your strengths, skills, goals, and personal qualities. Self-assessment is crucial to knowing what you have to offer an employer and to conveying it effectively. Try to come up with five unique strengths. Have examples of how you have used them professionally.
- Research the company in order to ask intelligent questions. An interview is suppose to be a dialogue; you want to learn about them just as they want to learn about you.
- Rehearse what you plan to say during the interview. Practice answers to commonly asked questions and determine how you will emphasize your strengths and skills.
- Dress professionally and conservatively. If you make a negative first impression, you may not be fairly considered for the job. Refer to Chapter 7 for dressing tips in the interview.

Success During the Interview

Chapter 7 covers what interviewers are looking for. Below are some additional tips to help you succeed in your interview.

- Arrive on time or ten minutes early. This will ensure you the full amount of time allotted and show that you are enthusiastic about the position.
- The first five minutes of the interview can be extremely important. To start your interview off right, offer a firm handshake and smile, make good eye contact, and say something to break the ice. "Nice to meet you," or something of that sort, should clear your throat nicely and prepare you for more substantive conversation.
- As you begin the interview, be aware of non-verbal behavior. Wait to sit until you are offered a chair. Look alert, speak in a clear, strong voice, try to stay relaxed, avoid nervous mannerisms, and try to be a good listener as well as a good talker.
- Be specific, concrete, and detailed in your answers. The more informa-tion you volunteer, the better the employer gets to know you and thereby is able to make a wise hiring decision. But *don't* be long-winded.
- Always have questions for the interviewer.
- Don't mention salary in a first interview unless the employer does. If asked, give a realistic range and add that opportunity is the most impor-tant factor for you.

- Offer examples of your work and references that will document your best qualities.
- Answer questions as truthfully as possible. Never appear to be "glossing over" anything. If the interviewer ventures into ticklish political or social questions, answer honestly but try not to say more than is necessary.
- Never make derogatory remarks about present or former employers or companies. Make sure you look very positive in the interviewer's eyes.

Follow-Up

The following suggestions will help you survive the "awful waiting" time after the interview.

- Don't get discouraged if no definite offer is made or specific salary discussed.
- If you feel the interview isn't going well, don't let your discouragement show. Occasionally an interviewer who is genuinely interested in you may seem to discourage you to test your reaction.
- At the end of the interview, ask when a hiring decision will be made. This is important not only because it reconfirms your interest in the position but also so you'll know when to expect a response.
- Send a thank-you letter to the interviewer: thank him or her for the time and effort; reiterate your skills and qualifications for the position; and make clear your interest in the job.
- Make notes on what you feel you could improve upon for your next interview and on what you feel went particularly well. After all, experience is only valuable to the extent that you're willing to learn from it.
- If offered the position, up to two weeks is a reasonable amount of time to make your decision. All employment offers deserve a written reply, whether or not you accept them.

You will learn a great deal about patience during the waiting period that follows an interview. The important point to remember during this time is that all your hopes shouldn't be dependent on one or two interviews. The job search is continuous and shouldn't stop until you have accepted an offer. Keeping all your options open is the best possible course.

Keep in contact with the company if they haven't responded by the date they indicated in the interview. Asking the status of your application is a legitimate question. This inquiry should be stated in a manner that is not pushy but shows your continued interest in the company.

Step 10: Make Sure This Is the Job for You

Start celebrating! You have received a job offer after working so diligently on the job search. But before you accept or decline, consider the offer carefully. Make sure the details of the offer are clear; preferably, get them in writing. Details should include starting date, salary and benefits, location, job description and responsibilities, and the date by which you must respond. Evaluating a job offer can be both exciting and difficult. We have provided the following information to assist you in making a job decision.

Negotiating Salary

Be aware of what other people in similar positions are making before accepting any offer. The *Occupational Outlook Handbook,* put out by the U.S. Department of Labor every two years, cites salary statistics by field. Another good source of information is *The American Almanac of Jobs and Salaries* by John Wright, published by Avon. Professional societies and associations frequently provide this sort of information too. It's one more good reason to belong to one.

When negotiating salary, proceed with care to prevent jeopardizing a positive relationship with your new employer. Here are some points in negotiating salaries:

- Be prepared with salary research before discussing any figures.
- Approach the session with trust and a willingness to compromise.
- Know when to stop. Don't push your luck.
- Be open to substituting other benefits in exchange for a higher salary.

The end result should be that both parties are happy with the outcome. For advice on how to get the salary you want, we recommend these books:

BOOKS ON SALARY NEGOTIATION

Chapman, Jack. *How to Make $1000 a Minute.* Berkeley, CA: Ten Speed Press, 1987.

Chastain, Sherry. *Winning the Salary Game: Salary Negotiation For Women.* New York: John Wiley & Sons, 1980.

Fisher, Roger, and William Levy. *Getting to Yes: Negotiating Agreement Without Giving In.* New York: Penguin Books, 1992.

Kennedy, Marilyn Moats. *Getting the Job You Want & The Money You're Worth.* American College of Executives, 1987.

Krannich, Ronald L., and Rae. *Salary Success: Know What You're Worth and Get It.* Woodbridge, VA: Impact Publications, 1990.

Compare the Offers on Paper

Don't blindly accept the first offer you receive. You've put a great deal of effort in the job search, so spend a little more time in comparing the relative merits of each offer. Below is a sample checklist to assist you in this endeavor. The idea is to list the factors that you consider important in any job, and then assign a rating for how well each offer fills the bill in each particular area.

We've listed some factors that should be considered before accepting any offer. Some may not be relevant to your situation. Others that we've left out may be of great importance to you. So feel free to make any additions, deletions, or changes you want. Assign a rating (1 being the lowest and 5 the highest) for each factor under each offer. Then total the scores.

The offer with the most points is not necessarily the one to accept. The chart doesn't take into account the fact that "responsibilities" may be more important to you than "career path," or that you promised yourself you'd never punch a time clock again. Nevertheless, looking at the pros and cons of each offer in black and white should help you make a much more methodical and logical decision.

Factor	Offer A	Offer B
Responsibilities	_____	_____
Company reputation	_____	_____
Salary	_____	_____
Vacation leave	_____	_____
Insurance/Pension	_____	_____
Profit sharing	_____	_____
Tuition reimbursement	_____	_____
On-the-job training	_____	_____
Career path advancement	_____	_____
Company future	_____	_____
Product/service quality	_____	_____
Location (housing market, schools, transportation)	_____	_____
Boss(es)	_____	_____
Co-workers	_____	_____
Travel	_____	_____
Overtime	_____	_____
Other	_____	_____
	_____	_____
TOTAL POINTS	_____	_____

Evaluating Job Offers

A job involves more than a title and salary. Before you accept any offer, be sure you understand what your responsibilities will be, what benefits you'll receive besides salary (insurance, profit sharing, vacation, tuition reimbursement, etc.), how much overtime is required (and whether you'll be paid for it), how much travel is involved in the job, who your supervisor will be, how many people you'll supervise, and where the position could lead (do people in this position get promoted?). In short, find out anything and everything you can to evaluate the offer.

The cost of living is essential in comparing job offers in different cities. The difference in the cost of living can mean living like royalty in Houston or struggling in New York, even if the salaries offered seem relatively close. To compare cost of living, check the Consumer Price Indexes provided by the Bureau of Labor Statistics.

It seems obvious that it's unwise to choose a job solely on the basis of salary. Consider all the factors, such as your boss and colleagues and the type of work you'll be doing, before making any final decision.

Corporate Cultures

Every company has a different corporate culture (philosophies and management style) and some fit better with your own personality than others. Thus it is important to research the company's culture in your career search. Specific companies are discussed in the following books:

Kanter, Rosabeth Moss, and Barry A. Stein. *Life in Organizations.* New York: Basic Books, 1979.

Levering, Robert, and Milton Moskowitz. *The 100 Best Companies To Work For In America.* New York: Doubleday, 1993.

Peters, Thomas J., and Robert H. Waterman, Jr. *In Search of Excellence.* New York: Warner Books, 1982.

Peters, Thomas J., and Nancy Austin. *Passion for Excellence.* New York: Random House, 1985.

Plunkett, Jack. *The Almanac of American Employers.* Boerne, TX: Corporate Jobs Outlook, 1994.

It is also possible to decipher a company's culture during the interview. The following are factors worth examining:

- What is the environment like? Look at the appearance of the office, the company newsletter, brochures, and bulletin boards.
- Who is on board? How does the company greet strangers, what kind of people work for them, and why is the company a success (or failure)?
- How are employees rewarded? Look at the benefits, awards, compensation, and recognition given to employees.
- What is the fashion statement? Look at the dress code. Are there different dress styles for levels of employment?
- How do people spend their time? Look at the ambience of the workplace and what an average day is like.
- How do managers behave? Look at the history of the company, how things get done, and the management style.

Is the Job a Dream or a Nightmare?

Dream jobs sometimes do turn into nightmare employment. It happens all the time. How do you avoid this possibility? Look for the eight danger signs of the "job from hell."

Financial problems and corporate turmoil. Prospective employees rarely do financial or management research on a company in which they are interested. It will behoove you to find out if the firm is financially sound and if there has been much turmoil within the company.

Layoffs indicate danger. Many companies try to convince new employees that recent layoffs will have no effect on their position. Don't believe it! A good indication of a job about to go bad is that mass layoffs have recently occurred.

Recent mergers or acquisitions can be another danger signal. Companies that have bought or merged with another company are usually trying to reduce expenses. And the easiest way for the corporate world to reduce expenses is to cut employees and reorganize. The chances of you working in the position you interviewed for will diminish with reorganization. Being new, you may also be one of the first to be laid off or transferred.

Word on the street. What is the informal word about your new potential workplace? Word of mouth is often a good source of inside information about the reality of working for a particular company. Try to eliminate gossip and scuttlebutt from those who are naturally and overly negative. But if a general consensus exists that a company is not good to its employees or that people are unusually unhappy, carefully weigh your decision.

Turnover within your position. How many people have worked in your new position during the last couple of years? Is your particular job one that experiences a great deal of turnover? High turnover should alert you to the possibility that either the job is horrible and no one can stand it or that no one is really capable of doing this job, including you. Percentages show that those who take jobs with high turnover rates are very likely to become a statistic as well.

Elusive or vague job description. A key danger signal is the absence of or vagueness in your job description. Look for a job where the duties are known up front. It's fine for some things about a job to be determined later, and you certainly want your responsibilities to be increased, but don't take a job in which you are not sure what your primary duties will be or to whom you will report.

"Bad boss" potential. Don't discount the boss's influence on your job performance or your satisfaction within a job. Most employees spend more waking time with a boss than with their spouse. Try to meet your boss before you accept the job and ask yourself if you are ready to live with him or her on a daily basis. As we have mentioned before, your boss should be a role model. He or she should help you grow and develop in your career. If you have doubts about your boss, you should have doubts about the job.

That gut feeling. Finally, you can never discount that deep-down feeling you get about your job offer. Even when the pay and benefits are great, you still might have mixed emotions about a particular job. Explore those emotions and find out why they are "mixed." They may be more than a premonition.

Even if a job looks like a winner, if you see one or more of these danger signs, do a little more research before you accept. Don't wind up a major loser.

five

Network, Network, Network: The Best Job-Search Technique

What's the difference between knowing a lot of people and having an influential network? If you're a smart job searcher, you will realize that knowing a lot of people is just the start. It is the process of staying in touch with people and building strong connections that creates an influential and powerful network. While the old axiom "it's not what you know but who you know" may be an overstatement for all job searches, savvy job seekers combine ingenuity and creativity to use who they know to help them find jobs in which they can use what they know.

For many people, networking has a negative connotation. It implies cocktail parties, insincere conversation, and golf games with people you don't really like. In reality, however, job networking is simply asking people you know for information about careers and employment. You may already be networking and not know it!

The Six Myths of Networking

In order to encourage more networking, let's start by debunking some common myths.

MYTH #1: People get jobs through ads and other formal announcements. The truth is that fewer than 20 percent of available jobs are ever advertised. The majority of jobs are in the "hidden job market." Mark S. Granovetter, a Harvard sociologist, reported to *Forbes* magazine that informal contacts, or networks, account for almost 75 percent of successful job searches. Agencies find about 9 percent of new jobs for professional and technical people, and ads yield about another 10 percent.

If those figures don't convince you to begin networking, how about these. A recent study found that employers preferred using networks to hire new employees because it reduced recruiting costs and decreased the risks associated with hiring a new, unknown employee. Furthermore, people who use networking are generally more satisfied with the job they land and tend to have higher incomes.

MYTH #2: Networking is so effective, you can ignore more traditional means of job searching, such as responding to ads. This is simply not true. As important as networking is to your job search, you will shorten the time you spend looking for a job if you use more methods. The average job seeker only uses a few of the available job-search techniques. No wonder job searches take so long! Networking complements your other techniques, not replaces them. Don't put all your eggs in one basket; use as many options as possible.

MYTH #3: Networking is only effective for people who are very assertive. If you were asking people for jobs, this might be true. However, networking is just asking people for information for your job search, which requires you to be polite but not overly assertive.

If you are uncomfortable contacting people, start your network with people you know well or with whom you have some connection: you go to the same church, you are both members of the same alumni association, etc. Talking with friends and family is less intimidating than approaching strangers. Networking in friendly territory will help you develop confidence in your approach and know what questions to ask.

MYTH #4: The job hunter's most important networking contacts within a company are in the HR department. If you limit your network to human resources personnel, you will be waiting a long time for a job. Only one person in four gets their job by relying strictly on personnel offices. Human resources people are there to help others hire. Find those "others."

The purpose of networking is to talk to as many people as possible. Sometimes people only tangentially related to the hiring process can provide you with valuable information about your industry, tips on companies that may be hiring, or names of other contacts.

MYTH #5: No one knows enough people to network effectively. Most people know an average of 200 people. Even if only 20 people you know can help you with your job search, those 20 can refer you to 400 additional people, and your network has taken off.

Certainly if you're moving to a new town, your list of contacts will be small. You must act to develop it. Find out about your local alumni association, join a church, join professional associations, and attend as many social functions as possible. Meet people!

MYTH #6: Once you've found a job, there is no need to keep up with your network. Absolutely false. Write a thank-you note immediately after meeting with someone who was helpful with your job search. Once you've landed a job, let your network know and periodically touch base with them.

Networking as a waiter

Eric, a recent college graduate, was interested in getting a job in the very competitive field of advertising. While waiting for interviews to roll in, he waited tables at a local pub in order to pay the bills.

One night, several months and part-time jobs after graduation, Eric struck up a conversation with a group of people that had stopped by after work. After learning that they worked for a large advertising agency, Eric told them about his job search, collected their business cards, and contacted the office the following week. Eric's personality, resume, and samples impressed the office staff so much that they invited him for an interview. He got the job.

Step-by-Step Guide to Networking

To begin the networking process, draw up a list of all the people you know who might help you gain access to someone who can hire you for the job you want. Naturally, the first sources, the ones at the top of your list, will be people you know personally: friends, colleagues, former clients, relatives, acquaintances, customers, and club or church members. Just about everyone you know, whether or not he or she is employed, can generate contacts for you.

Don't forget to talk with your banker, lawyer, insurance agent, dentist, and other people who provide you with services. It is the nature of their business to know lots of people who might help you in your search. Leave no stone unturned in your search for contacts. Go through your holiday-card list, college yearbook, club membership directories, and any other list you can think of.

The next step is to expand your network to include new people who can help you. The easiest way to do this is to ask each of the people you do know for the names of two or three other people who might be helpful in your job search.

Professional organizations are another resource. If you are changing careers, you should view professional organizations as essential to your job search. Most groups meet on a regular basis and are an excellent way to contact other people in your field. Some professional associations offer placement services to members. Many chambers of commerce publish directories of the professional and trade associations that meet in your area. Local business magazines and newspapers also publish times and locations for meetings of professional associations.

Your college alumni association is another resource to expand your network. Alumni club meetings provide opportunities to catch up on happenings with your alma mater and meet other professionals in your area. Additionally, some schools maintain alumni databases for the express purpose of networking. This is a valuable resource for both seasoned professionals and recent college grads looking for a job lead and a friendly face. Still other alumni associations offer resume referral services that you can join for a small fee.

The Information Interview

There are situations, however, when your existing network simply won't be adequate. If you're changing careers, you may not know enough people in your new field to help you. If you've just moved to a new location, your network may still be in Iowa. Your situation may require you to creatively build a new network. One of the best techniques for doing this is the "information interview."

Information interviewing is a technique for developing contacts by interviewing people for job-search information. This technique acknowledges that names of contacts are easy to find but relationships that can help you find a job require additional action on your part.

First, telephone or write to possible contacts whom you've identified through lists of acquaintances, professional associations, your alumni organization, or simply a cold call. Explain that you are very interested in his or her field, and arrange a twenty-minute appointment. Be very clear that you are not asking him or her for a job but only for information. Also, never ask new people out to lunch. It is too time-consuming and lunch isn't as important to the business person as it may be to the job searcher. Don't give someone a reason to turn you down. Twenty minutes is enough time for you to get information without imposing on your host.

The information interview is the time to ask your contact questions about the field, the job market, and job-hunting tips. Ask your contact to review your resume and make recommendations about how to present yourself or fill in gaps in your experience. Most importantly, ask your contact for the names of two or three other people to talk with, thus expanding your network. And always follow up with a thank-you letter.

QUESTIONS TO ASK IN AN INFORMATION INTERVIEW

Job Function Questions
What do people with a job like yours do?
What does your typical day consist of?
What do you like/dislike about your work?
Who are the key people in your field?
What skills are necessary for your position?

Company Questions
What has been the major achievement of this organization?
How often do you interact with top management?
What trends do you foresee for this organization and in the field?
What is the company's corporate culture like?
Who are your major competitors?

Career Field Questions
What is the growth potential in your field for the next five years?
What journals or magazines should I read?
What professional organizations do you recommend?
Who else would you recommend that I talk with?

Information interviews not only help build your network but they can identify career paths, potential employers, worthwhile professional associations, and weaknesses in your work or educational background. Most importantly, learning to glean information is a skill that will serve you throughout your life.

Example of an Information Interview Letter

66 W. Emerson St.
Evanston, IL 60208
(847) 555-3456

April 11, 1997

Dr. David Hart
President
Environmental Research Company
2020 Waukegan Road
Glenview, IL 60025

Dear Dr. Hart:

Dr. Young, with whom I have studied these past two years, suggested that you might be able to advise me of opportunities in the environmental engineering field.

I am about to graduate from the university with a B.S. in civil engineering, and I am a member of Phi Beta Kappa. For two of the last three summers, I have worked as an intern with the Air Pollution Control Association.

I am eager to begin work and would appreciate a few minutes of your time to discuss trends in environmental research and, as a newcomer, gain the benefit of your advice regarding a career. Exams are finished on June 6, and I would like to arrange a meeting with you shortly thereafter. I look forward to hearing from you and in any case will be in touch with your office next week.

Sincerely,

Richard Smith

Information interview letter tips:
- Keep it short and direct.
- Tell enough about yourself to demonstrate that you are sincere and qualified.
- Always conclude with a date when you'll call, and always call if they haven't called you by that date.

Admittedly, networking will not work in every situation. No amount of networking will help you land a job for which you do not have the minimum qualifications. Nor will networking work if you try to meet with people at a much higher professional level than your own. A CEO will likely be unwilling to help someone looking for an entry-level position. You can also make people unwilling to help you by being pushy and demanding. But if you avoid these pitfalls, you should develop a great network.

Do You Know Your Networking Net Worth?

To determine the net worth of your networking ability, take the following quiz to assess how you approach people at professional meetings, social events, and community functions. For each statement, circle Y for yes or N for no.

Y   N   1. I belong to at least one professional or trade association in which I can meet people in my field.

Y   N   2. In the past year, I have used my contacts to help at least two people meet someone of importance to them.

Y   N   3. In the last month, I have attended at least two functions in order to meet people who are potential professional contacts.

Y   N   4. When I meet new professional contacts, I ask them for a business card and make notes on the back about our conversation.

Y   N   5. When asked, "What kind of job are you looking for?" I can answer in two sentences or less.

Y   N   6. I keep in touch with former classmates and workmates.

Y   N   7. I have given colleagues information to help them solve a problem.

Y   N   8. I always know at least 25 professionals in my field well enough to call and say, "Hi, this is (my name)," and they know who I am.

Y   N   9. When attending professional or social functions, I introduce myself to new people and show interest in their careers.

Y   N   10. I am involved in at least one community or social organization outside work.

Count how many times you circled Y, then analyze your score:

0-4   You can make your job search easier by learning the basics of networking.

5-8   You can give and get even more out of your professional networks.

9-10   You're well on your way to feeling the power of networking in your job search!

Networking Etiquette

There are, of course, many ways in which to network, and for each method you must know the rules, or the etiquette, of networking.

On the Telephone. Since the purpose of networking is to establish a personal relationship with people who can help you with your job search, you will find that the telephone is more effective than letters to contact people. When calling, clearly state the purpose of your call and explain how you found the person's name and telephone number. Be sensitive about the time you call. In one study, employers indicated that Monday mornings and Friday afternoons were the worst times to try to reach them, for obvious reasons. The best times to call business people, this same survey said, are Tuesdays, Wednesdays, and Thursdays between 10:00 a.m. and 2:00 p.m.

The Twenty-Minute Meeting. When you make an appointment to meet with someone for information, many of the same rules apply as when interviewing for a job. Arrive a few minutes early; bring a copy of your resume; and be prepared with questions to ask. It is best not to ask to meet someone for the first time over lunch.

Thank-You Notes. The thank-you note is more than just a polite gesture. A well-written thank-you note enhances your credibility with your interviewee. In your thank-you note, reiterate key points of your conversation and explain how you intend to act on your contact's advice. Include a copy of your resume for his or her files. Make sure that your contact has your correct phone number and address so that he or she can contact you with additional information.

Networking On-line. On-line computer services can help you expand your network to mind-boggling numbers. Many of the main on-line services such as CompuServe and America On-line have discussion groups that can be useful for job searchers. Prodigy offers a careers bulletin board that is another way to do information interviews.

One caution, however, about using these services. Be careful about providing too much personal information such as your address, phone number, social security number, and so on, because you never know who is lurking on the Net. Additionally, people can easily misrepresent themselves, and you may not be corresponding with whom you think you are.

E-mail has become commonplace in the corporate world and presents another way to make networking contacts. "Netiquette," or etiquette on the Net, however, suggests that this is not always the best way to conduct informational exchanges. It is, however, a great way to confirm appointments and send thank-you notes.

CYBERTIPS ON NETWORKING

A few sources for networking on the Net include:

Interactive Employment Network
http://www.espan.com
Provides networking advice.

Forty-Plus Club
http://www.sirius.com/
Not-for-profit organization of skilled and experienced job-searching executives, managers, and professionals who share their knowledge and skills with each other. A great networking source.

Professional Organization Homepages. Many local and national professional organizations are developing sites on the Internet for their members. Often these include times of meetings and information on job openings or careers in that particular field. Ask your contacts if such sites exist within your field and look them up.

Listserves. Many professional organizations also maintain listserves, or E-mail mailing lists that members use to maintain on-going dialogues on issues within the field. This is an excellent way to get up-to-date information and to learn of people who can help you in your job search. Do not, however, ask people for jobs over the listserve. Find their E-mail address and write to those you are interested in talking to individually.

Don't forget the watering holes

For convivial networking, you can't beat the casual atmos-phere of one (or several) of Chicago's saloons on a Friday afternoon. Rick Kogan, once the *Chicago Tribune's* Mr. Night-Life, helped us with the following suggestions for imbibers and teetotalers alike. You can meet **architects** at Moonrakers (735 S. Dearborn) and The Berghoff (17 W. Adams). **Politicians** like The Berghoff, too, although politi-cians can be found everywhere meeting as many people as they can. The general **business crowd** can be found at Harry Caray's (33 W. Kinzie).

People in **advertising, journalism, or public relations** meet at the Billy Goat Tavern (430 N. Michigan Ave., lower level), Avanzare (161 E. Huron), and at hideaways along Rush St.

Attorneys frequent Jerome's (2450 N. Clark St.) and Sieben's Brewing Company (436 W. Ontario), while **artists** hang out at gallery openings, which are listed in Friday's *Tribune.* **Interior designers,** members of the furniture trades, and textile manufacturers meet at Shaw's Crab House (21 E. Hubbard) and Andy's Bar and Grill (11 E. Hubbard).

You can meet **financial wizards** at Broker's Inn (323 S. LaSalle St.) or at the Sign of the Trader in the lobby of the Board of Trade building (141 W. Jackson). **Accountants** add up the bills at the City Tavern (33 W. Monroe).

As a safe bet, restaurants or bars on the lower levels of professional buildings are generally good places to meet people from offices in the building, so if all else fails, try those.

Networking After You Land the Job

Networking doesn't end when you land the job. Keep people who are part of your network informed about your job search, and let them know when you finally land a job. Periodically touch base and let them know how things are working out with the new job.

Maintaining your network requires that you contribute as much as you receive. After you find your job—or even while you are looking for it—remember that your ideas, information, and contacts can help other people in your network. Often we have to train ourselves to offer such information because we don't think of ourselves as resources.

Sometimes people seem to walk into successful jobs or successful career changes. If you asked them how they did it, they would probably say they were in the right place at the right time. No doubt, some people do just get lucky, but others have high career awareness, or an idea of what their next career move or career change might be. Developing high career awareness means knowing what your next move is, planning for it, knowing who might be involved in helping you, and positioning yourself for it.

In other words, networking should become a part of your life and a part of your plans for your next career move. Knowing people in all types of career areas allows you to keep up with the possibilities and helps you position yourself to take the next step up the career ladder.

BOOKS ON NETWORKING

Numerous books have been written on job searching and networking. Here are a few good ones.

Krannich, R.L. and C.R. *Network Your Way to Job and Career Success.* Manassas, VA: Impact Publications, 1989.

Petras, Kathryn and Ross. *The Only Job Hunting Guide You'll Ever Need.* New York: Fireside, 1995.

Stoodley, Martha. *Information Interviewing: What It Is and How to Use It In Your Career.* Deerfield Beach, FL: Garrett Publishing, 1990.

Networking Resources in the Chicago Area

There follows a selected list of over 200 organized groups, ready-made for networking, forming relationships, and gleaning information about jobs and business in the Chicago area.

SELECTED PROFESSIONAL ORGANIZATIONS, TRADE GROUPS, NETWORKS, CLUBS, AND SOCIETIES

Advertising Agency Production Managers Club
35 W. Wacker Drive
Chicago, IL 60601
(312) 220-4354
Professional group for purchasers of graphic arts.

Advisory Counsel on Women's Affairs
510 N. Peshtigo Court, Suite 6A
Chicago, IL 60611
(312) 744-4427
Managers and advocates of improving the status of women in the Chicago area.

AFTRA
75 E. Wacker Drive, 14th floor
Chicago, IL 60601
(312) 372-8081
Labor union involved with radio and television performers.

Agate Club of Chicago
303 E. Wacker Drive, Suite 1318
Chicago, IL 60601
(312) 861-0600
Oldest club in the U.S. for consumer magazine sales reps.

Airline Employees Association
5600 S. Central Ave.
Chicago, IL 60638
(773) 767-3333

Air Transport Association of Chicago
1765 Commerce Drive, Suite 105
Elk Grove Village, IL 60007
(847) 439-0360

Alliance of American Insurers
1501 Woodfield Road, Suite 400 West
Schaumburg, IL 60173
(847) 330-8500
Trade association for property and casualty insurance companies.

American Architectural Manufacturers Association
1540 E. Dundee Road, Suite 310
Palatine, IL 60067
(847) 202-1350
Trade association of manufacturers of structural products and their suppliers.

American Association of Medical Assistants
20 N. Wacker Drive
Chicago, IL 60606
(312) 899-1500
Professional association; publishes educational materials.

American Assn. of University Women
2335 W. Touhy Ave., Suite 104
Chicago, IL 60645
(773) 262-8662
Engages in advocacy, action, and research; publishes monthly newsletter with job listings; sponsors meetings and seminars.

American Bar Association
750 N. Lake Shore Drive
Chicago, IL 60611
(312) 988-5000
Professional association for attorneys. Publishes magazines, journals, newspapers with want ads; maintains extensive library and research department; sponsors educational and informational seminars.

American Center for Design
233 E. Ontario St., Suite 500
Chicago, IL 60611
(312) 787-2018
Professional organization of people in graphic arts. Publishes *Creative Registry,* newsletter with job listings.

American Chemical Society
540 Frontage Road
Northfield, IL 60693
(847) 441-6383
Scientific, educational, and professional association of chemists and chemical engineers. Publishes newsletter with employment listings.

American College of Healthcare Executives
840 N. Lake Shore Drive
Chicago, IL 60611
(312) 943-0544
Professional association for hospital and health service administrators.

American Congress for Rehabilitation Medicine
5700 Old Orchard Road
Skokie, IL 60077
(847) 966-0095
Professional association; publishes monthly journal.

American Dental Association
211 E. Chicago Ave.
Chicago, IL 60611
(312) 440-2500

Professional association that promotes oral health of the public and provides member services and continuing education to the dental profession.

American Dental Hygienists
444 N. Michigan Ave.
Chicago, IL 60611
(312) 440-8900
Professional organization that features information related to dental hygiene.

American Dietetic Association
216 W. Jackson Blvd., Suite 800
Chicago, IL 60606
(312) 899-0040
Professional association of dietitians in hospitals, colleges, schools, day care centers, business, and industry. Holds workshops and seminars, promotes educational opportunities, publishes newsletter.

American Economic Development Council
9801 W. Higgins Road, Suite 540
Rosemont, IL 60018
(847) 692-9944
National organization of professional economic and industrial developers. Publishes monthly newsletter with career opportunities.

American Federation of Musicians/Chicago
Local 10-208
175 W. Washington St.
Chicago, IL 60602
(312) 782-0063

American Federation of Television and Radio Artists/SAG
75 E. Wacker Drive, 14th floor
Chicago, IL 60601
(312) 372-8081

American Hardware Manufacturers Association
801 N. Plaza Drive
Schaumburg, IL 60173-4977
(847) 605-1025
Trade association of manufacturers of products distributed through hardware wholesalers and manufacturers' reps.

American Health Information Management Association
919 N. Michigan Ave.
Chicago, IL 60611
(312) 787-2672
Association for health-records professionals. Newsletter, meetings.

American Hospital Association
840 N. Lake Shore Drive
Chicago, IL 60611
(312) 280-6000
Professional association for hospital employees.

American Institute of Architects
222 Merchandise Mart, Suite 1049
Chicago, IL 60654
(312) 670-7770
Chicago-area chapter of professional association for architects and associates.

American Institute of Banking
175 W. Jackson Blvd., Suite 2200
Chicago, IL 60604
(312) 347-3400
Sponsors evening courses and seminars leading to a certificate in banking.

American Institute of Graphic Arts/Chicago Chapter
2210 W. North Ave.
Chicago, IL 60647
(773) 489-1400

American Library Association
50 E. Huron St.

Chicago, IL 60611
(312) 944-6780
Professional association of librarians, libraries, trustees, and friends. Publishes *Booklist,* professional journals; maintains extensive research and information departments.

American Management Association
8655 W. Higgins Road
Chicago, IL 60631
(773) 693-5511
Focuses on business seminars for management personnel.

American Marketing Association
250 S. Wacker Drive, Suite 200
Chicago, IL 60606
(312) 648-0536
Association for marketing and research executives, sales and promotion managers, and advertising specialists. Organizes educational seminars and meetings; publishes monthly newspaper, "Marketing News," which carries employment listings.

American Medical Association
515 N. State St.
Chicago, IL 60610
(312) 464-5000
Professional association for doctors.

American Medical Technologists
710 Higgins Road
Park Ridge, IL 60068
(847) 823-5169
Professional association of medical technologists.

American Medical Writers Association
7016 S. Fairfield
Chicago, IL 60629-1915
(773) 471-3712
Chicago chapter of national organization of communicators in the health sciences. Holds monthly meetings, yearly educational seminars.

American Planning Association
1313 E. 60th St.
Chicago, IL 60637
(773) 955-9100
Professional organization of people
in urban planning and related fields.
Seminars, educational programs for
the public; publishes reports,
newsletters, and monthly magazine
with employment listings.

**American Red Cross Mid-America
Chapter**
43 E. Ohio St.
Chicago, IL 60611
(312) 440-2001
Provides disaster assistance, emergency communication, and safety
education.

American Society of Civil Engineers
Illinois Section
203 N. Wabash Ave., Room 100
Chicago, IL 60601
(312) 263-1606
Local chapter of a national. Local
meetings, newsletter.

**American Society of Design
Engineers**
P.O. Box 931
Arlington Heights, IL 60006
(847) 259-7120

**American Society of Interior
Designers**
620 Merchandise Mart Plaza
Chicago, IL 60654
(312) 467-5080
Professional society for interior
designers and associate members in
allied design fields. Sponsors educational seminars; publishes newsletter
with want ads.

**American Society of Journalists and
Authors/Midwest Chapter**
Jerry Reedy, President
3542 N. Pine Grove
Chicago, IL 60657

**American Society of Real Estate
Counselors**
430 N. Michigan Ave.
Chicago, IL 60611
(312) 329-8427
Trade association for real estate counselors, i.e., those who receive remu-
neration on a fee, rather than a commission, basis.

American Society of Safety Engineers
1800 E. Actin St.
Des Plaines, IL 60018
(847) 692-4121

**American Society for Training &
Development**
8 S. Michigan Ave., Suite 1400
Chicago, IL 60603
(312) 236-3327
Society for professionals in training,
education, and human resources
development.

**American Society of Women
Accountants**
625 Albino Lane
Mount Prospect, IL 60056
(847) 250-0090
Professional association for women
accountants and educators. Monthly
dinner meetings, job bank, publishes
newsletter, "The Coordinator."

**American Spa and Health Resort
Assn.**
P.O. Box 585
Lake Forest, IL 60045
(847) 234-8851
ASHRA promotes the public aware-
ness of spas/health resorts and sets
standards for membership.

American Women's Society of Certified Public Accountants
401 N. Michigan Ave.
Chicago, IL 60611
(312) 644-6610
Holds monthly meetings, offers specialized education, publishes monthly newsletter.

Amusement and Music Operators Assn.
401 N. Michigan Ave.
Chicago, IL 60611-4267
(312) 644-6610
Trade association for manufacturers, distributors, and operators of coin-operated amusement devices.

Appraisal Institute
875 N. Michigan Ave., Suite 2400
Chicago, IL 60611-1980
(312) 335-4110
A professional society of real estate appraisers.

Art Directors & Copy Writers Club of Chicago
116 W. Illinois
Chicago, IL 60610
(312) 321-9446 FAX number only

Association of Home Appliance Manufacturers
20 N. Wacker Drive, Suite 1500
Chicago, IL 60606
(312) 984-5800

Association of Information Technology Professionals
505 Busse Highway
Park Ridge, IL 60068-3191
(847) 825-8124
Local chapter of national organization for data processing installers, programmers, systems analysts, research specialists, and educators. Publishes newsletter with job listings.

Association of Legal Administrators
(312) 781-2135
Organization of administrators of law firms and corporate and government legal departments. Job placement service.

Association of Mental Health Administrators
60 Revere Drive, Suite 500
Northbrook, IL 60062
(847) 480-9626
Annual meeting, bi-monthly newsletter, quarterly management practices journal.

Association for Multi-Image
150 E. Ohio St.
Chicago, IL 60611
Contact by mail only.
Chicago chapter of national organization for film producers and dealers. Holds periodic meetings, educational seminars, publishes newsletter.

Association of Professional Landscape Designers
11 S. LaSalle, Suite 1400
Chicago, IL 60603
(312) 201-0101
Awards Professional Landscape Designer Certification.

Association for Theater in Higher Education
200 N. Michigan Ave., Suite 300
Chicago, IL 60601
(312) 541-2066
ATHE fosters interaction and the exchange of information among those engaged in all areas of theater research, performance, scholarship, and crafts.

Automotive Service Industry Assn.
25 Northwest Point Blvd., Suite 425
Elk Grove Village, IL 60007
(847) 228-1310

Multiple trade association of manufacturers, remanufacturers, warehouse distributors, and jobbers in the automobile industry. Holds annual trade show; provides career opportunity programs to schools and organizations; publishes "Business Opportunities," a bi-monthly guide to jobs in auto industry.

Bank Administration Institute
1 N. Franklin
Chicago, IL 60606
(312) 553-4600
Organization of bank administrators and their staffs. Educational seminars; publishes magazine with job listings.

Bank Marketing Association
309 W. Washington Blvd.
Chicago, IL 60606
(312) 782-1442
Professional organization for public relations and marketing executives for banks and related institutions. Sponsors workshops and seminars; maintains job search service; publishes "Community Bank Marketing," a newsletter with want ads, and *Bank Marketing Journal.*

Broadcast Advertising Club
325 W. Huron, Suite 403
Chicago, IL 60610
(312) 440-0540

Builders Association of Chicago
5 Westbrook Corporate Center
Westchester, IL 60154
(708) 409-0808
Trade association, representing general contractors.

Building Owners and Managers Association of Chicago
135 S. LaSalle St., Suite 1011
Chicago, IL 60603
(312) 236-5237
Association of building managers. Hosts meetings, publishes newsletter.

Business Professional Advertising Association/Illinois
121 Mohawk Drive
Clarendon Hills, IL 60514
(630) 323-5666

Cable Television and Communications Association of Illinois
2400 East Devon, Suite 317
Des Plaines, IL 60018
(847) 297-4520

Catholic Alumni Club
P.O. Box 41684
Chicago, IL 60641
(312) 726-0735
Social club for single Catholic college grads under 40. Holds meetings; sponsors social events; publishes newsletter.

Center for New Television
1440 N. Dayton
Chicago, IL 60622
(312) 951-6868
Membership group serves independent television producers, media professionals, and video artists.

Chicago Advertising Federation
225 N. Michigan Ave., 20th floor
Chicago, IL 60601
(312) 861-7051
Professional group for people in advertising and related fields. Holds monthly meetings; publishes newsletter with want ads; hosts seminars; sponsors charitable and social events.

Chicago Alliance of Business Employment and Training
14 E. Jackson Blvd.
Chicago, IL 60604
(312) 786-0890
Organization formed to help minorities and the disabled find jobs.

Chicago Architecture Foundation
224 S. Michigan Ave.
Chicago, IL 60604
(312) 922-3432
Not-for-profit organization to
increase knowledge of Chicago area
past, present, and future architecture.

**Chicago Area Broadcast Public
Affairs Association**
c/o WBBM-TV
630 McClurg Court
Chicago, IL 60611
Professional group for public affairs
journalists. Meetings, seminars; publishes newsletter with want ads.

Chicago Artists Coalition
5 W. Grand Ave.
Chicago, IL 60610
(312) 670-2060
Network of visual artists.

**Chicago Association of Business
Economists**
c/o Kemper Financial Services
120 S. LaSalle St.
Chicago, IL 60603
(312) 845-1755

**Chicago Association of Direct
Marketing**
200 N. Michigan Ave., Suite 300
Chicago, IL 60601
(312) 541-1272
Holds monthly meetings; sponsors
seminars; holds annual convention;
sponsors social programs.

**Chicago Association of Women
Business Owners**
200 N. Michigan Ave., Suite 300
Chicago, IL 60601
(312) 541-1272
National network group. Monthly
meetings, seminars, newsletter. For a
brochure call: (800) 892-9000.

**Chicago Audio Visual Producers
Assn.**
c/o Meeting Media
3100 Dundee Road, Suite 703
Northbrook, IL 60062
(847) 561-8160
Organization of people working
in A/V. Quarterly educational meetings, freelance talent directory for
members.

Chicago Bar Association
321 S. Plymouth Court
Chicago, IL 60604-3997
(312) 554-2000
Independent local professional association for lawyers.

Chicago Board of Realtors
520 N. Michigan Ave.
Chicago, IL 60611
(312) 222-2540
Professional group of licensed real
estate brokers. Meetings, educational
seminars; newsletter, information
brochures; real estate courses.

Chicago Bond Club
222 W. Adams St.
Chicago, IL 60606
(312) 236-1600

Chicago Book Clinic
11 S. LaSalle St., Suite 1400
Chicago, IL 60603
(312) 946-1700
Book production group. Monthly
meetings, courses in book publishing,
holds annual exhibit of award-win-
ning book designs.

**Chicago Chapter of Chartered Life
Underwriters**
65 E. Wacker Place, #1107
Chicago, IL 60601
(312) 853-0456
Newsletter, monthly meeting.
Continuing education courses.

Chicago Computer Society
P.O. Box 27
Deerfield, IL 60015
(847) 794-7737
Networking group for personal computer users. Meetings, special interest seminars, newsletter, private electronic bulletin board.

Chicago Convention and Tourism Bureau
2300 S. Lake Shore Drive
Chicago, IL 60616-1497
(312) 567-8500
Sponsors seminars; listing of conventions and trade shows in Chicago; publishes guides, maps, brochures about Chicago.

Chicago Cosmetologists Association
401 N. Michigan Ave.
Chicago, IL 60611
(312) 321-6809
Trade association of people working in sales of cosmetics.

Chicago Council on Foreign Relations
116 S. Michigan Ave.
Chicago, IL 60603
(312) 726-3860
Sponsors foreign trips and educational programs; Council Forum group hosts social and educational activities for members under 40.

Chicago Council of Lawyers
220 S. State St., Suite 800
Chicago, IL 60604
(312) 427-0710
Independent professional group for lawyers.

Chicago Finance Exchange
414 Plaza Drive, Suite 209
Westmont, IL 60559
(630) 655-0117
Network group for women in finance.

Chicago Foundation for Women
230 W. Superior, 4th floor
Chicago, IL 60610
(312) 266-1176
Professional organization.

Chicago Headline Club
455 N. Cityfront Plaza
Chicago, IL 60611
(312) 345-6100
National group of print and electronic journalists. Holds monthly meetings; sponsors seminars and awards; keeps active job file.

Chicago Home Economists in Business
5422 S. Ingleside Drive
Chicago, IL 60615
For job information send SASE to above address.
Home economists employed in industry. Holds monthly meetings; publishes newsletter.

Chicago's Fine Dining Association
405 N. Wabash Ave., Suite 3512
Chicago, IL 60611
(312) 467-7142
Organization of 23 of Chicago's top restaurants. Bi-monthly meetings, newsletter, job data.

Chicago Society of Association Executives
20 N. Wacker Drive, Suite 1456
Chicago, IL 60606
(312) 236-2288
Professional group. Meetings and seminars; maintains job referral service.

Chicago Software Association
2 N. Riverside Plaza, Suite 2400
Chicago, IL 60606
(312) 939-5355
Group lends support to the local technical community in industry, academics, service industries, and government.

Chicago Stock Exchange
40 S. LaSalle St.
Chicago, IL 60605-0000
(312) 663-2222
Members are securities brokers and
dealers in Illinois and surrounding
area.

Chicago Teachers' Center
770 N. Halsted St., Suite 420
Chicago, IL 60622
(312) 733-7330
Resource center for elementary and
secondary school teachers and educators.

Chicago Transportation Club
5412 W. Wilson Blvd.
Chicago, IL 60630-3933
(773) 282-2313
Social organization for anyone
involved in transportation business.

Chicago Women in Publishing
43 E. Ohio St., Suite 1022
Chicago, IL 60611
(312) 645-0083
Professional group open to women
interested in book and magazine
publishing. Holds monthly meetings;
publishes newsletter with job listings;
sponsors educational seminars.

Chicago Women's Travel Club
Attn: Ann Dorian
332 S. Michigan Ave.

Chicago, IL 60604
(312) 939-3993
Group of women travel professionals.

Chicagoland Chamber of Commerce
200 N. LaSalle St.
Chicago, IL 60601
(312) 494-6700
Publishes brochures dealing with all
aspects of business in Chicago; directory of largest employers; guides,
maps. Research and statistical division provides data about Chicago
metropolitan area.

Citizens for a Better Environment
407 S. Dearborn, Suite 1775
Chicago, IL 60605
(312) 939-1530

Citizen's Information Service
332 S. Michigan Ave.
Chicago, IL 60604
(312) 939-4636
Provides information about government and civic concerns.

City Club of Chicago
360 N. Michigan Ave., Suite 1903
Chicago, IL 60601
(312) 565-6500
Civic group founded in 1903. Hosts
meetings and debates; sponsors educational seminars.

Executive networking
The higher your rung on the corporate ladder, the greater
the chances that networking with executives outside your
own field will pay off. If you're looking for a top spot in
electronics, don't pass up a chance to discuss your credentials and employment needs with, say, the recruiting executive of an advertising firm. He or she just might have the
hidden connection that could land you a great job.

One hiring exec from a large corporation reports: "I network with recruiters from more industries than most people would think, both industries that are related to ours and those that are not. It helps to find out what talent is available. If one of my contacts has someone in a file they don't need and I do, they're happy to tell me about that person. And I work the same way."

Civic Federation
243 S. Wabash, Suite 850
Chicago, IL 60604
(312) 341-9603
Watchdog organization since 1894.

Commercial-Investment Real Estate Institute
430 N. Michigan Ave., Suite 600
Chicago, IL 60611-4092
(312) 321-4460
Functions as a professional association of real estate practitioners.

Contract Furnishings Council
1190 Merchandise Mart Plaza
Chicago, IL 60654
(312) 321-0563
Association of full-service contract furnishings dealers. Specialized education, placement service.

Decorating Products Assn. of Chicago
9944 Roberts Road
Palos Hills, IL 60465
(708) 923-0232
Retailers and distributors of wallpaper, paint, and other decorating products. Conducts surveys, promotes educational activities, publishes monthly magazine, *Decorating Retailer.*

Design Professionals Association
247 Bryant Ave.
Glen Ellyn, IL 60137
(630) 858-9500
Members are professionals involved in landscape design.

Dietary Managers Association
1 Pierce Plaza, Suite 1220 W
Itasca, IL 60143
(630) 775-9200
Sponsors continuing education courses for managers and supervisors; publishes bi-weekly newsletter.

Donors Forum of Chicago
208 S. LaSalle, Suite 740
Chicago, IL 60604
(312) 578-0090
Clearinghouse for information on philanthropic and non-profit charitable organizations in Chicago. Maintains research library, sponsors educational seminars, holds five meetings a year, publishes newsletter.

Economic Club of Chicago
20 N. Clark St., Suite 2720
Chicago, IL 60602
(312) 726-1628
Educational group for top executives.

Economic Development Council
135 S. LaSalle St., Suite 1140
Chicago, IL 60603
(312) 726-8787
Not-for-profit organization that records current events in the Chicago area. Hosts monthly luncheon with a guest speaker; publishes monthly newsletter.

Electronic Industries Association
222 S. Riverside Plaza, Room 2200
Chicago, IL 60606
(312) 648-2300
Trade association for manufacturers of radio, TV, video systems.

Electronic Representatives Organization
20 E. Huron St.
Chicago, IL 60611
(312) 649-1333
Electronic equipment sales reps' organization that holds biennial conferences in Chicago and around the country. Monthly newsletter.

Executives Club of Chicago
8 S. Michigan Ave., Suite 1604
Chicago, IL 60603
(312) 263-3500
81-year-old club. Weekly luncheons, sponsors charitable activities, maintains an informal job bank.

Fashion Group of Chicago
333 N. Michigan Ave., Suite 2032
Chicago, IL 60601
(312) 372-4811
Network group of models, designers, and retailers.

Financial Managers Society
230 W. Monroe St., Suite 2205
Chicago, IL 60606
(312) 578-1300
Technical information exchange for controllers. Publishes monthly newsletter, "Printout."

Food Equipment Manufacturers Assn.
401 N. Michigan Ave., Suite 2200
Chicago, IL 60611
(312) 644-6610
Manufacturers of commercial food service equipment and supplies for restaurant, hotel, and industrial use. Publishes monthly newsletter.

Foodservice Equipment Distributors Association
223 W. Jackson Blvd.
Chicago, IL 60606
(312) 427-9605
Trade association for distributors of food service equipment such as

ovens, ranges, china, silverware, etc., for hotels, restaurants and institutions.

Government Finance Officers Assn.
180 N. Michigan Ave.
Chicago, IL 60601
(312) 977-9700
Professional association of auditors, comptrollers, treasurers, directors of finance, and accounting officials of federal, state, provincial, and local governments in the U.S. and Canada.

Greater North Michigan Ave. Assn.
625 N. Michigan Ave., Suite 401
Chicago, IL 60611
(312) 642-3570
Provides development, protection, promotion for Michigan Avenue-based retailers, hotels, tenants, restaurants, community residents, and educational institutions.

Greater State Street Council
36 S. State St., Suite 902
Chicago, IL 60603
(312) 782-9160
Provides development, protection, promotion for State Street-based retailers, hotels, tenants, restaurants, and movie theaters; sponsors annual Santa Claus parade.

Healthcare Financial Management Association
2 Westbrook Corporate Center
Westchester, IL 60154
(708) 531-9600
Professional association of health care financial managers and those in related fields.

Home Builders Association of Greater Chicago
635 Butterfield Road, Suite 100
Oak Brook Terrace, IL 60181-4000
(630) 627-7575
Trade association of persons involved in all phases of the building industry.

Hotel-Motel Association of Illinois
27 E. Monroe St., Suite 700
Chicago, IL 60603
(312) 346-3135
Organization of management
employees of Chicago-area hostelries.

Human Resources Management Assn.
140 S. Dearborn, Suite 812
Chicago, IL 60603-5205
(312) 332-0143
Group of personnel professionals.
Meetings, bi-monthly newsletter.

Illinois Arts Council
100 W. Randolph St., Suite 10-500
Chicago, IL 60601
(312) 814-6750
Maintains information on local arts
organizations, including the Illinois
Creative Artists Registry.

Illinois Assn. of Mortgage Brokers
350 W. 22nd St., Suite 104
Lombard, IL 60148
(630) 916-7720

Illinois Bankers Association
111 N. Canal St.
Chicago, IL 60606
(312) 876-9900
Sponsors educational seminars; publishes *Illinois Banker* magazine.

Illinois CPA Society
222 S. Riverside Plaza, Suite 1600
Chicago, IL 60606
(312) 993-0393
Professional association. Sponsors
educational seminars.

Illinois Creative Artists Registry
c/o Illinois Arts Council
100 W. Randolph St., Suite 10-500
Chicago, IL 60601
(312) 814-6750
List made available to people and
organizations interested in hiring
people in the arts.

Illinois Federation of Teachers
714 Enterprise Drive
Oak Brook, IL 60521
(630) 571-0100
FAX: (630) 571-1204

Illinois Food Retailers Association
1919 S. Highland Ave.
Lombard, IL 60148
(630) 627-8100
Trade association of independent
grocers in Illinois. Meetings, newsletter with want ads.

Illinois Hospital Association
1151 E. Warrenville Road
Naperville, IL 60563
(630) 505-7777
Trade association of Illinois hospitals.

Illinois Manufacturers Association
209 W. Jackson Blvd.
Chicago, IL 60606
(312) 922-6275
Trade association. Sponsors seminars
and educational programs. Publishes
a newsletter and has meetings and
events.

Illinois Mortgage Bankers Association
11 S. LaSalle St., Suite 2155
Chicago, IL 60603
(312) 236-6208
Educational association for mortgage
bankers at commercial banks and
savings & loans. Seminars, meetings,
social events; publishes bi-monthly
newsletter with want ads.

Illinois Park and Recreation Assn.
1N141 County Farm Road
Winfield, IL 60190
(630) 752-0141
Organization of administrative and
recreational programming professionals working in park districts.
Educational seminars; annual conference; publishes bi-monthly magazine,
Illinois Parks and Recreation, with
want ads.

Illinois Physical Therapy Association
1010 Jorie Blvd., Suite 134
Oak Brook, IL 60521
(630) 571-1400
Professional organization of qualified physical therapists.

Illinois Restaurant Association
350 W. Ontario St., Suite 7W
Chicago, IL 60610
(312) 787-4000
Lobbying organization. Holds seminars and educational programs; publishes legislative newsletter and magazine.

Illinois Retail Merchants Association
19 S. LaSalle St., Suite 300
Chicago, IL 60603
(312) 726-4600
Trade association of small and large retailers located in Illinois.

Illinois State Chamber of Commerce
311 S. Wacker Drive, Suite 1500
Chicago, IL 60606-6619
(312) 987-7100
ISCC provides programs and services to help members control their cost of doing business.

Illinois Women's Press Association
129 Parkside
Chicago Heights, IL 60411
(708) 755-6576

Independent Accountants
Association of Illinois/Chicago
Chapter
P.O. Box 48-1080
Niles, IL 60714
(847) 470-4710

Independent Writers of Chicago
7855 Gross Point Road, Unit M
Skokie, IL 60077
(847) 676-3784
Network group for all freelance writers. Holds monthly meetings; sponsors seminars; provides group insurance; informal job bank.

Institute of Association Management
Companies
435 N. Michigan Ave., Suite 1717
Chicago, IL 60601-4067
(312) 644-0828
Membership consists of companies engaged in the management of two or more organizations on a professional client basis.

Institute of Electrical and Electronics
Engineers/Chicago
2460 Wisconsin Ave.
Downers Grove, IL 60515
(800) 898-4333

Institute of Environmental Sciences
940 E. Northwest Highway
Mount Prospect, IL 60056
(847) 255-1561

Institute of Food Technologists
221 N. LaSalle St., Suite 300
Chicago, IL 60601
(312) 782-8424
Chicago branch of worldwide organization of executives, educators, scientists, and engineers in the food technology industry.

Institute of Internal
Auditors/Chicago Chapter
c/o Jeff Suchomel, Quaker Oats
P.O. Box 049001
Chicago, IL 60604
(312) 222-7904

Institute of Management
Accountants
c/o Don Richter
24841 W. North Road
Lake Villa, IL 60046
(847) 559-7900, ext. 31

Institute of Real Estate Management
430 N. Michigan Ave., 7th floor
Chicago, IL 60611
(312) 32-6000
A professional society of real estate managers.

International Association of Business
Communicators
6211 N. Campbell
Chicago, IL 60659
Contact by phone only
(312) 332-0147
Sponsors monthly luncheons and
seminars; publishes newsletter; holds
annual convention.

Int'l. Hardware Distributors Assn.
401 N. Michigan Ave., Suite 2200
Chicago, IL 60611-4267
(312) 644-6610

International Interior Design Assn.
341 Merchandise Mart Plaza
Chicago, IL 60654
(312) 467-1950
Organization of interior and furnishings designers in the contract furniture industry.

Investment Analysts Society of
Chicago
330 S. Wells, Suite 1422
Chicago, IL 60606-7101
(312) 360-0382
Network group for financial analysts.

Kiwanis Club, District Office
10220 S. Cicero Ave.
Oak Lawn, IL 60453
(708) 857-7910
Federation of business and professional men's civic service clubs.

Lawyers for the Creative Arts
213 W. Institute Place, Suite 411
Chicago, IL 60610
(312) 944-2787
Free legal assistance and information
to artists and arts groups.

League of Chicago Theaters
67 E. Madison Ave., Suite 2116
Chicago, IL 60603
(312) 977-1730
Support group for Chicago's professional, community, and educational
theaters.

Lions Club International
300 22nd St.
Oak Brook, IL 60521-8842
(630) 571-5466
Fraternal organization involved in
civic and charitable activities.

Metropolitan Chicago Health Care
Council
222 S. Riverside Plaza, 19th floor
Chicago, IL 60606
(312) 906-6000
Trade association of Chicago-area
hospitals.

Midwest Healthcare Marketing Assn.
401 N. Michigan Ave.
Chicago, IL 60611-4267
(312) 644-6610

Midwest Women's Center
828 S. Wabash Ave., Suite 200
Chicago, IL 60605
(312) 922-8530
Non-profit service agency for women
seeking career help. Publishes
newsletter and *Illinois Women's
Directory;* maintains job bank; sponsors educational programs and career
development seminars.

Million Dollar Round Table
325 W. Touhy Ave.
Park Ridge, IL 60068
(847) 692-6378
Network group of successful insurance agents; publishes newsletter.

Municipal Bond Club of Chicago
c/o Brian Battle
Griffin, Kubik, Stevens and
Thompson
233 S. Wacker Drive, Suite 300
Chicago, IL 60606
(312) 441-2500
Holds annual outing, conducts a
municipal bond school, publishes
directory, holds occasional meetings
with speakers.

National Academy of Television Arts
and Sciences/Chicago Chapter
2648 N. Seminary Ave.
Chicago, IL 60614
(773) 281-3201

Nat. Assn. of Boat Manufacturers
401 N. Michigan Ave.
Chicago, IL 60611
(312) 836-4747
Members are makers of pleasure
boats.

Nat. Assn. General Merchandise Reps
401 N. Michigan Ave.
Chicago, IL 60611-4267
(312) 644-6610
Organization of manufacturers reps
selling drug, health, and beauty aids
to food chains and food items to
non-food chains and stores. Publishes
monthly newsletter.

National Association of Government
Communicators/Chicago Office
c/o Tom Laue, Mgr., External Affairs
Illinois Housing Dev. Authority
401 N. Michigan Ave., Suite 900
Chicago, IL 60611
(312) 836-5361

National Association of Independent
Insurance Adjusters
300 W. Washington St., Suite 805
Chicago, IL 60606
(312) 853-0808

National Association of Realtors
430 N. Michigan Ave.
Chicago, IL 60611
(312) 329-8200
Hosts seminars; publishes magazines
and educational materials; sponsors
conventions.

National Association of the
Remodeling Industry
175 E. Delaware
Chicago, IL 60611

(312) 266-8889
Hosts meetings, seminars, informational gatherings.

National Association of Retail
Dealers of America
10 E. 22nd St., Suite 310
Lombard, IL 60148
(630) 953-8950
Organization of retailers and dealers
of audio components, kitchen and
laundry appliances, and other household equipment. Sponsors sales and
management training and advertising
workshops; conducts surveys.

National Association of Sporting
Goods Wholesalers
P.O. Box 11344
Chicago, IL 60611
(312) 565-0233

National Association of Women in
Construction
P.O. Box 441
Lansing, IL 60438-0441
(800) 793-3204
Professional association for women.
Holds monthly meetings; seminars
and educational programs; newsletter.

National Black MBA Association
180 N. Michigan Ave., Suite 1515
Chicago, IL 60601
(312) 236-2622
Group for minority MBAs.Monthly
meetings, seminars, newsletter.

National Broadcast Association for
Community Affairs
401 N. Michigan Ave.
Chicago, IL 60611-4267
(312) 644-6610
NBACA is an organization for broadcast professionals dedicated to
strengthening community affairs programming.

National Electronic Distributors Assn.
35 E. Wacker Drive, Suite 1100
Chicago, IL 60601
(312) 558-9114
Trade organization of wholesale distributors of electronic parts, components, and consumer products.

National Family Business Council
1640 W. Kennedy Road
Lake Forest, IL 60045
(847) 295-1040
Open to all owners of family businesses. Monthly meetings; publishes newsletter.

Nat. Housewares Manufacturers Assn.
6400 Shafer Court, Suite 650
Rosemont, IL 60018
(847) 292-4200
Trade association of manufacturers and distributors of housewares.

National Human Resources Association
8 S. Michigan Ave., Suite 1000
Chicago, IL 60603
(312) 759-9101
Networking group of personnel professionals.

National Live Stock and Meat Board
444 N. Michigan Ave.
Chicago, IL 60611
(312) 467-5520
The Meat Board was formed to protect and increase demand for beef, pork, lamb, veal and processed meat products through consumer marketing programs.

National Marine Manufacturers
200 E. Randolph St., Suite 5100
Chicago, IL 60601-6436
(312) 946-6200
Manufacturers of pleasure boats, boating supplies, and marine engines.

National Network of Sales Professionals
P.O. Box 1611
Arlington Heights, IL 60006
(847) 705-2362
Organization for sales people, whether employees or independents.

National Organization for Women
30 E. Adams, Suite 401
Chicago, IL 60603
(312) 578-9531
Chicago chapter of national women's organization does electoral work; fund-raising; sponsors educational seminars; publishes local and national newsletters.

National PTA
330 N. Wabash St., Suite 2100
Chicago, IL 60611
(312) 670-6782
Conducts research, maintains standing committees and extensive publications list.

National Recreation and Parks Association/Chicago
c/o Great Lakes Regional Offices
650 W. Higgins Road
Hoffman Estates, IL 60195
(847) 843-7529

National Restaurant Association
150 N. Michigan Ave., Suite 2000
Chicago, IL 60601
(312) 853-2525
Trade association of restaurants, cafeterias, clubs, contract feeders, drive-ins, caterers, and institutional food services.

National Safety Council
1121 Spring Lake Drive
Itasca, IL 60143-3201
(630) 285-1121

Nat. Soc. of Fund-Raising Executives
414 Plaza Drive, Suite 209

Westmont, IL 60559
(630) 655-0134
Professional organization of
fund-raising and public relations
personnel, working in non-profit
organizations.

National Sporting Goods Association
1699 Wall St.
Mt. Prospect, IL 60056
(847) 439-4000
Trade association. Publishes newsletter with job listings.

Overseas Sales and Marketing Association of America
P.O. Box 37
Lake Bluff, IL 60044
(847) 234-1760
Members are export management
and trading companies.

Paper Industry Management
1699 Wall St., Suite 212
Mount Prospect, IL 60056
(847) 956-0250

Promotion Industry Club
1805 N. Mill St., Suite A
Naperville, IL 60563-1275
(630) 369-3772
P.C. members are manufacturers, distributors, and users of promotion
premiums.

Publicity Club of Chicago
435 N. Michigan
Chicago, IL 60611
(312) 670-4177
Professional association for people in
the communications industry.
Publishes monthly newsletter and
annual *Chicago Media Directory.*
Holds classes in P.R.

Public Relations Society of America
30 N. Michigan Ave., Suite 508
Chicago, IL 60602

(312) 372-7744
Professional association for public
relations practitioners.

Purchasing Management Association of Chicago
2250 E. Devon
Des Plaines, IL 60018
(847) 298-1940
Professional association. Sponsors
seminars and courses; maintains job
placement bureau.

Retail Advertising and Marketing
333 N. Michigan, Suite 300
Chicago, IL 60601
(312) 251-7262
International association devoted
exclusively to retail advertising and
marketing professionals.

Retail Merchants Association
19 S. LaSalle, Suite 300
Chicago, IL 60603
(312) 726-4600
Trade association of department,
chain, and mass merchandising and
specialty stores.

Rotary Club of Chicago
12 S. Michigan Ave.
Chicago, IL 60603
(312) 372-3900
Professional businessmen's club.
Promotes civic and charitable activities among members; holds monthly
meetings; maintains job listings.

Society of Human Resource Professionals
8 S. Michigan Ave., Suite 1000
Chicago, IL 60603
(312) 368-0188

Society of Women Engineers
P.O. Box 06532
Chicago, IL 60606-0532
(630) 713-7355

Professional organization for women in all areas of engineering.

Sports Foundation
c/o Ms. Pat Sinda
1699 Wall St., Suite 700
Mount Prospect, IL 60056-5708
(847) 439-4000

Television Bureau of Advertising/Chicago
c/o Tim Cornellie
18 Rivers Bend Drive
Lake Barrington, IL 60010
(847) 382-6296

Water Quality Association/Research Council
4151 Naperville Road
Lisle, IL 60532
(630) 505-0160

Western Society of Engineers
53 W. Jackson Blvd., Suite 1730
Chicago, IL 60604
Umbrella organization of engineering associations located in the Chicago area.

Women Employed
22 W. Monroe St., Suite 1400
Chicago, IL 60603
(312) 782-3902
Organization of working women that has helped thousands of women find jobs and develop short- and long-term career plans. Monthly seminars on essential career skills; monthly program meetings on topics of concern to working women.

Women Health Executives Network
P.O. Box 350
Kenilworth, IL 60043
(847) 256-4422
Professional group of health care executives, from department managers to presidents. Monthly meetings, newsletter with job listings.

Women in Cable
230 W. Monroe St., Suite 730
Chicago, IL 60606
(312) 634-2330
Network group for women working in cable TV. Holds meetings; conducts speakers bureau; publishes newsletter.

Women in Communications
P.O. Box 268611
Chicago, IL 60626
(773) 508-9424
Publishes newsletter with job listings; hosts seminars; holds monthly meetings.

Women in Design/Chicago
3712 N. Broadway
Chicago, IL 60613
(312) 409-9945
Group of professional graphic designers.

Women in Film and Television
676 N. LaSalle, Suite 400
Chicago, IL 60610
(312) 587-0949

Women in Franchising
53 W. Jackson Blvd., Suite 205
Chicago, IL 60604
(312) 431-1467

Women in International Trade
180 N. LaSalle St., Suite 2920
Chicago, IL 60601
(312) 641-1466
Group for management-level women who work in aspects of international trade. Educational programs, speakers, newsletter, special events.

Women in Management
30 N. Michigan Ave., Suite 506
Chicago, IL 60602
(312) 419-0171
Support group for professional women in management.

Women in the Director's Chair
3435 N. Sheffield, Suite 202
Chicago, IL 60657
(773) 281-4988

Women's Advertising Club of Chicago
30 N. Michigan Ave., Suite 508
Chicago, IL 60602
(312) 263-2215
Professional group for women in advertising and allied fields.

Women's Bar Association of Illinois
3223 Lake Ave., Suite 15C-148
Wilmette, IL 60091
(847) 853-1480
Professional association open to all women lawyers. Seminars, meetings.

Women's Council of Realtors
430 N. Michigan Ave.
Chicago, IL 60611
(312) 329-8569
Support system for women in real estate within the National Association of Realtors.

YMCA of Metropolitan Chicago
755 W. North Ave.
Chicago, IL 60610
(312) 280-3400
Recreation, education, and social services to men and women of all ages.

Young Executives Club of Chicago
111 N. Wabash Ave., Suite 702
Chicago, IL 60602-1905
(312) 853-0186
Network group for Chicago's future business leaders. Monthly luncheons with captains of industry.

Young Leadership Division
Jewish United Fund
1 S. Franklin St.
Chicago, IL 60606
(312) 346-6700, ext. 7626
Educational and social programs for adults under 40.

YWCA of Metropolitan Chicago
180 N. Wabash Ave., Suite 301
Chicago, IL 60601
(312) 372-6600
Career workshops.

You've already got lots of contacts

Networking paid off for Liz, a young woman eager to make her way in banking or a related industry. She told us why she's glad she took the time to talk with her friends and neighbors about her job search.

"I was having dinner with close friends and telling them about my job search," says Liz. "During the conversation, they mentioned a banker friend they thought might be hiring. As it turned out, the friend didn't have a job for me. But he suggested I come in, meet with him, and discuss some other possibilities. He put me in touch with an independent marketing firm, servicing the publishing industry. The owner of the firm was looking for someone with my exact qualifications. One thing led to another, and pretty soon I had landed exactly the position I wanted."

Developing the Perfect Resume

It seems almost impossible to write the *imperfect* resume, with over 125 books on the market today pertaining solely to resume writing. However, we still anguish over the process, believing it will secure us a job. Keep in mind that no one ever secured a job offer on the basis of a resume alone. The way to land a good position is to succeed in the interview. You have to convince a potential employer that you're the best person for the job. No piece of paper will ever do that for you—but having an excellent resume is a necessary first step.

The resume is an invitation enticing the employer to interview you. With a little success, and some luck, the employer will want to meet you after reading your resume. However, the most effective method of resume delivery is for you to first meet the employer in person; then provide your resume. We understand that this is not always possible.

The French word *résumé* means "a summing up." Thus the purpose of a resume is not to catalogue, in exact detail, your entire biography. You should be concise with your work experience, education, accomplishments, and affiliations. Your goal is to pique the employer's interest. A good rule of thumb is that the resume should be kept to one or at most two pages.

The Basics of a Good Resume

To develop a resume that entices a potential employer to want to meet you, we suggest the following tips:

1. *Tailor your resume to the potential job opening.* The astute job searcher should always research a potential employer and find out as much information as possible on the qualifications needed for a particular job and then tailor his

or her resume to match the qualifications. When listing your experience and education, concentrate on those items that demonstrate your ability to do the job you are applying for. Using a computer will facilitate this process of customizing each resume.

2. *Be concise.* Most employers don't have time to read a two-page resume and usually scan a resume within 10–20 seconds. Thus, you want to capture the reader's attention quickly. Only then will you get a more careful reading. This is not the time to demonstrate your impressive vocabulary. Instead, describe your experience in short, pithy phrases. Give figures and facts when describing your accomplishments. Your resume should read more like a chart than a chapter in a textbook. And it should look more like an ad than a legal document.

3. *Be honest.* Never lie, exaggerate, embellish, or deceive. Be honest about your education, accomplishments, and work experience. A deliberate lie can be grounds for termination and will likely turn up in a background search. If you have gaps between jobs, and gaps are not always as negative as some would have you believe, you may consider listing years worked rather than months.

4. *Have a professional presentation.* Today's high-quality computers allow you to prepare your own resume with the same professional results as paid resume preparers. A good rule of thumb: make your resume professional enough to send out on the potential employer's letterhead. If it isn't, it's probably not sharp enough.

Your resume should cover your most current work experiences (three to four jobs), with the name, location, and dates of employment plus a summary of your responsibilities relevant to the qualifications of the job you are seeking. Be sure to state your accomplishments on each job. Present your work history chronologically. Begin with your present position and work backward to your earlier jobs. If you haven't had that many jobs, organize your resume to emphasize the skills you've acquired through experience.

There are no hard and fast rules on what to include in your resume besides work experience, education, and special skills pertinent to the job for which you are applying. Professional affiliations may also be of interest to the employer. Do not list anything personal (such as marital status, date of birth, etc.) that could potentially screen you out. Salary history and references should not be included in your resume; these should be discussed in person during the interview.

Keep in mind that a resume is a sales tool. Make sure that it illustrates your unique strengths in a style and format *you* can be proud of. Be brief, tailor your experiences to the job you are seeking, and provide figures and facts to support your accomplishments.

Elements of a Resume

Here are the five main elements of a resume, with a brief description of each. All need not appear in the same order in every resume, and sometimes one or two are combined or left out, as you'll see in the sample resumes that follow.

NAME
Address
City, State, Zip
Phone
E-Mail Address (optional)

Objective: Employers use this information as a screening device or to assess a job match. It should grab the reader's attention and motivate him or her to read further. Make this relevant to the job for which you are applying!

Experience: The more impressive your work history, the more prominently you should display it. Use facts and figures to support accomplishments and goals reached.

List employment in reverse chronological order, putting the most promotable facts—employer or job title—first.

Give functional description of job if work history is strong and supports job objective.

List dates of employment last. They are the least important of all your information.

Skills: You may want to embed these in the employment section. Or, for career changers, list the skills section first. Highlight skills that are relevant to the potential job opening. Give short, results-oriented statements to support skills. Position your most marketable skills first.

Education: List in reverse chronological order, putting the most salable facts—school or degree—first. Mention honors or achievements, such as a high GPA or Dean's List.

Miscellaneous: Call this section anything applicable: Interests, Activities, Achievements, or Accomplishments.

Give only information that promotes your candidacy for the position for which you are applying.

References: Available upon request. Don't waste space on names and addresses. Have ready on a separate sheet.

Choosing a Resume Format

There are many different but equally acceptable ways to organize your resume. Every resume compiler and career counselor has his or her favorite method and style. The format you use should best present your strongest points and best convey your message to the potential employer. Resume books will use different terms for the various styles, but here are the three most popular types.

1. *The Chronological Resume* is the traditional style, most often used in the workplace and job search. It is also the resume style favored by most employers. That does not mean, however, that it is the most effective. A positive aspect of the chronological resume, aside from it being the traditional approach that employers may expect, is that it emphasizes past jobs that you wish your potential employer to notice. This resume is also very adaptable, with only the reverse chronological order of previous employment an essential ingredient.

2. *The Functional Resume* is most common among those reentering the job market after an absence, career changers, and those wishing to emphasize skills gained through non-work experience. This resume focuses on the many skills gained from employment and the accomplishments one has achieved. It shows a potential employer that you can do and have done a good job. What it doesn't necessarily emphasize is where you have done it and when.

3. *The Combination Resume* merges features of the functional and chronological resumes. This allows job seekers to emphasize accomplishments and skills while still maintaining the traditional format of reverse chronological order of positions held and organizations worked for. This format is perfect if your most current work is not your most impressive.

Sample After-College Chronological Resume

The Chronological Resume format is ideal for someone just graduating with little work experience. Here is a sample:

Michael King
2660 Golf Road
Schaumburg, IL 60025
(847) 555-0007

OBJECTIVE   Entry-level sales management position

EDUCATION   B.A., Political Science, May 1997.
DePaul University, Chicago, IL
Courses include: Business Law, Applied Probability, Statistics, Calculus, Economics, English, Creative Writing, French.

WORK   SALES MANAGEMENT INTERN. Summers 1995-97.
EXPERIENCE   **Bloomingdale's,** Chicago, IL
Managed the sales, distribution, pricing, shelving, and display of all shoes in the main store. Intensive on-the-job and educational training through the store's management training program.
CAMPUS REPRESENTATIVE. School years 1993-1995.
Office of Admissions, DePaul University
Organized and implemented an entire recruiting campaign for qualified high school minority students. Received a record number of minority student acceptances and matriculates.

ACTIVITIES   President, African-American Student Association
AND HONORS   Freshman Advisor
Tutor for high-risk high school students
National Collegiate Minority Leadership Award

REFERENCES   Available upon request.

Sample Career-Changing Functional Resume

The Functional Resume format is ideal for someone changing careers since it emphasizes skills rather than past employment. Here is a sample:

Kathy Lawrence
5532 W. Fullerton Street
Chicago, IL 60610
(773) 555-2436

OBJECTIVE   Office manager and systems administrator.

AREAS OF EXPERTISE
Administrative

- Maintained and managed departmental funds in excess of $350,000.
- Managed 18 administrative and technical staff.
- Developed annual operations plan and budget.

Organizational

- Set up procedures for assigned experiments and procured equipment for a research laboratory.
- Planned course syllabi to facilitate learning for students with assessed weaknesses.
- As a member of a consulting team, analyzed a major client's business requirements for management information as part of a reengineering project.

Computer and Systems

- Managed data processing functions for clients and generated accounting reports.
- Analyzed end-user requirements and designed systems to meet business requirements.
- Designed and produced customized applications.

WORK HISTORY   IBM Corp., Chicago, IL 1993-present
LAN Administrator for a 110-unit client-server network system
Analyst for internal computing systems
Computer Programmer and Systems Consultant
Cargill, Wilson, and Acree, Chicago, IL (1991-93)
Accounting Software and Systems Consultant
Oakton Community College (1988-91)
Instructor, Computer Science and Math Departments

EDUCATION	DePaul University, M.S., Management Information Systems (1988)
	New York University, B.A., Mathematics (1986) GPA 3.7/4.0
HONORS/ ACTIVITIES	Dean's List, three semesters
	Treasurer for non-profit organization
REFERENCES	Available upon request.

The power of verbs

Jeff B. has been a sales manager in Chicago for 20 years. During those years he has changed jobs seven times, enhancing his career with each move. Jeff realized early that using powerful, active verbs to describe his accomplishments made his resume stand out. Here are some sample verbs that job seekers in various career areas might use to help build a more effective resume.

Management
Controlled
Headed
Implemented

Methods and Controls
Restructured
Cataloged
Verified
Systematized

Public Relations/ Human Relations
Monitored
Handled
Sponsored
Integrated

Creative
Devised
Created
Originated
Conceived

Advertising/Promotion
Generated
Targeted
Tailored
Sparked

Communications
Produced
Edited
Consulted
Disseminated

Resourcefulness
Rectified
Pioneered
Achieved

Negotiations
Engineered
Mediated
Proposed
Negotiated

Sample Combination Resume

The Combination Resume allows you to use aspects of both the chronological and functional formats. This type is good for someone whose present work perhaps does not reflect his or her most impressive skills. Here is a sample:

Paul Wheaton
1042 N. Oakley
Chicago, IL 60606
(312) 555-0011

EDUCATION

Loyola University, Chicago, IL,
M.S., Information and Computer Science, December 1995, GPA 3.7/4.0

Notre Dame University, South Bend, IN,
A.B., Mathematics, May 1990, GPA 3.4/4.0

QUALIFICATIONS

Career-related Projects:
- Designed and implemented multi-tasking operating system for the IBM-PC.
- Implemented compiler for Pascal-like language.
- Designed electronic mail system using PSL/PSA specification.

Languages and Operating Systems:
- Proficient in Ada, Modula-2, Pascal, C+
- Thorough knowledge of IBM-PC hardware.
- Experienced in UNIX, MS-DOS, CP/M operating systems.

Hardware:
- IBM-PC (MS-DOS), Pyramid 90x (UNIX), Cyber 990 (NOS)

WORK EXPERIENCE

UNIX Programmer, Simms Programming Services, Chicago, IL 9/95-present.
Responsible for porting MS-DOS database applications to IBM-PC/AT running Xenix System V. System administration.
Computer Programmer, IBM Corp., Chicago, IL 10/92-9/95
Performed daily disk backup on Burroughs B-1955 machine. Executed database update programs and checks. User assistance.
Computer Operator, Computer Associates, Inc., Chicago, IL 8/90-9/92
Responsible for maintaining and operating computer systems.

REFERENCES

Available upon request.

Sample Combination Resume for Liberal Arts Major

As mentioned earlier, the Combination Resume allows you to use parts of both the chronological and functional formats. This type is good for liberal arts majors who have several career fields to select among because of their broad educational background. Since Laura (example resume follows) wanted to apply for jobs in broadcasting, magazine publishing, and writing speeches for a Congressman, she used the combination style to avoid writing several different resumes. Here is the sample:

Laura Clarkson

49 W. Davis Street

Skokie, IL 60212

(847) 555-0011

EDUCATION   B.A. Degree, June 1997. Major in English. Minor in psychology. University of Illinois, Chicago, IL
Activities:
Participated in University-in-Italy Program (Rome).
Member of University's Women's Cross Country Running.
Editor "Running Notes." Reporter for student newspaper.
Member of Chi Omega sorority. Rush Co-Chairperson.
Panhellenic Society representative.

EXPERIENCE   *University of Illinois Chicago,* Sports Information Office.
Administrative Intern, spring 1996 to present.
Reported on all school sports events. Managed post-game football press box operations. Published stories about school athletes. Wrote press releases.
Football Statistician, fall 1994 and fall 1995.
Compiled statistics. Wrote game summaries and weekly reports.
IBM, Chicago, IL
Public Relations Intern, summers 1994 and 1995.
Researched information for "IBM Computer's" student advertisements and special publications. Proofread copy and checked facts. Replied to reader correspondence. Coordinated IBM Computer's School Visitation Program.
Marshall Fields, Chicago, IL
Salesperson, Summer 1993.
Completed nightly closings, and maintained various departments in manager's absence. Rotated throughout store as needed. Highest sales for two months.

INTERESTS   Enjoy playing the piano and guitar, oil and watercolor painting. Avid runner. Have traveled in Europe and throughout the western U.S.

REFERENCES   Available upon request.

Resume Checklist

- Brainstorm a list of the skills and talents you want to convey. These may include character traits such as persistence and assertiveness; work skills such as fluency in languages and computer literacy; and transferable skills such as managing, motivating, and leading people, manipulating data, evaluating and analyzing systems.
- Prepare your resume on a computer and printer that give you the same results as a professionally typeset resume.
- Use heavyweight (at least 20 lb.), high-quality paper and a laser printer if at all possible. White, off-white, or light gray papers ($8^1/_2$ x 11 inches) are usually safe, conservative bets. However, if you are in theater, arts, or advertising, you can be a little more daring. If you have the budget, consider buying $9^1/_2$ x $12^1/_2$-inch envelopes so you won't have to fold your resume and cover letter.
- Be concise and brief in your wording.
- Avoid personal pronouns.
- Use active verbs to describe your accomplishments rather than your assigned duties.
- Arrange information in descending order of importance within each section of your resume.
- Be consistent in format and style.
- Tailor your skills and experience as much as possible to each potential job opening.
- Proofread your resume, and then have a few friends proofread it as well.
- Be selective in sending out your resume. Mass mailings usually only result in spending unnecessary time and money.

Using the Computer to Design Your Resume

Welcome to the high-tech world of resume writing. Even if you don't own your own computer, many libraries have them available, and copy stores such as Kinko's rent computer time. So there is no excuse to rule out the computer in designing your resume. There are certain advantages:

- You have the ability to save your resume on a disk, which simplifies editing it for a specific company or position. Revises and updates become simple.
- Computers offer a wide range of type faces, styles (bold, italics, and so on), and sizes. Combined with a laser printout, you can achieve a professional-looking resume at modest expense.

No matter what method you use to prepare your resume, *proofread* it before printing. Misspelled words or typing errors reflect badly on you even if it's not your fault. Recruit a friend to help read your resume, word for word and comma for comma. And don't make last minute changes after everyone has proofed it. Somehow, you *will* end up with an error.

Professional Resume Preparers

It is always better to prepare your own resume, as long as you have reasonable writing skills. However, if you have trouble condensing your writing style and you have no friends who can help, no access to a university career office or books on resumes, then a professional may be able to assist you.

Before choosing a professional resume service, try to get a recommendation from someone whose judgment you trust. Find out the minimum and maximum costs before employing any service. Ask whether the price includes only writing, or typesetting and printing as well. If changes are needed, will it cost extra? Finally, always shop around for the best services available. Don't forget that many career counselors and consultants also provide resume preparation; refer to Chapter 2.

The following are firms that will assist you in preparing your resume. Keep in mind that a listing in this book does not constitute an endorsement.

A-AAAction Communications
The John Hancock Center
175 E. Delaware, Suite 4806
Chicago, IL 60611
(312) 943-7195

A Advanced Resume Service
1900 E. Golf Road, Suite M100
Schaumburg, IL 60173
(847) 517-1088
e-mail: ADVRESUMES@aol.com
Free phone or fax consultation. Lifetime updates, mailings, and cover letters available.

A Better Resume
208 S. LaSalle St., Suite 168
Chicago, IL 60604
(312) 781-9590

A Better Resume Service
70 W. Madison St.
Chicago, IL 60606
(312) 332-6665
and:
80 River Oaks Center, Suite 802
Calumet City, IL 60409
(708) 730-1888
and:
7667 W. 95th St., Suite 307
Hickory Hills, IL 60457
(708) 599-8886

Allen & Associates
1300 E. Woodfield Road, Suite 300
Schaumburg, IL 60173
(847) 517-7792
Complete program, including broadcast letters and a research list.

Banner Personnel
122 S. Michigan Ave., Suite 1510
Chicago, IL 60603
(312) 704-6100

Bondar Executive Secretaries
5005 Newport Drive, Suite 800
Rolling Meadows, IL 60008
(847) 394-5055

CareerPro Resume and Job Consulting Service
10540 Western Ave., Suite 405
Chicago, IL 60406
(773) 779-3344

CareerPro Resume Services
29 E. Madison
Chicago, IL 60611
(312) 580-1977

Hunter Resumes
70 W. Madison
Chicago, IL 60606
(800) 767-2377

Joan Masters & Sons
875 N. Michigan Ave., Suite 3614
Chicago, IL 60611
(312) 787-3009

Professional Resumes
208 S. LaSalle, Suite 1681
Chicago, IL 60604
(312) 368-8888

Timesavers Secretarial Services
9822 Maynard Terrace
Niles, IL 60053
(847) 470-0231

Words by CEO
304 E. Lyndale
Northlake, IL 60164
(847) 562-8855

The laughing stock of the company

Make sure that you don't end up as fodder for employer
levity as did the following unfortunates:

One candidate wrote under Job Responsibilities:
"Assassinated store manager during busiest retail season."
What she meant to write was "assisted."

"Education: College, August 1890–May 1994."

"Here are my qualifications for you to overlook."

"Please call me after 5:30 p.m. because I am self-
employed and my employer does not know I am looking
for another job."

Reason for leaving last job? The candidate replied: "No
special reason." Another replied: "They insisted that all
employees get to work by 8:45 every morning. Couldn't
work under those conditions."

One applicant submitted a seven-page resume and
stated, "This resume is fairly long because I have a lot
to offer you."

Electronic Resume Issues

Tom Washington, author of *Resume Power: Selling Yourself on Paper,* provides some hints for preparing electronic resumes.

The term "electronic resumes" refers to the fact that more companies are electronically scanning resumes and storing information in computer databases. These resumes are then available in seconds when managers seek a person with just the right background. It also refers to the ability to send resumes electronically to electronic bulletin boards, enabling employers from all over the world to "discover" you.

Interviewer: Does an electronic resume have to be different from a traditional resume?

Tom: Yes and no. No, in the sense that the things that make any resume effective will make a scanned resume effective. Visually it still has to be easy to skim and read, and it should include results and contributions rather than just duties. Your results and contributions are the things that cause employers to want to meet you.

But, yes, the resume also needs to be different. To be effective your resume must be easy to scan into the computer database, and it needs to be easy to retrieve. Without being properly composed, some words or whole lines can become scrambled and thus difficult to read. You should do everything you can to avoid that.

In order to prevent your resume from getting "scrambled," it helps to understand how a resume is scanned. First the resume is placed within an electronic scanner, which sends a "picture" of the document to a computer with optical character read (OCR) software. The software then translates the picture into words.

To ensure that your resume is properly scanned, just follow these simple rules. Laser-printed resumes scan best. Avoid nine-pin dot matrix printers, although 24-pin dot matrix printers will produce acceptable quality. Avoid the use of italics and fancy fonts. Some scanners cannot read them properly. Stick with Times Roman, Bookman, Arial, Helvetica, Courier, or fonts that are closely related to these. Avoid the use of shading, columns, boxes, vertical lines, or underlining. All of these things can confuse scanners.

Inter.: What can people do to get their resume read?

Tom: The answer is to understand the importance of key words. When a job becomes available, decisions are made as to what kind of experience and knowledge is required. Then certain "key words" are selected. These key words are chosen because it is believed that virtually all highly qualified people will use these words in their resumes. For example, a manager needing a programmer in COBOL on a UNIX operating system, using an IBM AS400, would request that the computer search its database for resumes with those terms. Then a human will need to skim each resume selected by the database to determine if the person does in fact have the desired background. If so, a key will be punched, the resume will be printed out, and an interview will be arranged.

Inter.: How do people make sure their resumes contain the right key words?

Tom: Put yourself in the shoes of an employer who is looking for someone with your experience. If you were looking for someone like you, what key words would you look for? Then simply make sure those words appear somewhere in the resume. The computer doesn't care if they appear at the beginning or at the end; it will find them and cause these resumes to appear on the computer screen.

Inter.: Any other hints?

Tom: Try to think of the different ways an employer might look for key words. If you are an RN, make sure the acronym RN appears, but also find a place to spell it out—registered nurse. Be aware of synonyms. If you are an attorney, make sure the word lawyer also appears. Find ways to bring in the buzz words and jargon that are used in your field.

Here is a checklist for preparing the ideal scannable resume:

- Use 8¹/₂ x 11-inch paper, light color.
- Avoid dot matrix printouts. Laser prints scan easier.
- If using a computer, use the 12 point font size, and do not condense spacing between letters.
- Avoid using a newspaper-type format, columns, or graphics.
- Be sure to include your name at the top of the second page if your resume is two pages.
- Key words or accomplishments are often scanned; make sure your resume contains words related to the position for which you are applying. Use "hard vocabulary": "computer skills," "software packages," etc. Also avoid flowery language.

Resumix, a Silicon Valley, California, company provides a brochure, "Preparing the Ideal Scannable Resume." If you are interested, call Resumix at (408) 988-0444.

The Cover Letter Adds a Custom Touch

Never, never send your resume without a cover letter. Whether you are answering a want ad or following up an inquiry call or interview, you should always include a letter with your resume. Use your researching skills to locate the individual doing the hiring. Using the personal touch of addressing your cover letter to a real person will save you the headache of having your resume sent to H.R.'s stack of resumes, or possibly even being tossed out.

A good cover letter should be brief and interesting enough to grab the reader's attention. If you've spoken with the individual, you may want to remind him or her of the conversation. Or, if you and the person to whom you are writing know someone in common, be sure to mention it.

In the next paragraph or two, specify what you could contribute to the company in terms that indicate you've done your homework on the firm and the industry. Use figures and facts to support your accomplishments that are relevant to the job opening.

Finally, in the last paragraph, either request an interview or tell the reader that you will follow-up with a phone call within a week to arrange a mutually convenient meeting.

Sample Cover Letter

52 Lake Street
Wilmette, IL 60212

August 12, 1997

Ms. Jacqueline Doe
Wide World Publishing Company
22 Central Blvd
Chicago, IL 60606

Dear Ms. Doe:

As an honors graduate of Northern Illinois University with two years of copy editing and feature-writing experience with the *Chicago Weekly*, I am confident that I would make a successful editorial assistant with Wide World.

Besides my strong editorial background, I offer considerable business experience. I have held summer jobs in an insurance company, a law firm, and a data processing company. My familiarity with word processing should prove particularly useful to Wide World now that you have become fully automated.

I would like to interview with you as soon as possible and would be happy to check in with your office about an appointment. If you prefer, your office can contact me between the hours of 11 a.m. and 3 p.m. at (847) 555-6886.

Sincerely,

Mary Baker

Sample Cover Letter in Reply to Want Ad

34 Park Blvd.
Round Lake, IL 60057
(847) 555-2468

May 15, 1997

Mr. Tom White, Manager
Human Resources
Armstrong Consulting
69 West Street
Chicago, IL 60617

Dear Mr. White:

My background seems ideal for your advertisement in the May 13 issue of the *Chicago Tribune* for an experienced accountant. My five years of experience in a small accounting firm in Rosemont has prepared me to move on to a more challenging position.

As you can see from my resume, my experience includes not only basic accounting work but also some consulting with a few of our firm's larger clients. This experience combined with an appetite for hard work, an enthusiastic style, and a desire to succeed makes me a strong candidate for your consideration. I assisted the company in expanding its clientele by 30%.

I would appreciate the opportunity to discuss how my background could meet the needs of Armstrong Consulting. I will call you within a week to arrange a convenient time to meet.

Sincerely,

Stacy Barnes

Sample Networking Cover Letter

560 Central Blvd.
Chicago, IL 60657
(312) 555-6886

December 2, 1997

Mr. James King
3-Q Inc.
45 Houston St.
Arlington Hts., IL 60006

Dear Jim:

Just when everything seemed to be going smoothly at my job, the company gave us a Christmas present that nobody wanted: management announced that half the department will be laid off before the new year. Nobody knows yet just which heads are going to roll. But whether or not my name is on the list, I am definitely back in the job market.

I have already lined up a few interviews. But knowing how uncertain job hunting can be, I can use all the contacts I can get. You know my record—both from when we worked together at 3-Q and since then. But in case you've forgotten the details, I've enclosed my resume. I know that you often hear of job openings as you work your way about Chicago. I'd certainly appreciate your passing along any leads you think might be worthwhile.

My best to you and Susan for the Holidays.

Cordially,

Tom Johnson

Enclosure

Do's and don'ts for cover letters

Do:

- Send a resume with every cover letter.
- Use high-quality, high-rag content paper.
- Target an individual person about the job opening.
- Be brief and interesting enough to capture the reader's attention.
- Tailor your experiences to meet the potential job opening.
- Use acceptable business format; letter should be well spaced on the page.
- Have someone check your letter for grammar, spelling, and formatting mistakes.
- Have an agenda in the letter and follow-up in the amount of time you specified.

Don't:

- Send your first draft of a letter just so you can meet the deadline.
- Send your letter to the president of the company simply because you don't know the name of the hiring authority.
- Include information that can be found on your resume.
- Give only one possible time to meet.
- Call the company four times a day after you have sent the letter.

CYBERTIPS FOR RESUME AND COVER LETTER WRITING

Using the Net to find more sample resumes and cover letters is a good place to start. Many of the job-search services or college career center homepages also have tips on resume and cover letter writing. Some on-line services will also post your resume for employer perusal.

Career Channel—The Job Search
http://riceinfo.rice.edu/projects/careers/Channel/seven.html

Catapult Job Search Guides
http://www.wm.edu/catapult/jsguides.html

Cover Letters by the Rensselaer Polytechnic Institute Writing Center
http://www.rpi.edu/dept/llc/writecenter/web/text/coverltr.html

Interactive Employment Network
http://www.espan.com

Resumes On-Line
http://199.94.216.72:81/online.html

Resumes from Yahoo
http://www.yahoo.com/Business/Employment/Resumes/Individual_Resumes

RECOMMENDED BOOKS ON RESUME WRITING

The following books are full of all the how-to information you'll need to prepare an effective resume and most are available from bookstores or your local library.

Corwin, Leonard. *Your Resume: Key to a Better Job.* New York: Arco, 1988.

Fournier, Myra, and Jeffrey Spin. *Encyclopedia of Job-Winning Resumes.* Ridgefield, CT: Round Lake Publishers, 1991.

Hahn, Harley, and Rick Stout. *The Internet Yellow Pages.* Berkeley, CA: Osborne McGraw-Hill, 1994.

Jackson, Tom. *The Perfect Resume.* New York: Anchor/Doubleday, 1990.

Kennedy, Joyce Lain, and Thomas J. Morrow. *Electronic Resume Revolution.* New York: James Wiley & Sons, 1994.

Krannich, Ronald L., and William J. Banis. *High Impact Resumes and Letters.* Manassas, VA: Impact Publications, 1994.

Lewis, Adele. *How to Write a Better Resume.* Woodbury, NY: Barron's, 1993.

Nadler, Burton Jay. *Liberal Arts Power: How to Sell It on Your Resume.* Princeton, NJ: Peterson's Guides, 1989.

Parker, Yana. *Damn Good Resumes.* Berkeley, CA: Ten Speed Press, 1989.

Provenzano, Steven. *Top Secret Resumes and Cover Letters.* Chicago: Dearborn Publishing, 1995.

Smith, Michael H. *The Resume Writer's Handbook.* New York: Harper and Row, 1994.

Weinstein, Bob. *Resumes Don't Get Jobs: The Realities and Myths of Job Hunting.* New York: McGraw-Hill, 1993.

Yate, Martin. *Resumes That Knock 'em Dead.* Holbrook, MA: Bob Adams, 1992.

seven

The Killer Interview

Your networking paid off and your resume was a success. You are now ready to take the next step in your job search. Unfortunately, though, your resume won't automatically grant you a job, and all the contacts in the world won't do you any good if you don't handle yourself well in an interview. All interviews have the same goal: to convince the interviewer that he or she should hire you or recommend that you be hired. That is what counts. Remember, this interview is all that stands between you and the job, so make it a *killer* interview. This chapter will guide you through the steps and give you an idea of what to expect and what to avoid when interviewing.

Dr. Bob's Six Steps to a Killer Interview

STEP 1: Preparing for the Interview

Good preparation shows ambition and zeal and is a key part of interviewing that is often forgotten. The more you prepare, the more you will be relaxed and comfortable with the interview. Additionally, the more you prepare, the greater your chance of impressing someone with your knowledge of the company and the interview process.

Researching the company before the interview is a must in your preparation. You should be familiar with the following company information before your interview begins:

- The interviewer's name.
- General information about the company, such as the location of the home office, number of plants/stores and their locations, names of parent company, subsidiaries, etc.

- Organizational structure, type of supervision, type of training program.
- Philosophy, goals, and image.
- Financial details, including sales volume, stock price, percent of annual growth in earnings per share, recent profits, etc.
- The competition in the industry and the company's place in it.
- The products or services marketed by the company, including recent media coverage of them.
- Career path in your field.
- Recent news items regarding the company or the industry. It is especially important to check the *Wall Street Journal's* business section to see if the company you are interviewing with is mentioned on the morning of the interview. Be prepared to speak on many aspects of the company.

Researching the Company via the World Wide Web

One of the easiest ways to research a company or organization is to do so over the Net. While not every organization has a WWW address, more and more companies are beginning to see the benefits of a homepage. Increasingly, companies are posting employment opportunities on their Web pages. Library Net addresses, mentioned in Chapter 4, are a good place to check. Try a few of these sites for starters:

Commercial Services on the Net—Open Market
http://www.directory.net
A very large index of commercial Web sites. You should be able to find a company Web page here if it exists.

Computer Related Companies
http://www.xnet.com/~blatura/computer.shtml
An excellent list of U.S. computer-related company Web pages.

Corporate Web Registry—Hoover's Company Profiles
http://www.hoovers.com/bizreg.html
Links to over 1,100 corporate Web sites, combined with extensive information about many corporations, including history, current business, personnel, and office locations. A wonderful resource.

Hot 1000 List
http://techweb.cmp.com/techweb/ia/hot1000/hot1.html
This list includes any homepages officially established by or for the companies comprising the Fortune 1,000.

Industrial Companies
http://www.xnet.com/~blatura/industry.shtml
A fine list of U.S. industrial company Web pages.

Public Companies
http://networth.galt.com/www/home/insider/publicco.htm
This list includes any homepages officially established by or for the company. As we go to press, the list contains more than 700 public companies.

The BigBook Directory
http://www.bigbook.com
Contains 11 million business addresses, phone numbers, and maps. If you need directions to your interview, click on the company name to see a map of the surrounding area, including streets.

Another part of preparation is constructing a list of questions to ask the interviewer at the end of the meeting. Producing a list of questions and asking intelligent questions about the company indicates that you're prepared and that you did your research. We include a list of possible questions for you to ask later in this chapter.

Practicing Before Your Interview
Another key part of preparation and of conducting the most successful of interviews is to practice the interview as much and in as many ways as possible. This can take many forms. However, the best way is to build a list of the questions you feel will be asked and to make sure that you know how to answer them and have answered them out loud to yourself or to someone helping you with a mock interview. Practice your answers and multiple variations of them and you will be much better prepared for the interview.

STEP 2: Dressing Right: Interviewing Fashion Do's and Don'ts

Never underestimate the power of a sharply dressed man or woman during an interview. Proper attire is a key ingredient to a good first impression with your prospective employer. Hygiene is equally important. Shaving should be done the morning before the interview. Perfume and cologne should be low key. Keep the hair trimmed, fingernails clean, and let your credentials and charm do the rest.

The Career-Dressed Woman
Within reason, a variety of conservative colors are appropriate for most interview situations. Many tasteful suits are available in black, brown, teal, taupe, olive, forest, maroon, burgundy, and plum. When selecting a suit, especially if you are on a limited budget, focus on classic cuts and styles. The proper fit is just as essential as the suit itself. A good suit should last at least five years. Try to select a high-quality fabric such as wool or wool gabardine. These are the coolest fabrics—making them appropriate not only for the stress of interviewing but also for everyday wear year-round.

If the shoe fits wear it! We see countless well-dressed women with shoes with run-down heels and scraped up toes. Don't brainwash yourself by thinking that they are only shoes and nobody looks at your feet anyway. Shoes are one of those make-or-break elements of your wardrobe. Make sure the local shoe repair has done a good job at keeping yours new-looking.

Keep it feminine: a lot of women still hold the idea that professional means masculine. Not true. Women's professional attire has come into its own since the late '80s and early '90s, when stiffly tailored dark suits paired with floppy bows and ties were all the rage. These have been replaced with soft scarves, unique pins, and more attractive colors and styles.

Keep in mind when selecting professional clothing that "feminine" in no way means "sleazy." Tight skirts, too high heels, and low-cut blouses are never appropriate, no matter how conservative their color or casual the office.

The bottom line is that much of business is influenced by image. You may not get that job because you look great, but not looking good may be a reason why you don't get hired.

The Career-Dressed Man

On your big shopping spree for the proper suit, try to be conservative, not flashy. Stick with darker colors like navy blue, dark gray, or black. Single-breasted vs. double-breasted? Whatever you look best in is what you should buy. Usually single-breasted is more conservative and probably best for interviewing.

Shirts and ties are very important in the construction of the perfect suit. Your dress shirts should be comfortable and fit properly around the neck. Tight shirts in the neck area tend to make you resemble Baby Huey or the Pillsbury Doughboy.

The tie can say a lot about the individual, so when choosing your tie be careful and take your time. Try to steer yourself toward the 100% silk ties; they tend to portray a more professional look. Don't allow the tie to overpower your suit with loud colors and crazy patterns. The proper length is also vital in choosing the right tie. Too short a tie makes you look silly. Once knotted, a tie should reach over your belt buckle. Anything higher is not acceptable.

Dress socks are a must. No thick socks and no athletic socks; this is your career, not a gymnasium. Coordinated color socks are essential and they should come over the calf so that when you sit down, you aren't flashing skin between the top of the sock and trouser cuff.

Polished wing-tip shoes are always safe. Make sure that your shoes are as shiny as a new dime. As is the case with women's shoes, your shoes can say a lot about you and should not be in a state of disrepair.

Common Dressing Mistakes Made by Men

Now that you are an expert on career dressing, here are a few mistakes made by men in their quest to dress to impress:

- The belt and suspenders faux pas. You only need one or the other to keep your pants up.

- Make sure that you are not wearing high-water pants. The length of the pant leg should reach the middle of your shoe.
- No knit ties. They went out some years ago with leisure suits.
- Iron your shirt. Wrinkles are not in style.
- No gaudy rings or chains. Save them for bar hopping or the discos. The fact remains that clothes make a difference in our society. One might wish that impressions did not count, but they do!

How to dress

A friend of ours who wanted to break into investment banking finally landed her first big interview with Merrill Lynch. It was fairly easy for her to do her homework on a company of that size. Two days before the interview, however, it suddenly dawned on her that she had no idea how to dress. How did she solve her problem?

"It was pretty easy, actually, and fun, too," says Laura. "All I did was go and hang around outside the office for 15 minutes at lunch time to see what everybody else was wearing."

However, we recommend that even if the office attire is casual, one should still dress professionally. One career counselor recommends that one should "always dress one step above the attire of those in the office where you are interviewing."

STEP 3: The First Impression

The first impression, whether we like it or not, is important in a successful interview. Start off the interview right! Arriving at least ten minutes early helps you relax a little rather than rushing into the meeting all tense and harried. Remember to treat the receptionist, secretary, and anyone else you meet the same way you would treat any potential boss. Be friendly and professional. They often have input into the selection of candidates.

The beginning of the interview is crucial. Many experts feel that the decision to hire you is made during the first four minutes. The rest of the interview is used to justify this earlier decision. Four things are important in creating that first impression. First, a firm handshake, for both men and women, is important. Second, try to make eye contact with the interviewer as much as possible—but don't have a staredown. Third, try to convey a positive attitude with a friendly smile; never underestimate yourself—past jobs and education have equipped you with valuable skills. And finally, say something simple early on to get those first words out of your mouth: "Very nice to meet you" should suffice. It is also important to address your interviewer by last name unless instructed to do otherwise.

STEP 4: Express Yourself

The bulk of the interview is designed for you to answer questions posed by the interviewer. Here are a few tips:

- Be aware of your non-verbal behavior. Wait to sit until you are offered a chair. Look alert, speak in a clear, strong voice, and stay relaxed. Make good eye contact, avoid nervous mannerisms, and try to be a good listener as well as a good talker. Smile.
- Follow the interviewer's lead, but try to get the interviewer to describe the position and duties to you fairly early in the interview so that you can later relate your background and skills in context.
- Be specific, concrete, and detailed in your answers. The more information you volunteer, the better the employer gets to know you and thereby is able to make a wise hiring decision.
- Don't mention salary in a first interview unless the employer does. If asked, give a realistic range and add that the opportunity is the most important factor for you.
- Offer examples of your work and references that will document your best qualities.
- Answer questions as truthfully and as frankly as you can. Never appear to be "glossing over" anything. On the other hand, stick to the point and don't over-answer questions. The interviewer may steer the interview into ticklish political or social questions. If this occurs, answer honestly, trying not to say more than is necessary.
- Never make derogatory remarks about present or former employers or companies.

Questions You May Be Asked During an Interview

Bear in mind that all questions you are asked during an interview serve a specific purpose. Try to put yourself in the interviewer's shoes. Imagine why he or she is asking the questions, and try to provide the answers that, while never dishonest, present you in the most desirable light. Direct your responses toward the particular position for which you are applying. What follows are some questions that employers often ask during interviews. As we mentioned earlier, it is advisable to rehearse answers to these questions prior to your interview so you can appear relaxed and confident.

Ice Breakers

These are designed to put you at ease and to see how well you engage in informal conversation. Be yourself, act natural, and be friendly.

a. Did you have any trouble finding your way here?
b. How was your plane flight?
c. Can you believe this weather?
d. I see you're from Omaha. Why do you want to work here?

Work History and Education

These are to assess whether your background and skills are appropriate for the position. Talk about your skills coherently and relate them to the job to be filled. Give specific examples of how you used certain skills in the past. Remember that questions you are asked concerning your past will help the employer determine how you might react and make decisions in the future.

a. *Tell me about yourself.
b. Tell me about the most satisfying job/internship you've ever held.
c. Tell me about the best boss you ever had. The worst.
d. What have you learned from some of the jobs you've held?
e. For what achievements were you recognized by your superiors at your last position?
f. What are you looking for in an employer?
g. What are you seeking in a position?
h. Why did you choose to get a degree in the area that you did?
i. In what activities have you participated outside of work (or class)?
j. How did you finance your education?
k. *What do you like/dislike about your current (or last) job?

Ambitions and Plans

These are questions to evaluate your ambition, how clearly you have thought about your future goals, their feasibility, and how actively you seek to meet them.

a. Are you a joiner or more individually centered? A leader or a group member? A committee member or chairperson? (There isn't necessarily a wrong answer to this type of question. Keep in mind that a ship full of captains will flounder just as badly as a ship with none at all.)
b. What job in our company would you choose if you were free to do so?
c. What does success mean to you? How do you judge it?
d. Assuming you are hired for this job, what do you see as your future?
e. What personal characteristics do you think are necessary for success in this field?

*Note: Questions marked with an asterisk (*) are among the toughest to answer. Further on in this chapter, the "15 Toughest Interview Questions" are treated in some depth so you can "ace" them when the time comes.

    f. How far will you go to get ahead in your career?

    g. Are you willing to prove yourself as a staff member of our firm? How do you envision your role?

    h. Are you willing to work overtime?

    i. *Where do you see yourself five years from now?

    j. How much money do you hope to earn in five years? Ten years?

Company or Organization

These questions are to determine if you have conscientiously researched the company and if you would be a "match" for them. They also indicate your interest in the company.

    a. Do you prefer working for a small or large organization?

    b. Do you prefer a private or non-private organization? Why?

    c. What do you know about our organization?

    d. *Why are you interested in this company?

    e. What kind of work are you interested in doing for us?

    f. What do you feel our organization has to offer you?

    g. *Why do you think you can contribute to our company?

Values and Self-Assessment

These help the interviewer get to know you better and to determine how well you understand yourself. They also help to inform the interviewer of what motivates you.

    a. What kinds of personal satisfactions do you hope to gain through work?

    b. If you had unlimited funds, what would you do?

    c. *If you could live during any time in history, when and where would you live?

    d. What motivates you?

    e. What are your strengths and weaknesses?

    f. How would you describe yourself?

    g. What do you do with your free time?

    h. What kind of people do you like to work with?

    i. How do you adapt to other cultures?

    j. *What is your greatest achievement?

    k. *How do you manage stress?

How to Handle Objections During the Interview

It is not uncommon to face objections in an interview. It may be that the interviewer believes you lack some skills required. Don't panic! If you keep a level head, you will be able to recover. For example, one woman was applying for an assistant buyer position in the fragrance department of a retail operation although she had never sold perfumes. Her background was in shoes. The interviewer didn't feel she had enough knowledge of perfumes. But by the end of the interview, she had swayed the interviewer with facts of her past achievements as a salesperson, convincing him that skilled people are capable of learning any product line. She even discussed trends in the fragrance industry, which she had researched in a trade magazine—surprising the interviewer, who didn't expect her to know much about the subject.

If an interviewer appears to have an objection to hiring you, ask what it is. With this knowledge, you may be able to change the interviewer's mind or redefine the job description to fit your qualifications.

STEP 5: Questions, You Must Have Questions

A typical interviewer comment toward the close of an interview is to ask if you have any questions. Never just say "no." Keep a list of questions in mind to ask. Sometimes even the worst of interviews can be salvaged by good questions. If you believe that most questions were answered during the interview, try the "not-really-a-question" tactic. This might be a statement such as, "As I mentioned, I believe that my creativity and attention to detail are my strengths. How do you think these would fit into the organization?" Here are a few other questions you might ask.

Questions to Ask Interviewers
- What would a normal working day be like?
- About how many individuals go through your program each year?
- How much contact is there with management?
- During training, are employees transferred among functional fields?
- How soon could I expect to be advanced to the next level in the career path?
- How much travel is normally expected?
- Will I be expected to meet certain deadlines? How frequent are they?
- How often are performance reviews given?
- How much decision-making authority is given after one year?
- Does the company provide any educational benefits?
- How frequently do you relocate professional employees?
- Have any new product lines/services been announced recently?
- What are the essential skills/qualities necessary for an employee to succeed in this position?
- Where are the last two people who held this position (did they leave the company or get promoted)?
- What role would my job play in helping the company achieve its corporate mission and make a profit?
- What are the five most important duties of this job?
- Why did you join the company? What is it about the company that keeps you here?
- What has the company's growth pattern been over the past five years?

At the conclusion of the interview, ask when a hiring decision will be made. This is important not only because it reconfirms your interest in the position but also so you'll know when, realistically, to expect a response. Don't forget, of course, to thank your interviewer for his or her time and to make clear your interest in the position if you feel there may be any doubt about this point.

STEP 6: The Aftermath

As soon as you leave the interview and have a chance, take notes on what you feel you could improve upon for your next interview and on what you feel went particularly well. After all, experience is only valuable to the extent that you're willing to learn from it. It also helps to make a note of something in the interview you might use in your thank-you letter.

The All Important Thank-You Letter

Always follow up each interview with a prompt thank-you letter—written the same day, if possible. The purpose of the letter is to supplement the presentation you made. Thank the interviewer for his or her hospitality. Express continued interest in the position, and mention up to three additional points to sell yourself further. Highlight how your specific experience or knowledge is directly applicable to the company's immediate needs, and if you forgot to mention something important in the interview, say it now. If possible, try to comment on something the interviewer said. Use that comment to show how your interests and skills perfectly match what they're looking for.

The thank-you letter should be sent A.S.A.P.! Your name should remain in front of the interviewer as much as possible. Sending the letter immediately will demonstrate how serious you are about the position. It may well be the final factor in helping you land the job.

Get the most from your references

References should remain confidential and never revealed until a company is close to making you an offer and you want to receive one.

Always brief your references before you supply an interviewer with their names and numbers. Tell the references what company you're interviewing with and what the job is. Give them some background on the company and the responsibilities you'll be asked to handle.

Your references will then be in a position to help sell your abilities. Finally, don't abuse your references. If you give their names too often, they may lose enthusiasm for your cause.

Waiting

Now the waiting begins. Try not to be too impatient, and remember that for the time being no answer is better than a rejection. There could be many reasons why you haven't heard from the company. It could be that the interview process has not concluded, or that other commitments have kept the company from making a decision. The most important point to remember during this time is that all your hopes shouldn't be pinned on one or two interviews. The job search is continuous and shouldn't stop until you have accepted a job offer. Keeping all your options open is the best possible plan.

However, if much time has passed and you haven't heard anything from a company in which you are particularly interested, a telephone call or letter asking about the status of your application is appropriate. This inquiry should be stated in a manner that is not pushy but shows your continued interest in the firm. Remember that waiting is an integral part of the job hunt, but a demonstration of your continued interest is appropriate.

Many job seekers experience a kind of euphoria after a good interview. Under the impression that a job offer is imminent, a candidate may discontinue the search. This is a serious mistake. The hiring decision may take weeks or may not be made at all. On average, about six weeks elapse between the time a person makes initial contact with a company and receives a final answer. If you let up on your job search, you will prolong it. Maintain a constant sense of urgency. Get on with the next interview. Your search isn't over until an offer is accepted and you actually begin your new job.

15 Toughest Interview Questions—and How To Answer Them

1. Tell me about yourself. This question, in one form or another, is one of the most likely to be asked. It is also one of the most likely questions to be answered poorly. Answer it without going into your personal life or family background. Stick to your professional and educational background and how it applies to the job you are interested in. Focus on your strengths and—especially with this question—remember to keep your response brief.

2. Teach me how to do something. This question is sometimes used in a consulting or sales company interview. One candidate responded by verbally teaching the interviewer how to play tennis. The subject of the lesson isn't what matters but, rather, the teaching presentation. The interviewer is assessing how well you would do in front of a client. Do you have the skills to impress or persuade a person, and are you articulate and sophisticated in your presentation? Most importantly, can you think on your feet?

3. Should city buses be free? You are probably wondering what free buses have to do with you getting the job. Nothing! Instead, the interviewer wants to see how you think the question through. The interviewer doesn't expect you to have expertise in this area and wants dialogue to occur. Don't be afraid to ask questions to determine whether you are heading in the right direction. Always modify your thinking with whatever information the interview may provide to you. Keep in mind that analytical ability is important but so are enthusiasm and creativity.

4. Do you know how to operate a Macintosh computer? On your resume you listed PC knowledge, but you have no experience with the Mac. Then why did the interviewer ask this question? Either the company uses Macs or the interviewer wanted to pull a weakness from your resume. Rather than bluntly saying "no," rephrase your response as: "I have gained a good deal of experience on the PC and with many programs. I feel comfortable with computers, and the transition to the Mac should be fairly easy."

5. Why do you think you can contribute to our company? Most candidates will answer in a typical manner that they are energetic, motivated, and a hard worker. This may or may not be true, but every interviewer has heard this response. What is more effective is to respond with examples or facts from your past experiences that draw the interviewer a picture of how you are a go-getter. This is an excellent question to prepare for, as it gives you an idea of what makes you unique from all other qualified candidates on the market.

6. If you could live during any time in history, when and where would you live? This is an off-the-wall question but it will occur sometimes. The interviewer probably doesn't expect a specific answer. And he may not let you off the hook after you give your answer. Feel free to give yourself time to think before answering; a pensive pause can sometimes even help an interview. Whatever your answer, have a reason for choosing it because almost certainly the interviewer will follow up with, "Why did you choose that?" At work the unexpected happens, and the interviewer wants to see how you deal with it.

7. What is your greatest achievement? This question allows the interviewer to assess both values and skills. What you select as your achievement will express what is important to you. And at the same time your narrative will reveal skills you have acquired. The interviewer will be interested in listening for skills necessary for the job opening.

8. Do you think your grades were a good indication of your academic achievement? If you were an A student, you can respond enthusiastically, "Yes!" However, those of us who had less than fantastic grades will respond differently. There are many reasons you may not have had high grades. For example: you worked full time while attending school or you were involved in many outside organizations. Turn the answer into a positive by explaining the benefits you received from the trade-offs of working and attending school. Emphasize your common sense and creativity rather than your grades. Besides, grades are not everything.

9. Why are you interested in this company? If you've done your homework on the company, you shouldn't sweat over this question. This is your opportunity to show how well your skills and values match that of the company's.

10. What do you like/dislike about your current (or last) job? You need to be alert when answering this question. Criticizing a former employer could send the message that you are a troublemaker or have a negative attitude, which could spell the end to your prospects with this company. Be as positive about your work experience as possible. Emphasize what you contributed and learned from the company. Even a negative experience can be translated into challenges and learning opportunities.

11. Describe how you dealt with a difficult problem. Try to be as positive as you can, and focus on the approach you used rather than any negative outcomes. For example, describe how you examined the problem, developed several alternative solutions, and implemented the solutions. Emphasize any positive outcomes from your solutions.

12. Where do you see yourself five years from now? Be realistic in your answer rather than trying to impress the interviewer. You can reiterate your goals to advance while still being a team player. And you can add that new opportunities are bound to arise within the company, which will also affect what you would like to be doing five years from now. Emphasize how the current job you are interviewing for will prepare you for five-year goals.

13. How do you manage stress? Listen carefully to the question. This isn't asking "can" you manage stress, but rather "how." The basic answer to this question involves giving an example of how you maintained your cool, pulled everyone together, and came up with a positive result, all without becoming overwhelmed.

14. What can you do for our company that someone else cannot? Similar to Question 5, this question usually will come after a description of the job has been provided. You need to reiterate what skills you have that pertain to the position and the company overall. Reemphasize those qualities that you feel are unique and how they might help the organization.

15. Could you explain these gaps in your work history? You may have gaps in your work history for many legitimate reasons. What you want to express is that you enjoy working and that when things aren't going as planned (maybe you were laid off) you are challenged to learn and overcome. Be sure to describe any studying or volunteer work that you may have done while unemployed.

Nine Interview Styles to Watch For

The interviewing process can be tricky at times. Most applicants are clueless as to how the interview will go or what it will entail. Many job seekers and career changers will eventually encounter some of these interview types. Knowing a little about each of them is certainly advantageous. Knowing what to expect will boost your confidence and dry out those nervous, sweaty palms.

Behavioral Interviewing. A new technique for interviewing, behavioral interviewing assumes that past behavior predicts future performance. You can easily recognize when an interviewer is using "behavioral interviewing" because you will be asked questions about how you have worked in the past. For example, "Tell me about a time where you successfully learned a new software package"; or, "Tell me about a conflict you had with a co-worker and how you dealt with it." The employer expects you to tell short stories about yourself to give more insight into how you behave at work.

The best strategy to use when answering behavioral interview questions is the STAR technique. STAR stands for situation, task, action, result. First, describe the situation and task you were assigned in order to set the stage. Next, review the action you took. Plan to spend the most time on this part of the answer because your past performance is what the employer is most interested in. Finally, emphasize the results, the outcome of your actions.

Situation: "I was assigned sales manager for a new product my company was introducing."

Task: "I was to develop a marketing plan to determine best sales techniques."

Action: "I created a market survey instrument and conducted a campaign to assess consumer preference. I also conducted blind taste tests at local supermarkets."

Result: "The result was a successful marketing campaign that saw sales of our product skyrocket by 42%."

With STAR, you are able to convince the employer that you are capable of performing the open job by demonstrating your past success.

The Analytical Interview. The analytical interview is designed to let the interviewer see you think on your feet. The interviewer will ask you challenging questions to see how you analyze and perform under pressure. You may hear some off-the-wall questions like the examples below. In some cases you may be given a pen and paper, but don't be surprised if you're not. Most of the time the interviewer is looking for an answer that is simply in the ball park. If you are totally stumped and caught off guard by the question, think creatively. You also are better off answering humorously than not at all. Remember, the interviewer is interested in your thinking process, not just in how you derived the answer. Here are some questions that may put you on the spot.

- Why are manhole covers round?
- What are the number of square yards of pizza eaten in the U.S. each year?
- How many gas stations would you estimate there are in the United States?

How much does a 747 weigh?

D.N. Meehan, a senior scientist at a large firm, was interviewing a young man. Meehan asked the candidate to estimate the weight of a fully loaded 747 at takeoff. It's pretty obvious that coming up with the correct answer would be very difficult for almost anyone. Since the applicant was not versed in aviation, he felt he would have to come up with something creative and unique in order to leave a lasting impression on the interviewer. The candidate asked if he could use anything in the room and then proceeded to use Meehan's computer. It was a surprise to Meehan when the candidate turned on the "flight simulator" game and came up with the correct answer.

Tennis, anyone?

Theo Johnson, a student at Northwestern University, was asked "How many matches need to be played in a single elimination tennis tournament if there are 256 participants?" Eagerly, Theo began using his math background and developed an equation to solve the problem. Several minutes later, he had his answer. The interviewer, however, was not as impressed as Theo was. The interviewer said that it was quite simple: "There are 255 matches. Each match has one loser and everyone loses once except the winner."

Stress Interviewing. The stress interview is like a horror film. It is more interesting to see than to be in. The intent of the interviewer is to determine how well you can handle pressure or a crisis situation.

Usually, the interviewee doesn't recognize a stress situation. For example, a candidate was taken to lunch by two recruiters. The recruiters informed the candidate that he didn't have the qualifications for the job, and then they began talking among themselves. In reality, they were seeing how he would respond to rejection since the position was in sales, which required dealing with stress and rejection.

Your best strategy for the stress interview is to recognize questions in disguise. Rather than becoming hostile, relax and attempt to present your case to the employer. There are endless cases where the interviewee allows the discussion to get under his skin and make his blood boil. Instead, be humble and try to ignore anything that offends you. Even though questions are designed to insult you, view this as a challenge and answer candidly.

No stress interviewing information would be complete without at least one horror story. A director of a business school placement office told us one that injects new meaning into the word stress. A candidate was interviewing with a Wall Street firm that was known for challenging interviews. He walked into a large boardroom, and at the end of the table, a partner, holding a newspaper in front of his face, said, "Get my attention." Thinking quickly, the candidate took out his lighter and set the newspaper on fire. We're not sure if he got the job, but he did get the partner's attention.

The Manhattan, Kansas, Interview. This type of interview occurs more often than you are aware of since it forms a hidden agenda within the interview itself. We often hear interviewers talk about how they would feel about a candidate if they were stuck with him or her in the airport in Manhattan, Kansas, or anywhere else for that matter, for twenty-four hours. Would you be pals or get on each other's nerves? Many times this assessment is based solely on personality and fit with the interviewer's personality. However, it does serve as a reminder that it is the interviewer who is recommending you for the job, not someone else in the company. You must impress your interviewer while also showing that you're a pretty good person to have around.

Stream of Consciousness Interviewing. This interview goes something like this: "Well let me tell you something about the company, we are located downtown, which is a great place for lunch, as a matter of fact I found a wonderful little restaurant last week that served wonderful pasta, it tasted just like something I had in Italy last year, Italy, now that's a great place to visit, I went there with my sister and we had a blast, Milan, Rome, and Florence, the art is wonderful."

Are you starting to get the picture? Just because you know how to interview doesn't mean your interviewer does. Sometimes you need to learn how to control the interview. For first timers this can be extremely difficult. You also need to be sure that you do not embarrass or insult your interviewer. One way to insert yourself into the stream of consciousness interview is to ask questions about the company and quickly follow up with statements about how your particular strengths would work well in that environment. This type of interview is a real challenge. Make sure that the interviewer leaves with a positive impression of who you are rather than just a feeling of having told a good story.

The Epicurean Interview. If you are in an all-day interview and someone offers to take you to lunch, it may not be as relaxing as it sounds. This is not your moment to put your interviewing skills on the back burner. When going to lunch during the interview process, never let your killer-interview guard down. While conversation may be informal, evaluation is still present. Here are some Epicurean hints for the lunch interview:

- Don't order the most expensive item simply because you are not paying. It is best to order something in the medium price range. Also, don't worry about saving money by ordering the cheapest item; order what you want within reason.
- Stay away from spaghetti, spinach, and shrimp dishes or any other dish that could give you embarrassment. It can be extremely awkward trying to work a piece of food out from between your teeth or slurping up a long pasta noodle.
- If you don't drink alcohol, this is not the time to begin. And if you do drink, we recommend you wait until you have the job. If you must drink, limit yourself to just one. It is best to be as alert as possible during the lunch interview.
- Try to relax. Finding common interests between the interviewer and yourself will help lighten the conversation.

Dear Dr. Bob

How about sharing an interesting Epicurean experience with us.— Sincerely, The Epicurean Club.

Dear Epicurean Club
A student I worked with told me a story about going to a classy restaurant with a potential employer. Having talked a great deal and eaten only a little during the meal, the student decided to order what she thought was a simple dessert. But being a classy restaurant where swank desserts were served, she received a large, flaming dessert. In fact, it was such a large, flaming dessert that the waiter set the plant hanging over the table on fire. Needless to say, the student made a burning impression on the employer. Bon appetit!

The Athletic Interview. From time to time athleticism, or at least some degree of fitness, can help during an interview. I recall one interview where I was told to meet my potential employer on a popular street corner in New York City. We were to meet and then go someplace to talk. As my luck would have it, by the time the interviewer showed up, he was late for a train at Penn Station. However, he was still interested in talking with me, so in business suits and briefcases we jogged to the station. He made his train and I got a second interview. Always be ready for the unexpected, even if it takes a little more out of you than you expected.

The Grunge Interview. We have talked about proper dress during the interview. There are still those, however, who believe that the best way to interview is to feel comfortable with yourself and your dress. In other words, be yourself and the job is bound to come. Wrong! Take this one opportunity to blend in with those that are interviewing you, and do not make an issue or statement with your clothes. Once you get the job and they see what a great employee you are, they will better understand your dressing desires and requirements. No matter how cool it looks to grunge dress and no matter how comfortable you feel, take our advice and hang up the blue jeans for a few hours.

Dr. Bob's Friendly Interview. As I finished up this section on interviewing, a staff member alerted me to the fact that I had not included my own style of interviewing: the "friendly interview," in which the employer is quite pleasant and lulls you into thinking that he likes everyone. The idea is to catch you off guard with a simple question that might reveal more than you planned about who you are. The way to handle this (and every interview) is to understand that your interview face must be on at all times, always presenting your best side. We all know that everyone has weaknesses; the interview, however, is not the time to let people know about them.

A Few Final Tips on Interviewing

In many ways an interview is like a first date. You can't predict how it will turn out. However, like a date, you can prepare yourself to make the best impression possible. You can also assess whether the company is a good match for you. Just as your first date may not be your best, likewise your first interview may not be your best.

However, you can learn from your mistakes and correct them in future interviews. Most importantly, don't forget to follow up. If you had the dream date, you wouldn't forget to call again—so must you write the "thank-you letter" to the potential employer.

Rejected? How Can It Happen?

Remember that the world is full of rejections and failures. What would motivate us to improve if we didn't have past failures? Everybody flunks at some point in their life; nobody is perfect. To give you a flavor of how to really fail an interview, here are some major employer turn-offs (provided by the Lindquist-Endicott Report, Northwestern University):

Sloppy appearance. Like it or not, people form lasting impressions of you within the first seconds of the interview. When dressing for an interview, pay close attention to details.

Arrogant attitude. If employers had to sum up the qualities they are looking for in candidates in two words, they would likely be "team player." They want people whose first loyalty is to the company and who are willing to work for the good of the group. Arrogant individualists have no place in this environment.

Limited knowledge about the company or the field. No greater turn-off than to expect the employer to tell you about his or her company. One of Procter and Gamble's favorite interview questions is, "Which of the P&G products is your favorite?" Simple question, but it surprises many.

Asking about the salary or benefits too early. Asking about the salary too early in the interview says nothing about what you can do for the company, only what you want from them. You don't want the employer to think that you are selfish with a one-way mind.

Lack of clarity in long-range goals. Employers want to know why you want a particular job and where you want to go with it. Demonstrate that you have some sort of career plan and that plan fits in with the company's goals.

Failure to ask for the job. Interviewing is like a sales presentation. After you have spent time marketing yourself, don't forget to close the deal. Ask for the job and let them know you are interested.

How to Bounce Back from Rejection

Do these lines sound familiar? "You're really not the right one." "We liked you, but we've decided not to hire right now." "You really don't have the experience we are looking for." "You are overqualified." These phrases occur more often than we would like. It's important to keep your sanity and courage during the interview process.

Anger, stress, guilt, fear, and anxiety are unfortunate companions to any job search. The strategy, therefore, is to learn to deal with rejection in a healthy and constructive manner and not let it distort your judgment. Develop methods to compensate for the beating your ego may take during the job search. Family and friends can be an excellent source for encouragement and positive support. Don't forget to eat well and exercise to relieve the stress involved in the job search. Be persistent and don't give up! Eddie Rickenbacker once said, "Try like hell to win, but don't cry if you lose." This should be one of your mottoes.

What Do Interviewers Really Want To See?

General Personality. Ambition, poise, sincerity, trustworthiness, initiative, and interest in the firm. (General intelligence is assumed.) Different firms look for different kinds of people, personalities, style, appearance, abilities, and technical skills. Always check the job specifications. Don't waste time talking about a job you can't do or for which you don't have the minimum qualifications.

Personal Appearance. A neat, attractive appearance makes a good impression and demonstrates professionalism.

Work Experience. Again, this varies from job to job, so check job specifications. Be able to articulate the importance of what you did in terms of the job for which you are interviewing and in terms of your own growth or learning. Even if the work experience is unrelated to your new field, employers look upon knowledge of the work environment as an asset.

Verbal Communication Skills. The ability to express yourself articulately is very important. This includes the ability to listen effectively, verbalize thoughts clearly, and express yourself confidently.

Skills. The interviewer will evaluate your skills for the job, such as organization, analysis, and research. It is important to emphasize the skills that you feel the employer is seeking and to give specific examples of how you developed them. This is the main reason why it is important to engage in self-assessment prior to the interview.

Goals/Motivation. Employers will assess your ability to articulate your short-term and long-term goals. You should seem ambitious yet realistic about the training and qualifications needed to advance. Demonstrate your interest in the functional area or industry and a desire to succeed and work hard.

Knowledge of the Interviewer's Company and Industry. At a minimum, you are expected to have done some homework on the company. Don't waste interview time asking questions you could have found answers to in printed material. Know the firm's position and character relative to others in the same industry. General awareness of media coverage of a firm and its industry is usually expected.

CYBERTIPS ON INTERVIEWING

As with most aspects of the job search, the Internet is full of sites with tips on interviewing and the latest in interviewing news. We have listed a few below:

Career Channel
http://riceinfo.rice.edu/projects/careers/Channel/seven/Interview/text/The.interview.html

Career Magazine
http://www.careermag.com/careermag/newsarts/interviewing.html

BOOKS ON INTERVIEWING

Biegelein, J.I. *Make Your Job Interview a Success*. New York: Arco, 1994.

Danna, Jo. *Winning the Job Interview Game: Tips for the High-Tech Era*. Briarwood, NY: Palamino Press, 1986.

Fear, Richard A. *The Evaluation Interview*. New York: McGraw-Hill, 1990.

King, Julie Adair. *The Smart Woman's Guide to Interviewing and Salary Negotiation*. Hawthorne, NJ: Career Press, 1993.

Krannich, Caryl R. *Interview for Success*. Mannassas, VA: Impact, 1995.

Marcus, John J. *The Complete Job Interview Handbook*. New York: Harper & Row, 1994.

Medley, H. Anthony. *Sweaty Palms: The Neglected Art of Being Interviewed*. Berkeley, CA: Ten Speed Press, 1992.

Pettus, Theodore. *One On One—Win the Interview, Win the Job*. New York: Random House, 1981.

Smart, Bradford D. *The Smart Interviewer*. New York: John Wiley & Sons, 1990.

Stewart, Charles J., and William B. Cash. *Interviewing Principles and Practices*. Dubuque, IA: William C. Brown Publishers, 1994.

Yate, Martin. *Knock 'em Dead*. Holbrook, MA: Adams Publishing, 1995.

Summer, Temporary, and Part-Time Jobs

For some, getting a job is seen as a summer only or as a temporary proposition. If that is the case, this is the chapter for you. First, summer jobs.

Summer Jobs—Findable and Rewarding

Summer provides the unique opportunity for students to brainstorm about careers that strike their interest. This is an experimental time in which the employer takes only a limited risk. But, how does one go about finding a summer job?

Finding a summer job is very similar to finding a permanent job. Persistence and positive attitude are keys for the high school or college job seeker just as they are for the full-time worker. Here are a few simple hints for prospective summer job seekers.

Set realistic expectations. Don't expect to get rich with summer work and, most importantly, realize that you won't get to the top after a week's work. Some progress can be expected, but summer jobbers should realize that they aren't on the same totem pole as permanent workers.

Have the right attitude. Nothing impresses an employer more than the right attitude. What do they want in an employee? Someone who is loyal, respectful, polite, punctual, enthusiastic, and hardworking. Remember that the number of people who really have all these qualities is small. If you can demonstrate your willingness to be the right person, you may get the job.

Dress right. Dress is a real issue with the summer job seeker. The best way to dress for summer jobs is somewhere between a suit and tie, as parents might encourage, and jeans and T-shirt, as friends might suggest. A collared shirt with slacks or khakis for guys, and slacks or skirt for young women are certainly acceptable. Additionally, wear leather shoes, not sneakers.

Be persistent. As a job seeker you can't be persistent enough. A true key to success in a summer job search is to keep trying, often with the same employer. Many summer success stories come from young people who visit their top five summer job sites of choice once a week until they get a job. One common mistake made by summer job seekers is to stop looking once they think they have a job. Even if an interview goes well or an employer says they like you, you must keep going until you have an actual job offer.

Interview well. Hopefully, after all your searching and preparation, your final challenge will be the interview. But don't be too worried; after all, if you get the interview, you do have a good chance of getting the job, or else the company wouldn't be wasting their time with you. For a successful interview, keep in mind these familiar guidelines: (1) Give specific reasons why you are right for the job; (2) Try to relate every question to your strengths of being loyal, enthusiastic, and other desirable qualities; (3) Inject a little humor into your otherwise serious and hardworking nature—but don't overkill on the comedy; and finally (4) Ask lots of questions to demonstrate your interest in the position.

As you go out into the summer job market, there are a few areas that can present stumbling blocks to your search. These include fear of risk; failing to contact the right person within the company; and taking no for an answer. (In other words, not being persistent enough.) If, on the other hand, you avoid these common traps, you will most likely find yourself on your way to a rewarding summer job experience.

If you are hesitant about working during the summer because you would rather be sitting by the pool, consider the many non-indoor summer opportunities. A summer job doesn't have to be inside an office or fast-food restaurant. There are paid internships offered by non-profit organizations that are not the typical office job environment.

As with any summer job, finding a good one requires starting your search as early as possible. The application process alone takes time, not to mention the research portion.

Dr. Bob's Six-Step Summer Job System

How do you get a job for the summer? Our tried and true system has worked for students and others for years.

1. **Know what you want to do.** Try to make a decision about what you want to do as early as possible. The sooner you decide, the sooner you can begin your search. Don't forget, the Career Center at your school provides resources and counseling to students. (See Chapter 2 for information on choosing a career.)
2. **Develop a resume.** It is important to accomplish this as early as possible since companies and application deadlines are as early as December for some summer jobs. (See Chapter 6 for details on resume and cover letter writing.)
3. **Write a cover letter.** A good cover letter is essential—it directs attention to your resume. Don't forget to have your resume and cover letter critiqued by a friend and career counselor, if possible.
4. **Do research and make contacts.** This step takes the longest, but hard work here can really pay off. Information interviews (see Chapter 5) with people in your field can help develop contacts. Don't forget your Alumni Office to develop a list of prospective employers. Make as many contacts as possible, and as soon as you have your contact list, begin mailing letters and resumes. A helpful tip is to send your letters in batches so you can track them efficiently and follow up each one with a letter.
5. **Follow-up and persistence.** This is the most important step! Make sure that for every letter you send out, for every person you talk to, and for every potential job site you visit, you continue to call back and let them know you are interested. Failure to follow up is disastrous for many a summer job searcher.
6. **Schedule interviews.** As part of your follow-up, try to schedule interviews. Give your letters time to arrive, then follow up with a phone call. This will keep you a step ahead of most college students, who don't start looking for summer jobs until school is out. Finally, make sure you know how to perform the "killer" interview discussed in Chapter 7.

Jobs without salaries

VISTA—Volunteers in Service To America—is a national service program aimed at alleviating poverty in America's cities and towns. They produce a bi-weekly electronic bulletin featuring immediate assignment openings, program updates, and national service news of interest to career centers, volunteer offices, libraries, professional groups, and potential volunteers. To request an information brochure or application, call (800) 942-2677.

Top 11 Summer Internships in the Chicago Area

The following is a list of paid summer internships that generally accept applicants from all walks of life—from recent college grads to career changers to people re-entering the workforce.

Abbott Laboratories
100 Abbott Park Road
Abbott Park, IL 60064
(847) 937-6100

Ameritech Corp.
30 S. Wacker Drive
Chicago, IL 60606
(312) 750-5000

Amoco Corp.
2000 E. Randolph Drive
Chicago, IL 60601
(312) 856-6111

Andersen Consulting
69 W. Washington St.
Chicago, IL 60602
(312) 580-0069

Art Institute of Chicago
111 S. Michigan Ave.
Chicago, IL 60603
(312) 433-3600

Leo Burnett and Company
35 W. Wacker Drive
Chicago, IL 60601
(312) 220-5959

Chicago Board of Trade
141 W. Jackson Blvd.
Chicago, IL 60604
(312) 435-3500

Deloitte and Touche Consulting Group
2 Prudential Plaza
180 N. Stetson St.
Chicago, IL 60601
(312) 946-3000

Hewitt Associates LLP
100 Half Day Road
Lincolnshire, IL 60069
(847) 295-5000

Motorola, Inc.
1303 E. Algonquin Road
Schaumburg, IL 60196
(847) 576-5000

UAL Corporation
P.O. Box 66919
Chicago, IL 60666
(847) 700-4000

RECOMMENDED SOURCES AND GUIDES FOR INTERNSHIPS

The Academy of Television Arts and Sciences
Student Internship Program, 5220 Lankershim Blvd., North Hollywood, CA
91601, (818) 754-2830 (provides internships in the media field).

The American Institute of Architects
Director, Education Programs, 1735 New York Ave., N.W., Washington, DC
20006 (provides information on architectural internships).

Inroads, Inc.
100 South Broadway, P.O. Box 8766, Suite 700, St. Louis, MO 63102 (African-
American, Native American, and Hispanic-American students can intern in the
areas of business, engineering, and science).

National Audubon Society
Government Affairs Internship Program, 666 Pennsylvania Ave., S.E.,
Washington, DC 20003, (202) 547-9009 (provides internships in resource con-
servation and wildlife management).

National Directory of Internships
National Society for Internships and Experiential Education, 122 St. Mary's St.,
Raleigh, NC 27605 (provides information on internships in a variety of areas).

National Institutes of Health
Summer Internship Program, Office of Education, Bldg. 10, Room 1C129, 9000
Rockville Pike, Bethesda, MD 20892, (301) 402-2176 (provides internships
working alongside influential scientists).

Oldman, Mark, and Samer Hamadeh. *The Princeton Review; America's Top 100
Internships.* New York: Villard Books, 1995.

Summer Job Hunting on the Net

Be sure and use your computer in your summer job search. Below are a few
sources to get you started.

Career Mosaic
http://www.careermosaic.com/cm/
Lists job opportunities for cooperative education or internships.

CareerNet—Career Resource Center
http://www.careers.org
Be sure to look to CareerNet for links to current jobs, employer sites, newsgroups, and government sites throughout the year.

Cooperative Education/Internships
http://www.wpi.edu/Academics/IMS/Library/jobguide/coop.html
Lists cooperative education, internships, and summer work with links to other sources.

JobTrak
http://www.jobtrak.com
An excellent place to look for jobs posted at member colleges and universities. You'll need a password, however. Check with your college placement or career office. JobTrak recently posted more than 1,000 internships for its member schools.

National Internships
http://campus.net/busemp/nintern/
Student internships and part-time jobs in: Washington, DC; New York City; Northern and Southern CA; Seattle; Texas; and many other places. Job opportunities in the private, non-profit, and government sectors.

Online Career Center
http://occ.com/occ
Try a keyword search on "internship" to get just a list of these.

Peace Corps
http://www.clark.net/pub/peace/PeaceCorps.html>
Students can examine frequently asked questions about working for the Peace Corps; timelines for the application process; a list of countries where volunteers are assigned; and a description of the domestic program.

Peterson's Education Center
http://www.petersons.com
Check this new resource for internship opportunities at colleges and universities nationwide. You will also find information on summer job opportunities.

Summer Urban Ministry Opportunities Directory
http://www.fileshop.com/iugm/sumr-dir.html
Lists national and international positions.

Temporary/Part-Time Jobs

Locating part-time work in your chosen field is ideal since you can continue to develop your network of contacts. Many professionals can freelance. An administrative assistant, for example, might be able to find part-time work at a law firm. An accountant might be able to do taxes on a part-time basis and still gain access to new referrals.

Another option is independent contracting. For example, if you're a computer programmer and the company you're interviewing with can't justify hiring someone full time because there isn't enough work, suggests that they hire you on a temporary basis for specific projects. Or offer to come in one or two days a week. Or suggest that you work on an as-needed basis. The advantage to the company is that they don't have to pay you benefits (except those you're able to negotiate). The advantage to you is income and experience in your chosen field.

People with technical skills can work themselves into becoming full-time freelancers in precisely this manner. They might even talk an employer OUT of hiring them full time and negotiate contract work in order to maintain the freedom of their self-employed status.

Below are some agencies that may assist you in your search for a temporary job.

CHICAGO'S 25 HIGHEST-VOLUME TEMPORARY EMPLOYMENT AGENCIES

Adia Personnel Services
540 N. Michigan Ave., Suite 206
Chicago, IL 60611
(312) 644-2342

America's TempCorps
186 N. York Road
Elmhurst, IL 60126
(630) 530-1595

Banner Temporary Service
122 S. Michigan Ave., Suite 1510
Chicago, IL 60603
(312) 704-6000

Beco Group
2200 S. Prospect St.
Park Ridge, IL 60068
(847) 825-8000

C. Berger & Co.
327 E. Gundersen Drive
Carol Stream, IL 60188
(630) 653-1115

C. R. Temporaries Ltd.
300 N. Martingale St., Suite 440
Schaumburg, IL 60173
(847) 619-1600

Debbie Temps
1419 Lake-Cook Road
Deerfield, IL 60015
(847) 940-4477

Employee Leasing
801 Asbury Drive
Buffalo Grove, IL 60089
(847) 913-2010

Robert Half International
205 N. Michigan Ave., Suite 330
Chicago, IL 60601
(312) 616-8200

Interim Personnel
1200 Harger Road, Suite 217
Oak Brook, IL 60521
(630) 571-3906

Kelly Temporary Services
1101 W. 31st St., Suite 240
Downers Grove, IL 60515
(630) 964-8488

MacTemps
230 N. Michigan Ave. 30th floor
Chicago, IL 60601
(312) 332-6868

Manpower Temporary Services
500 Park Blvd.
Itasca, IL 60143
(847) 773-1323

Richard Michael Temps
55 W. Monroe St., Suite 1010
Chicago, IL 60603
(312) 558-9070

Norrell Services
10255 W. Higgins Road, Suite 440
Rosemont, IL 60018
(847) 299-4200

Olsten of Chicago
16 W. Ontario St.
Chicago, IL 60610
(312) 944-3880

Paige Temporary
5215 Old Orchard Road
Skokie, IL 60077
(847) 966-0111

Paladin/Chicago
875 N. Michigan Ave., Suite 3218
Chicago, IL 60611
(312) 654-2600

Preferred Staffing
1600 Golf Road
Rolling Meadows, IL 60008
(847) 981-8140

Romac International
20 N. Wacker Drive, Suite 3810
Chicago, IL 60606
(312) 419-8367

Salem Services
Two TransAm Plaza Drive, Suite 170
Oakbrook Terrace, IL 60181
(630) 932-7000

Staffing Consultants
55 E. Monroe St.
Chicago, IL 60603
(312) 419-8899

Stivers Temporary Personnel
200 W. Monroe St.
Chicago, IL 60606
(312) 558-3550

Talent Tree Staffing Services
2 N. La Salle St., Suite 950
Chicago, IL 60622
(312) 855-1390

Tech Temps
2000 Spring Road, Suite 202
Oak Brook, IL 60521
(630) 574-4884

Temping in Today's Market

Temporary hires, independent contractors, leased employees, and part-timers constitute about 20% of today's workforce. If this trend continues, nearly one-third of all employees may be working on an as-needed basis within the next ten years. The U.S. Department of Labor projects that 1.3 million new temporary jobs will be created between 1992 and 2005.

One recent survey of 150 human resource executives conducted by the Office Team found that 78% viewed a consistent record of temporary employment equivalent to full-time work. And more than one-third of the temps surveyed at one agency were offered jobs as a result of temp assignments.

Temping is not only a means to pay the bills while looking for a full-time job but it can also be a way to get your foot in the door. A temp position gives you the opportunity to demonstrate your initiative and skills while also allowing you to test the waters of a company before committing to them.

The sheer number of temp agencies in Chicagoland is overwhelming and you will probably only want to work with several. Consult the following Web site, which offers lists of local agencies, advice on working with them, and reviews of people's personal experiences with particular agencies.

http://www.best.com:80/~ezy/redguide.html/

RECOMMENDED READING ON TEMPORARY/PART-TIME JOBS

Canape, Charlene. *The Part-Time Solution: The New Strategy for Managing Motherhood*. New York: Harper Collins, 1990.

Hawes, Gene R. *College Board Guide to Going to College While Working: Strategies for Success*. New York: College Entrance Examination Board (distributed by College Board Publications), 1985.

Magid, Renee Y. *When Mothers and Fathers Work: Creative Strategies for Balancing Career and Family*. New York: AMACOM, 1987.

Paradis, Adrain A. *Opportunities in Part-Time and Summer Jobs*. Lincolnwood, IL: VGM Career Horizons, 1987.

Rothberg and Cook. *Part-Time Professional*. Washington, DC: Acropolis Books, 1985.

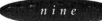

nine

How To Handle a New Job and Workplace

A new job, new colleagues, and a new desk—this is what the job search was all about. How do you handle the new job? Well, let the job experts give you some advice.

Walking into your new everyday life, seeing all those new colleagues, and concentrating on fitting into the atmosphere can be overwhelming. But it is important to keep your cool, stay focused, and be yourself. It is natural to be nervous, but how that nervousness manifests itself is important. Showing too much apprehension or bumbling about a bit too much can give others, and cost you, a bad first impression.

How Significant Is the First Day on the Job?

The first day at work can certainly be one of the most important days during your time at a particular company. This is the day that you begin to establish who you are and what you can contribute to the organization. The first day can show your employer a lot. It will give him or her an idea of what you are going to be like as an employee and how you will fit into the workplace.

In order to ease some of the restraint you may be feeling or cure some of those first-day butterflies, here are some tips that will enable you to feel more comfortable. For starters, promptness is essential and says a lot to the employer. This is important for more than just the first day. If you are constantly late, it reveals a sense of irresponsibility and may cause you some grief down the road.

Once you arrive at work on time, determining your duties and what is expected of you is vital. Take a little time to settle in, but try to get on the job soon, and show enthusiasm and contentment with your new job.

185

You might want to meet with your boss early in the day. This will show motivation and eagerness and will contribute early on to a good first impression. It will also give you an idea of some of the expectations that the company has for you. This and subsequent meetings should help you determine what drives the company and your superiors.

Learn the chain of command and assess the importance of teamwork. Ask about the long-term goals of the company so you can assess your role in it. Keep in mind on your first day that the old saying is true: you never get a second chance to make a first impression.

First Day Do's and Don'ts

It is important to keep in mind some rudimentary but very significant factors in terms of your on-the-job performance. We have formed a Top Ten list that should guide you through a successful first day on the job.

1. **DON'T** expect the red carpet to roll out for you. Employees may not even be expecting you, and special treatment may not be forthcoming.

2. **DON'T** imagine rewarding accomplishments and important responsibilities to await you on your first day. Be prepared for paperwork and orientations.

3. **DON'T** stress. Just take it one step at a time. The company knows you are new and will help you get acclimated; they want you to perform well.

4. **DON'T** be afraid to ask questions, and make sure you realize that no question is a stupid question.

5. **DON'T** be overwhelmed with all the new information. Concentrate on grasping the major points or the most urgent.

6. **DO** enjoy yourself. Think of your job as a challenge and a way to gain new skills for the future.

7. **DO** be prepared. Show everybody that you have your head on straight, can plan ahead, and know what you are doing.

8. **DO** get involved. Interpersonal communication within a company is very important. Be a part of the team, and show other employees that you have some good ideas.

9. **DO** be confident. You were hired because you are qualified. Don't let anything get in your way and make you think otherwise. If the company believes in you, then by all means you should believe in yourself.

10. **DO** stay focused. Try to maintain a working attitude throughout the day. Daydreaming and other distractions will hinder your professional image. Try not to incorporate your personal life with your professional life for the security of your career.

Adjusting Over the Long Run

A new job can be very intimidating and can fill you with mixed emotions about a career. Here are some helpful hints that will enable you to adjust to the company, fit in, and, most importantly, make an impact as a valuable employee.

Develop good communication skills. Has it come to your attention that most top-notch people in a company seem to know one another? Interpersonal communication is a key ingredient in making your job more productive and pleasant. Listen as well to everybody's input, not just those higher up on the career ladder. Keep in mind that you spend a large portion of your life with your workmates, and most of them have something to offer.

Take risks. Don't be afraid to take risks. A leader will have developed enough self-confidence so that taking a few calculated risks is worth the possible payoff. Overcoming skepticism and taking risks can even be the turning point of a career. Just remember to weigh all the options and be prepared for negative as well as positive results.

Work hard. A hard worker always seems to have a brighter future than someone who settles for being just adequate. Let the company know that you are the "go to" person. If you portray that hard-working image, the next step for most supervisors is to trust you with additional duties.

Honesty is the best policy. Try not to make excuses to bail yourself out of hot water. You are better off apologizing and admitting the fact that you made a mistake. Most importantly, never point your finger at other employees. You will only look foolish and cowardly. You want to set a good example, not be the bad example.

Maintaining a Good Relationship with the Boss

Here are some helpful tips to assist you in maintaining a good relationship with your boss.

- Think of your boss as a customer for the product you are trying to sell: yourself. Keep in mind that there is no such thing as impressing your boss too much.

- Value and respect your boss' time. Managers must handle a number of things all at once. If you see that your boss is busy, try to solve the problem yourself or seek assistance from another employee. Freeing your boss from trivial concerns will make everyone's life easier.
- Be open to advice. Don't be offended when your supervisor tries to steer you in the right direction. Make room for criticism, and view it as information that can make you a more effective employee.
- Never make your boss look foolish. Don't challenge his or her judgment in front of other employees. If you feel that you're right, talk to the boss privately. Involving others will just result in dispute and cause havoc.
- Always make your boss look good. Try to keep him/her informed of new issues and ideas. Remember that the better you do, the better the boss looks; and the better the boss looks, the better your career will be.
- Tell your boss about your career objectives or plans for the future. Inform him/her about your ideas and goals of accomplishment. Be optimistic, not skeptical, when discussing career plans with the head person.
- When confrontation with the boss is necessary, try to find an ice-breaking technique to reduce tension. Try to find a common goal or interest in solving the problem. This brings people together and makes them more open to discussion and less defensive.
- Always listen to your boss, but never let him/her walk all over you. Even though you may not have the final say, your judgments deserve to be heard.

A good professional relationship with the boss is vital in terms of job happiness and success. But don't look for the boss to be either perfect or your good buddy. A boss should be a role model and a leader, the person we answer to and respect.

Dear Dr. Bob

Lately, I've noticed my boss taking all the credit for my hard work. He never mentions my name when receiving glowing remarks about a project. What should I do?
—Unrecognized Employee

Dear Unrecognized Employee
Your situation is an age-old one. We are supposed to make our bosses look good and hope they will return the favor. Unfortunately, that hasn't happened in your case. I am one that believes "what goes around, comes around" and eventually your efforts will be rewarded. You will have other jobs and other bosses, but your ability will stay with

you. In the meantime, use subtle techniques for claiming what is due. Make sure your name appears on written reports. When people praise your boss, mention how hard the whole department has worked as well. In due time, you will receive your just recognition.

Creativity and Innovation in Your Career

Corporations want individuals that can be assets and contribute to the company. New ideas and different approaches are always encouraged. Be creative. Show the company that you have the zeal and ability to bring new concepts into the company. Try not to be a routine employee who comes to work, takes care of her responsibilities, and leaves work exactly on time everyday.

Don't hesitate when you think you have a new idea that might help the company. The reality is that many companies do not recognize the value of the creative process but only the "bottom line" result. Here are a few tips for breaking your own barriers to creativity.

Postpone judgment. Explore an idea before promoting or nixing it. Even a patently unrealistic idea may lead to a workable solution to a problem.

Look for the second right answer. Avoid the trap of committing too soon to a single solution to a problem. Always look for the second, less obvious answer.

Take risks. How many models for an airplane did Orville and Wilbur Wright fail with before they found one that worked? Think about that the next time you are hesitant in something.

Look for unlikely connections. Computer guru Steve Jobs once said that when he worked for Atari he applied what he learned about movement from a modern dance class in college to the development of video games. Talk about an unlikely connection!

Allow yourself to be foolish. Kids have a leg up on us when it comes to creativity because they are encouraged to be foolish. Creativity flourishes when you allow your mind to romp. Some experts even suggest keeping toys in your office or home to encourage your playful side.

Creativity is within everyone's grasp. It comes out not when you do something that no one has done before but when you do something that *you* have never done before. Recognizing the barriers you yourself have erected to the creative process is the first step to unleashing your potential. Your career and success can only be enhanced once this is done.

Romance in the Office: A Definite Don't

Many dedicated corporate types have found Cupid's arrow piercing their briefcases and setting their hearts aflutter under their banker pinstripes. What's a person to do when love hits in the workplace? The logical, reasonable answer is, "Don't do it!" But rarely is romance logical or reasonable.

Let's face it. Being in proximity with others for an extended period of time makes the workplace fertile ground for romance to blossom. You share common interests, talk frequently, and may even have similar problems. Next thing you know, you find Mr. or Ms. Right directly under your nose. If you are indeed smitten by a co-worker, we offer a few words of advice about relationships in the workplace.

- Know the company's policy on dating co-workers. Some companies consider it unprofessional or even a conflict of interest. However, it is unlikely that your organization will have a written policy prohibiting such relationships.
- Remember that the workplace is for work. Heated romances should remain outside the workplace.
- Be prepared for people to gossip. Romance is juicy stuff — especially for those who don't have it. There are no easy answers about how to handle gossip. It's best to ignore harmless gossip and to confront people spreading malicious stories (there is harm in a rumor that you or your significant other is pregnant!).
- Think about how to handle the break-up. No one wants to think about the end of a relationship, especially when it is just beginning. However, the number-one workplace hazard is a vindictive ex. Understand that if things don't work out, it is likely that you will still work together. Make sure you are ready for that possibility.
- Finally, never date the boss. Regardless of how professionally you conduct yourself in the office, every action or decision you make will be viewed by others through the lens of your relationship. Additionally, having an ex-significant other for a boss can be terribly awkward.
- If a romance goes sour, there is always the risk of sexual harassment. When one person in a relationship has greater authority over the other, the possibility of sexual harassment exists.

The easiest course is to avoid workplace romances altogether. However, love is capricious, and you may well find that one special person just across the hall. If that's the case, even Cupid understands the importance of separating love and work.

Keeping Your Career on the High Road

Becoming successful and happy is the ultimate dream of those who are trying to get their foot in the door. A true success story involves hard work and a positive professional attitude. Here are some tips that will enable you to take that first step toward a new and fulfilling life.

1. Always maintain a good professional relationship with your co-workers and peers. Knowing a wide array of people is certainly advantageous and can become very helpful when you need a favor or some assistance.
2. Find a mentor, somebody who can develop the best in you and advance your interests in the company.
3. Try to concentrate on small, easy projects at first. Conquering your first assignment will give the company a good initial vision of your work abilities. This will also alleviate the pressures a little and add to your self-esteem and believability.
4. Cater to your clients. Be straightforward and candid with them. Make them see that you are fair and treat them as people not profit figures. Try to value their time by being flexible with your schedule.
5. Never assume that a certain issue is not your job. Try to do whatever you can to make your department and the company work. Even if you are not responsible for certain areas, it won't hinder your career if you attempt to find answers when a problem affects you.
6. Take on as many responsibilities and as much work as you can handle. The operative phrase here, however, is "as much work as you can handle." Willingly accepting additional projects and assignments can ingratiate you with your boss only if you complete them in a timely and professional manner.
7. Accept criticism as a form of information that can make you a better employee. When constructively criticized, determine and take the actions that can correct the problem.
8. Never get stuck in one job. Always look to move forward. If you feel that you don't have a future at a certain company, keep your eyes open for other opportunities. Make sure you gain more and more skills and credibility as you progress.
9. Be a leader. Emphasize your willingness to help others. Gaining leadership status can be challenging, but it will definitely broaden your career in the long run.
10. Stay current on issues in your field. Keeping current enables you to assess the stability of your current job and to predict your next career move.
11. Good people are hard to find. No matter how cliché, it's true. If you excel, you will be in an elite group and in demand by employers.

Keep Your Network Alive

Ideally, this book will help you achieve your dream job. But remember that the average person changes jobs five to eight times in their career. Thus, after you've landed a job, it is important that you notify your network people of your new position and thank them for their assistance. Don't throw away those business cards you worked so hard to accumulate. After all, you never know when you may need to ask them for help again. You've spent months building up a network of professional contacts. Keep your network alive.

Make a "New Year's Resolution" to weigh all aspects of your job annually. Evaluate your current situation and the progress you are making (as measured by increased salary, responsibilities, and skills). Compare the result with what you want from your life's career. Even though you may be completely satisfied in your new job, remember that circumstances can change overnight, and you must always be prepared for the unexpected.

We hope you make good use of the job-search techniques outlined in this book. Perhaps the next time you talk to an unemployed person or someone seeking a new job, you will look at that person with new insight gained from your own job search and career successes. We hope you'll gladly share what you've learned from these pages about how to get a job.

Where Chicago Works

T his chapter contains the names, addresses, and phone numbers of the Chicago area's top employers of white-collar workers. The companies are arranged in categories according to the major products they manufacture and the major services they provide.

This listing is intended to help you survey the major potential employers in fields that interest you as well as selected smaller enterprises. It is selective, not exhaustive. We have not, for example, listed all the advertising agencies in the area as you can find that information in the Yellow Pages. We have simply listed the largest ones potentially offering the most jobs. In addition, we've included many firms whose corporate operations are outside of Chicago proper just in case commuting is not a factor in your job search.

The purpose of this chapter is to get you started, both looking and thinking. This is the kickoff, not the final gun. Browse through the whole chapter, and take some time to check out areas that are unfamiliar to you. Many white-collar skills are transferable. People with marketing, management, data processing, accounting, administrative, secretarial, and other talents are needed in a huge variety of businesses.

Ask yourself in what area your skills could be marketed. Use your imagination, especially if you're in a so-called specialized field. A dietitian, for instance, might look first under Health Care, or maybe Hospitality. But what about insurance companies, museums, retail stores, or the scores of other places that run their own dining rooms for employees or the public? What about food and consumer magazines? Who invents all those recipes and tests those products?

The tips and insider interviews that are scattered throughout this chapter are designed to nudge your creativity and suggest additional ideas for your job search. Much more detailed information on the area's top employers and other, smaller companies can be found in the directories and other resources suggested in Chapter 4. We can't stress strongly enough that you have to do your homework when you're looking for a job, both to unearth places that might need a person with your particular talents and to succeed in the interview once you've lined up a meeting with the hiring authority.

A word about hiring authorities: if you've read Chapter 7, you know that the name of the game is to meet the person with the power to hire you, or get as close to that person as you can. You don't want to go to the chairman or the personnel director if the person who actually makes the decision is the marketing manager or customer service director.

Just where are those employers located, anyway? Obviously, we can't list every possible hiring authority in the Chicago area. If we tried, you'd need a wagon to haul this book around. Besides, directories go out of date-even those that are regularly and conscientiously revised. So always double-check a contact you get from a book or magazine, including this one. Call the company's switchboard to confirm who heads a particular department or division.

To give you an overview of the breadth, depth, and structure of Chicagoland's economy, we've provided categorical lists by major industry or function. Obviously, you'll encounter redundancy among our lists since large organizations tend to be diversified. Further, simple classification of employers has become nearly impossible given the vast numbers of mergers and acquisitions that have occurred. Actually, redundancy in classifying employers benefits you, the job seeker, by providing multiple ways to think about work and employment.

The Chicago area's top employers are arranged in the following categories:

Accounting/Auditing
Advertising Agencies/Public Relations/Media Services
Aerospace/Defense
Apparel/Fashion/Cosmetics
Architectural Firms
Associations and Association Management
Automobile/Truck/Transportation Equipment
Banks: Commercial and Savings/Credit Unions
Broadcasting
Chemicals
Computers: Hardware/Software
Computers: Information Management/Consulting
Construction/Contractors
Consulting: Financial/Health Care/Human Resources/Management/Marketing
Educational Institutions
Electronics/Telecommunications
Energy/Oil/Gas/Plastics
Engineering
Entertainment
Environmental Services
Food/Beverage Producers and Distributors

Furniture/Housewares/Household Textiles
Government
Health Care: HMOs & PPOs/Hospitals
Hospitality: Hotels/ Restaurants
Insurance
Law Firms
Museums/Theaters/Cultural Institutions/Fundraising
Paper and Allied Products
Pharmaceuticals/Medical Products
Printing
Publishing
Real Estate
Retailers/Wholesalers
Social Services
Sports/Recreation
Stock Brokers/Financial Services
Travel/Shipping/Transportation
Utilities

Here, then, are the Chicago area's greatest opportunities. Note that in many cases, nearby employers are listed with Chicago employers.

Accounting/Auditing

WEB SITES:

http://www.kentis.com/index.html/
is the accounting professionals resource
center; links to homepages of CPAs.

http://unf.edu/students/jmayer/arl.html
links to resources for accountants and
auditors.

http://mail.eskimo.com/~pretzl/
has accounting employment opportunities
and resume bank.

PROFESSIONAL ORGANIZATIONS:

For networking in accounting and related
fields, check out these local professional
organizations listed in Chapter 5. Also see
"Banks" and "Stock Brokers."

**American Women's Society of Certified
Public Accountants
Illinois CPA Society**

For additional information, contact:

**American Institute of Certified Public
Accountants**
1211 Avenue of the Americas
New York, NY 10036
(212) 596-6200

American Institute of CPAs
Harbor Cite Financial Center, 210 Plaza
Three
Jersey City, NJ 07311
(201) 938-3000

American Society of Women Accountants
1255 Lynnfield Road, Suite 257
Memphis, TN 38119
(901) 680-0470

CPA Associates
201 Route 17 North, 4th floor
Rutherford, NJ 07070-2574
(201) 804-8686

Institute of Management Accountants
10 Paragon Drive
Montvale, NJ 07645
(201) 573-9000

**National Association of Black
Accountants**
7249A Hanover Pkwy.
Greenbelt, MD 20770
(301) 474-6222

National Society of Public Accountants
1010 N. Fairfax St.
Alexandria, VA 22314
(703) 549-6400

PROFESSIONAL PUBLICATIONS:

Accounting Review
Cash Flow
The CPA Journal
D & B Reports
Journal of Accountancy
Management Accounting
National Public Accountant
The Practical Accountant
The Woman CPA

DIRECTORIES:

Accountants Directory (American Business
Directories, Inc., Omaha, NE)
Accounting Firms and Practitioners
(American Institute of Certified Public
Accountants, New York, NY)
*Emerson's Directory of Leading U.S.
Accounting Firms* (Emerson's, Seattle,
WA)
*National Directory of Certified Public
Accountants* (Peter Norback Publishing
Co., Princeton, NJ)
Who Audits America (Data Financial Press,
Menlo Park, CA)

Employers:

Altschuler Melvoin & Glasser
30 S. Wacker Drive, Suite 2600
Chicago, IL 60606
(312) 207-2800
320 professional staff

Arthur Andersen
33 W. Monroe St.
Chicago, IL 60603
(312) 580-0033
1,538 professional staff

Bansley & Kiener
125 S. Wacker Drive
Chicago, IL 60606
(312) 263-2700
77 professional staff

BDO Seidman
205 N. Michigan Ave., Suite 2100
Chicago, IL 60601
(312) 856-9100
132 professional staff

Blackman Kallick Bartelstein
300 S. Riverside Plaza, Suite 660
Chicago, IL 60606
(312) 207-1040
150 professional staff

Checkers Simon & Rosner
1 S. Wacker Drive, Suite 1700
Chicago, IL 60606
(312) 346-4242
196 professional staff

Coopers & Lybrand
203 N. La Salle St.
Chicago, IL 60601
(312) 701-5500
1,116 professional staff

Crowe Chizek & Co.
1 Mid America Plaza
Oak Brook, IL 60522
(630) 574-7878
145 professional staff

Deloitte & Touche
180 N. Stetson Ave.
Chicago, IL 60601
(312) 946-3000
860 professional staff

Ernst & Young
233 S. Wacker Drive
Chicago, IL 60606
(312) 879-2000
1,206 professional staff

Friedman Eisenstein Raemer Schwartz
401 N. Michigan Ave., Suite 2600
Chicago, IL 60611
(312) 644-6000
222 professional staff

Frost Ruttenberg & Rothblatt
5750 Old Orchard Road, Suite 200
Skokie, IL 60077
(847) 470-8120
76 professional staff

Gleeson Sklar Sawyers & Cumpata
5550 W. Touhy Ave., Suite 300
Skokie, IL 60077
(847) 673-4500
75 professional staff

Grant Thornton
1 Prudential Plaza, Suite 700
Chicago, IL 60601
(312) 856-0200
265 professional staff

Klayman & Korman
8750 W. Bryn Mawr Ave.
Chicago, IL 60631
(773) 693-6000
73 professional staff

KPMG Peat Marwick
303 E. Wacker Drive
Chicago, IL 60601
(312) 938-1000
995 professional staff

Kupferberg Goldberg & Neimark
111 E. Wacker Drive, Suite 1400
Chicago, IL 60601
(312) 819-4300
85 professional staff

Leventhal, Kenneth, & Co.
31 N. Franklin St., Suite 2100
Chicago, IL 60606
(312) 879-6500
76 professional staff

McGladrey & Pullen
1699 E. Woodfield Road, Suite 300
Schaumburg, IL 60173
(847) 517-7070
254 professional staff

Miller Cooper & Co. Ltd.
650 Dundee Road, Suite 250
Northbrook, IL 60062
(847) 205-5000
86 professional staff

Ostrow Reisin Berk & Abrams Ltd.
455 N. Cityfront Plaza Drive
Chicago, IL 60611
(312) 670-7444
78 professional staff

Price Waterhouse
200 E. Randolph Drive
Chicago, IL 60601
(312) 540-1500
820 professional staff

Rootberg, Philip, & Co.
250 S. Wacker Drive, Suite 800
Chicago, IL 60606
(312) 930-9600
96 professional staff

Thomas Havey & Co.
30 N. La Salle St., Suite 4200
Chicago, IL 60602
(312) 368-0500
169 professional staff

Wolf & Co.
2100 Clearwater Drive
Oak Brook, IL 60521
(630) 574-7800
78 professional staff

Accounting firms big and small

We talked with Richard Craig, a Certified Public Accountant, now a Senior Vice President in finance at a leading data processing firm. We asked how he began his career in accounting and about the advantages and disadvantages associated with the size of the firm you work for.

Said Craig, "I started at Touche Ross (now Deloitte & Touche), one of the big eight (now the big six) accounting firms. Usually, working for a larger firm means learning a specific task. Staffs are larger, so each job is more specialized. You don't usually handle as many components of a job as you would in a smaller firm. You sometimes have more opportunity for hands-on experience in a smaller firm and gain more general management experience," Craig advised.

"But regardless of the size of the firm where you begin your career, if you wish to advance you should remain flexible through the first five years. If your job is not what you expected, be willing to make a change.

"Also, if you want a manager's position, you may have to move around to gain general managerial experience. Sometimes, that will mean a transfer to a department that would not necessarily be your first choice. But if the position rounds out your background, it is usually worth at least a temporary stay."

Advertising Agencies/Public Relations/Media Services

WEB SITES:

http://www.commercepark.com/AAAA/
AAAA.html
American Association of Advertising
Agencies

http://www.adage.com/
is the site for *Ad Age Magazine.*

PROFESSIONAL ORGANIZATIONS:

For networking in advertising and related fields, check out these local professional organizations listed in Chapter 5. Also see "Consulting: Marketing."

Advertising Agency Production
  Managers Club
Business Professional Advertising
  Association
Chicago Advertising Federation
Chicago Association of Direct Marketing
Promotion Industry Club

For additional information, contact:

Advertising Council, The
Chicago Office
740 N. Rush St.
Chicago, IL 60611
(312) 751-8055

American Advertising Federation
1400 K St., N.W., Suite 1000
Washington, DC 20005
(800) 999-2231

American Mail Marketing Association
1333 F St., Suite 710
Washington, DC 20005
(202) 347-0055

**American Association of Advertising
Agencies**
666 3rd Ave., 13th floor
New York, NY 10017
(212) 682-2500

**International Association of Business
Communicators**
1 Hallidie Plaza, Suite 600
San Francisco, CA 94102
(415) 433-3400

Marketing Research Association
2189 Silas Deane Highway, Suite 5
Rocky Hill, CT 06067
(203) 257-4008

Public Relations Society of America
33 Irving Place, 3rd floor
New York, NY 1003
(212) 995-2230

Women in Communications
10605 Judicial Drive, Suite A-4
Fairfax, VA 22030
(703) 359-9000

Women Executives in Public Relations
P.O. Box 609
Westport, CT 06881
(203) 226-4947

PROFESSIONAL PUBLICATIONS:

Advertising Age
Adweek
Brandweek
Direct Marketing Magazine
Jack O'Dwyer's Newsletter

Journal of Advertising Research
Madison Ave.
Marketing News
Potentials in Marketing

DIRECTORIES:

Standard Directory of Advertisers (National
Register Publishing Co., New Provi-
dence, NJ)
Standard Directory of Advertising Agencies
(National Register Publishing Co., New
Providence, NJ)

For those interested in the advertising
field, the industry's *Red Book*, or *Standard
Directory of Advertising Agencies*, is useful
in finding a specific contact in your area
of interest. For example, an artist would
contact the agency's Art Director or
Creative Director. The directory is
available at most libraries.

Employers, Advertising Agencies

Abelson-Taylor
35 E. Wacker Drive, Suite 900
Chicago, IL 60601
(312) 781-1700

Academy Advertising/Marketing
6625 N. Avondale Ave.
Chicago, IL 60631
(773) 792-0200

Arian, Lowe & Travis
343 W. Erie St., Suite 520
Chicago, IL 60610
(312) 787-3300

Arocom Marketing Group
225 W. Washington St., Suite 2200
Chicago, IL 60606
(312) 419-7102

Associated Advertisers
930 N. York Road, Suite 130
Hinsdale, IL 60521
(630) 655-6070

Austin Knight, Inc.-Midwest Region
303 W. Erie St.
Chicago, IL 60610
(312) 337-5599

Ayer, N.W., & Partners Chicago
515 N. State St., Suite 2100
Chicago, IL 60610
(312) 644-2937

Baker Advertising
1912 N. Cleveland
Chicago, IL 60614
(312) 944-6316

Bates Advertising USA
737 N. Michigan Ave., Suite 2030
Chicago, IL 60611
(312) 664-0200

Bayer Bess Vanderwarker
225 N. Michigan Ave., Suite 1900
Chicago, IL 60601
(312) 861-3800

BB&A/AD-Dimensions
2021 Midwest Road
Oak Brook, IL 60521
(630) 889-4150

BBDO Chicago
410 N. Michigan Ave.
Chicago, IL 60611
(312) 337-7860

BB&L/TMP
420 N. Wabash
Chicago, IL 60611
(312) 467-9350

**Bender, Browning, Dolby & Sanderson
Advertising**
444 N. Michigan Ave., Suite 1400
Chicago, IL 60611
(312) 644-9600

Bennet, Walter, Communications
20 N. Wacker Drive
Chicago, IL 60606
(312) 372-1131

Bently, Barnes & Lynn
420 N. Wabash Ave.
Chicago, IL 60611
(312) 467-9350

BJK&E Media Group
625 N. Michigan Ave.

Chicago, IL 60611
(312) 988-2000
Advertising and public relations.

Bozell Worldwide
625 N. Michigan Ave., Suite 2700
Chicago, IL 60611
(312) 988-2000
Advertising and public relations.

Brandt, Robert, & Associates
806 York Road
Hinsdale, IL 60521
(630) 325-2000

Brown, E.H., Advertising
20 N. Wacker Drive, Suite 1865
Chicago, IL 60606-2996
(312) 372-9494

Brown/LMC Group/Chicago
222 W. Hubbard St., Suite 408
Chicago, IL 60610
(312) 527-3919

Burnett, Leo, and Company
35 W. Wacker Drive
Chicago, IL 60601
(312) 220-5959

Burrell Communications Group
20 N. Michigan Ave.
Chicago, IL 60602
(312) 443-8600
Advertising and public relations.

Campbell Mithun Esty
737 N. Michigan Ave.
Chicago, IL 60611
(312) 266-5100

Circle Advertising
10500 W. 153rd St.
Orland Park, IL 60462
(708) 349-3300

Corbett HealthConnect
211 E. Chicago Ave.
Chicago, IL 60611-2660
(312) 664-5310

Cramer-Krasselt/Direct
225 N. Michigan Ave.
Chicago, IL 60601
(312) 616-9600

Cravit, David, & Associates Advertising
737 N. Michigan Ave.
Chicago, IL 60611
(312) 266-5100

Creative Marketing International Corp.
31W001 North Ave.
West Chicago, IL 60185
(630) 293-9600

D'Arcy Masius Benton & Bowles
200 E. Randolph Drive
Chicago, IL 60601
(312) 861-5000

DB Advertising Associates
848 E. 58th St.
Chicago, IL 60637
(773) 947-3313

DDB Needham Chicago
303 E. Wacker Drive
Chicago, IL 60601
(312) 861-0200

Direct Edge Marketing
875 N. Michigan Ave., Suite 2800
Chicago, IL 60611
(312) 397-3200

Doremus & Company
10 S. Riverside Plaza
Chicago, IL 60606
(312) 321-1377

DraftDirect Worldwide
142 E. Ontario
Chicago, IL 60611-2818
(312) 944-3500

Eicoff, A., & Co.
401 N. Michigan Ave., Suite 400
Chicago, IL 60611
(312) 527-7100

Eire Partners
230 W. Superior St., Suite 600
Chicago, IL 60610
(312) 335-4330

EJL Advertising/Chicago
401 N. Michigan Ave.
Chicago, IL 60611
(312) 828-0400

Esrock Advertising
14550 S. 94th Ave.
Orland Park, IL 60462
(708) 349-8400

FCB Direct
101 E. Erie St.
Chicago, IL 60611-2897
(312) 751-7000

Flair Communications
214 W. Erie St.
Chicago, IL 60610
(312) 943-5959

Food Group, The (Chicago)
980 N. Michigan Ave.,
Suite 1212
Chicago, IL 60611
(312) 482-9266

Foote, Cone & Belding
101 E. Erie St.
Chicago, IL 60611-2897
(312) 751-7000

Gams Chicago
360 N. Michigan Ave.
Chicago, IL 60601
(312) 236-8768

Garfield, Linn & Company
142 E. Ontario St.
Chicago, IL 60611
(312) 943-1900

Goble & Associates
800 S. Wells St., Suite 200
Chicago, IL 60607
(312) 431-2900

Grant/Jacoby
737 N. Michigan Ave.
Chicago, IL 60611
(312) 664-2055
Advertising and public relations.

Grey Directory Marketing
222 Hubbard St.
Chicago, IL 60610
(312) 222-0025

GSP Marketing Services
320 W. Ohio

Chicago, IL 60610
(312) 944-3000
Direct marketing agency.

Hamilton Communications
727 N. Hudson
Chicago, IL 60610
(312) 642-1825
Advertising and public relations.

Hodes, Bernard, Advertising
10 S. Riverside Plaza
Chicago, IL 60606
(312) 258-9000

Interbrand Schechter
303 E. Wacker Drive
Chicago, IL 60601
(312) 240-9700
Marketing agency.

Italia/Gal Advertising
308 W. Erie, Suite 400
Chicago, IL 60610
(312) 787-8786

Jordan Tamraz Caruso Advertising
1419 N. Wells St.
Chicago, IL 60610-1395
(312) 951-2000

Keroff & Rosenberg Advertising
444 N. Wabash
Chicago, IL 60611
(312) 321-9000

Ketchum Advertising & Public Relations
111 N. Canal St.
Chicago, IL 60606-7272
(312) 715-9200
Advertising and public relations.

Kryl & Company
2 N. Riverside Plaza, Suite 2400
Chicago, IL 60606-2704
(312) 466-0270
Direct marketing agency.

Levy, Jack, Associates
1 E. Erie St.
Chicago, IL 60611
(312) 337-7800
Advertising and public relations.

Lintas Campbell-Ewald
980 N. Michigan Ave., Suite 1060
Chicago, IL 60611
(312) 587-2650

Lois/USA Chicago
2300 Merchandise Mart
Chicago, IL 60654
(312) 527-5030

Marketing Support
200 E. Randolph St., Suite 5000
Chicago, IL 60601
(312) 565-0044
Marketing agency.

McCann Healthcare
625 N. Michigan Ave., 8th floor
Chicago, IL 60611
(312) 266-9200

McConnaughy Stein Schmidt Brown
401 E. Illinois St., Suite 500
Chicago, IL 60611
(312) 321-8000

McKinney Advertising & Public Relations
430 W. Erie
Chicago, IL 60610
(312) 944-6784
Advertising and public relations.

Miller Advertising Agency
1 Northfield Plaza, Suite 300
Northfield, IL 60093
(847) 441-2618

Nahser, Frank, Inc.
10 S. Riverside Plaza
Chicago, IL 60606
(312) 845-5000

Noble & Associates/Chicago
515 N. State St., 29th floor
Chicago, IL 60610
(312) 644-4600

Ogilvy & Mather
1 Illinois Center
111 E. Wacker
Chicago, IL 60601-4208
(312) 856-8200

Potentia Healthcare Communications Partners
211 E. Chicago Ave., Suite 920
Chicago, IL 60611-2660
(312) 988-1300

Rapp Collins/Chicago
10 S. Riverside Plaza, Suite 1920
Chicago, IL 60606
(312) 454-0660

Rhea & Kaiser Advertising
400 E. Diehl Road
Naperville, IL 60563-1342
(630) 505-1100

Riney & Partners Heartland
224 S. Michigan Ave., Suite 700
Chicago, IL 60604
(312) 697-5700

Rubin Response Services
1111 Plaza Drive
Schaumburg, IL 60173
(847) 619-9800
Direct response company.

Saatchi & Saatchi Pacific/Chicago Field
300 Park Blvd., Suite 307
Itasca, IL 60143
(630) 775-9701

Sander Allen Advertising
230 N. Michigan Ave.
Chicago, IL 60601
(312) 444-1771

Shaker Advertising Agency
1100 Lake St.
Oak Park, IL 60301
(708) 383-5320

Slack Myers & Barshinger
444 N. Michigan Ave., #900
Chicago, IL 60611
(312) 527-0777
Advertising and public relations.

Tatham Euro RSCG
980 N. Michigan Ave.
Chicago, IL 60611
(312) 337-4400

TBWA Chiat/Day Chicago
1111 W. 22nd St.
Oak Brook, IL 60521
(630) 574-8030

Thompson, J. Walter, USA
900 N. Michigan Ave.
Chicago, IL 60611
(312) 951-4000

TMP Worldwide
420 N. Wabash
Chicago, IL 60611
(312) 467-9350

True North Communications
101 E. Erie St.
Chicago, IL 60611-2897
(312) 751-7227

Wahlstrom/Chicago
101 E. Erie St.
Chicago, IL 60611
(312) 943-0200

Wells Rich Greene BDDP/Chicago
111 E. Wacker Drive
Chicago, IL 60601
(312) 938-0900

Young & Rubicam Chicago
1 S. Wacker Drive, Suite 1800
Chicago, IL 60606
(312) 845-4000

Zimmerman & Partners Advertising
645 N. Michigan Ave., Suite 800
Chicago, IL 60611
(312) 573-1063

Employers: Public Relations Firms

Bozell Worldwide
625 N. Michigan Ave., Suite 2700
Chicago, IL 60611
(312) 988-2000
Advertising and public relations.

Burrell Communications Group
20 N. Michigan Ave.
Chicago, IL 60602
(312) 443-8600
Advertising and public relations.

Burson Marsteller
1 E. Wacker Drive
Chicago, IL 60601
(312) 329-9292

Cramer-Krasselt
225 N. Michigan Ave.
Chicago, IL 60601
(312) 616-9600

Cushman, Aaron D. & Associates
25 E. Wacker Drive, Suite 850
Chicago, IL 60601
(312) 263-2500

Diederichs, Janet, & Assoc.
333 N. Michigan Ave.
Chicago, IL 60611
(312) 346-7886

Dragonette Inc.
205 W. Wacker Drive, Suite 2200
Chicago, IL 60601
(312) 424-5300

Edelman Worldwide
200 E. Randolph St.
Chicago, IL 60601
(312) 240-3000

Fleishman Hillard/Chicago
875 N. Michigan Ave., Suite 3300
Chicago, IL 60611
(312) 751-8878

Financial Relations Board
875 N. Michigan Ave.
Chicago, IL 60611
(312) 266-7800

Gibbs & Soell
2500 W. Higgins Road, Suite 850
Hoffmann Estates, IL 60195
(847) 519-9150

Golin/Harris
500 N. Michigan Ave.
Chicago, IL 60611
(312) 836-7100

Grant/Jacoby
737 N. Michigan Ave.
Chicago, IL 60611

(312) 664-2055
Advertising and public relations.

Hamilton Communications
727 N. Hudson
Chicago, IL 60610
(312) 642-1825
Advertising and public relations.

Hill & Knowlton
900 N. Michigan Ave., Suite 2100
Chicago, IL 60611
(312) 255-1200

Janis, Martin, & Co.
919 N. Michigan Ave.
Chicago, IL 60611
(312) 943-1100

Jasculca/Terman & Associates
730 N. Franklin St., Suite 510
Chicago, IL 60606-7272
(312) 337-7400

Ketchum Advertising & Public Relations
111 N. Canal St.
Chicago, IL 60606-7272
(312) 715-9200
Advertising and public relations.

Korshak, Margie
875 N. Michigan Ave., Suite 2750
Chicago, IL 60611
(312) 751-2121

Levy, Jack, Associates
1 E. Erie
Chicago, IL 60611
(312) 337-7800
Advertising and public relations.

Lipman Hearne, Inc.
303 E. Wacker Drive, Suite 1030
Chicago, IL 60601
(312) 946-1900

Manning, Selvage & Lee
303 E. Wacker Drive, Suite 440
Chicago, IL 60601
(312) 819-3535

Ogilvie Adams & Rinehart
900 N. Michigan Ave., Suite 2750
Chicago, IL 60611
(312) 988-2684

Porter Novelli
303 E. Wacker Drive
Chicago, IL 60601
(312) 856-8888

Posner McGrath Ltd.
300 Tri-State International, Suite 270
Lincolnshire, IL 60069
(847) 405-0800

Public Communications
35 E. Wacker Drive, Suite 1254
Chicago, IL 60601
(312) 558-1770

Ruder& Finn
444 N. Michigan Ave.
Chicago, IL 60611
(312) 644-8600

Selz, Seabold
221 N. LaSalle St.
Chicago, IL 60601
(312) 372-7090

Slack Myers & Barshinger
444 N. Michigan Ave., #900
Chicago, IL 60611
(312) 527-0777
Advertising and public relations.

Ury, Bernard & Assoc.
105 W. Madison St.
Chicago, IL 60602
(312) 726-3668

Weiser Walek Group
150 S. Wacker Drive, Suite 3000
Chicago, IL 60606
(312) 368-1500

Williams, L.C., & Associates
180 N. Stetson Ave., Suite 1500
Chicago, IL 60601
(312) 565-3900

Employers: Media Services Firms

Blair TV
455 N. Cityfront Plaza Drive
Chicago, IL 60611
(312) 321-6600
Television station representatives.

Bohbot Communications of Illinois
875 N. Michigan Ave.
Chicago, IL 60611
(312) 944-4040

CPM, Inc.
515 N. State St., Suite 2200
Chicago, IL 60610-4320
(312) 527-2100

International Communications (Chicago)
333 W. Wacker Drive, Suite 700
Chicago, IL 60606
(312) 444-2788

Kelly, Scott & Madison
35 E. Wacker Drive, Suite 1150
Chicago, IL 60601
(312) 977-0772

Outdoor Services
737 N. Michigan Ave., Suite 1201
Chicago, IL 60611
(312) 397-6700

Petry Television
410 N. Michigan Ave.
Chicago, IL 60611
(312) 644-9660
Television station representatives.

Quantum Media International
875 N. Michigan Ave.
Chicago, IL 60611
(312) 944-7588

SMY Media
333 N. Michigan Ave.
Chicago, IL 60601
(312) 621-9600

Western International Media Corporation
737 N. Michigan Ave., Suite 1200
Chicago, IL 60611
(312) 397-6711

Aerospace/Defense

WEB SITES:

http://www.well.com/user/css/
AIA.HTML
is the homepage of the American
Aerospace Industries Association.

http://www.galcit.caltech.edu/~aure/
htmls/aerolinks.html
links to aeronautics resources.

http://brad.net/aero_outlook/
discusses industry trends; links to
associations, journals, and government
agencies.

PROFESSIONAL ORGANIZATIONS:

For information in aerospace and related
fields, you can contact:

Aerospace Education Foundation
1501 Lee Highway
Arlington, VA 22209
(703) 247-5839

Areospace Electrical Society
P.O. Box 24883, Village Station
Los Angeles, CA 90024

**Aerospace Industries Association of
America**
1250 I St., N.W.
Washington, DC 20005
(202) 371-8400

**American Institute of Aeronautics and
Astronautics**
370 L'Enfant Promenade, S.W.
Washington, DC 20024
(703) 264-7500

**International Association of Machinists
& Aerospace Workers**
9000 Machinists Place
Upper Marlboro, MD 20772
(301) 967-4500

Society of Senior Aerospace Executives
1100 15th St., N.W., Suite 300
Washington, DC 20005
(202) 289-0500

Women in Aerospace
922 Pennsylvania Ave., S.E.
Washington, DC 20003
(202) 547-9451

PROFESSIONAL PUBLICATIONS:

Aerospace Daily
Aerospace Engineering
Air Jobs Digest
Aviation Week and Space Technology
Business and Commercial Aviation
Space Commerce Week

DIRECTORIES:

Aviation Week & Space Technology,
   Marketing Directory Issue (McGraw-Hill
   Publishing Co., New York, NY)
International ABC Aerospace Directory
   (Jane's Information Group, Alexandria,
   VA)

Employers:

Aircraft Gear Corp.
6633 W. 65th St.
Bedford Park, IL 60638
(708) 594-2100
Precision aircraft, missile gearing & gear
assembly

Barnes & Reinecke
425 E. Algonquin Road
Arlington Heights, IL 60005
(847) 640-7200
Design engineering and logistics services
for military and automotive applications.

CEF Industries-Calco Division
320 S. Church St.
Addison, IL 60101
(630) 628-2299
Aircraft accessories, fractional high-
temperature motors.

IIT Research Institute
10 W. 35th St.
Chicago, IL 60616
(312) 567-4000
Provider of contract research and development.

Motorola, Inc. / Communications Sector
1299 E. Algonquin Road
Schaumburg, IL 60196
(847) 576-5000
Manufacturer of command control and communications systems.

Northrop Grumman Corp. / Electronics Systems and Integration Division
600 Hicks Road
Rolling Meadows, IL 60008
(847) 259-9600
Manufacturer of electronic systems, electronic warfare equipment and transportation systems; and provider of related services.

Scot, Inc.
2525 Curtiss St.
Downers Grove, IL 60515
(630) 969-0620
Explosive actuated devices, escape systems & missiles.

Apparel/Fashion/Cosmetics

WEB SITES:

http://www.apparelex.com/
has links to over 26,000 apparel and textile companies.

PROFESSIONAL ORGANIZATIONS:

For networking in the apparel and fashion industries and related fields, check out this local professional organization listed in Chapter 5:

Chicago Cosmetologists Association

For additional information, you can contact:

American Apparel Manufacturers Association
2500 Wilson Blvd., Suite 301
Arlington, VA 22201
(703) 524-1864

Apparel Industry Board
350 N. Orleans St.
Chicago, IL 60657
(312) 836-1041

Cosmetic, Toiletry, and Fragrance Association
1101 17th St., N.W., Suite 300
Washington, DC 20036
(202) 331-1770

Council of Fashion Designers of America (CFDA)
1412 Broadway
New York, NY 10018
(212) 302-1821

Fashion Group of Chicago
333 N. Michigan Ave., Suite 2032
Chicago, IL 60601
(312) 372-4811

International Association of Clothing Designers
475 Park Ave. South
New York, NY 10016
(212) 685-6602

PROFESSIONAL PUBLICATIONS:

Apparel Industry Magazine
Beauty Fashion
Cosmetic World News
Cosmetics and Toiletries
Fashion Newsletter
New York Apparel News
Women's Wear Daily

DIRECTORIES:

Apparel Industry Sourcebook (Denyse & Co., Inc., North Hollywood, CA)
Apparel Trades Book (Dun & Bradstreet, Inc., New York, NY)
Beauty Fashion, Fragrance Directory issue (Beauty Fashion, Inc. New York, NY)
Garment Manufacturer's Index (Klevens Publications, Littlerock, CA)
Membership Directory (American Apparel Manufacturers Association, Arlington, VA)
Wholesale/Manufacturers Apparel Directory (American Business Lists, Omaha, NE)
Who's Who: The CFTA Membership Directory (Cosmetic, Toiletry, and Fragrance Assoc., Washington, DC)

Employers:

Alberto Culver
2525 Armitage Ave.
Melrose Park, IL 60160
(708) 450-3000
Diversified manufacturer of cosmetics and foods.

Artra Group
500 Central Ave.
Northfield, IL 60093
(847) 441-6650
Distributor of costume jewelry.

Avon Products
6901 Golf Road
Morton Grove, IL 60053
(708) 966-0200
World's largest distributor of cosmetics, fragrances, and jewelry via in-home sales.

Caron, Inc.
350 W. Kinzie
Chicago, IL 60610
(312) 670-3700
Women's suits, dresses & sportswear.

Choi Brothers
3401 W. Division
Chicago, IL 60651
(773) 489-2800
Industrial uniforms.

Cosmetique, Inc.
200 Corporate Woods Parkway
Vernon Hills, IL 60061
(847) 913-9099
National beauty continuity club.

Farley Industries
233 S. Wacker Drive, Suite 5000
Chicago, IL 60606
(312) 876-1724
Manufacturer of Fruit of the Loom
underwear and activewear.

Florsheim Shoe Co.
Div. of Interco, Inc.
130 S. Canal St.
Chicago, IL 60606
(312) 559-2500
Men's shoes.

Hartmarx Corp.
101 N. Wacker Drive
Chicago, IL 60606
(312) 372-6300
Men's suits.

Helene Curtis Industries
325 N. Wells St.
Chicago, IL 60619
(312) 661-0222
Manufacturer of cosmetics and hair
preparations.

Heyman Corp.
6045 W. Howard St.
Niles, IL 60714
(847) 647-0909
Children's clothing.

Howard, Don, Industries
4245 N. Knox
Chicago, IL 60641
(312) 263-6700
Maternity clothes & lingerie.

Humphreys' Inc.
2009 W. Hastings
Chicago, IL 60608
(312) 997-2358
Leather belts, wallets, suspenders, caps &
jewelry.

Integrity Uniform Co.
3801 W. Lawrence Ave.
Chicago, IL 60625
(773) 463-2626
Uniforms.

Johnson & Johnson
901 E. Kankakee River Drive
Wilmington, IL 60481
(815) 476-2123
Products for health and personal care.

Johnson Products, Co.
8522 S. Lafayette Ave.
Chicago, IL 60620
(773) 483-4100
Cosmetics.

Magid Glove & Safety Manufacturing Co.
2060 N. Kolmar Ave.
Chicago, IL 60639
(773) 384-2070
Safety clothing, aprons, glasses & gloves.

Marilyn Miglin
112 E. Oak St.
Chicago, IL 60611
(312) 943-1120
Cosmetics, skin care, and fragrance
products.

O'Bryan Brothers
4220 W. Belmont Ave.
Chicago, IL 60641
(773) 283-3000
Manufacturer of women's lingerie.

Oxxford Clothes
1220 W. Van Buren St.
Chicago, IL 60607
(312) 829-3600
Men's clothing.

Royal Knitting Mills
2007 S. California Ave.
Chicago, IL 60608
(773) 247-6300
Knit outerwear.

Rubens & Marble
2340 N. Racine Ave.
Chicago, IL 60614
(773) 348-6200
Infant underwear.

Rubin Manufacturing
2241 S. Halsted St.
Chicago, IL 60608
(312) 738-0222
Industrial protective clothing & outerwear.

Schuessler Knitting Mills
1523 N. Fremont St.
Chicago, IL 60622
(312) 642-1490
Knitted hats.

Soft Sheen Products
1000 E. 87th St.
Chicago, IL 60619
(773) 978-0700
Cosmetics.

Contracting for a career in fashion

We asked Gary Randazzo, president of a mid-sized contractor of women's apparel, to explain the lines of distribution in the apparel, or garment, industry. "Contractors are the first step in a long and often confusing line of distribution for a garment," says Randazzo. "Contractors put the goods together for manufacturers who do not have their own shops. This is what is known as piece work, assembling garments that have been cut and need only to be sewn together. Some contractors do the actual cutting of the material and construct the garment from the pattern to finished product. The public is generally not aware that contractors even exist, but they are a very important part of the chain.

"Once a garment has been finished, it is usually sent back to the manufacturer for sale to a wholesaler. It is then sold to the retail market. In some instances, large apparel companies can be considered wholesalers and manufacturers. They may also operate retail arms."

We asked if working for a contractor can help round out your experience in the garment industry. "Absolutely. After working for even a small contractor you can move to quality control, product management, and even inventory control for manufacturers or wholesalers. Also, you learn the business from the ground up: working on the shop floor examining dresses, dealing with employees, making contacts with wholesalers and manufacturers. That experience is invaluable in any part of the industry."

Architectural Firms

WEB SITES:

http://arch.buffalo.edu:8001/internet/
h_firms.html
links to firms and services.

http://archpropplan.auckland.ac.nz/
misc/sources3.html
links to architectural organizations and newsgroups.

http://199.170.0.130/carprof.htm
discusses careers in architecture.

PROFESSIONAL ORGANIZATIONS:

For networking in architecture and related fields, check out these local professional organizations listed in Chapter 5. Also see "Construction" and "Engineering."

American Architectural Manufacturers
   Association
American Institute of Architects,
   Chicago Chapter
Builders Association of Chicago
Chicago Architecture Foundation

For additional information, you can write or call:

American Institute of Architects
1735 New York Ave., N.W.
Washington, DC 20006
(202) 626-7300

Society of American Registered
Architects
1245 S. Highland Ave.
Lombard, IL 60148
(630) 932-4622

PROFESSIONAL PUBLICATIONS:

AIA Journal
Architecture
Architectural Record
Architectural Review
Building Design & Construction
Progressive Architecture

DIRECTORIES:

AIA Membership Directory (American
   Institute of Architects, Washington, DC)
Architects Directory (American Business
   Directories, Inc., Omaha, NE)
*International Directory of Architects and
   Architecture* (St. James Press, Detroit, MI)
Penguin Directory of Architecture (Viking
   Penguin, New York, NY)
*Society of American Registered Architects
   National Membership Directory* (Society
   of American Registered Architects,
   Lombard, IL)

Employers:

Balsam/Olson Group
1 S. 376 Summit Ave.
Oakbrook Terrace, IL 60181
(630) 629-9800

BCA Architects
150 N. Wacker Drive
Chicago, IL 60601
(312) 578-9502

Belluschi, Anthony, Architects
55 W. Monroe, Suite 200
Chicago, IL 60603
(312) 236-6751

Bernheim, Kahn & Elisco
5 Revere Drive,
Northbrook, IL 60062
(847) 480-1333

Booth & Hansen
555 S. Dearborn St.
Chicago, IL 60605
(312) 427-0300

Cox, James, Associates
345 N. Canal
Chicago, IL 60606
(312) 454-0060

DeStafano and Partners
445 E. Illinois St.
Chicago, IL 60611
(312) 836-4321

Edwards & Kelcey
1480 Northwest Highway, Suite 408
Park Ridge, IL 60068
(847) 297-1172

Epstein, A., & Sons International
600 W. Fulton St.
Chicago, IL 60661-1199
(312) 454-9100

Frega, John Victor, Associates, Ltd.
411 S. Wells St.
Chicago, IL 60607
(312) 663-0640

Fujikawa Johnson & Associates
111 E. Wacker Drive, Suite 3015
Chicago, IL 60601
(312) 565-2727

Green Hiltscher Shapiro
1021 W. Adams, Suite 300
Chicago, IL 60607
(312) 243-8230

Hansen, Lind, Meyer
35 E. Wacker Drive, Suite 1600
Chicago, IL 60601
(312) 609-1300

Holabird & Root
300 W. Adams St.
Chicago, IL 60606
(312) 726-5960

HSW, Ltd. Architects & Planners
137 N. Wabash Ave., Suite 504
Chicago, IL 60602
(312) 263-2338

Jenkins Group CFO
300 Park Blvd., Suite 250
Itasca, IL 60143
(630) 250-9100

Kirkegaard, R. Lawrence, & Associates
4910 Main St.
Downers Grove, IL 60515
(630) 810-5980

Knight, Lester B., & Associates
549 W. Randolph St.
Chicago, IL 60661
(312) 346-2100

Legat Architects
24 N. Chapel St.
Waukegan, IL 60085
(847) 662-3535

Loebel, Schlossman & Hackl
130 E. Randolph, Suite 3400
Chicago, IL 60601
(312) 565-1800

Loewenberg Associates
875 N. Dearborn, Suite 350
Chicago, IL 60610
(312) 440-9600

Lohan Associates
225 N. Michigan Ave., Suite 800
Chicago, IL 60601
(312) 938-4455

McClier
401 E. Illinois St., Suite 625
Chicago, IL 60611
(312) 836-7700

Murphy/Jahn
35 E. Wacker Drive, 3rd floor
Chicago, IL 60601
(312) 427-7300

Nagle & Hartray
1 IBM Plaza, Suite 2301
Chicago, IL 60611
(312) 832-6900

**O'Donnell, Wicklund, Pigozzi &
Peterson Architects**
570 Lake Cook Road
Deerfield, IL 60015
(847) 940-9600

Otis Associates
1450 E. American Lane, Suite 1300
Schaumburg, IL 60173
(847) 517-7100

Perkins & Will
330 N. Wabash Ave., Suite 3600
Chicago, IL 60611
(312) 755-0770

Schipporeit, Inc.
351 W. Hubbard St.
Chicago, IL 60610
(312) 670-4480

Schuler & Shook
213 W. Institute Place
Chicago, IL 60610
(312) 944-8230

Skidmore, Owings & Merrill
224 S. Michigan Ave., Suite 1000
Chicago, IL 60604
(312) 554-9090

Solomon, Cordwell, Buenz & Associates
57 W. Grand Ave., Suite 800
Chicago, IL 60610
(312) 245-5250

STS Consultants
111 Pfingston Road
P.O. Box 10019
Northbrook, IL 60062
(847) 272-6520

Tigerman/McCurry Associates
444 N. Wells St.
Chicago, IL 60610
(312) 644-5880

VOA Associates
224 S. Michigan Ave., Suite 1400
Chicago, IL 60604
(312) 554-1400

Weese, Harry, & Associates
10 W. Hubbard St.
Chicago, IL 60610
(312) 467-7030

Wight & Co.
814 Ogden Ave.
Downers Grove, IL 60515
(708) 969-7000

Zisook, Edmond N., & Associates
176 W. Adams St., Suite 1900
Chicago, IL 60603
(312) 332-3347

Associations and Association Management

Association management—a great place to start for liberal arts grads

Associations—trade organizations, individual membership societies, and voluntary organizations—are often an overlooked job market. Associations offer a variety of positions in administration, marketing, public relations, finance, publishing, membership, government relations, education, information systems, and events planning. You can work for the association itself—and Chicago is headquarters to some of the largest organizations—or for an association management firm, and wear a lot of hats.

WEB SITES:

http://www.asaenet.org/new/ nrindex.html
is the site for the American Society of Association Executives..

PROFESSIONAL ORGANIZATIONS:

For information on associations and association management, you can contact:

American Society of Association Executives
1575 I St., N.W.
Washington, DC 20005
(202) 626-2723
Publishes two on-line newsletters, *ASAE Career Opps* and *CEO Job Opportunities Update,* listing job openings nationwide. See their Web site listed above.

PROFESSIONAL PUBLICATIONS:

Association Leader
Association Management
Leadership: the Magazine for Volunteer Assn. Leaders

DIRECTORIES:

Who's Who in Association Management
(American Society of Assn. Executives, Washington, DC)

Employers:

American Academy of Orthopaedic Surgeons
6300 N. River Road
Rosemont, IL 60018
(847) 823-7186

American Academy of Pediatrics
141 Northwest Point Blvd.
Elk Grove Village, IL 60009
(847) 228-5005

American Bar Association
750 N. Lake Shore Drive
Chicago, IL 60611
(312) 988-5000

American College of Surgeons
55 E. Erie St.
Chicago, IL 60611
(312) 664-4050

American Dental Association
211 E. Chicago Ave.
Chicago, IL 60611
(312) 440-2500

American Dietetic Association
216 W. Jackson Blvd.
Chicago, IL 60606
(312) 899-0040

American Hospital Association
1 N. Franklin St.
Chicago, IL 60606
(312) 422-3000

American Library Association
50 E. Huron St.
Chicago, IL 60611
(312) 944-6780

American Medical Association
515 N. State St.
Chicago, IL 60610
(312) 464-5000

American Soc. of Clinical Pathologists
2100 W. Harrison St.
Chicago, IL 60612
(312) 738-1336

Bostrom Corp.
435 N. Michigan Ave.
Chicago, IL 60611
(312) 644-0828
Association management.

College of American Pathologists
325 Waukegan Road
Northfield, IL 60093
(847) 832-7000

Gas Research Institute
8600 W. Bryn Mawr Ave.
Chicago, IL 60631
(773) 399-8100

International Assn. of Lions Clubs
300 22nd St.
Oak Brook, IL 60521
(630) 571-5466

McRand, Inc.
1 Westminster Place
Lake Forest, IL 60045
(847) 295-3300
Conference management services.

Metropolitan Chicago Health Care Council
222 S. Riverside Plaza
Chicago, IL 60606
(312) 906-6000

Murphy & Murphy
325 W. Huron St.
Chicago, IL 60610
(312) 440-0540
Association management.

National Assn. of Independent Insurers
2600 River Road
Des Plaines, IL 60018
(847) 297-7800

National Assn. of Realtors
430 N. Michigan Ave.
Chicago, IL 60601
(312) 329-8200

National Futures Association
200 W. Madison St., Suite 1600
Chicago, IL 60606
(312) 781-1300

Rotary International
1560 Sherman Ave.
Evanston, IL 60201
(847) 866-3000

Sherwood Group
60 Revere Drive
Northbrook, IL 60022
(847) 480-9080
Association management.

Smith, Bucklin & Associates
401 N. Michigan Ave.
Chicago, IL 60611
(312) 644-6610
Association management.

Automobile/Truck/Transportation Equipment

WEB SITES:

http://autocenter.com/cache/index/
Directory/index.html
is a directory of automotive
manufacturers.

http://www.catalog.com/miata/
carinfo.html
contains links to automotive sites and
companies.

PROFESSIONAL ORGANIZATIONS:

For information on the automotive
industry, you can contact:

**ASIA (Automotive Service Industry
Assn.)**
25 N.W. Point
Elk Grove Village, IL 60007
(847) 228-1310

**MEMA (Motor Equipment Manufactur-
ers Assn.)**
1225 New York Ave., N.W., Suite 300
Washington, D.C. 20005
(202) 393-6362

PROFESSIONAL PUBLICATIONS:

Automotive Marketing
Automotive News
Ward's Automotive Reports

DIRECTORIES:

ASIA Membership Directory (Automotive
  Service Industry Assoc., Elk Grove
  Village, IL)
Automotive News, Market Data Book Issue
  (Crain Communications, Detroit, MI)
Ward's Automotive Yearbook (Ward's
  Communications, Detroit, MI)

Employers:

Borg-Warner Corp.
200 S. Michigan Ave.
Chicago, IL 60603
(312) 322-8500
Diversified manufacturer of automotive
components.

Capsonic Group
1401 Howard St.
Elk Grove Village, IL 60007
(847) 888-7530
Automotive switches.

Cardwell Westinghouse
8400 S. Stewart Ave.
Chicago, IL 60620
(773) 483-7575
Railroad parts & braking systems.

Commercial-Cam Co.
1444 S. Wolf Road
Wheeling, IL 60090
(847) 459-5200
Index drives, overload clutches & cams,
indexing conveyors.

Darley, W. S., & Co.
2000 Anson Drive
Melrose Park, IL 60160
(708) 345-8050
Fire protection & police equipment,
pumps & brass goods.

Dynagear, Inc.
2500 Curtiss St.
Downers Grove, IL 60515
(630) 969-1008
Automotive timing gears, sprockets &
chains.

Electro-Motive
9301 W. 55th St.
La Grange, IL 60525
(708) 387-6000
Diesel & electric locomotives, engines, oil
drilling equipment.

Fel-Pro, Inc.
7450 N. McCormick Blvd.
Skokie, IL 60076
(847) 674-7700
Gaskets, packings, rubber products, seals, sealers, adhesives.

Filtran
875 Seegers Road
P.O. Box 328
Des Plaines, IL 60016
(847) 635-6670
Automatic transmission filters & automotive stampings.

Ford Motor Co.
12600 S. Torrence Ave.
Chicago, IL 60633
(773) 646-3100
Automobiles.

Ford Motor Co., Stamping Plant
1000 E. Lincoln Highway
Chicago Heights, IL 60411
(708) 757-5700
Automobile body stamping.

Hendrickson Spring
2441 W. 48th St.
Chicago, IL 60632
(773) 376-1200
Truck & trailer springs.

Midas International Corp.
225 S. Michigan Ave.
Chicago, IL 60603
(312) 565-7500
National chain of muffler and brake shops.

Navistar International Corp.
455 Cityfront Plaza Drive
Chicago, IL 60611
(312) 836-2000
Diversified manufacturer of trucks and tractors.

North American Gear & Axle
1020 W. 119th St.
Chicago, IL 60643
(773) 821-5450
Automotive gears & heat treating.

Pines Trailer
2555 S. Blue Island Ave.
Chicago, IL 60608
(773) 254-5533
Semi-trailers.

Precision Universal Joint
3440 N. Kedzie
Chicago, IL 60618
(773) 478-0404
Automotive universal joints.

Sate-Lite Manufacturing Co.
6230 Gross Point Road
Niles, IL 60714
(847) 647-1515
Plastic injection molding, automobile & bicycle parts.

Thrall Car Manufacturing Co.
2521 State St.
P.O. Box 218
Chicago Heights, IL 60411
(708) 757-5900
Railroad cars & equipment.

Whitney, J.C., Co.
1104 S. Wabash Ave.
Chicago, IL 60605
(312) 431-6000
Catalog retailer of auto parts.

Trading information at trade shows

Trade shows, those large industry gatherings that fill the hotels, make restaurant reservations tough to get, and tie up traffic around Chicago's McCormick Place exhibition hall, provide excellent opportunities for savvy job hunters. Although most are restricted to "the trade"—meaning people already working in a particular industry or its customers—many will let you register for a day upon paying a small fee. Here are some of the largest trade shows often held in Chicago, and their sponsoring organizations to call for information:

National Restaurant Show (May)   National Restaurant Assn. (312) 853-2525

World Sports Expo (July)   National Sporting Goods Assn. (847) 439-4000

National Hardware Show (August)   American Hardware Mfg. Assn. (708) 605-1025

International Housewares Show (January)   National Housewares Mfg. Assn. (708) 292-4200

American Booksellers Assn. (June)   American Booksellers Assn. (914) 591-2665

National Premium Incentive Show (September)   Hall-Erickson Co. (630) 850-7779

Chicago's McCormick Place and its satellite buildings host more trade shows than any other exhibition halls. You can find out about upcoming shows by calling the Trade Show Scheduling Hotline at (312) 791-6500.

Banks: Commercial and Savings/Credit Unions

WEB SITES:

http://www.wiso.gwdg.de/ifbg/
bank_usa.html
links to homepages of US banks.

http://www.cybercash.com/
directory.html
is a directory of consumer banks.

http://www.bankrate.com/bankrate/
rates/xrefindx.htm
lists names of financial institutions with
Web sites.

PROFESSIONAL ORGANIZATIONS:

For networking in the banking industry
and related fields, check out these local
professional organizations listed in
Chapter 5. Also see **"Stock Brokers/
Financial Services."**
American Institute of Banking
Bank Administration Institute
Bank Marketing Association
Chicago Finance Exchange
Government Finance Officers
    Association
Illinois Association of Mortgage Brokers
Illinois Bankers Association

For additional information, you can
contact:

American Bankers Association
1120 Connecticut Ave., N.W.
Washington, DC 20036
(202) 663-5000

Bank Marketing Association
1120 Connecticut Ave.
Washington, D.C. 20036
(202) 663-5422

Financial Management Association
College of Business Administration
University of South Florida
Tampa, FL 33620
(813) 974-2084

Financial Women International
7910 Woodmony Ave., Suite 1430
Bethesda, MD 20814
(301) 657-8288

**Mortgage Bankers Association of
America**
1125 15th St., N.W.
Washington, DC 20005
(202) 861-6500

National Bankers Association
1802 T St., N.W.
Washington, DC 20009
(202) 588-5432

PROFESSIONAL PUBLICATIONS:

ABA Banking Journal
American Banker
Bank Letter
Bank Management
Bank Marketing Magazine
Bankers Magazine
Bankers Monthly
*Barron's National Business and Financial
    Weekly*

DIRECTORIES:

American Bank Directory (McFadden
    Business Publications, Norcross, GA)
*Directory of American Savings and Loan
    Associations* (T.K. Sanderson Organiza-
    tion, Baltimore, MD)
Financial Yellow Book (Monitor Publish-
    ing, New York, NY)
Money Market Directory (Money Market
    Directories, Charlottesville, VA)
Moody's Bank and Finance Manual
    (Moody's Investors Service, New York,
    NY)
Polk's Bank Directory (R.L. Polk, Nashville,
    TN)
Rand McNally Bankers Directory (Rand
    McNally, Chicago, IL)
Savings and Loan Association Directory
    (American Business Directories, Omaha,
    NE)
Who's Who in International Banking (Reed
    Reference Publishing, New Providence,
    NJ)

Employers, Commercial Banks:

Amalgamated Bank of Chicago
1 W. Monroe St.
Chicago, IL 60603
(312) 822-3000

**American National Bank & Trust
Company of Chicago**
33 W. La Salle St.
Chicago, IL 60602-2651
(312) 661-5000
21 Branches

BankAmerica
231 S. LaSalle St.
Chicago, IL 60697
(312) 828-2345

Bank One, Chicago
800 Davis St.
P.O. Box 712
Evanston, IL 60204-0712
(847) 866-5500
21 Branches

Bank of Northern Illinois
1 S. Genesee St.
Waukegan, IL 60085-5602
(847) 623-3800
5 Branches

Beverly Bank
1357 W. 103rd St.
Chicago, IL 60643-2395
(773) 881-2200
5 Branches

Chicago Title and Trust Co.
171 N. Clark St.
Chicago, IL 60602
(312) 223-2000

Cole Taylor Bank
850 W. Jackson Blvd.
Chicago, IL 60607-3078
(312) 738-2000
9 Branches

Columbia National Bank of Chicago
5250 W. Harlem Ave.
Chicago, IL 60656-1804
(773) 775-6800
7 Branches

Comerica Bank-Illinois
3044 Rose St.
Franklin Park, IL 60131-2714
(847) 202-3333
26 Branches

Federal Reserve Bank
230 S. LaSalle St.
Chicago, IL 60604
(312) 322-5322

First Bank
410 N. Michigan Ave.
P.O. Box 8102
Chicago, IL 60680-8102
(312) 836-6500
9 Branches

**First National Bank of Chicago/NBD
Bank**
1 First National Plaza
Chicago, IL 60670
(312) 732-4000
91 Branches

First National Bank
100 1st National Plaza
Chicago Heights, IL 60411-3539
(708) 754-3100
5 Branches

Firstar Bank Illinois
30 N. Michigan Ave.
P.O. Box 528
Chicago, IL 60690-0528
(312) 641-1000
43 Branches

Grand National Bank
265 Virginia St.
Crystal Lake, IL 60014-8736
(815) 459-4600
5 Branches

Harris Bank Barrington
201 S. Grove Ave.
Barrington, IL 60010-4493
(847) 381-4000
7 Branches

Harris Bank Libertyville
354 W. Milwaukee Ave.
Libertyville, IL 60048-2252
(847) 362-3500
4 Branches

Harris Bank Palatine
50 W. Brockway St.
P.O. Box 39
Palatine, IL 60078-0039
(847) 359-1070
7 Branches

Harris Bank Roselle
110 E. Irving Park Road
P.O. Box 72200
Roselle, IL 60172-0200
(630) 980-2700
4 Branches

Harris Bank St. Charles
1 E. Main St.
Saint Charles, IL 60174-1981
(630) 377-4100
5 Branches

Harris Trust & Savings Bank
111 W. Monroe St.
Chicago, IL 60690-0755
(312) 461-2121
9 Branches

Heritage Bank
12015 Western Ave.
Blue Island, IL 60406-1100
(708) 385-2900
14 Branches

LaSalle Bank
139 W. Cass Ave.
P.O. Box 215
Westmont, IL 60559-0215
(630) 964-1000
5 Branches

LaSalle Bank Lake View
3201 W. Ashland Ave.
Chicago, IL 60657-2182
(773) 525-2180
5 Branches

LaSalle National Bank
135 S. La Salle St.
Chicago, IL 60690-0729
(312) 443-2300

LaSalle Northwest National Bank
4747 W. Irving Park Road
Chicago, IL 60641-2791
(773) 777-7700
10 Branches

Marquette National Bank
6316 S. Western Ave.
Chicago, IL 60636-2491
(773) 476-5100
11 Branches

Mid-City National Bank of Chicago
2 Mid-City Plaza, Madison & Halsted Sts.
Chicago, IL 60607
(312) 421-7600
10 Branches

NBD Bank
211 S. Wheaton Ave.
P.O. Box 687
Wheaton, IL 60189-0687
(630) 665-2600
64 Branches

North Community Bank
3639 W. Broadway St.
Chicago, IL 60613-4489
(773) 248-9500
9 Branches

Northern Trust Bank
8501 W. Higgins Road
Chicago, IL 60631-2801
(773) 693-5555
5 Branches

Northern Trust Bank
265 Deerpath Road
Lake Forest, IL 60045
(847) 615-4183

Northern Trust Bank
1 Oakbrook Terrace
Oakbrook Terrace, IL 60521
(630) 691-2299

Northern Trust Bank
62 Green Bay Road
Winnetka, IL 60093
(847) 446-6300

Northern Trust Company
50 S. La Salle St.
Chicago, IL 60603-1003
(312) 630-6000
53 Branches

Oak Brook Bank
1400 16th St.
Oak Brook, IL 60521-1300

(630) 571-1050
9 Branches

Old Kent Bank
105 S. York St.
P.O. Box 8618
Elmhurst, IL 60126-8618
(630) 941-5200
25 Branches

Republic Bank of Chicago
1510 75th St.
Darien, IL 60561-4407
(630) 241-4500
7 Branches

Seaway National Bank
645 E. 87th St.
Chicago, IL 60619
(773) 487-4800

South Shore Bank
7054 S. Jeffrey Blvd.
Chicago, IL 60637
(773) 288-1000

Success National Bank
1 Marriott Drive
Lincolnshire, IL 60069-3703
(847) 634-4200
6 Branches

U.S. Bank
17130 Torrence Ave.
Lansing, IL 60438
(708) 474-1010
5 Branches

West Suburban Bank
701-711 S. Meyers Road
Lombard, IL 60148
(630) 629-4200
9 Branches

West Suburban Bank of Carol Stream/ Stratford Square
355 W. Army Trail Road
Bloomingdale, IL 60108-1397
(630) 351-0600
5 Branches

Employers, Savings Banks:

Advance Bank
2320 Thorton Road

Lansing, IL 60438
(708) 474-1600
11 Branches

Avondale Federal Savings Bank
20 W. Clark St.
Chicago, IL 60602-4109
(312) 782-6200
5 Branches

Bell Federal Savings & Loan Association
79 W. Monroe St.
Chicago, IL 60603-4901
(312) 346-1000
13 Branches

Financial Federal Trust & Savings Bank of Olympia Fields
21110 Western Ave.
Olympia Fields, IL 60461-1985
(708) 747-2000
5 Branches

Hinsdale Federal Bank for Savings
1 Grant Square
P.O. Box 386
Hinsdale, IL 60522-0386
(630) 323-1776
9 Branches

Household International
2700 Sanders Road
Prospect Heights, IL 60070
(847) 564-5000
61 Branches

LaSalle Cragin Bank
5200 W. Fullerton Ave.
Chicago, IL 60639-1479
(773) 889-1000
25 Branches

LaSalle Talman Bank
135 S. LaSalle St.
Chicago, IL 60603
(312) 443-2000
59 Branches

Mid America Federal Savings Bank
55th & Holmes, Suite 300
Clarendon Hills, IL 60514
(630) 325-7300
12 Branches

Northwestern Savings Bank
2300 W. Western Ave.
Chicago, IL 60647-3196
(773) 489-2300
5 Branches

Regency Savings Bank
1 Naperville Plaza
P.O. Box 3018
Naperville, IL 60566-7018
(630) 357-4500
11 Branches

St. Paul Federal Bank for Savings
6700 W. North Ave.
Chicago, IL 60635-3937
(773) 622-5000
52 Branches

Suburban Federal Savings
154th St. at Broadway
P.O. Box 1076
Harvey, IL 60426-7076
(708) 333-2200
12 Branches

Superior Bank FSB
440 Ogden Ave.
Hinsdale, IL 60521
(630) 323-2900
8 Branches

TCF Bank Illinois
1420 Kensington Road, Suite 320
Oak Brook, IL 60521-2171
(630) 571-3332
31 Branches

Employers, Credit Unions:

Air Line Pilots Association Federal Credit Union
825 Midway Drive
Willowbrook, IL 60521
(630) 789-2575

AT&T Teletype Federal Credit Union
5550 W. Touhy Ave., Suite 102
Skokie, IL 60077-3254
(847) 676-8000

Baxter Credit Union
1425 Lake Cook Road
Deerfield, IL 60015-5213
(847) 940-6300

Chicago Municipal Employees Credit Union
180 W. La Salle St., Suite 410
Chicago, IL 60601-2504
(312) 236-2326

Chicago Patrolmens Federal Credit Union
203 W. Wabash Ave., 2nd floor
Chicago, IL 60601
(312) 726-8814

Consumers Cooperative Credit Union
2750 Washington St.
Waukegan, IL 60085-4900
(847) 623-3636

DuPage Schools Credit Union
401 S. Carlton
Wheaton, IL 60187
(630) 668-3440

Edison Credit Union
300 W. Adams St., Suite 330
Chicago, IL 60606-5170
(312) 332-6357

Federal Center Employees Credit Union
230 S. Dearborn St., Suite 2962
Chicago, IL 60604-1601
(312) 922-5310

Motorola Employees Credit Union
1205 E. Algonquin Road
Schaumburg, IL 60196-1065
(847) 576-5000

United Air Lines Employees Credit Union
125 E. Algonquin Road
Arlington Heights, IL 60005-4617
(847) 700-8700

United Bell Credit Union
309 W. Washington St., Suite 350
Chicago, IL 60606-3202
(312) 332-3311

United Credit Union
4444 S. Pulaski Road
Chicago, IL 60632-4011
(773) 376-6000

Zenith Federal Credit Union
1900 W. Austin Ave.
Chicago, IL 60639-5001
(773) 745-3241

Broadcasting

WEB SITES:

http://www.yahoo.com/text/
Business_and_Economy/Companies/
Media/Television/
links to networks, cable, and local
stations.

http://radio.aiss.uiuc.edu/~rrb/
stations.html
is a guide to radio station sites.

PROFESSIONAL ORGANIZATIONS:

For networking in radio, television, and
related fields, check out these local professional organizations listed in Chapter 5.

AFTRA
American Women in Radio and
    Television
Association for Multi Image
Broadcast Cable Financial Management
    Association
Center for New Television
Chicago Area Broadcast Public Affairs
    Association
Chicago Audio Visual Producers
    Association
Chicago Headline Club
National Broadcast Association for
    Community Affairs

For additional information, contact:

**American Federation of Television and
Radio Artists**
260 Madison Ave.
New York, NY 10016
(212) 532-0800

American Radio Association
17 Battery Place, Room 1443
New York, NY 10004
(212) 809-0600

Corporation for Public Broadcasting
901 E St., N.W.
Washington DC 20004
(202) 879-9600

**National Academy of Television Arts and
Sciences**
111 W. 57th St.
New York, NY 10019
(212) 586-8424

**National Association of African-
American Sportwriters and Broadcasters**
21 Bedford St.
Wyandanch, NY 11798
(516) 491-7774

National Association of Broadcasters
1771 N St., N.W.
Washington, DC 20036
(202) 429-5300

**National Association of Television
Program Executives**
2425 Olympic Blvd., Suite 550E
Santa Monica, CA 90404
(310) 453-4440

National Cable Television Association
1724 Massachusetts Ave., N.W.
Washington DC 20036
(202) 775-3550

National Radio Broadcasters Association
2033 M St., N.W.
Washington, DC 20036
(202) 429-5420

PROFESSIONAL PUBLICATIONS:

Billboard
Broadcast Communications
Broadcasting and Cable
Broadcasting Magazine
Cable World
Communications News
Radio World
Ross Reports
Television Broadcast
TV Radio Age
Variety

DIRECTORIES:

BPI TV News Contacts (BPI Media Services, New York, NY)

Broadcasting Cable Source Book (Broadcasting Publishing Co., Washington, DC)

Broadcasting and Cable Yearbook (R.R. Bowker, New Providence, NJ))

Cable Programming Resource Directory: A Guide to Community TV Production

Facilities and Programming Services and Outlets (Broadcasting Publications, Washington, DC)

Gale Directory of Publications and Broadcast Media (Gale Research, Detroit, MI)

Television and Cable Fact Book (Warren Publishing, Washington, DC)

Who's Who in Television (Packard House, Beverly Hills, CA)

Breaking into broadcasting

We asked a radio station executive how to get started in broadcasting.

"Persevere," she says. "One of my first interviews was with the personnel director of a television station in Peoria. 'Do you realize,' he said, 'that Northwestern graduated hundreds of communications majors last year alone? There aren't that many job openings in the whole state.'

"That was a sobering thought. It discourages a lot of people. But you have to keep in there. Send out resumes, read the trades, see who's switching formats, and all that. Do anything on the side that might result in a good lead. The year after I graduated from college, I took a news writing course taught at Columbia College. In Chicago there are a lot of broadcasting professionals teaching there; taking a course from a working professional can lead to valuable contacts.

"Another important point is to treat your contacts with respect. Broadcasting is a volatile business. You can't afford to burn a lot of bridges or alienate a lot of people. Somebody can be your assistant one day and your boss the next."

Employers, Broadcasting Companies:

American Broadcasting Companies
190 N. State St.
Chicago, IL 60601
(312) 750-7777
Owns and operates WLS-TV, WLS-AM radio, WLS-FM radio, WYTZ-FM radio; local and network news bureaus; local, network, and spot sales offices.

Broadcasting Partners
800 S. Wells
Chicago, IL 60607
(312) 360-9000
Owns and operates WVAZ-FM radio.

Burnham Broadcasting
980 N. Michigan Ave., Suite 1200
Chicago, IL 60611
(312) 787-9800
Owns and operates various network affiliates.

CBS, Inc.
630 N. McClurg Court
Chicago, IL 60611
(312) 944-6000
Owns and operates WBBM-TV, WBBM-AM radio, WBBM-FM radio; local and network news bureaus; local, network, and spot sales offices.

Century Broadcasting Corporation
875 N. Michigan Ave., Suite 3650
Chicago, IL 60611
(312) 922-1000

Colby Broadcast Corporation
6405 Olcott Ave.
Hammond, IN 46320
(219) 844-1230
Owns and operates WJOB-AM radio.

Combined Broadcasting
541 N. Fairbanks, Suite 1100
Chicago, IL 60611
(312) 440-1851
Owns and operates WGBO-TV.

Cox Enterprises
150 N. Michigan Ave., Suite 1040
Chicago, IL 60601
(312) 781-7300
Owns and operates WCKG-FM radio.

Evergreen Media
875 N. Michigan Ave., Suite 3750
Chicago, IL 60611
(312) 440-5270
Owns and operates WLUP-FM. WNUA-FM, and WLUP-AM radio.

Fastpitch USA
P.O. Box 1190
St. Charles, IL 60174
(630) 377-7917
Cable TV "magazine" producer.

Fox Television Stations
205 N. Michigan Ave.
Chicago, IL 60601
(312) 565-5532
Owns and operates WFLD-TV.

Gannett Media Sales
444 N. Michigan Ave.

Chicago, IL 60604
(312) 527-0552
Owns WGCI-FM radio.

GK Sportsflash
1376 W. Grand Ave.
Chicago, IL 60622
(312) 563-0777
Video sports and news producer.

Illiana Broadcasters
2915 Bernice Road
Lansing, IL 60438
(708) 895-1400
Operates WJPC-FM radio.

Infinity Broadcasting Co.
180 N. Michigan Ave., Suite 1200
Chicago, IL 60601
(312) 977-1800
Owns and operates WUSN-FM, WJJD-AM, and WJMK-FM radio.

Intersport Television
414 W. Orleans Plaza, Suite 600
Chicago, IL 60610
(312) 661-0616
Cable TV program producer.

Jones Spacelink
1107 E. Roosevelt Road
Wheaton, IL 60187
(630) 260-8808
Cable TV outlet.

Major Broadcasting
130 E. Randolph, Suite 2303
Chicago, IL 60601
(312) 591-4600
Owns and operates WFYR-FM radio.

Major Networks
101 W. Grand Ave.
Chicago, IL 60610
(312) 755-1300
Radio broadcaster and program producer.

Major Sports Marketing
101 W. Grand Ave.
Chicago, IL 60610
(312) 755-1300
Radio broadcaster.

Metrovision Southwest Cook County
7720 W. 98th St.
Hickory Hills, IL 60457
(708) 430-4840
Cable TV outlet.

Metrowest Corporation
2151 N. Elston Ave.
Chicago, IL 60614
(773) 276-5050
Owns and operates WPWR-TV.

Midway Broadcasting Corporation
3350 S. Kedzie Ave.
Chicago, IL 60623
(773) 247-6200

National Broadcasting Co.
NBC Tower
454 N. Columbus Drive
Chicago, IL 60611
(312) 836-5555
Owns and operates WMAQ-TV and
WKQX-FM radio; local and network news
bureaus; local, network, and spot sales
offices.

Northern Illinois Broadcasting Co.
1140 W. Erie St.
Chicago, IL 60622
(312) 633-9700
Owns and operates WNIB-FM radio.

One-on-One Sports Network
1935 Techny Road, Suite 18
Northbrook, IL 60062
(847) 509-1661
Radio broadcaster.

Sportlite Films
Video Division
2970 Lake Shore Drive
Chicago, IL 60657-5644
(773) 477-1517
TV broadcaster.

Sportschannel Chicago
820 W. Madison St.
Oak Park, IL 60302
(708) 524-9444
TV broadcaster and cable TV
programmer.

Tichenor Media Systems
625 N. Michigan Ave., 3rd floor
Chicago, IL 60611
(312) 649-0105
Owns and operates WOJO-FM radio and
WIND-AM radio.

Tribune Broadcasting Co.
2501 W. Bradley Place
Chicago, IL 60618
(773) 528-2311
Owns and operates WGN-TV and WGN-
AM radio.

United Training Media
Div. of United Learning
6633 W. Howard St.
Niles, IL 60714
(847) 647-0600
TV program producer and program
distributor.

Viacom International
150 N. Michigan Ave., Suite 1135
Chicago, IL 60601
(312) 329-8840
Owns and operates WLIT-FM radio.

Westinghouse Broadcasting Co.
NBC Tower
455 N. City Front Plaza
Chicago, IL 60611
(312) 670-6767
Owns and operates WMAQ-AM, WXRT-
FM, and WSCR-AM. radio.

Worldwide Entertainment
500 Davis St.
Evanston, IL 60201
(847) 475-2398
Owns and operates WTMX-FM radio.

Employers, TV Stations and Bureaus:

CBS News
630 N. McClurg Court
Chicago, IL 60611
(312) 951-3313
National news bureau.

NBC News
454 N. Columbus Drive
Chicago, IL 60611-5555
(312) 836-5564
National news bureau.

WBBM-TV
630 N. McClurg Court
Chicago, IL 60654
(312) 944-6000
CBS-owned television station.

WCFC-TV
38 S. Peoria
Chicago, IL 60607
(312) 433-3838
Christian-oriented television station.

WCIU-TV
26 N. Halsted
Chicago, IL 60661
(312) 705-2600
Ethnic issue-oriented television station.

WEHS-TV
100 S. Sangamon, Suite 300
Chicago, IL 60607
(312) 829-8860
The Home Shopping Network.

WGBO-TV
541 N. Fairbanks Court, 11th floor
Chicago, IL 60611
(312) 670-1000
Spanish-format television station.

WGN-TV
Subsidiary of Tribune Broadcasting Co.
2501 Bradley Place
Chicago, IL 60618
(773) 528-2311
TV superstation.

WLS-TV
190 N. State St.
Chicago, IL 60601
(312) 750-7777
ABC-owned television station.

WMAQ-TV
454 N. Columbus Drive
Chicago, IL 60611-5555
(312) 836-5555
NBC-owned television station.

WPWR-TV
2151 N. Elston Ave.
Chicago, IL 60614
(773) 276-5050
UPN-affiliated television station.

WSNS-TV
430 W. Grant Place
Chicago, IL 60625
(773) 583-5000
Spanish-format television station.

WTTW Television
5400 N. St. Louis Ave.
Chicago, IL 60625
(773) 583-5000
Educational station; PBS outlet.

WYCC-TV
7500 S. Pulaski Road
Chicago, IL 60652
(773) 838-7878
Operates Channel 20 for the City Colleges of Chicago.

Employers, Radio Stations:

WBBM-AM Radio
630 N. McClurg Court
Chicago, IL 60611
(312) 944-6000
CBS owned station.

WBEZ Radio
848 E. Grand Ave.
Chicago, IL 60611
(312) 832-9150
Local public radio station; carries NPR.

WCBR-FM
120 W. University Drive
Arlington Hts., IL 60004
(847) 255-5800

WCKG-FM/WYSY-FM
2 Prudential Plaza, Suite 1040
Chicago, IL 60601
(312) 240-7900
Cox Broadcasting station.

WFMT-FM Radio
303 E. Wacker Drive
Chicago, IL 60601
(312) 565-5000
Local fine arts station.

WGCI-AM
332 S. Michigan Ave., Suite 600
Chicago, IL 60604
(312) 427-4800

WGN-AM Radio
435 N. Michigan Ave.
Chicago, IL 60611
(312) 222-4700
Chicago Tribune-owned clear channel
station.

WJJD-AM, WJMK-FM Radio
180 N. Michigan Ave., Suite 1200
Chicago, IL 60601
(312) 977-1800
Infinity Broadcasting owned station.

WKQX-FM
Merchandise Mart
Chicago, IL 60654
(312) 527-8348

WLIT-FM Radio
150 N. Michigan Ave., Suite 1135
Chicago, IL 60601
(312) 329-9002
Viacom-owned station.

WLS-AM, WLS-FM Radio
190 N. State St.
Chicago, IL 60601
(312) 984-0890
ABC-owned stations.

WLUP-FM Radio
875 N. Michigan Ave., Suite 3750
Chicago, IL 60611
(312) 440-5270
Evergreen Media Corp. station.

WMAQ-AM Radio
NBC Tower
455 N. City Front Plaza
Chicago, IL 60611
(312) 245-6000
Westinghouse-owned station.

WMVP-AM Radio
875 W. Michigan Ave., Suite 3750
Chicago, IL 60611
(312) 440-5270
24-hour sports radio programming.

WNUA-FM
444 N. Michigan Ave.
Chicago, IL 60611
(312) 645-9550
Pyramid-owned station.

WPNT Radio
875 N. Michigan Ave., Suite 1510
Chicago, IL 60611
(312) 440-8200

WSCR Sports Radio
4949 W. Belmont Ave.
Chicago, IL 60641
(773) 777-1700
24-hour sports radio programming.

WVON-AM Radio
3350 S. Kedzie Ave.
Chicago, IL 60623
(312) 247-6200

WXRT-FM
4949 W. Belmont Ave.
Chicago, IL 60641
(773) 777-1700
Diamond-owned station.

Employers, Syndicators and Cable:

Cable News Network (CNN)
435 N. Michigan Ave.
Chicago, IL 60611
(312) 645-8555
National news bureau.

CEN
1400 E. Touhy, Suite 260
Des Plaines, IL 60018-3305
(847) 390-8700
Central Educational Network.

Chicago Access Network Television
322 S, Green St.
Chicago, IL 60607
(312) 738-1400
Cable channels including Hotline 21,
CAN-CALL 42, and FYI Chicago TV27.

CLTV News
2000 York Road
Oak Brook, IL 60521
(630) 368-4000
ChicagoLand Television cable station.

CNBC
141 W. Jackson, Suite 1771
Chicago, IL 60604
(312) 341-3016
National news bureau.

ITFS
155 E. Superior
Chicago, IL 60611
(312) 751-8277
Instructional Television Fixed Service.

Jenny Jones Show
NBC Tower
454 N. Columbus
Chicago, IL 60611
(312) 836-9400
Syndicated talk show.

Jerry Springer Show
454 N. Columbus
Chicago, IL 60611
(312) 321-5350
Syndicated talk show.

Oprah Winfrey Show
Harpo Studios
110 N. Carpenter St.
Chicago, IL 60607
(312) 633-0808
Syndicated talk show.

Chemicals

WEB SITES:

**http://www.yahoo.com/
Business_and_Economy/Companies/
Chemicals/**
lists chemical companies and sites.

**http://nearnet.gnn.com/wic/
chem.06.html**
is the homepage of the American
Chemical Society.

PROFESSIONAL ORGANIZATIONS:

For networking in the chemical industry
and related fields, check out this professional organization listed in Chapter 5:

American Chemical Society

For additional information, you can
contact:

American Chemical Society
1155 16th St., N.W.
Washington, DC 20036
(202) 872-4600

Chemical Manufacturers Association
1300 Wilson Blvd.
Arlington, VA 22209
(703) 741-5000

**National Organization for the
Professional Advancements of Black
Chemists and Chemical Engineers**
525 College St., N.W.
Washington, D.C. 20059
(202) 667-1699

PROFESSIONAL PUBLICATIONS:

CFTA Newsletter
Chemical Business
Chemical Industry Update
Chemical Week

DIRECTORIES:

Chem Sources-U.S.A. (Chemical Sources
  International, Clemson, SC)
Chemclopedia (American Chemical
  Society, Washington, DC)
Chemical and Engineering News, Career
  Opportunities Issue (American
  Chemical Society, Washington, DC)
Chemical Week, Buyer's Guide Issue
  (McGraw-Hill, New York, NY)
*Chemical Week: Financial Survey of the 300
  Largest Companies* (McGraw-Hill, New
  York, NY)

Employers:

Abbott Laboratories
1401 Sheridan Road
North Chicago, IL 60064
(847) 937-6100

Akzo Nobel Chemicals
8201 W. 47th St.
McCook, IL 60525
(708) 447-7990

Amersham Life Sciences
2636 S.Clearbrook Drive
Arlington Heights, IL 60005
(847) 593-6300

Benjamin Moore & Co.
North & 25th Avenues
Melrose Park, IL 60160
(708) 343-3100

Dial Corp.
6200 W. 51st St.
Chicago, IL 60638
(312) 458-4890

Henkel Corp.
P.O. Box 191
Kankakee, IL 60901
(815) 932-6751

INX International
1419-1443 W. Carroll Ave.
Chicago, IL 60607
(312) 421-0675

Kester Solder Co.
515 E. Touhy Ave.
Des Plaines, IL 60018
(847) 297-1600

Koppers Industries
3900 S. Laramie Ave.
Cicero, IL 60650
(708) 656-5900

Morton Automotive Coatings
2701 E. 170th St.
Lansing, IL 60438
(708) 474-7000

Morton International
1645 S. Kilbourn Ave.
Chicago, IL 60623
(773) 521-7000

Nalco Chemical Co.
6216 W. 66th Place
Bedford Park, IL 60638
(708) 496-5000

PPG Specialty Surfactants
3938 Porett Drive
Gurnee, IL 60031
(847) 244-3410

Rhone-Poulenc Basic Chemicals Co.
1101 Arnold St.
Chicago Heights, IL 60411
(708) 757-6111

Sherwin-Williams Co.
11541 S. Champlain Ave.
Chicago, IL 60628
(773) 821-3106

Stepan Co.
22 W. Frontage Road
Northfield, IL 60093
(847) 446-7500

Sun Chemical Corp.
135 W. Lake St.
Northlake, IL 60164
(708) 562-0550

TEC Incorporated
315 S. Hicks Road
Palatine, IL 60067
(847) 358-9500

Turtle Wax
1550 N. Fremont
Chicago, IL 60622
(312) 751-3400

UOP
25 E. Algonquin Road
Des Plaines, IL 60017
(847) 391-2000

Velsicol Chemical Corp.
10400 W. Higgins Road
Rosemont, IL 60018
(708) 298-9000

Computers: Hardware/Software

WEB SITES:

http://www.zdnet.com/~zdi/tblazer/
compani.html
lists sites of hardware manufacturers and software developers.

http://www.stars.com/Jobs.html
lists computer opportunities related to Web development.

PROFESSIONAL ORGANIZATIONS:

For networking in the computer industry, check out this local professional organization listed in Chapter 5. Also see **"Computers: Information Management/ Consulting."**

Chicago Computer Society

For additional information, contact:

Computer and Communications Industry Association
666 11th St., N.W.
Washington DC 20001
(202) 783-0070

Data Processing Management Association
505 Busse Highway
Park Ridge, IL 60068
(847) 825-8124

Information Industry Association
555 New Jersey Ave., N.W., Suite 800
Washington, DC 20001
(202) 986-0280

Information Technology Association of America
1616 N. Ft. Myer Drive, Suite 1300
Arlington, VA 22209
(703) 522-5055

Software Publishers Association
1730 M St., N.W., Suite. 700

Washington, DC 20036
(202) 452-1600

PROFESSIONAL PUBLICATIONS:

BYTE
Computer Industry Report
Computer World
Datamation
InfoWorld
Journal of Software Maintenance
PC Computing
PC Letter
PC Magazine
PC Week
Software Magazine

DIRECTORIES:

Data Communications Buyers Guide (McGraw-Hill, New York, NY)
Data Sources: Hardware-Data Communications Directory (Ziff-Davis, New York, NY)
Data Sources: Software Directory (Ziff-Davis, New York, NY)
Datapro Directory of Microcomputer Software (Datapro Information Services Group, Delran, NJ)
Engineering, Science and Computer Jobs (Peterson's Guides, Princeton, NJ)
Guide to High Technology Companies (Corp. Technology Information Services, Woburn, MA)
ICP Software Directory (International Computer Programs, Indianapolis, IN)
Membership Directory (Information Technology Assoc. of America, Arlington, VA)
Software Publishers' Catalog Annual (Meckler Corp., Westport, CT)

Employers:

Ambassador Office Equipment
425 N. Martingale Road
Schaumburg, IL 60173
(847) 706-3400
Exclusive U.S. distributor of Canon office and computer equipment.

Arthur Andersen Worldwide
33 W. Monroe
Chicago, IL 60602
(312) 580-0069
Developer of integrated manufacturing,
distribution and financial system software.

Andrew Corp.
10500 W. 153rd St.
Orland Park, IL 60462
(708) 349-3300
Manufacturer of antenna systems;
developer of emulation and file transfer
utility software.

Anixter International
2 N. Riverside Plaza
Chicago, IL 60606
(312) 902-1515
Networking and cabling materials.

Applied Systems
200 Applied Parkway
University Park, IL 60466
(708) 534-5575
Developer of software for insurance.

BACG
3030 Warrenville Road, Suite 300
Lisle, IL 60532
(630) 505-5775
Developer of physical distribution
software.

Bell & Howell Co. / Scanner Division
6800 N. McCormick Road
Chicago, IL 60645
(847) 675-7600
Manufacturer of bar code, optical, and
optical character recognition scanners.

CCC Information Services
444 Merchandise Mart Plaza
Chicago, IL 60654
(312) 222-4636
Software systems for the insurance and
automotive services industries.

CCH Incorporated
2700 Lake Cook Road
Riverwoods, IL 60015
(847) 267-7000
Developer of accounting software.

C Gate Software
600 E. Diehl Road
Naperville, IL 60563
(630) 505-3300
Developer of data management and
protection software for LANs.

Cimlinc, Inc.
1222 Hamilton Pkwy.
Itasca, IL 60143
(630) 250-0090
Software for UNIX and X Windows
workstations.

**Cincinnati Bell Information Systems /
Mobile Division**
2 Pierce Place, Suite 200
Itasca, IL 60143
(630) 775-1700
Developer of cellular phone system
software.

Coin Controls
1850 Howard St.
Elk Grove Village, IL 60007
(847) 228-1810
Manufacturer of coin validation and
payout equipment.

Comdisco, Inc.
6111 N. River Road
Rosemont, IL 60018
(847) 698-3000
Provider of computer data services.

Comsi, Inc.
600 Hunter Drive, Suite 100
Oak Brook, IL 60521
(630) 571-6600
Programming.

Cyborg Systems
2 N. Riverside Plaza
Chicago, IL 60606
(312) 454-1865
Developer of personnel and payroll
software.

Dainippon Screen (USA)
5110 Tollview Drive
Rolling Meadows, IL 60008
(847) 870-7400
Distributor of graphics arts computer
systems and equipment.

Delphi Information Systems
3501 Algonquin Road, Suite 500
Rolling Meadows, IL 60008
(847) 506-3100
Developer of insurance agency management software.

Dick, A.B., Co.
5700 W. Touhy Ave.
Niles, IL 60714
(847) 779-1900
Manufacturer of presses, microfiche machines, and digital cameras.

Disc Manufacturing
1 E. Wacker Drive
Chicago, IL 60601
(312) 467-6755
Manufacturer of compact disks, including CD-ROM, CD audio, and CD-I.

DocuMail Systems Co.
6802 N. McCormick Road
Lincolnwood, IL 60645
(847) 675-7600
Manufacturer of postal automation systems.

Document Management Products Co.
6800 N. McCormick Road
Chicago, IL 60645
(847) 675-7600
Manufacturer of microfilm and optical disks.

Domino Amjet
1290 Lakeside Drive
Gurnee, IL 60031
(847) 244-2501
Manufacturer of inkjet printers and related equipment.

Donnelley, R.R., and Sons Co. / Information Resources Sector
77 W. Wacker Drive
Chicago, IL 60601
(312) 326-8000
Provider of database management services; CD-ROM information management solutions; and geographic and demographic consumer information.

Dukane Corp. / Audio Visual Products Division
2900 Dukane Drive
Saint Charles, IL 60174
(630) 584-2300
Manufacturer of professional presentation equipment.

Enterprise Systems
1400 S. Wolf Road, Suite 500
Wheeling, IL 60090
(847) 537-4800
Developer of hospital management software.

General Binding Corp.
1 GBC Plaza
Northbrook, IL 60062
(847) 272-3700
Manufacturer and marketer of business machines.

Grayhill
561 Hillgrove Ave.
La Grange, IL 60525
(708) 354-1040
Manufacturer of control products.

IBM Corporation
330 N. Wabash Ave.
Chicago, IL 60611
(312) 245-2000
World's largest manufacturer and marketer of information technology.

IIT Research Institute
10 W. 35th St.
Chicago, IL 60616
(312) 567-4000
Provider of contract research and development in the areas of artificial intelligence, robotics, and electronics.

Interlake Corporation / Material Handling Group
1240 E. Diehl Road
Naperville, IL 60563
(630) 245-8800
Developer of warehouse management software.

Internet Systems Corp.
2 Prudential Plaza
Chicago, IL 60601
(312) 540-0100
Developer of banking and financial
software.

Landis and Staefa
1000 Deerfield Pkwy.
Buffalo Grove, IL 60089
(847) 215-1000
Developer of facilities management
software.

Law Bulletin Information Network
415 N. State Parkway
Chicago, IL 60610
(312) 644-7800
Provider of computer on-line services.

May & Speh
1501 Opus Place
Downers Grove, IL 60515
(630) 964-1501
Provider of systems management services.

Medicus Systems Corporation
1 Rotary Center, Suite 400
Evanston, IL 60201
(847) 570-7500
Developer of specialized health care
software.

Methode Electronics
7444 W. Wilson Ave.
Harwood Heights, IL 60656
(708) 867-9600
Energy Controls.

Molex
2222 Wellington Court
Lisle, IL 60532
(630) 969-4550
Manufactures connectors, cable assem-
blies, and other areas of technology.

National Education Training Group
1751 W. Diehl Road
Naperville, IL 60563
(630) 369-3000
Training and informational services.

NB / Microseal Corp.
2000 Lewis Ave.
Zion, IL 60099
(847) 872-1666
Manufacturer of micrographic systems;
developer of imaging software.

**Omron Electronics / Control Compo-
nents Division**
1 E. Commerce Drive
Schaumburg, IL 60173
(847) 843-7900
Manufacturer of IC chip card readers and
other technical equipment.

**Phoenix Technologies, Ltd. / Eclipse
Software Division**
3 First National Plaza
70 W. Madison
Chicago, IL 60602
(312) 541-0260
Developer of fax send, receive, and
management software for Windows.

Pitney Bowes / Software Systems
4343 Commerce Court, Suite 500
Lisle, IL 60532
(630) 505-0572
Developer of mailing list management
software.

Platinum Technology
1815 S. Meyers Road
Oak Brook Terrace, IL 60181
(630) 620-5000
Developer of mainframe and client-server
software.

Quantra Corporation
707 Skokie Blvd.
Northbrook, IL 60062
(847) 291-4000
Developer of real estate portfolio management software.,

**Resource Information Management
Systems**
500 Technology Drive
Naperville, IL 60566
(630) 369-5300
Developer of health plan administration
software.

**Rockwell Telecommunications /
Switching Systems Division**
1431 Opus Place
Downers Grove, IL 60515
(630) 960-8000
Manufacturer of automatic call distribution systems.

SEI Information Technologies
212 E. Ohio, Suite 200
Chicago, IL 60611
(312) 440-8300
Provider of software and computerization consulting services.

SHL Systemhouse Corp. / Midwest Region
300 S. Wacker Drive, Suite 2500
Chicago, IL 60606
(312) 939-0099
Provider of computer and systems integration services for UNIX software systems.

Siemens Medical Systems / Nuclear Medicine Group
2501 N. Barrington Road
Hoffman Estates, IL 60195
(847) 304-7700
Manufacturer of nuclear medicine imaging systems.

Society For Visual Education
6677 N. Northwest Highway
Chicago, IL 60613
(773) 775-9550
Developer of educational software for grades K-8.

Softnet Systems
717 Forest Ave.
Lake Forest, IL 60045
(847) 266-8150
Developer of health care software.

SPSS
444 N. Michigan Ave., Suite 3000
Chicago, IL 60611
(312) 329-2400
Developer of statistical software.

Spyglass, Inc.
1230 E. Diehl Road, Suite 304
Naperville, IL 60563
(630) 505-1010
Developer of software for browsing the Internet.

Stenograph Corp.
1500 Bishop Court
Mount Prospect, IL 60056
(847) 803-1400
Manufacturer of computer-driven legal transcription products and systems.

Sun Electric Corp.
1 Sun Parkway
Crystal Lake, IL 60014
(815) 459-7700
Manufacturer of electronic and computerized automotive test and service equipment.

SunGard Investment Systems
11 Salt Creek Lane
Hinsdale, IL 60521
(630) 920-3100
Developer of financial and portfolio management software.

Systems and Programming Resources
2015 Spring Road, Suite 750
Oak Brook, IL 60521
(630) 990-2040
Provider of custom applications software programming services.

TDK Corp. of America
1600 Feehanville Drive
Mount Prospect, IL 60056
(847) 803-6100
Manufacturer of electrical and electronic equipment.

Technology Solutions Co.
205 N. Michigan Ave., Suite 1500
Chicago, IL 60601
(312) 228-4500
Provider of systems integration, custom applications, and systems software programming.

U.S. Robotics
8100 N. McCormick Blvd.
Skokie, IL 60076
(847) 982-5010
Manufacturer of data communications products and systems.

VisionTek
1175 Lakeside Drive
Gurnee, IL 60031
(847) 360-7500
Manufacturer of printer and computer memory boards and cards.

Whittman-Hart, LP
311 S. Wacker Drive, Suite 3500
Chicago, IL 60606
(312) 922-9200
Provider of custom applications software programming.

Williams Electronics Games
3401 N. California Ave.
Chicago, IL 60618
(773) 961-1000
Manufacturer of electronic games, including arcade video games and pinball machines.

Zebra Technologies Corp.
333 Corporate Woods Pkwy.
Vernon Hills, IL 60061
(847) 634-6700
Manufacturer of programmable thermal and thermal transfer bar code printers.

Computers: Information Management/Consulting

WEB SITES:

http://www.acm.ndsu.nodak.edu/ ~acmco/
discusses careers in computer consulting.

http://204.252.76.40/0002c2a.html
is a news update on the information services industry.

http://www.wdn.com/aop/
is the homepage for the Assocation of Online Professionals.

PROFESSIONAL ORGANIZATIONS:

For local networking groups, see the preceding section. For additional information, contact the following organizations. Also see **"Computers: Hardware/Software."**

American Society for Information Science
8720 Georgia Ave., Suite. 501
Silver Spring, MD 20910
(301) 495-0900

Association for Computing Machinery
1515 Broadway
New York, NY 10036
(212) 869-7440

Association of Independent Information Professionals
245 5th Ave., Suite 2103
New York, NY 10016
(212) 779-1855

IEEE Computer Society
1730 Massachusetts Ave., N.W.
Washington, DC 20036
(202) 371-0101

Information Industry Association
1625 Massachusetts Ave. N.W., Suite 700
Washington, DC 20036
(202) 986-0280

ITI Information Technology Industry Council
1250 I St., N.W., Suite 200
Washington, DC 20005
(202) 737-8888

Society for Information Management
401 N. Michigan Ave.
Chicago, IL 60611
(312) 644-6610

Women in Information Processing
P.O. Box 39173
Washington, DC 20016
(202) 328-6161

PROFESSIONAL PUBLICATIONS:

CIO: The Magazine for Information Executives
Computer Communications Review
Computerworld: Newsweekly for Information Systems Management
Data Communications
EDI News
Information Processing and Management
InformationWEEK
Internet Business Report
Link-Up
Network World
Networking Management
Online

DIRECTORIES:

Computers and Computing Information Resources Directory (Gale Research, Detroit, MI)
Data Sources (Ziff-Davis Publishing, New York, NY)
Directory of Top Computer Executives (Applied Computer Research, Phoenix, AZ)
Information Industry Directory (Gale Research, Detroit, MI)
Information Sources (Information Industry Association, Washington, DC)

Networking in new media

For get-togethers in cyberspace try these sites:

Worldwide Web Artists Consortium

(212) 358-8220

http://wwwac.org

Webgirls: networking for cyberfemales

(212) 642-8012

asherman@interport.net

ECHO (East Coast Hangout)

(212) 292-0900

info@echonyc.com

Employers:

Abacus Data Systems
3601 Algonquin Road
Rolling Meadows, IL 60008
(847) 632-0303

ABS Associates
1930 N. Thoreau Drive
Schaumburg, IL 60173
(847) 437-8700

ADP Dealer Services
1950 Hassell Road
Hoffman Estates, IL 60195-2308
(847) 397-1700

Ameritech Health Connections
33 W. Wacker Drive, Suite 2900
Chicago, IL 60606
(312) 460-2700

Andersen Consulting
69 W. Washington St.
Chicago, IL 60602
(312) 372-7100

Beilfuss, C. W., & Associates
2221 Camden Court, Suite 310
Oak Brook, IL 60521
(630) 990-0830

Benesch, Alfred, & Co.
205 N. Michigan Ave., Suite 2400
Chicago, IL 60601
(312) 565-0450

Borri, Brenda, Co.
625 N. Michigan Ave.

Chicago, IL 60622
(312) 440-0177

Business Systems Solutions
1400 Lake Cook Road
Buffalo Grove, IL 60089
(847) 459-3800

CCH, Inc.
2700 Lake Cook Road
Riverwoods, IL 60015
(847) 267-7000

ComCoTec
2505 S. Finley Road, Suite 110
Lombard, IL 60148
(630) 268-3600

Communications Technology Group
6600 Lincoln Ave., Suite 306
Lincolnwood, IL 60645
(847) 675-7800

Communitech
321 Bond St.
Elk Grove Village, IL 60007
(847) 439-4333

Computer Support Centre
1920 Thoreau Drive, Suite 150
Schaumburg, IL 60173
(847) 397-8000

Concepts Dynamics
1821 Walden Office, Suite 500
Schaumburg, IL 60173
(847) 397-4400

Datair Employee Benefit Systems
735 N. Cass
Westmont, IL 60559-1100
(630) 325-2600

Delphi Information Systems
3501 Algonquin Road, Suite 500
Rolling Meadows, IL 60008
(847) 506-3100

Distribution Sciences
1700 Higgins Road, Suite 280
Des Plaines, IL 60018
(847) 699-6620

Dunn Systems
4301 W. Touhy Ave.
Lincolnwood, IL 60646
(847) 673-0900

Fipsco
1090 Executive Way
Des Plaines, IL 60018
(847) 803-4700

FutureSource
955 Parkview Blvd.
Lombard, IL 60148
(630) 620-8444

Greenbrier & Russel
1450 E. American Lane
Schaumburg, IL 60173
(847) 706-4000

Information Retrieval Companies
312 W. Randolph St., Suite 610
Chicago, IL 60606
(312) 726-7587

Insurance Information Technologies
377 E. Butterfield Road, Suite 800
Lombard, IL 60148
(630) 434-9200

ISI Infortext
1050 N. National Parkway
Schaumburg, IL 60173
(847) 490-1155

Kenwood Associates
333 W. Wacker Drive
Chicago, IL 60606
(312) 857-1500

Kupferberg, Goldberg & Neimark
111 E. Wacker Drive, Suite 1400
Chicago, IL 60601
(312) 819-4300

Lante Corporation
35 W. Wacker Drive, Suite 3200
Chicago, IL 60601
(312) 236-5100

Links Technology Corp.
3930 N. Pine Grove
Chicago, IL 60613
(312) 461-9301

Liocs Corp.
246 E. Janata Blvd.
Lombard, IL 60148
(630) 953-2220

Magnetic Media Information Services
655 W. Irving Park, Suite 5516
Chicago, IL 60613
(312) 266-2624

Metamor Technologies
223 W. Erie St.
Chicago, IL 60610
(312) 638-2667

Microsystems Engineering Co.
2500 Highland Ave., Suite 350
Lombard, IL 60148
(630) 261-0111

New Logic
1200 Riverside Plaza, Suite 1654
Chicago, IL 60606
(312) 648-1200

New Media
280 W. Shuman Boulevard
Naperville, IL 60563
(630) 355-4404

Platinum Technology
1815 S. Meyers Road
Oakbrook Terrace, IL 60181
(630) 620-5000

Programming Services
3 Golf Center, Suite 247
Hoffman Estates, IL 60195
(847) 991-1228

Quantra Corporation
707 Skokie Blvd., 7th floor
Northbrook, IL 60062
(847) 291-4000

Real Time Software
2340 Des Plaines River Road
Des Plaines, IL 60018
(847) 698-4000

Reed Industry Solutions Group
600 Hunter Drive, Suite 100
Oak Brook, IL 60521
(630) 571-6600

Resource Information Management Systems
500 Technology Drive
Naperville, IL 60540
(630) 369-5300

Retail Data
142 E. Ontario St., Suite 550
Chicago, IL 60611
(312) 787-6755

Revere Group, Ltd.
5 Revere Drive, Suite 320
Northbrook, IL 60062
(847) 291-2500

Rohde, Harry, Management Systems
360 W. Butterfield Road, Suite 160
Elmhurst, IL 60126
(630) 834-0600

Rolfe & Nolan
120 S. Riverside Plaza, Suite 1430
Chicago, IL 60606
(312) 559-0250

SEI Information Technology
450 E. Ohio St.
Chicago, IL 60611
(312) 440-8300

Sentinel Technologies
2550 Warrenville Road
Downers Grove, IL 60515
(630) 769-4300

Software Options & Systems
1935 S. Plum Grove Road, Suite 332
Palatine, IL 60067
(847) 358-2130

Subject Wills & Co.
1420 Kensington Road, Suite 110
Oak Brook, IL 60521
(630) 572-0240

Swiderski Electronics
1200 Greenleaf
Elk Grove Village, IL 60007
(847) 364-1900

System Software Associates
500 W. Madison St., Suite 3200
Chicago, IL 60661
(312) 258-6000

Systems House
10500 Lunt Ave., Suite 104
Rosemont, IL 60018
(847) 390-6300

Tallgrass Systems, Ltd.
15222 S. LaGrange Road
Orland Park, IL 60462
(708) 349-2212

Tech Law Automation Partners
10 S. Wacker Drive, Suite 2100
Chicago, IL 60606
(312) 578-8900

Technology Solutions Company
205 N. Michigan Ave., Suite 1500
Chicago, IL 60601
(312) 819-2250

Tenman Systems
1699 Wall St., Suite 500
Mount Prospect, IL 60056
(847) 290-7500

Triangle Technologies
144 Branding Lane
Downers Grove, IL 60515
(630) 969-8200

Trilogy Consulting Corp.
850 S. Greenbay Road
Waukegan, IL 60085
(847) 244-9520

Wallace Computer Services
4600 W. Roosevelt Road
Hillside, IL 60162
(708) 449-8600

Booting up big $$$ in computer sales

Philip Daniels competes in the fast lane as a computer sales engineer. His clients are Fortune 500 companies, and his products are communications boards, controllers, and disk and tape subsystems manufactured by a relatively new specialty company. "It's an emotionally and physically stressful environment where I constantly have to prove myself," says Philip.

We asked how he got there and what keeps him successful.

"I use every skill and all the experience I've ever had," said the former teacher and editorial assistant for a steel company's community relations department. "When I decided to go back to school for an associate's degree in computers, I needed a job as well. So I sold cars, and that provided invaluable marketing and people experience, plus communications skills that are absolutely essential in my present business.

"Once I got into computer courses, I realized I couldn't settle for a $25,000 programming job and began laying more plans. And, incidentally, you must prepare yourself for the entry position in this field. My first job—strictly commission—was with a small systems house, and within a year I was director of marketing with a sales staff of six. I got a total overview of the business so that I could talk from that perspective on my next round of interviews.

"I used an employment agent who specializes in computer sales to get this position and was very specific with him about my requirements."

Asked to explain his current success, Philip responds: "I'd have to say the number one factor is technical expertise—with sales ability second. I read, listen, and pick brains to stay on top of the products and a changing market place so that my company provides a service to the client by sending me. By the way, with little more education than a $25,000 programmer, I'll make at least three times that this year. And the perks are great, too."

Construction/Contractors

WEB SITES:

http://www.copywriter.com/ab/
constr.html
lists bulletin boards and discussion groups
for the industry; offers links to others
industry sites including Construction
Online.

http://scescape.com/worldlibrary/
business/companies/construct/html
links to construction companies.

PROFESSIONAL ORGANIZATIONS:

For networking in the construction
industry and related fields, check out the
following local professional organizations
listed in Chapter 5. Also see "**Engineering.**"

American Economic Development
   Council
Builders Association of Chicago

For additional information, you can
contact:

Associated Builders and Contractors
1300 N. 17th St., 8th floor
Rosslyn, VA 22209
(703) 812-2000

**Associated General Contractors of
America**
1957 E St., N.W.
Washington, DC 20006
(202) 393-2040
Building Service Contractors

Association International
10201 Lee Highway, Suite 225
Fairfax, VA 22030
(703) 359-7090

**Construction Management Association
of America**
7918 Jones Bridge Drive, Suite 540
McLean, Va 22102
(703) 356-2622

Construction Specifications Institute
601 Madison St.

Alexandria, VA 22314
(703) 684-0300

**National Association of Home Builders
of the U.S.**
1201 15th St., N.W.
Washington, DC 20005
(202) 822-0200

**National Association of Minority
Contractors**
1333 F St., N.W., Suite 500
Washington, DC 20004
(202) 347-8259

**National Association of Women in
Construction**
327 S. Adams St.
Fort Worth, TX 76104

PROFESSIONAL PUBLICATIONS:

Builder
Builder and Contractor
Building Design and Construction
*Building: The Facilities Construction and
   Management Journal*
Construction Review
Constructor
Pit and Quarry

DIRECTORIES:

*Associated Builders & Contractors
   Membership Directory* (Associated
   Builders & Contractors, Washington,
   DC)
Blue Book of Major Homebuilders (LSI
   Systems, Inc., Crofton, MD)
Construction Equipment: Construction
   Giants (Cahners Publishing, Des Plaines,
   IL)
Constructor, Directory Issue (Associated
   General Contractors of America,
   Washington, DC)
Directory of Construction Associations
   (Metadata, Inc., New York, NY)
ENR Directory of Contractors (McGraw-
   Hill, New York, NY)

Guide to Information Sources in the Construction Industry (Construction Products Manufacturers Council, Arlington, VA)

Employers:

Amsted Industries
Boulevard Towers South, 44th floor
205 N. Michigan Ave.
Chicago, IL 6060l
(312) 645-1700

Baker Heavy & Highway Co.
118 S. Clinton St., Suite 350
Chicago, IL 60606
(312) 876-1444

Bartkus & Associates
819 S. Wabash
Chicago, IL 60605
(312) 663-4141

Benesch, Alfred, Engineers
205 N. Michigan Ave. #2400
Chicago, IL 60601
(312) 565-0450

Benson, Ragnar
250 S. Northwest Highway
Park Ridge, IL 60068
(847) 698-4900

Capitol Construction Group
1000 Capitol Drive, Suite 200
Wheeling, IL 60090
(847) 215-2500

Chicago Bridge & Iron Co.
1501 N. Division St.
Plainfield, IL 60544
(815) 439-6000

Crane Construction Co.
343 Wainwright Drive
Northbrook, IL 60062
(847) 291-3400

Crane/Fiat
1235 Hartrey Ave.
Evanston, IL 60202
(847) 864-7600

Envirodyne Engineers
168 N. Clinton St.
Chicago, IL 60606
(312) 648-1700

Epstein, A., & Sons, International
600 W. Fulton St.
Chicago, IL 60606
(312) 454-9100

Falcon Building Products
2 N. Riverside Place, Suite 1100
Chicago, IL 60606
(312) 906-9700

First Alert
3901 Liberty St.
Aurora, IL 60504
(630) 851-7330
Manufacturer of a large range of home safety products.

Fischbach & Moore
1619 S. Michigan Ave.
Chicago, IL 60616
(312) 360-9381
Electrical contractors.

Fluor Daniel
200 W. Monroe St., Floor 22
Chicago, IL 60606
(312) 368-3500

Gerber Plumbing Fixtures Corp.
4600 W. Touhy Ave.
Chicago, IL 60646
(847) 675-6570
Retail and wholesale plumbing.

Gilbane Building Co.
8725 W. Higgins Road., Suite 700
Chicago, IL 60631
(773) 693-9200

Greeley & Hansen
100 S. Wacker Drive, Suite 1400
Chicago, IL 60606
(312) 558-9000

Harza Engineering Co.
233 S. Wacker Drive
Chicago, IL 60606
(312) 831-3000

Hyre Electric Co.
2320 W. Ogden Ave.
Chicago, IL 60608

(312) 738-7200
Electrical contractors.

Inland Steel Industries
30 W. Monroe St.
Chicago, IL 60603
(312) 346-0300
Produces and markets steel.

Kennedy, George A., & Associates
6 N. Michigan Ave., Suite 414
Chicago, IL 60602
(312) 332-7060

Kenny-Kiewit-Shea
2100 N. River Road
River Grove, IL 60171
(708) 649-4600

Materials Service Corporation
222 N. LaSalle
Chicago, IL 60601-1090
(312) 372-3600

McHugh, James, Construction
2222 S. Indiana Ave.
Chicago, IL 60616
(312) 842-8400

Mertes Contracting Corp.
1741 N. California Ave.
Chicago, IL 60647
(773) 276-0480

Meyne Co.
1755 W. Armitage Ave.
Chicago, IL 60622
(773) 862-2000

Morse/Diesel
Western Region Office
125 S. Wacker Drive, Suite 200
Chicago, IL 60606
(312) 541-1600

O'Donnell Wicklund Pigozzi & Peterson
570 Lake Cook Road
Deerfield, IL 60015
(847) 940-9600

O'Neil, W.E., Construction
2751 N. Clybourn Ave.
Chicago, IL 60614
(773) 327-1611

Opus North Corporation
9700 W. Higgins Road, Suite 900
Rosemont, IL 60018
(847) 318-1600

Paschen Contractors
2739 N. Elston Ave.
Chicago, IL 60647
(773) 278-4700

Pepper Companies
643 N. Orleans St.
Chicago, IL 60610
(312) 266-4703

Power Contracting & Engineering Corporation
2360 N. Palmer Drive
Schaumburg, IL 60173
(847) 925-1300

Sargent & Lundy
55 E. Monroe St.
Chicago, IL 60603
(312) 269-2000

Schal Associates
200 W. Hubbard St.
Chicago, IL 60610
(312) 245-1000

Soil Testing Services
111 Pfingston Road
Northbrook, IL 60062
(847) 272-6520

Sundance Homes
1375 E. Woodfield Road, Suite 600
Schaumburg, IL 60173
(847) 255-5555
Developer of single-family homes.

Turner Construction Co.
230 S. LaSalle
Chicago, IL 60604
(312) 693-8702

WMX Technologies
3003 Butterfield Road
Oak Brook, IL 60521
(630) 572-8800

Consulting: Financial/Health Care/Human Resources/ Management/Marketing

PROFESSIONAL ORGANIZATIONS:

For networking in consulting and related fields, you can check out these professional organizations listed in Chapter 5:

American Planning Association
American Society for Training and Development

For additional information, you can write or call:

Association of Management Consulting Firms (ACME)
230 Park Ave.
New York, NY 10169
(212) 949-6571

Institute of Management Consultants
521 5th Ave.
New York, NY 10175
(212) 697-8262

National Management Association
2210 Arbor Blvd.
Dayton, OH 45439
(513) 294-0421

PROFESSIONAL PUBLICATIONS:

Academy of Management Review
ACME Newsletter
Business Quarterly
Corporate Risk Management
Executive
Harvard Business Review

DIRECTORIES:

ACME Directory (Association of Management Consultants, New York, NY)
Consultants and Consulting Organizations Directory (Gale Research, Detroit, MI)
Directory of Management Consultants (Kennedy & Kennedy, Fitzwilliam, NH)
Dun's Consultants Directory (Dun &

Bradstreet, Parsippany, NY)
IMC Directory (Institute of Management Consultants, New York, NY)

Employers, Financial Consulting:

Abrix Group, the
2860 River Road, Suite 200
Des Plaines, IL 60018
(847) 297-8300
Specializes in physicians and dentists.

Arthur Andersen Consulting
33 W. Monroe St.
Chicago, IL 60603
(312) 580-0033
Consulting arm of the accounting firm.

Blair Clay & Co.
8124 S. Indiana Ave., Suite 1W
Chicago, IL 60619
(773) 874-3674
Specializes in computer technology.

Capitol Control Group Limited
750 Lake Cook Road, 1st floor
Buffalo Grove, IL 60089
(847) 459-4770
Specializes in employee benefit planning services.

CHI/COR Information Management
300 S. Wacker Drive
Chicago, IL 60606
(312) 322-0150

Coopers & Lybrand Consulting
203 N. LaSalle St.
Chicago, IL 60601
(312) 701-5500
Consulting arm of the accounting firm.

Corporate Finance Group
208 S. LaSalle St., Suite 510
Chicago, IL 60604
(312) 855-9291

DeLoitte & Touche/Fantus
1 N. Franklin St., Suite 2620
Chicago, IL 60601
(312) 460-0234
Consulting in general business, strategic marketing, and site selection.

Duff & Phelps Financial Consulting Co.
55 E. Monroe St., Suite 3600
Chicago, IL 60603
(312) 263-2610

Ellis, Richard, Inc.
3 First National Plaza, Suite 1750
Chicago, IL 60602
(312) 899-1900
Real estate consulting.

Ernst & Young
233 S. Wacker Drive
Chicago, IL 60606
(312) 879-2000
Consulting arm of the accounting firm.

Francorp
20200 Governors Drive
Olympia Fields, IL 60461
(708) 481-2900
Specializes in franchise development.

Friedman Eisenstein Raemer & Schwartz
401 N. Michigan Ave.
Chicago, IL 60601
(312) 644-6000

Gallagher, Arthur J., & Company
2 Pierce Place
Itasca, IL 60143
(630) 773-3800
Benefits consulting.

Harper, E.B., & Company
222 Wisconsin Ave., Suite 202
Lake Forest, IL 60045
(847) 295-3191
Acquisitions consulting.

Hewitt Associates
100 Half Day Road
Lincolnshire, IL 60069
(847) 295-5000
Specializes in employee benefit and compensation programs.

Holzman Post Ludwig & Schwartz
125 S. Wilde Road
Arlington Heights, IL 60005
(847) 392-2999
Retirement and savings plan consulting.

Kaufman, Hall & Associates
1 Northfield Plaza
Northfield, IL 60093
(847) 441-8780
Health care consulting.

KPMG Peat Marwick
303 E. Wacker Drive
Chicago, IL 60601
(312) 938-1000
Consulting arm of the accounting firm.

Management Compensation Group
520 Lake Cook Road, Suite 150
Deerfield, IL 60015
(847) 374-1000

McGladrey & Pullen
1699 E. Woodfield Road, Suite 300
Schaumburg, IL 60173
(847) 517-7070

Price Waterhouse
200 E. Randolph St.
Chicago, IL 60601
(312) 540-1500
Consulting arm of the accounting firm.

Shepro Braun Consulting
30 W. Monroe St., 3rd floor
Chicago, IL 60603
(312) 443-1316

Unum America
233 S. Wacker Drive., Suite 4300
Chicago, IL 60606
(312) 655-8160
Consultants in welfare plans and employee benefits.

Employers, Health Care Consulting:

Care Communications
101 E. Ontario
Chicago, IL 60611
(312) 943-0463

Caremark International
2211 Sanders Road
Northbrook, IL 60062
(847) 559-4700
Manages health care services and
physician practices.

Carnow, Conibear & Associates, Ltd.
333 W. Wacker Drive, Suite 1400
Chicago, IL 60606
(312) 782-4486

Dorenfest, Sheldon I., & Associates
515 N. State St., Suite 1801
Chicago, IL 60610
(312) 464-3000

Jensen, Rolf, & Associates
549 W. Randolph, 5th floor
Chicago, IL 60661-2208
(312) 831-8200

McCann Health Care
625 N. Michigan Ave.
Chicago, IL 60611
(312) 266-9200

Medicus Systems Corporation
1 Rotary Center, Suite 400
Evanston, IL 60201
(847) 570-7500

Morell & Associates
5 Revere Drive, Suite 200
Northbrook, IL 60062
(847) 498-7363

Occusafe, Incorporated
1040 S. Milwaukee Ave.
Wheeling, IL 60090
(847) 459-4800

Schanilec, J.L., & Associates
582 Revere Ave.
Westmont, IL 60559
(630) 323-0540

Smith, Herman, Associates
203 N. LaSalle St.
Chicago, IL 60601
(312) 701-5500
Hospital and health care consulting
division of Coopers & Lybrand.

Tribrook Group
999 Oakmont Plaza Drive, Suite 600
Westmont, IL 60559
(630) 990-8070

Zirn, B. Howard, & Associates
9801 W. Higgins Road, 8th floor
Rosemont, IL 60018
(847) 433-6205

Employers, Human Resources Consulting:

Cambridge Outplacement International
1 N. Frankiln St.
Chicago, IL 60603
(312) 251-0400

Challenger, Gray & Christmas
150 S. Wacker Drive, 27th floor
Chicago, IL 60606
(312) 332-5790

Cook Associates
212 W. Kinzie St.
Chicago, IL 60610
(312) 329-0900

Corporate Educational Services
1 Tower Lane, Suite 1000
Oakbrook Terrace, IL 60181
(630) 574-1999

Drake Beam Morin
55 W. Monroe St.
Chicago, IL 60602
(312) 578-4200

Employee Development Institute
Triton College
2000 5th Ave.
River Grove, IL 60171
(708) 456-0300

Felicity Group, Ltd.
40 E. 9th St., Suite 1601
Chicago, IL 60605
(312) 663-0202

Ferguson Partners Limited
200 W. Madison St., Suite 2720
Chicago, IL 60606
(312) 368-5040

Karp, William, Consulting Company
111 E. Chestnut St.
Chicago, IL 60611
(630) 766-7007

RHR International Company
220 Gerry Drive
Wood Dale, IL 60191
(312) 642-3452

Witt/Kieffer, Ford, Hadelman & Lloyd
2015 Spring Road, Suite 510
Oak Brook, IL 60521
(630) 990-1370

Employers, Management Consulting:

AM Consulting
123 N. Wacker Drive
Chicago, IL 60606
(312) 701-4800

AM & G Consulting Services
30 S. Wacker Drive, Suite 2400
Chicago, IL 60606
(312) 207-2800

Andersen Consulting
69 W. Washington St.
Chicago, IL 60602
(312) 580-0069
Consulting arm of the accounting firm.

Automated Concepts
8770 W. Bryn Mawr Ave.
Chicago, IL 60631
(773) 380-4200

Booz Allen & Hamilton
225 W. Wacker Drive, Suite 1700
Chicago, IL 60606
(312) 346-1900

Boston Consulting Group
200 S. Wacker Drive
Chicago, IL 60606
(312) 638-2667

Cara Corp.
1900 Spring Road, Suite 450
Oak Brook, IL 60521
(630) 990-2272

CFC Planmetrics
8600 W. Bryn Mawr, Suite 400N
Chicago, IL 60631
(773) 693-0200

Consulting
2021 Spring Road, Suite 200
Oak Brook, IL 60521
(630) 574-0100

Deloitte & Touche Consulting Group
180 N. Stetson Ave.
Chicago, IL 60601
(312) 946-3000
Consulting arm of the accounting firm.

Elan Associates
79 W. Monroe, Suite 1320
Chicago, IL 60603
(312) 782-6496

Interactive Business Systems
2625 Butterfield Road, Suite 114W
Oak Brook, IL 60521
(630) 571-9100

Interim Technology
823 Commerce Drive
Oak Brook, IL 60521
(630) 574-3030

International Profit Assocs.
1477 Barclay Blvd.
Buffalo Grove, IL 60089
(847) 993-3300

Keane Consulting
901 Warrenville Road
Lisle, IL 60532
(630) 852-5577

Kearney, A.T.
222 W. Adams
Chicago, IL 60606
(312) 648-0111

May, George S., Co.
303 S. Northwest Highway
Park Ridge, IL 60068
(847) 825-8806

McKinsey & Co.
1 First National Plaza
Chicago, IL 60603
(312) 551-3500

Metzler & Associates
520 Lake Cook Road
Deerfield, IL 60015
(847) 945-0001
Utilities consulting.

SPR Inc.
2015 Spring Road, Suite 750
Oak Brook, IL 60521
(630) 990-2040

New Resources Corp.
3315 Algonquin Road, Suite 500
Rolling Meadows, IL 60008
(847) 797-5800

Closing the deal on sales

Jim Coburg put in a long and successful stint as a salesman for Xerox, got an MBA, and went to work as district manager for Unisys in Northbrook, then a comparatively risky, aggressive new computer company. We asked him about the differences between selling for a giant and taking a risk with a relatively unknown firm.

"Xerox is probably fairly typical of any large corporation," says Jim, "in that they are very structured. It was a good place to work, but it didn't provide much opportunity for individual decision making. A company like Unisys offered a fantastic chance to exercise some entrepreneurial skills. The corporation set general goals, but it was up to me how I met them. I tried out different marketing techniques, divided up the territory in new ways, created teams, whatever."

We asked Jim what it takes to be a good salesperson.

"A lot of people think that salesmen are forever buying people lunches and playing golf," says Jim. "But to be really successful, you have to work hard. I don't necessarily mean 80 hours a week. You need to put in sufficient time to do the things that are necessary. A second important requirement is an absolutely thorough understanding of the products you're selling. Not only your own products but also your competitors'.

"In high-level selling, sales people have to be especially sharp about interpersonal skills. There's an old saying, and it's true: people don't buy from companies, they buy from people. When you're selling systems that range upward of $5 million, you're also selling yourself. It's important that your clients feel you'll be around even after the sale to handle any problems that might come up. To establish that kind of rapport, you have to look the part and be very articulate. It also helps if you have good written communication skills."

Employers, Marketing Consulting:

Arbitron Co.
311 S. Wacker Drive
Chicago, IL 60606
(312) 913-6220
Market research.

Broh, Irwin, & Associates
1011 E. Touhy Ave.
Des Plaines, IL 60018
(847) 297-7515

Conway Milliken
875 N. Michigan Ave., Suite 2511
Chicago, IL 60611
(312) 787-4060
Market research.

Creative & Responsive Research Services
500 N. Michigan Ave.
Chicago, IL 60611
(312) 828-9200
Market research.

Econometrics
303 E. Wacker Drive, Suite 1230
Chicago, IL 60601
(312) 616-1099
Market research.

Gallup Organization
120 N. LaSalle St., Suite 3500
Chicago, IL 60602
(312) 357-0199
Market research.

Heakin Research
3615 Park Drive, Suite 101
Olympia Fields, IL 60461
(708) 503-0100
Market research.

HR Associates
223 Burlington Ave.
Clarendon Hills, IL 60514
(630) 789-0444
Market research.

Information Resources
150 N. Clinton St.
Chicago, IL 60661
(312) 726-1221

Koch International
1040 S. Milwaukee Ave.

Wheeling, IL 60090
(847) 459-1100

Market Facts
3040 W. Salt Creek Lane
Arlington Hts., IL 60005
(847) 590-7000
Market research.

Mid-America Research
999 N. Elmhurst Road
Mount Prospect, IL 60056
(847) 392-0800
Market research.

Mobium Creative Group
414 N. Orleans, Suite 610
Chicago, IL 60610
(312) 527-0500
Marketing design firm.

National Opinion Research Center
1155 E. 60th St.
Chicago, IL 60637
(773) 753-7500
Market research.

Nielsen Media Research
205 N. Michigan Ave., Suite 2315
Chicago, IL 60601
(312) 819-5500
Market research.

Street-Smart Marketing
430 E. Northwest Highway
Palatine, IL 60067
(847) 705-8882
Marketing program planning.

Technomic Consultants International
500 Skokie Blvd., Suite 575
Northbrook, IL 60062
(847) 291-1212
Strategic market planning.

Tyson Kirk Tyson International, Ltd.
4343 Commerce Court, Suite 615
Lisle, IL 60532
(630) 969-0100

Whittman-Hart
311 S. Wacker Drive
Chicago, IL 60606
(312) 922-9200

Educational Institutions

WEB SITES:

http://www.cps.kiz.il.us/
Chicago public schools.

http://www.ucls.uchicago.edu/cais/
Chicago area private schools.

http://cpl.lib.uic.edu/005colleges/
005colleges.html
Illinois colleges and universities.

http://www.petersons.com:8080/
links to public and private schools,
colleges, and universities, arranged by
geography.

http://chronicle.ment.edu/
is the homepage of *ACADEME This Week;*
lists job opportunities.

PROFESSIONAL ORGANIZATIONS:

For networking in education and related
fields, contact these local organizations
listed in Chapter 5.

American Association of University
    Women
American Library Association
Chicago's Teachers' Center
Illinois Federation of Teachers

For more information you can contact:

American Association of School
Administrators
1801 N. Moore St.
Arlington, VA 22209
(703) 528-0700

American Federation of School
Administrators
1729 21st St., N.W.
Washington, DC 20009
(202) 986-4209

Association of School Business Officials
11401 N. Shore Drive
Reston, VA 22090
(703) 478-0405

College and University Personnel
Association
1233 20th St., N.W., Suite 301
Washington, DC 20036
(202) 429-0311

National Education Association
of the U.S.
1201 16th St., N.W.
Washington, DC 20036
(202) 833-4000

PROFESSIONAL PUBLICATIONS:

Academe
Chronicle of Higher Education
Education Week
Executive Educator
Technology & Learning

DIRECTORIES:

Bricker's International Directory of
    University Executive Programs (Peterson's
    Guides, Princeton, NJ)
College Blue Book (Macmillan Publishing
    Co., New York, NY)
Faculty White Pages (Gale Research,
    Detroit, MI)
Patterson's Elementary Education (Educa-
    tional Directories, Mount Prospect, IL)
Peterson's Guide to Four Year Colleges
    (Peterson's Guides, Princeton, NJ)
Peterson's Guide to Independent Secondary
    Schools (Peterson's Guides, Princeton,
    NJ)
Who's Who in American Education (Reed
    Reference Publishing, New Providence,
    NJ)

A quick tip

If you are interested in an academic or administrative position with a college or university, it sometimes helps to contact the Dean of your discipline as well as the personnel office. Contact local boards of education, including the **Chicago Board of Education** (312) 939-1860, and the **Archdiocese of Chicago** (312) 751-5200, for information on local schools. Private schools may not require certification to obtain a teaching position.

Employers, Two-Year Colleges:

City Colleges of Chicago
226 W. Jackson Blvd.
Chicago, IL 60606
(312) 553-2510

College of DuPage
22nd St. & Lambert Road
Glen Ellyn, IL 60137
(630) 858-2800

Harper College
1200 W. Algonquin Road
Palatine, IL 60067-7398
(847) 925-6000

Moraine Valley Community College
10900 S. 88th Ave.
Palos Hills, IL 60465-0937
(708) 974-4300

Morris, Robert, College of Chicago
180 N. LaSalle St.
Chicago, IL 60601-2501
(312) 836-4888

Oakton Community College
1600 E. Golf Road
Des Plaines, IL 60016-1268
(847) 635-1600

Triton College
2000 5th Ave.
River Grove, IL 60171-1995
(708) 456-0300

Employers, Four-Year Colleges and Universities:

Art Institute of Chicago, School of the
37 S. Wabash
Chicago, IL 60603-3103
(312) 899-5100

Barat College
700 E. Westleigh Road
Lake Forest, IL 60045-3297
(847) 234-3000

Chicago-Kent College of Law
565 W. Adams St.
Chicago, IL 60606
(312) 906-5000

Chicago State University
95th St. at King Drive
Chicago, IL 60628
(773) 995-2000

Columbia College
600 S. Michigan Ave.
Chicago, IL 60605-1997
(312) 663-1600

DePaul University
1 E. Jackson Blvd.
Chicago, IL 60604-2287
(312) 362-8000

DeVry Institute of Technology
3300 N. Campbell Ave.
Chicago, IL 60618-5994
(773) 929-8500

Elmhurst College
190 Prospect
Elmhurst, IL 60126-3296
(630) 617-3500

**Finch University of Health Sciences/
Chicago Medical School**
3333 Green Bay Road
North Chicago, IL 60064-3037
(847) 578-3000

Governors State University
University Parkway
University Park, IL 60466
(708) 534-5000

Harrington Institute of Interior Design
410 S. Michigan Ave.
Chicago, IL 60605-1496
(312) 939-4975

Illinois Institute of Technology
IIT Center
Chicago, IL 60616
(312) 567-3000

Keller Graduate School of Management
10 S. Riverside Plaza
Chicago, IL 60606
(312) 454-0880

Kendall College
2408 Orrington Ave.
Evanston, IL 60201-2899
(847) 866-1300

Lake Forest College
555 N. Sheridan Road
Lake Forest, IL 60045-2399
(847) 234-3100

Lewis University
Route 53
Romeoville, IL 60441
(815) 838-0500

Loyola University of Chicago
820 N. Michigan Ave.
Chicago, IL 60611-2196
(312) 915-6000

Marshall, John, Law School
315 S. Plymouth Court
Chicago, IL 60604
(312) 427-2737

National-Louis University
2840 Sheridan Road
Evanston, IL 60201-1730
(847) 475-1100

North Central College
30 N. Brainard St.
Naperville, IL 60566-7063
(630) 637-5100

North Park College
3225 W. Foster Ave.
Chicago, IL 60625-4895
(773) 244-6200

Northeastern Illinois University
5500 N. St. Louis Ave.
Chicago, IL 60625-4699
(312) 583-4050

Northwestern University
633 Clark St.
Evanston, IL 60208
(847) 491-3741

Northwestern University
Chicago Campus
340 E. Superior St.
Chicago, IL 60611
(312) 503-8649

Ray College of Design
350 N. Orleans St.
Chicago, IL 60610
(312) 280-3500

Roosevelt University
430 S. Michigan Ave.
Chicago, IL 60605-1394
(312) 341-3500

Rosary College
7900 W. Division St.
River Forest, IL 60305-1099
(708) 366-2490

Spertus Institute
618 S. Michigan Ave.
Chicago, IL 60605
(312) 922-9012

University of Chicago
5801 Ellis Ave.
Chicago, IL 60637-1513
(773) 702-1234

University of Illinois at Chicago
1140 S. Paulina
Chicago, IL 60612
(312) 996-7000

Electronics/Telecommunications

WEB SITES:

http://arioch.gsfc.nasa.gov/wwwvl/ ee.html
is the Web's virtual electrical engineering library.

http://www.wiltel.com/library/ library.html
is a telecommunications library.

http://www.utsi.com/telecomm.html
links to telecom companies.

http://www.spp.umich.edu/telecom/ online-pubs.html
links to telecom companies and on-line publications.

PROFESSIONAL ORGANIZATIONS:

For networking in electronics, telecommunications, and the office automation systems field, you can contact the following local organization listed in Chapter 5. Also see **"Computers."**

Illinois Manufacturers Association

For more information you can contact:

American Electronics Association
5201 Great American Pkwy., Suite 520
Santa Clara, CA 95054
(408) 987-4200

Electronics Industries Association
2500 Wilson Blvd.
Arlington, VA 22201
(703) 907-7500

IEEE (Institute of Electronic and Electrical Engineers)
1730 Massachusetts Ave., N.W.
Washington, DC 20036
(202) 371-0101

Multimedia Telecommunications Association
2000 M St., N.W., Suite 550
Washington, DC 20036
(202) 296-9800

Telecommunications Association
74 New Montgomery St., Suite 230
San Francisco, CA 94105
(415) 777-4647

PROFESSIONAL PUBLICATIONS:

Cellular Business
Communications Daily
Communications News
CTI For Management
Electrical World
Electronic Business
Electronic News
Electronics
Technology News of America
tele.com
Telecommunications Magazine
Telephony
Wireless

DIRECTORIES:

American Electronics Association Directory (American Electronics Association, Santa Clara, CA)
Corporate Technology Directory (Corporate Technology Information Services, Woburn, MA)
Directory & Buyers Guide (Telephony, Chicago, IL)
EIA Trade Directory & Membership List (Electronics Industries Assoc., Washington, DC)
Fairchild's Electronics Industry Financial Directory (Fairchild Publications, New York, NY)
Sourcebook (North American Telecommunications Association, Washington, DC)

Telecommunications Directory (Gale Research, Detroit, MI)

Telecommunications Sourcebook (North American Telecommunications Association, Washington, DC)

U.S. Electronic Industry Directory (Harris Publishing Co., Twinsburg, OH)

Employers:

360 Communications Co.
8725 W. Higgins Road
Chicago, IL 60631
(773) 399-2500

AT & T Corporation
227 W. Monroe
Chicago, Il 60602
(312) 236-6636

Advantis
231 N. Martingale Road
Schaumburg, IL 60173
(847) 240-3000
Provider of electronic data interchange services.

Ameritech Corp.
30 S. Wacker Drive
Chicago, IL 60606
(312) 750-5000

Ameritech Illinois
225 W. Randolph St.
Chicago, IL 60606
(312) 727-9411

Ameritech Information Industry
350 N. Orleans St.
Chicago, IL 60654
(312) 335-2900

Ameritech Services
2000 W. Ameritech Center
Hoffman Estates, IL 60196
(847) 248-2000

Andrew Corp.
10500 W. 153rd St.
Orland Park, IL 60462
(708) 349-3300

Appliance Control Technology
1431 Jeffrey Drive
Addison, IL 60101
(630) 916-0900

ARDIS
300 Knightsbridge Pkwy.
Lincolnshire, IL 60069
(847) 913-1215

Bell & Howell Company
6800 McCormick Road
Chicago, IL 60645-2797
(800) 338-0034

Bio-logic Systems Corporation
1 Bio-logic Plaza
Mundelein, IL 60060
(847) 949-5200

BRK Brands
780 McClure Road
Aurora, IL 60504
(630) 851-7330

Charles Industries, Ltd. / Wescom Division
5600 Apollo Drive
Rolling Meadows, IL 60008
(847) 806-6300

Circuit Systems
2350 E. Lunt Ave.
Elk Grove Village, IL 60007
(847) 439-1999

Cobra Electronics
6500 W. Cortland
Chicago, IL 60635
(773) 889-8870

Cole-Parmer Instrument Co.
625 E. Bunker Court
Vernon Hills, IL 60061
(847) 549-7600

Compaq Computer Corporation
425 N. Martingale Road
Schaumburg, IL 60173
(847) 330-3325

Dainippon Screen (USA)
5110 Tollview Drive
Rolling Meadows, IL 60008
(847) 870-7400

Digital Equipment Corp.
1124 Tower Road
Schaumburg, IL 60173
(847) 718-6500

Dukane Corp.
2900 DuKane Drive
St. Charles, IL 60174
(630) 584-2300

Dynapar
1675 Delany Road
Gurnee, IL 60031
(847) 662-2666

Federal Signal Corp. / Federal Sign Division
140 E. Tower Drive
Burr Ridge, IL 60521
(630) 887-6802

Grayhill, Inc.
561 Hillgrove Ave.
La Grange, IL 60525
(708) 354-1040

GTE Airfone Incorporated
2809 Butterfield Road
Oak Brook, IL 60522
(630) 572-1800

Honeywell
1500 W. Dundee Road
Arlington Heights, IL 60004
(847) 797-4000

IBM Corporation
1 IBM Plaza, 26th floor
Chicago, IL 60611
(312) 245-2000

IIT Research Institute
10 W. 35th St.
Chicago, IL 60616
(312) 567-4000

International Jensen
25 Tristate Int'l Office Center, Suite 400
Lincolnshire, IL 60069
(847) 317-3700

Knowles Electronics
1151 Maplewood Drive
Itasca, IL 60143
(630) 250-5100

Leica Inc.
111 Deer Lake Road
Deerfield, IL 60015
(847) 405-0123

MFS Telecom
1 Tower Lane, Suite 1600
Oakbrook Terrace, IL 60181
(630) 218-7200

Molex, Inc.
2222 Wellington Court
Lisle, IL 60532
(630) 969-4550
Electrical connectors, sockets, and terminals.

Motorola
1301 E. Algonquin Road
Schaumburg, IL 60196
(847) 576-1000

Motorola
Communications Sector
1299 E. Algonquin Road
Schaumburg, IL 60196
(847) 576-5000

Motorola / Cellular Group
425 N. Martingale Road
Schaumburg, IL 60173
(847) 632-5000

Network MCI Conferencing
8750 W. Bryn Mawr Ave., Suite 900
Chicago, IL 60631
(773) 399-1610

Nuclear Data
150 Spring Lake Drive
Itasca, IL 60143
(630) 285-3000

Oce-Bruning
1800 Bruning Drive West
Itasca, IL 60143
(630) 351-2900

RELTEC Corp.
Reliable Electric Division
11333 W. Addison St.
Franklin Park, IL 60131
(847) 455-8010

Richardson Electronics Ltd.
40W267 Keslinger Road
La Fox, IL 60147
(630) 208-2200

Robertshaw Controls Company
Electronic Controls Division
1431 Jeffrey Drive
Addison, IL 60101
(630) 916-0900

Rockwell Telecommunications
8245 S. Lemont Road
Darien, IL 60561
(630) 985-0638

**Rockwell Telecommunications /
Switching Systems Division**
1431 Opus Place
Downers Grove, IL 60515
(630) 960-8000

Sprint Telecommunications
5600 N. River Road
Rosemont, IL 60018
(800) 767-7774

Square D Co.
1415 S. Roselle
Palatine, IL 60067
(847) 397-2600

Stenograph Corp.
1500 Bishop Court
Mount Prospect, IL 60056
(847) 803-1400

Stewart-Warner Instrument Corp.
580 Slawin Court
Mount Prospect, IL 60056
(847) 803-0200

Talk-A-Phone Co.
5013 N. Kedzie Ave.
Chicago, IL 60625
(773) 539-1100

Telephone and Data Systems
30 N. La Salle St., Suite 4000
Chicago, IL 60602
(312) 630-1900

Tellabs
1000 Remington Blvd.
Bolingbrook, IL 60440
(630) 378-8800

Teltrend, Inc.
620 Stetson Ave.
Saint Charles, IL 60174
(630) 377-1700

Teradyne, Inc.
1405 Lake Cook Road
Deerfield, IL 60015
(847) 940-9000

U.S. Robotics
8100 N. McCormick Blvd.
Skokie, IL 60076
(847) 982-5010

Unisys Corporation
230 S. Dearborn St.
Chicago, IL 60604
(800) 874-8647

United States Cellular Corp.
8410 W. Bryn Mawr Ave., Suite 700
Chicago, IL 60631
(773) 399-8900

Weber Marking Systems
711 W. Algonquin Road
Arlington Heights, IL 60005
(847) 364-8500

Xerox Corporation
3000 Des Plaines Ave.
Des Plaines, IL 60018
(847) 297-3600

Zenith Electronics Corp.
1000 Milwaukee Ave.
Glenview, IL 60025
(847) 391-7000

Energy/Oil/Gas/Plastics

WEB SITES:

**http://www.oilnetwork.com/
services.html**
is a network of oil companies on the
Internet; also maintains a job center.

http://www.pennwell.com/ogj.html
is the homepage of *Oil and Gas Journal.*

http://www.utsi.com/oil_gas.html
links to oil and gas industry sites.

http://www.echi.com/live/visit/visit.html
is The Plastics Network; connects to
companies and directories.

PROFESSIONAL ORGANIZATIONS:

For networking in oil, gas, plastics, and
related fields, check out these following
local professional organizations listed in
Chapter 5. Also see **"Chemicals"** and
"Engineering."
American Chemical Society
Gas Research Institute

For more information, you can contact:

American Gas Association
1515 Wilson Blvd.
Arlington, VA 22209
(703) 841-8400

American Nuclear Society
555 N. Kensington Ave.
La Grange Park, IL 60525
(708) 352-6611

American Petroleum Institute
1220 L St., N.W.
Washington, DC 20005
(202) 682-8000

**Petroleum Industry Research
Foundation**
122 E. 42nd St.
New York, NY 10168
(212) 867-0052

Society of Plastics Engineers
14 Fairfield Drive
Brookfield, CT 06804
(860) 775-0471

Society of the Plastics Industry
1275 K St., N.W.
Washington, DC 20005
(202) 371-5200

PROFESSIONAL PUBLICATIONS:

Drilling Contractor
Gas Industries Magazine
Lundberg Letter
Modern Plastics
National Petroleum News
Oil Daily
Oil and Gas Journal
Plastics World
World Oil

DIRECTORIES:

Energy Job Finder (Mainstream Access,
New York, NY)
Gas Industry Training Directory (American
Gas Association, Arlington, VA)
International Petroleum Encyclopedia
(PennWell Publishing Co., Tulsa, OK)
Modern Plastics, Encyclopedia Issue
(McGraw-Hill, New York, NY)
National Petroleum News-Market Facts
(Adams/Hunter Publishing Co., Elk
Grove Village, IL)
Oil and Gas Directory (Geophysical
Directory, Inc., Houston, TX)
Plastics World, Directory Issue (Cahners,
Newton, MA)
US Oil Industry Directory (Penwell
Publishing, Tulsa, OK)

Employers:

Amoco Oil Co.
200 E. Randolph St.
Chicago, IL 60601
(312) 856-6111

Ashland Oil
6428 Joliet Road
Countryside, IL 60525
(708) 579-2880

CF Industries
1 Salem Lake Drive
Long Grove, IL 60047
(847) 438-9500

Charles Marine Products
5600 Apollo Drive
Rolling Meadows, IL 60008
(847) 806-6300

Clark Oil & Refining Co.
131st and Kedzie Ave.
Blue Island, IL 60406
(708) 385-5000

Combustion Engineering
750 E. Diehl, Suite 135
Naperville, IL 60563
(630) 505-2440

Crane, John, Inc.
6400 Oakton St.
Morton Grove, IL 60053
(847) 967-2400

Indeck Energy Services
1130 Lake Cook Road, Suite 300
Buffalo Grove, IL 60089
(847) 520-3212

Institute of Gas Technology
1700 S. Mount Prospect Road
Des Plaines, IL 60018
(847) 768-0500

Martin Oil Service
P.O. Box 298
Blue Island, IL 60406
(708) 385-6500

Mobil Oil Corporation
I-55 and Arsenal Road
Joliet, IL 60434
(815) 423-5571

Parker Hannifin Corp.
2445 S. 25th Ave.
Broadview, IL 60153
(708) 681-6300

Texaco, Inc.
3030 Warrenville Road, Suite 260
Lisle, IL 60532
(630) 505-9339

Torco Holdings
111 E. Wacker Drive, Suite 1300
Chicago, IL 60601-4402
(312) 616-1700

Vapor Mark IV
Transportation Products Group
6420 W. Howard St.
Niles, IL 60714
(847) 967-8300

Engineering

WEB SITES:

http://www.webcreations.com/bolton/
is a job-search page for engineers.

http://www.techweb.comp.com/current
is a job listing and career information site
for technical careers.

http://www.ieee.org/jobs.html
lists engineering jobs.

PROFESSIONAL ORGANIZATIONS:

For networking in engineering and related
fields, check out the following local
professional organizations listed in
Chapter 5. Also see **"Construction."**

American Society of Design Engineering
American Society of Safety Engineers
Institute of Electrical & Electronics
   Engineers/Chicago

For more information, you can contact:

American Society of Civil Engineers
345 E. 47th St.
New York, NY 10017
(212) 705-7496

American Society of Mechanical
Engineers
345 E.47th St.
New York, NY 10017
(212) 705-7722

Association for Facilities Engineering
8180 Corporate Park Drive, Suite 305
Cincinnati, OH 45242
(513) 489-2473

IEEE (Institute of Electrical and
Electronic Engineers)
345 E. 47th St.
New York, NY 10017
(212) 705-7900

National Society of Professional
Engineers
1420 King St.
Alexandria, VA 22314
(703) 684-2800

National Society of Women Engineers
1420 King St.
Alexandria, VA 22314
(703) 684-2800

Society of Women Engineers
120 Wall St., 11th floor
New York, NY 10005
(212) 509-9577

PROFESSIONAL PUBLICATIONS:

Building Design and Construction
Chemical Engineering
Civil Engineering News
Electronic Engineering Times
Engineering News Record

DIRECTORIES:

Directory of Contract Service Firms (C.E.
   Publications, Kenmore, WA)
Engineering, Science and Computer Jobs
   (Peterson's Guides, Princeton, NJ)
IEEE Membership Directory (Institute of
   Electrical and Electronics Engineers,
   New York, NY)
Official Register (American Society of Civil
   Engineers, New York, NY)
Professional Engineering Directory
   (National Society of Professional
   Engineers, Alexandria, VA)
Who's Who in Engineering (American
   Association of Engineering Societies,
   Washington, DC)

Employers:

Barnes & Reinecke
2201 Estes Ave.
Elk Grove Village, IL 60007
(847) 640-7200

Broutman. L. J., & Associates, Ltd.
3424 S. State St.
Chicago, IL 60616
(312) 842-4100

Cara Corp.
1900 Spring Road, Suite 450
Oak Brook, IL 60521
(630) 990-2272

Chicago Testing Laboratory
3360 Commercial Ave.
Northbrook, IL 60062
(847) 498-6400

Consoer Townsend & Assoc.
303 E. Wacker Drive
Chicago, IL 60601
(312) 938-0300

Construction Technology Laboratories
5420 Old Orchard Road
Skokie, IL 60077
(847) 965-7500

Consulting Engineers Group
55 E. Euclid Ave., Suite 420
Mount Prospect, IL 60056
(847) 255-5200

Corbpro Companies
931 W. Albion
Schaumburg, IL 60193
(847) 980-8770

ECOS Environmental Solutions
205 W. Harrison
Oak Park, IL 60304
(708) 383-2505

Epstein, A., & Sons
600 W. Fulton St.
Chicago, IL 60607
(312) 454-9100

Energon
33 N. La Salle St., Suite 2400
Chicago, IL 60602
(312) 443-5700

Grumman/Butkus Associates
500 Davis St., Suite 500
Evanston, IL 60201
(847) 328-3555

Harza Engineering Company
233 S. Wacker Drive
Chicago, IL 60606
(312) 831-3000

Hoyer-Schlesinger-Turner
300 W. Adams St.
Chicago, IL 60606
(312) 263-0556

Hunt, Robert W., Company
Oak Creek Center
580 Waters Edge
Lombard, IL 60148
(630) 691-4333

Northview Laboratories
1880 Holste Road
Northbrook, IL 60062
(847) 564-8181

Packer Engineering
North Washington at I-88
Naperville, IL 60566
(630) 505-5722

Sargent & Lundy
55 E. Monroe St.
Chicago, IL 60603
(312) 269-2000

Silliker Laboratories Group
900 Maple Road
Homewood, IL 60430
(708) 957-7878

Teng & Associates
205 N. Michigan Ave.
Chicago, IL 60601
(312) 616-0000

Wiss, Janney, Elstner Associates
330 Pfingsten Road
Northbrook, IL 60062
(847) 272-7400

Entertainment

WEB SITES:

http://www.fleethouse.com/fhcanada/
western/bc/van/entertan/hqe/vrhq-
lnk.htm
is a comprehensive guide to theater, film,
television, and music industries.

http://www.ern.com/ern.htm
has links to companies and individuals in
the entertainment industry.

http://www.ose.com/ose/
links to the entertainment and music
industries.

http://www.ircam.fr/divers/theatre-
e.html
is a guide to theater resources.

PROFESSIONAL ORGANIZATIONS:

For networking in the entertainment
industry, check out the following local
professional organizations listed in
Chapter 5. Also see **"Broadcasting"** and
**"Museums/Theaters/Cultural
Institutions."**

AFTRA
American Women in Radio and
  Television
Association for Multi-Image
Association for Theatre in Higher
  Education
Center for New Television
Chicago Area Broadcast Public Affairs
  Association
Chicago Audio Visual Producers
  Association
National Broadcast Association for
  Community Affairs

For more information, you can contact:

**Academy of Motion Picture Arts and
Sciences**
8949 Wilshire Blvd.
Beverly Hills, CA 90211
(310) 247-3000

American Film Institute
Kennedy Center for the Performing Arts
Washington, DC 20566
(202) 828-4000

Film Arts Foundation
346 9th St., 2nd Floor
San Francisco, CA 94103
(415) 552-8760

**Recording Industry Association of
America**
1020 19th St., N.W., Suite 200
Washington, DC 20036
(202) 775-0101

PROFESSIONAL PUBLICATIONS:

American Theatre
Backstage
Billboard
*Daily Variety: News of the Entertainment
  Industry*
Film Journal
On Location Magazine
Show Business News
Stage Managers Directory
Theater Times
Variety

DIRECTORIES:

*Back Stage Film/Tape/Syndication
  Directory* (Back Stage Publications, New
  York, NY)
Blue Book (Hollywood Reporter, Holly-
  wood, CA)
Film Producers, Studios, and Agents Guide
  (Lone Eagle, Beverly Hills, CA)
*Music Address Book: How to Reach Anyone
  Who's Anyone in the Music Business*
  (HarperCollins, NY)
Music Business Handbook & Career Guide
  (Sherwood Co., Los Angeles, CA)
New York Theatrical Sourcebook (Broad-
  way Press, Shelter Island, NY)
Who's Who in the Motion Picture Industry
  (Packard House, Beverly Hills, CA)
Who's Who in Television (Packard House,
  Beverly Hills, CA)

Breaking into film production

Tracey Barnett was working in public relations when she decided to break into film production. Although she didn't know anyone in the industry when she began, today she is a successful freelance production manager. We asked her how she did it.

"Most important was my desire to do it," says Tracey, "and I didn't get discouraged. I began by making a few contacts in the industry through people I knew in related fields. Then I set up interviews with these contacts. At the end of each interview, I asked for the names of three to five other contacts. This strategy opened a lot of doors for me. I followed up each interview with a phone call. I also kept in touch with my contacts on a monthly basis."

We asked Tracey what jobs are available for beginners in the film business and what qualifications are needed for those jobs.

"Entry-level positions include production assistant, stylist, assistant wardrobe manager, and grip," says Tracey. "There are no special requirements for these jobs. You don't need a degree in film to work in the business. In fact, people with film degrees begin at the same level as everybody else. What does count is intelligence and the ability to get things done quickly and efficiently. You need to think on your feet and be able to anticipate what needs to be done."

According to Tracey, freelance production assistants begin at about $150-$200 per day. More experienced production assistants can make as much as $300 per day. "But keep in mind that as a freelancer, you don't have the security of a regular paycheck," says Tracey. "You may not work every day." She advises those who need a more reliable income to look for a staff position in the industry.

Tracey advises those who want to break into the film business to keep at it: "Don't count your inexperience as a negative. Tenacity and enthusiasm will get you the first job. Approach your contacts and keep approaching them—over and over and over again."

Employers:

A Plus Talent Agency
680 N. Lake Shore Drive
Chicago, IL 60611
(312) 943-8315

Ambassador Talent Agents
203 N. Wabash Ave., Suite 2210
Chicago, IL 60601
(312) 641-3491

Aria
1017 W. Washington St., Suite 2A
Chicago, IL 60607
(312) 243-9400
Talent agency.

Chicago Film Office
1 N. LaSalle St., Suite 2165
Chicago, IL 60602
(312) 744-6415

Cineplex Odeon
70 E. Lake St.
Chicago, IL 60601
(312) 726-5300
Movie theater chain.

City of Chicago Department of Special Events
121 N. LaSalle, Room 703
Chicago, IL 60602
(312) 744-3315

Cultural Center, City of Chicago
78 E. Washington
Chicago, IL 60602
(312) 744-1742

David & Lee Model Management
70 W. Hubbard, Suite 200
Chicago, IL 60610
(312) 661-0500

Drama Group
330 202nd St.
Chicago Heights, IL 60411
(708) 754-5000
Theatrical agency.

Du Page Symphony Orchestra
P.O. Box 488
Glen Ellyn, IL 60138
(630) 858-4042

Elite Model Management
212 W. Superior, Suite 406
Chicago, IL 60610
(312) 943-3226

ETA, Inc.
7558 S. Chicago Ave.
Chicago, IL 60619
(773) 752-3955
Talent agency.

Geddes Agency
1925 N. Clybourn, Suite 402
Chicago, IL 60614
(312) 787-8333
Talent agency.

Hamilton, Shirley
333 E. Ontario St.
Chicago, IL 60611
(312) 787-4700
Talent and model agency.

Harpo Entertainment Group
110 N. Carpenter St.
Chicago, IL 60607
(312) 591-9595
Film and television production, including "Oprah!"

Harrise Davidson Associates
65 E. Wacker Drive, Suite 2401
Chicago, IL 60601
(312) 782-4480
Talent agency.

Jam Productions
207 W. Goethe St.
Chicago, IL 60610
(312) 266-6262
Booking agency & concert promoters.

Jefferson & Associates
1050 N. State St.
Chicago, IL 60610
(312) 337-1930
Talent agency.

Johnson, Suzanne
108 W. Oak St.
Chicago, IL 60610
(312) 943-8315
Talent agency.

Jenny Jones Show
454 N. Columbus Drive
Chicago, IL 60654
(312) 836-9400
Television program producer.

Leo's Dancewear
1900 N. Narragansett Ave.
Chicago, IL 60639
(773) 745-5600
Dancing supplies; shoes, costumes,
theatrical equipment & supplies.

Lily's Talent Agency
5962 N. Elston Ave.
Chicago, IL 60646
(773) 792-1160

Lorence, Emilia, Ltd.
619 N. Wabash
Chicago, IL 60611
(312) 787-2033
Talent agency.

M & R Amusement Companies
8707 Skokie Blvd.
Skokie, IL 60077
(847) 673-5600
Movie theater chain.

McCall Model & Talent
6933 S. Crandon, Suite 4C
Chicago, IL 60649
(773) 667-0611

Medinah Temple
600 N. Wabash Ave.
Chicago, IL 60611
(312) 266-5000
Theatrical facility.

National Talent Network
6326 N. Lincoln Ave.
Chicago, IL 60659
(773) 539-8575
Talent agency.

Nouvelle Talent Management
P.O. Box 578100
Chicago, IL 60657-8100
(312) 944-1133
Talent agency.

Petry Television
410 N. Michigan Ave.
Chicago, IL 60611
(312) 644-9660
Television station representatives.

Pheasant Run Resort
4051 E. Main St.
St. Charles, IL 60174
(630) 584-6300
Hotel, restaurants, and theater.

Phoenix Talent
332 S. Michigan Ave., Suite 1847
Chicago, IL 60604
(312) 667-0611
Talent agency.

Ravinia Festival Association
400 Iris Lane
Highland Park, IL 60035
(773) 728-4642 Chicago number
Three-month summer festival, featuring
the Chicago Symphony, world-renowned
classical and pop artists, dance, and
drama.

Renown Productions
3355 N. Drake Ave.
Chicago, IL 60618
(773) 509-9898
Prop supplier to theaters.

Rosemont Horizon
6920 Mannheim Road
Rosemont, IL 60018
(847) 635-6601
Indoor arena, booking big-name acts and
sports events.

Salazar & Navas
367 W. Chicago Ave.
Chicago, IL 60610
(312) 751-3419
Talent agency.

Screen Actors Guild
75 E. Wacker, 14th floor
Chicago, IL 60601
(312) 372-8081
Union.

Second City Theater
1616 N. Wells St.
Chicago, IL 60614
(312) 337-3992
The improvisational troupe that launched the careers of Mike Nichols, David Steinberg, Joan Rivers, John Belushi, and other nationally known performers.

Stewart Talent Management
212 W. Superior St., Suite 407
Chicago, IL 60610
(312) 943-3131

Vic
3145 N. Sheffield Ave.
Chicago, IL 60657
(773) 472-0449
Theater.

Walker, Don, Productions
360 N. Michigan Ave.
Chicago, IL 60601
(312) 332-1975
Entertainment bureau.

Williams-Gerard Productions
420 N. Wabash Ave.
Chicago, IL 60611
(312) 467-5560

Wolf, Paulette, Events & Entertainment
4020 W. Glenlake Ave.
Chicago, IL 60646
(773) 463-0040
Theatrical manager & producer.

Environmental Services

WEB SITES:

http://envirolink.org/envirowebs.html
links to publications, organizations, government, and industry sites.

http://www.econet.apc.org/econet/
links to industry news and organizations.

PROFESSIONAL ORGANIZATIONS:

For networking in environmental fields, check out the following local professional organizations listed in Chapter 5. See also "Engineering."

Citizens for a Better Environment
Institute of Environmental Sciences
Water Quality Association Research
  Council

For more information, contact:

Alliance for Environmental Education
10751 Ambassador Drive
Manassas, VA 22110
(703) 335-1025

Environmental Careers Organization
286 Congress St., 3rd floor
Boston, MA 02210
(617) 426-4783

National Association of Environmental Professionals
5165 MacArthur Blvd., N.W.
Washington, DC 20016
(202) 966-1500

National Wildlife Federation
1400 16th St., N.W.
Washington DC 20036
(202) 797-6800

Sierra Club
730 Polk St.
San Francisco, CA 94109
(415) 776-2400

Water Environment Federation
601 Wythe St.
Alexandria, VA 22314
(703) 684-2400

PROFESSIONAL PUBLICATIONS:

E, The Environmental Magazine
Ecology USA
Environmental Action
Environmental Business Journal
Environment Report
Environmental Science and Technology
Environmental Times
EPA Journal
Pollution Engineering
Water and Waste Digest

DIRECTORIES:

The Complete Guide to Environmental Careers (The CEIP Fund, Island Press, Washington, DC)
Conservation Directory (National Wildlife Federation, Washington, DC)
Directory of National Environmental Organizations (U.S. Environmental Directories, St. Paul, MN)
EI Environmental Services Directory (Environmental Information Ltd., Bloomington, MN)
The Environmental Career Guide (John Wiley & Sons, New York)
Environmental Industries Marketplace and *Gale Environmental Sourcebook* (Gale Research, Detroit, MI)
Green at Work: Finding a Business Career That Works for the Environment (Island Press, Washington, DC)

A "growth" industry

An environmental consultant friend of ours says the enforcement of federal regulations and emphasis on compliance with hazardous waste removal and clean air and water acts has put increased demands on her office. Opportunities for lawyers, engineers, and environmentalists are growing in large corporations and non-profit organizations. As she says, "It's a growth industry."

Employers, Private Sector:

Aires Consulting Group
1550 Hubbard Drive
Batavia, IL 60510
(630) 879-3006
Consulting firm.

American Waste Processing
P.O. Box 306
Maywood, IL 60153
(708) 681-3999
Consultants in hazardous waste management, treatment, and disposal.

Arro Laboratory
Caton Farm Road
Crest Hill, IL 60434
(815) 727-5436
Microbiological and chemical analysis.

Barton-Aschman
300 W. Washington St.
Chicago, IL 60606
(312) 917-3000
Consulting services in transportation and land development.

Browning-Ferris Industries
630 S. Hicks Road
Palatine, IL 60067
(847) 251-8759
Refuse disposal depots & plants.

Carnow Conibear & Associates
333 N. Wacker Drive
Chicago, IL 60606
(312) 782-4486
Property transfer audits, groundwater management, remedial design, risk assessments, and geotechnology surveys.

Chemical Waste Management
3003 Butterfield Road
Oak Brook, IL 60521
(630) 218-1500
Hazardous waste management.

Clarke Outdoor Spraying Co.
159 N. Garden Ave.
Roselle, IL 60172
(630) 894-2000
Pest control, pesticides & agricultural chemicals.

Clean Air Engineering
246 N. Woodwork Lane
Palatine, IL 60067
(847) 991-3300
Air pollution measurement, regulatory and policy analysis, and model development.

Clean Harbors of Chicago
11800 S. Stony Island Ave.
Chicago, IL 60617
(773) 646-6202
24-hr. emergency response; aqueous waste treatment, transport, disposal; lab chemical packaging and disposal; analytic testing services; training for hazardous material handling.

Commercial Testing & Engineering Company
1919 S. Highland Ave., Suite 210-B
Lombard, IL 60148
(630) 953-9300
Technical consulting on raw materials testing for coal, ores, and trace elements.

Consoer Townsend Environdyne Engineers
303 E. Wacker Drive, Suite 600
Chicago, IL 60601
(312) 938-0300
Multi-faceted consulting firm in environmental, manufacturing, and engineering services.

Ecology and Environment
111 W. Jackson Blvd.
Chicago, IL 60604
(312) 578-9243
Hazardous waste.

Emcom Co.
603 E. Diehl Road, Suite 123
Naperville, IL 60563
(708) 505-9450
Hazardous and solid waste consultation, design, development and operation; environmental and water evaluation and monitoring.

Envirodyne Engineers
168 N. Clinton St.
Chicago, IL 60606
(312) 648-1700
Provides planning and consulting engineering for major infrastructure improvements.

Greeley & Hansen
100 S. Wacker Drive
Chicago, IL 60606
(312) 558-9000
Offers sanitary and environmental engineering studies, designs, and construction services.

Harding Lawson Associates
1 Tower Lane
Oakbrook Terrace, IL 60181
(630) 571-2162
Consulting firm.

Heritage Environmental Services
1319 Marquette Drive
Romeoville, IL 60441
(815) 378-1600
Treatment; environmental engineering; laboratory services; transportation.

JMS Environmental Associates Ltd.
32 W. Burlington Ave.
Westmont, IL 60559
(630) 655-8500
Asbestos and environmental consulting and testing.

McIlvaine Company
2970 Maria Ave.
Northbrook, IL 60062
(847) 272-0010
Offers market research and technical consulting for world pollution control industry.

Mostardi-Platt Associates
945 Oaklawn Ave.
Elmhurst, IL 60126
(630) 993-9000
Environmental consultants in air pollution source compliance.

National Registry of Environmental Professionals
1253 Roosevelt Ave.
Glenview, IL 60025
(847) 724-6631
Environmental and energy consultants.

Northshore Waste Control
105 Skokie Valley Road
Highland Park, IL 60035
(847) 234-2760
Garbage collection.

Occusafe
1040 S. Milwaukee Ave.
Wheeling, IL 60090
(847) 459-4800
Assists clients toward resolutions of toxic and hazardous materials problems.

RCM Laboratories
9431 Ogden Ave.
Brookfield, IL 60513
(708) 485-8600
Environmental services for regulatory compliance and management.

RERC Environmental
2 N. LaSalle
Chicago, IL 60602
(312) 346-5467

Seeco Consultants
7350 Duvan Drive
Tinley Park, IL 60477
(708) 429-1666
Solid and hazardous waste; site assessments, tank management.

STS Consultants, Ltd.
111 Pfingsten Road
Northbrook, IL 60062
(847) 272-6520
Provides geotechnical and environmental consulting, and water resources and construction materials.

Wheelabrator
1501 E. Woodfield Road, Suite 200-West
Schaumburg, IL 60173
(847) 706-6900
Engineering consulting services for energy systems and pollution control applications.

WMX Technologies
3003 Butterfield Road
Oak Brook, IL 60521
(630) 572-8800
Formerly Waste Management Corp., provides refuse systems.

Employers, Government:

Department of Energy
Regional office of federal agency:
9800 South Cass Ave.
Argonne, IL 60439
(630) 252-2001

Environmental Protection Agency
401 M Street, S.W.
Washington, DC 20460
Contact: EPA Recruitment and Employment Center
(202) 382-3305
Regional administrators:
J.C. Kluczynski Federal Building
Chicago, IL 60604
(312) 353-2000
Federal government agency, recruits nationwide.

Illinois Pollution Control Board
100 W. Randolph
Chicago, IL 60601
(312) 814-3620
State agency acting through education, legislation, and planning.

Illinois State Dept. of Conservation
524 S. 2nd St.
Springfield, IL 62701-1787
(217) 785-4037
State government agency for conservation of natural resources, enforcement of state laws, and management of natural wildlife programs.

Employers, Not-For-Profit:

Citizens for a Better Environment
407 S. Dearborn, Suite 1775
Chicago, IL 60605
(312) 939-1530

Friends of the Parks
407 S. Dearborn, Suite 1590
Chicago, IL 60605
(312) 922-3307

Great Lakes Protection Fund
35 E. Wacker Drive
Chicago, IL, 60601
(312) 201-0660
Operates a $100-million endowment, established by the eight Great Lakes governors, to sponsor research and education projects.

Food/Beverage Producers and Distributors

Mouth-watering opportunities in food service management

Paula Hall, manager of the dietary department of a suburban hospital, sees the food service industry as a growing field with tremendous potential. The many hospitals in the Chicago area offer varied opportunities in food services, according to Paula. Some jobs, such as clinical or administrative dietitian, require a college degree in nutrition. Many do not.

Besides registered dietitians, Paula's staff includes food service supervisors, who manage the personnel who prepare food; diet technicians, who prepare and implement menus based on information about the patient; diet aides, who do such tasks as delivering meals to patients; a chef and cooking staff; and a food purchasing agent.

Paula is optimistic about employment prospects in the food service industry as a whole. "There are tremendous opportunities for those with culinary arts skills, and for hotel or restaurant food service managers. Opportunities exist in food equipment companies, public and private schools, contract food companies, food service consulting firms, even in banks and law firms downtown. Right now the possibilities in food marketing are phenomenal.

"The nutritional needs of the growing elderly population," Paula adds, "will also create many new jobs in the food service business as hospitals and other organizations become involved in the field of long-term care."

WEB SITES:

http://www.pvo.com/~pvo-plus/
provides a directory of food and beverage businesses, industry professionals, events, and an interactive bulletin board.

http://www.fmi.org
Food Marketing Institute

http://wwwfpi.org/fpi
Food Service and Packaging Institute

http://www.snax.com
Snack Food Association

http://www.Tmrinc.com/ifpd
International Food Products Directory

PROFESSIONAL ORGANIZATIONS:

For information about the food industry and related fields, contact the following professional organizations. Also see **"Hospitality"** for a list of Chicago-area restaurant chains.

American Institute of Food Distribution
28-12 Broadway
Fairlawn, NJ 07410
(201) 791-5570

Association of Food Industries
5 Ravine Drive
Matawan, NJ 07747
(908) 583-8188

Food Marketing Institute
800 Connecticut Ave., N.W.
Washington, DC 20006
(202) 452-8444

National Association of Beverage Retailers
5101 River Road, Suite 108
Bethesda, MD 20816
(301) 656-1494

National Association for the Specialty Food Trade
8 W. 40th St.
New York, NY 10018
(212) 482-6440

National Frozen Foods Association
4755 Linglestown Road
Harrisburg, PA 17112
(717) 657-8601

National Soft Drink Association
1101 16th St., N.W.
Washington, DC 20036
(202) 463-6732

Wine & Spirits Wholesalers of America
1023 15th St., N.W.
Washington, DC 20005
(202) 371-9792

PROFESSIONAL PUBLICATIONS:

Beverage World
Brewing Industry News
Fancy Food
Food and Beverage Marketing
Food Industry News
Food Management
Food and Wine
Foodservice Product News

Frozen Food Age
Journal of Food Products Marketing
Lempert Report
Wines and Vines

DIRECTORIES:

Hereld's 5000: The Directory of Leading U.S. Food, Confectionery and Beverage Manufacturers (SIC Publishing Co., Hamden, CT)
Impact Yearbook: A Directory of the Wine and Spirits Industry (M. Shanken Communications, New York, NY)
National Beverage Marketing Directory (Beverage Marketing Corp., New York, NY)
NFBA Directory (National Food Brokers Association, Washington, DC)
Thomas Food Industry Register (Thomas Publishing Co., New York, NY)
Wines and Vines Directory of the Wine Industry in North America (Hiaring Co., San Rafael, CA)

Employers:

Allen, J. W., & Co.
555 Allendale Drive
Wheeling, IL 60090
(847) 459-5400
Bakery ingredients, mixes, icings, fruit fillings, and frozen cake products.

Alpha/Rosen/Maryanne Baking Co.
4545 W. Lyndale St.
Chicago, IL 60639
(773) 489-5400
Buns & bread.

American Home Products
5151 W. 73rd St.
Chicago, IL 60638
(773) 767-8460
Manufactures Anacin, Chef Boy-ar-dee, Brach's candy, Woolite, PAM, Easy-Off, and many other familiar products.

American Licorice Co.
3701 W. 128th Place
Alsip, IL 60658
(773) 264-3600
Confectionery.

American Meat Packing
3946 S. Normal Ave.
Chicago, IL 60609
(773) 538-7000
Meat processing & packing.

Amos & Montgomery Food Business Group
461 W. Fullerton Ave.
Elmhurst, IL 60126
(630) 941-3320
Provides management assistance to food processors and retailers in food marketing and as national sales/marketing agents.

Appetizers
2555 N. Elston Ave.
Chicago, IL 60647
(773) 227-0400
Frozen hors d'oeuvres.

Aramark
2000 Spring Road, Suite 300
Oak Brook, IL 60521
(630) 572-2800
Providers of institutional food services; also services vending machines.

Archibald Candy Co./Fannie May Candies
1137 W. Jackson Blvd.
Chicago, IL 60607
(312) 243-3700

Armanetti
15127 S. 73rd Ave., Suite A1
Orland Park, IL 60462
(708) 429-4422
Retail liquor store chain.

Armour-Swift-Eckrich Dry Sausage Plant
410 Kirk Road
St. Charles, IL 60174
(630) 584-5900
Sausage & salami processing.

Bake-Line Products
1 Bake-Line Plaza
Des Plaines, IL 60016
(847) 699-1000
Cookies & baked goods.

Barton Brands
55 E. Monroe St., Suite 1700
Chicago, IL 60603
(312) 346-9200
Distills, blends, bottles, and distributes alcoholic beverages.

Berg, David, & Vienna Co.
2501 N. Damen Ave.
Chicago, IL 60647
(312) 278-5195
Manufacturer of hot dogs and other sausage products.

Bernard Food Industries
1125 Hartrey Ave.
Evanston, IL 60204
(847) 869-5222
Distributer of retail food products.

Borden
2301 Shermer Road
Northbrook, IL 60062
(847) 498-6200
Manufactures products including Wylers lemonade mix, Borden milk and cheese, Elmer's Glue, Walltex wall coverings, Cracker Jack snacks, and Mystic Tape.

Brach, E. J., Corp.
401 N. Cicero Ave.
Chicago, IL 60644
(773) 626-1200
Candies & confectionery products.

Bruss Co.
3548 N. Kostner Ave.
Chicago, IL 60641
(773) 282-2900
Meat products.

Buddig, Carl, & Co.
50 W. Taft Drive
South Holland, IL 60473
(708) 339-7300
Processed meat & sausage.

Butera's Finer Foods
1 Clocktower Plaza
Elgin, IL 60120
(708) 966-2770
Retail grocery chain.

Canteen Corp.
216 W. Diversey
Elmhurst, IL 60126
(773) 626-7370 Chicago number
Services vending machines; operates
restaurants.

Central Grocers Cooperative
3701 N. Centrella St.
Franklin Park, IL 60131
(847) 678-0660

C&K Snacks
6850 W. 63rd St.
Chicago, IL 60638
(773) 586-5020
Wholesale beer and snacks distributor.

Certified Grocers of Illinois
1 Certified Drive
Hodgkins, IL 60525
(708) 579-2100
Wholesale grocers.

Clark Products
950 Arthur Ave.
Elk Grove Village, IL 60007
(847) 956-1730
Food-service distributor and manufacturer.

Coca-Cola Bottling Co. of Chicago
7400 N. Oak Park Ave.
Niles, IL 60714
(847) 647-0200
Carbonated beverages.

Colonial Baking Co.
2435 Church Road
Aurora, IL 60504
(630) 851-3111
Baked breads & rolls.

Continental Distributing
9800 W. Balmoral Ave.
Rosemont, IL 60018
(847) 671-7700
Wholesaler of wines and spirits.

Corn Products
6500 Archer Road
Argo, IL 60501
(708) 563-2400

Dean Foods Company
3600 N. River Road
Franklin Park, IL 60131
(312) 625-6200 Chicago number
Major dairy and specialty foods manufacturer.

Diversifoods
910 Sherwood Drive, Suite 13
Lake Bluff, IL 60044
(847) 234-3407
Fast-food franchiser and restaurant
operator, including Burger King,
Godfather's Pizza, Chart House restaurants, Luther's Bar-B-Q, and Moxie's.

Dominick's Finer Foods
505 Railroad Ave.
Northlake, IL 60164
(708) 562-1000
Retail supermarkets and drug stores.

Don, Edward, & Company
2500 S. Harlem Ave.
North Riverside, IL 60546
(708) 442-9400
Distributor of food service equipment and
supplies.

Eby Brown Co.
1001 Sullivan Road
Aurora, IL 60507
(630) 897-8792
Wholesaler of tobacco and candy
distributor.

Fantasy-Blanke Baer Corp.
205 Alexandra Way
Carol Stream, IL 60188
(630) 462-5000
Flavor ingredient systems.

Farley Candy Co.
2945 W. 31st St.
Chicago, IL 60623
(773) 254-0900
Confectionery.

General Mills
704 W. Washington St.
West Chicago, IL 60185
(630) 231-1140
Dry food products.

Georgia Nut Co.
7500 N. Linder Ave.
Skokie, IL 60077
(847) 674-3717
Chocolate bars & roast nuts.

Golden Grain Co.
7700 W. 71st St.
Bridgeview, IL 60455
(708) 458-7020
Pasta, rice, & pasta mixes.

Gonnella Baking Co.
2002-14 W. Erie St.
Chicago, IL 60612
(312) 733-2020
Bread products.

Griffith Laboratories Worldwide
12200 S. Central Ave.
Alsip, IL 60658
(708) 371-0900
Processed meat, baked goods & frozen
food ingredients.

Guernsey Dell
4300 S. Morgan St.
Chicago, IL 60609
(773) 927-4000
Toffees, syrups, background flavors,
chocolate & praline nuts.

Heinemann's Bakeries
3925 W. 43rd St.
Chicago, IL 60632
(773) 523-5000
Bakery products.

Hinckley & Schmitt
6055 S. Harlem Ave.
Chicago, IL 60638
(773) 586-8600
Bottled water.

Hollymatic Corporation
600 E. Plainsfield Road
Countryside, IL 60525
(708) 579-3700
Producer of food processing and portion-
ing equipment.

Hostess Cake Co.
9555 W. Soreng Ave.
Schiller Park, IL 60176
(847) 678-0491

Houston Foods
3501 Mount Prospect Road
Franklin Park, IL 60131
(847) 957-9191
Specialty foods and gift packages.

Hyde Park Cooperative Society
1526 E. 55th St.
Chicago, IL 60615
(773) 667-1444
Three-store supermarket chain.

Interstate Brands Corp.
40 E. Garfield Blvd.
Chicago, IL 60615
(773) 536-7700
Butternut bread, buns & rolls.

Jay's Foods
825 E. 99th St.
Chicago, IL 60628
(773) 731-8400
Potato chips, popcorn & snack foods.

Jel Sert Co.
Highway 59 & Conde St.
West Chicago, IL 60185
(630) 231-7590
Beverage powders, confections & freezer
bars.

Jewel Companies
1955 W. North Ave.
Melrose Park, IL 60160
(708) 531-6000
Retail supermarket chain.

Jim Beam Corporation
510 Lake Cook Road
Deerfield, IL 60015
(847) 948-8888
Distills, blends, bottles, and distributes
alcoholic beverages.

Karp & Sons
1301 Estes Ave.
Elk Grove Village, IL 60007

(847) 593-5700
Baking supplies, jelly, flavors, extracts, fudges, and jams.

Katy Industries
853 Dundee Ave.
Elgin, IL 60120
(312) 379-1121 Chicago number
Large food processor.

Keebler Company
1 Hollow Tree Lane
Elmhurst, IL 60126
(630) 833-2900
Major producer and marketer of cookies, biscuits, and other bakery goods.

Kraft/General Foods Corporation
3 Lakes Drive
Northfield, IL 60093
(847) 646-2000
Producer and marketer of packaged grocery products including Maxwell House coffee, Jell-O, Kool-Aid, and Birdseye frozen foods.

Kronos-Central Products
4501 District Blvd.
Chicago, IL 60632
(773) 847-2250
Gyros, pita bread, & prepared sandwiches.

Land O'Frost
16850 Chicago Ave.
Lansing, IL 60438
(708) 474-7100
Meat & shelf-stable food packing & processing.

Leaf
1155 N. Cicero Ave.
Chicago, IL 60651
(773) 745-6200
Manufacturer of gum and candy.

Long, W. E., Co.
300 W. Washington St.
Chicago, IL 60606
(312) 726-4606
Cooperative for wholesale bakery members.

M&M Mars Candy Co.
2019 N. Oak Park Ave.
Chicago, IL 60635
(773) 637-3000
Manufacturer of a broad range of candy and confectionery products.

Miniat, Ed
945 W. 38th St.
Chicago, IL 60609
(773) 927-9200
Manufactures wholesale meats and oils.

Nabisco
7300 S. Kedzie Ave.
Chicago, IL 60629
(773) 925-4300
Producer of cookies, crackers, and cereals.

National Baking Co.
5001 W. Polk St.
Chicago, IL 60644
(773) 261-6000
Rolls & bread.

Nestle Foods
650 E. Diehl Road
Naperville, IL 60563
(708) 505-5388
Diversified manufacturer and marketer of food and liquor products including Fleischmann's beverages, Chase & Sanborn coffee, Planter's nuts, Curtiss candy, and Melville confections.

New Process Baking Co.
2883 S. Hillock Ave.
Chicago, IL 60608
(773) 376-7700

Newly Weds Foods
4140 W. Fullerton Ave.
Chicago, IL 60639
(773) 489-7000
Batter & breading mixes, bread crumbs, cracker meal, and English muffins.

Orval Kent Food Co.
120 W. Palatine Road
Wheeling, IL 60090
(847) 459-9000
Large manufacturer and distributor of refrigerated perishable salads.

Parco Foods
2200 W. 138th St.
Blue Island, IL 60406
(708) 371-9200
Cookies & crackers.

Park Corp.
511 Lake Zurich Road
Barrington, IL 60010
(847) 381-8550
Coffee, food, & detergent packaging.

Paterno Imports
2701 S. Western Ave.
Chicago, IL 60608
(773) 247-7070

Pepperidge Farm
230 2nd St.
Downers Grove, IL 60515
(630) 968-4000
Bread, rolls, & stuffing.

Pepsi-Cola General Bottlers
3 Crossroads of Commerce
3501 Algonquin Ave.
Rolling Meadows, IL 60008
(847) 253-1000

Pillsbury Co.
915 E. Pleasant St.
Belvidere, IL 61008
(815) 547-5311
Corn & peas, frozen packaging & processing.

Precision/Milani
2150 N. 15th Ave.
Melrose Park, IL 60160
(708) 216-0706
Specialty foods.

Quaker Oats Co.
321 N. Clark St.
Chicago, IL 60610
(312) 222-7111
Manufacturer and marketer of Gatorade, Snapple, and Quaker Oats cereals.

Rose Packing Co.
65 S. Barrington Road
Barrington, IL 60010
(847) 381-5700
Manufactures and sells pork products.

Royal Crown Bottling Co. of Chicago
2801 W. 47th St.
Chicago, IL 60632
(773) 376-7000
Carbonated beverages.

Rykoff-Sexton
1050 Warrenville Road
Lisle, IL 60532
(630) 964-1414
Leading manufacturer and distributor of food products to restaurants, hotels, schools, supermarkets, and the travel industry.

Rymer Foods
4600 S. Packers Ave.
Chicago, IL 60609
(773) 254-7530
Portion-controlled entrees for restaurants, institutions, and supermarket customers.

Salerno
7777 N. Caldwell Ave.
Niles, IL 60714
(847) 967-6200
Cookies & crackers.

Sanfilippo, John B., & Son
2299 Busse Road
Elk Grove Village, IL 60007
(847) 593-2300
Processes and packages nuts and candy.

Sara Lee Corporation
3 First National Plaza
Chicago, IL 60602
(312) 726-2600
Headquarters location for major manufacturer and marketer of consumer packaged goods including foods and candies; owns Booth Fisheries and Kitchens of Sara Lee.

Select Canfields
50 E. 89th Place
Chicago, IL 60619
(773) 483-7000
Produces and distributes beverages.

Shurfine-Central Corporation
2100 N. Mannheim Road
Northlake, IL 60164
(708) 681-2000
Food distributor to independent grocers.

Southland Corp.
205 S. Northwest Highway
Park Ridge, IL 60068
(847) 692-2240
Owns and operates the area's 7-11
convenience stores.

Superior Tea & Coffee Co.
990 Supreme Drive
Bensenville, IL 60106
(773) 489-1000 (Chicago number)
Producer and distributor of coffee, salad
dressings, syrups, and vending machine
products.

Sysco Food Services, Chicago
250 Weiboldt Drive
Des Plaines, IL 60016
(847) 699-5400
Distributes products to the food-service
industry.

Tootsie Roll Industries
7401 S. Cicero Ave.
Chicago, IL 60629
(773) 838-3400
Major domestic candy producer.

Topco Associates
7711 W. Gross Point Road
Skokie, IL 60077
(847) 676-3030
Large grocery products cooperative.

Treasure Island Food Marts
3460 N. Broadway
Chicago, IL 60077
(773) 327-4265
Retail grocery chain.

Turano Bakery
6501 W. Roosevelt Road
Berwyn, IL 60402
(708) 788-9220
Bread & pastries.

Vienna Sausage Manufacturing Co.
2501 N. Damen Ave.
Chicago, IL 60647
(773) 278-7800
Manufactures hot dogs, delicatessen-style
meats, cheesecake, pickles, soups, and
institutional foods.

Vincent Foods
135 S. LaSalle
Chicago, IL 60603
(312) 782-1838
Diversified food specialty company
engaged in the manufacture and distribution of food and food service products.

Vitner, C.J.
4202 W. 45th St.
Chicago, IL 60632
(773) 523-7900
Produces and distributes snack foods.

White Hen Pantry
660 Industrial Drive
Elmhurst, IL 60126
(630) 833-3100
Chain of convenience stores.

Wilton Enterprises
2240 W. 75th St.
Woodridge, IL 60517
(630) 963-7100
Develops and markets foods and kitchen
products.

World's Finest Chocolate
4801 S. Lawndale Ave.
Chicago, IL 60632
(773) 847-4600
Chocolate and confectionery products

Wrigley, Wm., Co.
410 N. Michigan Ave.
Chicago, IL 60611
(312) 644-2121
World's largest producer of chewing gum.

Furniture/Housewares/Household Textiles

WEB SITES:

http://www.cyspacemalls.com/ahf/index/html
American Home Furnishings

http://www.homefurnish.com/services.htm
Home Furnishing Netquarters

http://www.appliance.com/app/assoc.htm
National Association of Home Appliance Manufacturers

http://www.homefurnish.com/NHFA
National Home Furnishings Association

PROFESSIONAL ORGANIZATIONS:

For networking in furniture and housewares, check out these local professional organizations listed in Chapter 5:
American Society of Design Engineers
American Society of Interior Designers
Association of Home Appliance Manufacturers
Decorating Products Association of Chicago
National Housewares Manufacturers Association

For additional information, you can write or call:

American Furniture Manufacturers Association
P.O. Box HP-7
High Point, NC 27261
(910) 884-5000

International Home Furnishings Marketing Association
300 S. Main
High Point, NC 27260
(910) 889-0203

Textile Distributers Association
45 W. 36th St.
New York, NY 10018
(212) 563-0400

Textile Research Institute
P.O. Box 625
Princeton, NJ 08540
(609) 924-3150

United Textile Workers of America
P.O. Box 749
Voorhees, NJ 08043
(609) 772-9699

PROFESSIONAL PUBLICATIONS:

Discount Store News
Furniture Executive, The
Gifts & Decorative Accessories
HFD—Retail Home Furnishings
Home Furnishings Review
Housewares Magazine
Textile Hi-Lights
Textile Research Journal
Textile World

DIRECTORIES:

Davison's Textile Blue Book (Davison Publishing Co., Ridgewood, NJ)
Fairchild's Textile & Apparel Financial Directory (Fairchild Publications, New York, NY)
Furniture Manufacturers Directory (American Business Directories, Inc., Omaha, NE)
Merchandise Mart Buyers Guide (MMPI Management, Chicago, IL)
Who's Who in Furniture Distribution (National Wholesale Furniture Association, High Point, NC)

Employers:

All-Steel
P.O. Box 871
Aurora, IL 60507
(630) 859-2600
Metal office furniture.

Baker Knapp & Tubbs
6-187 Merchandise Mart
Chicago, IL 60654
(312) 337-7144
Residential and office furniture.

Brunswick Corporaton
1 North Field Court
Lake Forest, IL 60045-4811
(847) 735-4700
Manufactures pool tables, leisure
products.

Chicago Faucet
2100 S. Clear Water Drive
Des Plaines, IL 60018
(847) 803-5000
Manufacturer of bathroom and kitchen
fixtures.

Coleman Safety and Security Products
2820 Thatcher Road
Downers Grove, IL 60515
(630) 963-1550
Residential smoke detectors, door chimes
& thermostats.

Cooper Industries
400 Busse Road
Elk Grove Village, IL 60007
(847) 956-8400
Manufacturer of recessed and track
lighting systems.

Ekco Housewares
9234 W. Belmont Ave.
Franklin Park, IL 60131
(847) 678-8600
Bakeware, barware, and other household
products.

Elkay Manufacturing Co.
2222 Camden Court
Oak Brook, IL 60521
(630) 574-8484
Manufactures sinks, water coolers, and
faucets.

Excello Ltd.
1400 W. Fulton St.
Chicago, IL 60607
(312) 738-2211
Industrial textiles.

**Harper Leather Goods
Manufacturing Co.**
1050 W. 40th St.
Chicago, IL 60609
(773) 376-2662
Leather specialties, dog collars & rawhide
products.

Harris Marcus Lamps
3757 S. Ashland Ave.
Chicago, IL 60609
(773) 247-7500
Residential lighting fixtures, table lamps,
tables, chairs.

Health-o-Meter Products
7400 W. 100th Place
Bridgeview, IL 60455
(708) 598-9100
Bathroom scales.

Herman Miller
321 Merchandise Mart
Chicago, IL 60654
(312) 822-0140
Contract furniture for offices.

Holly Hunt Ltd.
1728 Merchandise Mart
Chicago, IL 60654
(312) 661-1900
Prepresents numerous furniture lines.

Jefferson Industries
2100 S. Marshall Blvd.
Chicago, IL 60623
(773) 277-6100
Carpet mats & runners.

Juno Lighting
2001 S. Mount Prospect Road
Des Plaines, IL 60017
(847) 827-9880

Kimball International
825 Merchandise Mart
Chicago, IL 60654
(312) 644-8144
Office furniture.

Knoll Group, The
1111 Merchandise Mart
Chicago, IL 60654
(312) 454-6920
Contract furniture for office and home.

Midwest Canvas Corp.
4635 W. Lake St.
Chicago, IL 60644
(773) 287-4400
Canvas products.

Ozite Manufacturing, Co.
1755 Butterfield Road
Libertyville, IL 60048
(847) 362-8210
Specialty textiles.

Pillowtex-Globe Corp.
3025 W. 47th St.
Chicago, IL 60632
(773) 376-2232
Bed pillows & down comforters.

Reflector Hardware Corp.
1400 N. 25th Ave.
Melrose Park, IL 60160
(708) 345-2500
Store fixtures, office and library furniture.

Regal Manufacturing Co.
1735 W. Diversey Pkwy.
Chicago, IL 60614
(773) 477-8780
Disposable industrial & health care
coveralls & accessories.

Salton/Maxim Housewares
550 Business Center Drive
Mt. Prospect, IL 60056
(847) 803-4600
Manufacturer of kitchen appliances,
personal care products.

St. Charles Manufacturing
1611 E. Main St.
St. Charles, IL 60174
(630) 584-3800
Manufacturer of custom kitchens.

Schnadig Corporation
1111 E. Touhy Ave.

Des Palines, IL 60018
(847) 803-6000
Manufacturer of upholstered furniture.

Schumacher Fabrics & Wallpaper
6-133 Merchandise Mart
Chicago, IL 60654
(312) 527-4650

Sealy Mattress Co.
111 N. Canal St., Suite 500
Chicago, IL 60606
(312) 559-0500
Manufacturer of bedding.

Selfix Inc.
4501 W. 47th St.
Chicago, IL 60632
(773) 890-1010
Housewares, organizers, home improve-
ment products.

Serta
2800 River Road, Suite 500
Des Plaines, IL 60018
(847) 699-9300
Manufacturer of bedding.

Shelby Williams Industries
11-111 Merchandise Mart
Chicago, IL 60654
(312) 527-3593
Contract furniture manufacturer.

Steelcase, Stow & Davis
1032 Merchandise Mart
Chicago, IL 60654
(312) 321-3500
Contract office furniture.

Stiffel Co.
700 N. Kingsbury St.
Chicago, IL 60610
(312) 664-9200
Lamps & lamp shades.

System Sensor
3825 Ohio Ave.
St. Charles, IL 60174
(630) 377-6363
Fire alarms & smoke detectors.

Triangle Home Products
945 E. 93rd St.
Chicago, IL 60619
(773) 374-4400
Bathroom cabinets, range hoods, and
other household products.

Weber-Stephens Products
200 E. Daniels Road

Palatine, IL 60067
(847) 934-5700
Barbeque grills.

Wilton International
2240 W. 75th Street
Woodridge, IL 60517
(630) 963-7100
Consumer products and home accessories.

Government

WEB SITES:

http://www.ci.chi.il.us/worksmart/
Works Mart Directory of (Chicago) City
Services
Provides alphabetical and categorical
listings of all Chicago city departments,
including their addresses, phone and Fax
numbers, programs, services, and bureaus.
This is the site to use when seeking contact
information on City of Chicago agencies
and departments.

http://www.state.il.us/
State of Illinois Site
Covers all 58 state agencies and offices
from Aging to Veterans Affairs, plus
employment services, educational
institutions, tourism, libraries, museums,
legislative information, and the capital
complex.

http://il.jobsearch.org/
Illinois Department of Employment
Security
Allows users to search for jobs on-line and
to locate regional employment offices.
The serious job seeker should use this site
regularly to make sure that job opportuni-
ties are not missed.

http://www.ajb.dni.us/
America's Job Bank (AJB)
Formerly known as the Interstate Job
Bank, AJB links 1,800 state employment

services which list approximately 250,000
jobs. About 5% of these jobs are in
government.

Other government Web cites include:

**http://lcweb.loc.gov/global/executive/
general_resources.html**
links to federal government sites.

**http://www.law.vill.edu/Fed-Agency/
fedwebloc.html**
lists over 200 federal government Web
servers.

**http://www.wpi.edu/Academics/IMS/
Library/jobguide/gov.html**
lists government job openings.

PROFESSIONAL ORGANIZATIONS:

For networking in government and related
fields, contact these local professional
organizations listed in Chapter 5.
**American Economic Development
  Council**
American Planning Association
Association of Legal Administrators
**Government Finance Officers
  Association**

For additional information about jobs in
government and related fields, you can
contact the following organizations:

**American Federation of Government
Employees**
80 F St., N.W.

Washington, DC 20001
(202) 737-8700

American Federation of State, County and Municipal Employees
1625 L St., N.W.
Washington, DC 20036
(202) 452-4800

Illinois Development Council
617 Indian Hill Road
Deerfield, IL 60035
(847) 317-0034

Metropolitan Housing Development Corp.
8 S. Michigan Ave.
Chicago, IL 60602
(312) 236-9673

National Association of Government Employees
2011 Crystal Drive, Suite 206
Arlington, VA 22202
(703) 979-0290

Northeast Illinois Planning Commission
222 S. Riverside Plaza
Chicago, IL 60605
(312) 454-0400

PROFESSIONAL PUBLICATIONS:

AFSCME Leader
City and State
Federal Employee News Digest
Federal Jobs Digest
Federal Staffing Digest
Federal Times
Government Executive
The Government Manager
The Public Employee Magazine
Public Employee Press

DIRECTORIES:

Braddock's Federal-State-Local Government Directory (Braddock Communications, Alexandria, VA)

165,000 Jobs! More than anywhere else
Who is the largest employer in Chicago? You guessed it. Government! Here's the breakdown on the top four:

Chicago, City of
121 N. La Salle St.
Chicago, IL 60602
(312) 744-4000
41,300 employees

Cook County
118 N. Clark St.
Chicago, IL 60602
(312) 443-6400
27,800 employees

Illinois, State of
100 W. Randolph St.
Chicago, IL 60601
(312) 814-6660
22,500 employees

U.S. Government
3230 S. Dearborn St.
Chicago, IL 60604
(800) 688-9889
73,500 employees

Public Employment

Although government has been downsizing, especially at the federal level, good opportunities exist if you know where to look. To illustrate, in Chapter 1 we cited a 4.4% projected decrease in federal employment between 1992 and 2005. What will happen to those functions and all that work? Through block grants, some of it will get passed on to state and local governments, whose employment increases are expected to be 11.74% and 10.38%, respectively, during the same period. Furthermore, while the total federal government may be downsizing, specific agencies may be growing. For example, the Immigration and Naturalization Service currently is recruiting heavily for border agents while other agencies are under a hiring freeze.

Here's some basic advice about seeking government employment. Don't treat the government as a monolithic employer that is highly centralized in its employment practices. It isn't! Government has decentralized its employment functions. Treat each government agency as an independent employer as you would any private-sector enterprise. Be prepared to play the long game. Government hiring procedures can be painfully slow. And don't assume that government hiring is any more objective than private sector practices. It isn't! Remember that human beings, not the government, make hiring decisions. So, network, network, network!

Public-sector information is pervasive on the Web. You should be able to find whatever information you need on the Internet in order to target your government job search. So, instead of listing information that is readily available on the Web, check out the sites listed at the beginning of this section, especially for State of Illinois employment. Contact information on local municipalities is given below.

Employers, Federal:

Chicago Service Center
U. S. Office of Personnel Management
219 S. Dearborn, 30th floor
Chicago, IL 60604
(312) 353-6234
http://www.usajobs.opm.gov/
Federal positions are posted to this Web site along with general information and an on-line employment application. Job listings can be searched by occupation and location. The general information page covers: how to apply for federal jobs; salary and benefits; veteran's information; and student employment. The site gets lots of use and tends to have slow response times during peak hours. However, using the OPM site is the most efficient way to obtain information about federal employment. Like many other agencies, OPM has been downsized and it does not have sufficient staff to provide job seekers with personal attention.

Employers, County:

Cook County
118 N. Clark St.
Chicago, IL 60602
(312) 443-6400

DeKalb County
100 E. Sycamore St.

Sycamore, IL 60178
(815) 895-7149

DuPage County
412 N. County Farm Road
Wheaton, Il 60187
(630) 682-7000
http://www.co.dupage.il.us/

Lake County
18 N. County St.
Waukegan, IL 60085
(847) 360-6600
http://www.co.lake.il.us/

Employers, Municipal:

We've provided contact information on
the largest municipalities that are most
likely to have the greatest number of
opportunities.

Arlington Heights, City of
33 S. Arlington Heights Road
Arlington Heights, IL 60005
(847) 253-2340

Aurora, City of
44 E. Downers Place
Aurora, IL 60505
(630) 892-8811

Berwyn, City of
6700 26th St.
Berwyn, IL 60402
(708) 788-2660

Calumet City
P.O. Box 1519
Calumet City, IL 60409
(708) 891-8100

Chicago Heights, City of
1601 Chicago Road
Chicago Heights, IL 60411
(708) 756-5300

Cicero, City of
4937 W. 25th St.
Cicero, IL 60650
(708) 656-3600

Des Plaines, City of
1420 Miner St.
Des Plaines, IL 60016
(847) 391-5300

Elgin, City of
150 Dexter Court
Elgin, IL 60120
(847) 931-5615
http://nsn.nslsius.org/elghome/cityelg/

Elmhurst, City of
119 Schiller St.
Elmhurst, Il 60126
(630) 530-3000
http://www.elmhurst.org/govern.html

Evanston, City of
2100 Ridge Ave.
Evanston, IL 60201
(847) 328-2100
http://chicago.digitalcity.com/evanston

Harvey, City of
P.O. Box 1539
Harvey, IL 60426
(708) 339-4200

Highland Park, City of
107 St. Johns Ave.
Highland Park, IL 60035
(847) 432-0800

Lake Forest, City of
220 E. Deerpath
Lake Forest, IL 60045
(847) 234-2600

Naperville, City of
P.O. Box 3020
Naperville, IL 60566
(630) 420-6111
http://www.naperville.il.us/

Oak Brook, City of
1200 Oak Brook Road
Oak Brook, IL 60521
(630) 990-3000

Oak Forest, City of
15440 S. Central Ave.
Oak Forest, Il 60452
(708) 687-4050

Oak Lawn, City of
5252 Dumke Lane
Oak Lawn, Il 60453
(708) 636-4400

Oak Park, City of
105 Oak Park Ave.
Oak Park, IL 60301
(708) 383-8005

Park Ridge, City of
505 Butler Place
Park Ridge, Il 60068
(847) 318-5200

Rolling Meadows, City of
3600 Kirchoff Road
Rolling Meadows, IL 60008
(847) 394-8500

St. Charles, City of
2 E. Main St.
St. Charles, IL 60174
(630) 377-4400

Schaumburg, City of
25 Illinois Blvd.
Hoffman Estates, IL
(708) 884-0030

Skokie, City of
5127 W Oakton St.
Skokie, IL 60077
(847) 673-0500

Waukegan, City of
160 N. Utica
Waukegan, IL 60085
(847) 360-9000

West Chicago, City of
475 Main
West Chicago, IL 60185
(630) 293-2200
http://city.wheaton.lib.il.us/cow/index.html

Wheaton, City of
303 W. Wesley St.
Wheaton, IL 60187
(630) 260-2000

Winnetka, City of
510 Green Bay Road
Winnetka, IL 60093
(847) 501-6000

Health Care: HMOs & PPOs/Hospitals

WEB SITES:

http://debra.dgbt.doc.ca/~mike/
healthnet/key.html
links to health care resources.

http://demonmac.mgh.harvard.edu/
hospitalweb.html
is a comprehensive list of hospitals on
the Web.

http://www.nscnet.com/jobheath.htm
lists health care employment opportunities.

PROFESSIONAL ORGANIZATIONS:

For networking in health care and related
fields, check out the following local
professional organizations listed in
Chapter 5:

American Association of Medical
    Assistants
American Dental Association
American Dental Hygienists
American Hospital Association
American Medical Association
American Medical Technologists
Illinois Hospital Association
Illinois Physical Therapy Association
Midwest Healthcare Marketing
    Association

For additional information, you can
contact:

American Association of Health Plans
1129 20th St., N.W., Suite 600
Washington, DC 20036
(202) 778-3200

American Dental Association
211 E. Chicago Ave.
Chicago, IL 60611
(312) 440-2500

American Health Care Association
1201 L St., N.W.
Washington, DC 20005
(202) 842-4444

American Hospital Association
1 N. Franklin St.
Chicago, IL 60606
(312) 422-3000

American Medical Association
515 N. State St.
Chicago, IL 60610
(312) 464-5000

American Public Health Association
1015 15th St., N.W.
Washington, DC 20005
(202) 789-5600

National Association for Home Care
519 C St., N.E., Stanton Park
Washington, DC 20002
(202) 547-7424

National Association of Social Workers
750 1st St., N.E.
Washington, DC 20002
(202) 408-8600

**National Council of Community Mental
Health Centers**
12300 Twinbrook Pkwy., Suite 320
Rockville, MD 20852
(301) 984-6200

PROFESSIONAL PUBLICATIONS:

ADA News
AHA Guide
American Journal of Nursing
American Journal of Public Health
Business and Health
The Dental Assistant
Health News Daily
Healthcare Executive
Healthcare Marketing Report
HMO Magazine
Home Care News
Home Health Line
Hospital Practice
Hospitals
*JAMA (Journal of the American Medical
    Association)*
Managed Care Outlook
Modern Healthcare

DIRECTORIES:

AHA Guide to the Health Care Field
 (American Hospital Association,
 Chicago, IL)
Blue Book Digest of HMOs (National
 Association of Employers on Health
 Care Action, Boca Raton, FL)
*Directory of Health Care Coalitions in the
 U.S.* (American Hospital Association,
 Chicago, IL)
Directory of Hospitals (SMG Marketing
 Group, Chicago, IL)
*Encyclopedia of Medical Organizations and
 Agencies* (Gale Research, Detroit, MI)
HMO/PPO Directory (Medical Economics
 Data, Montvale, NJ)
*Home Health Agency Report and Directory
 and Home Health Agency Chain
 Directory* (SMG Marketing Group,
 Chicago, IL)
KBL Healthcare Handbook (KBL
 Healthcare, New York, NY)
Managed Health Care Directory (American
 Managed Care and Review Association,
 Washington, DC)

Employers, HMOs and PPOs:

Aetna Health Plans
100 N. Riverside Plaza
Chicago, IL 60606
(312) 441-3000

BCI HMO
233 N. Michigan Ave.
Chicago, IL 60601
(312) 938-6600

Blue Cross/Blue Shield of Illinois
233 N. Michigan Ave.
Chicago, IL 60601
(312) 938-7974

Blue Cross HMO
1515 W. 22nd St.
Oak Brook, IL 60521
(630) 586-0400

Celtic Life Insurance Co.
233 S. Wacker Drive, Suite 700
Chicago, IL 60606
(312) 332-5401

Cigna Health Care of Illinois
1700 W. Higgins Road
Des Plaines, IL 60018
(847) 699-5600

CNA Managed Care-Illinois
333 S. Wabash Ave.
Chicago, IL 60685
(312) 822-5000

Compass Health Care Plans
9801 W. Higgins Road
Rosemont, IL 60019
(847) 292-2273

CompDent
770 N. Halsted St., Suite 308
Chicago, IL 60622
(312) 829-1296

FHP Great Lakes
1 Lincoln Center, Suite 700
Oak Brook, IL 60181
(630) 916-8400

FHP TakeCare Health Plan
of Illinois
1 Lincoln Center, Suite 700
Oak Brook, IL 60181
(630) 916-8400

**First Common Wealth, Ltd. Health
Services Corp.**
444 N. Wells, Suite 600
Chicago, IL 60610
(312) 644-1800

**Group Insurance Administration of
Illinois**
850 W. Jackson, Suite 600
Chicago, IL 60607
(312) 829-1556

Health Preferred of Mid America
2400 E. Devon Ave., Suite 188
Des Plaines, IL 60018
(800) 221-9212

HealthCare Compare Corp.
3200 Highland Ave.
Downers Grove, IL 60515
(630) 241-7900

HealthNetwork
1420 Kensington Road, Suite 203
Oak Brook, IL 60521-2143
(630) 954-2900

HealthStar
7257 N. Lincoln Ave.
Lincolnwood, IL 60646
(847) 673-3164

HMO Illinois
233 N. Michigan Ave.
Chicago, IL 60601
(800) 772-6897

Humana Health Plans
2545 S. M. L. King Drive
Chicago, IL 60616
(312) 808-3810

Illinois Masonic Community Health Plan
836 W. Wellington
Chicago, IL 60657
(773) 296-7014

Laborcare
7366 N. Lincoln Ave., Suite 304
Lincolnwood, IL 60646
(847) 675-7320

Maxicare Health Plans of the Midwest
111 E. Wacker Drive, Suite 1500
Chicago, IL 60601
(312) 616-4700

Medview Services-Illinois
555 W. Madison St.
Chicago, IL 60661
(312) 902-3765

MetLife Healthcare Network of Illinois
1900 E. Golf Road, Suite 501
Schaumburg, IL 60173
(847) 619-2222

MetLife Insurance
200 E. Randolph Drive, Suite 6836
Chicago, IL 60601-6804
(312) 861-3000

Midwest Business Medical Association
3201 Old Glenview Road, Suite 200
Wilmette, IL 60091
(847) 853-6262

New York Life/Sanus Health Plan
1111 W. 22nd St.
Oak Brook, IL 60521
(630) 368-1800

PHCS (Private Healthcare Systems)
9399 W. Higgins Road, Suite 500
Rosemont, IL 60018
(847) 292-6700

Preferred Plan
10600 W. Higgins Road, Suite 405
Rosemont, IL 60018
(847) 564-0235

Principal Health Care of Illinois
1 Lincoln Center, Suite 1040
Oak Brook, IL 60181
(800) 888-2310

Rush Health Plans
33 E. Congress Pkwy., Suite 600
Chicago, IL 60605
(312) 787-4778

Rush Prudential Health Plans
Sears Tower, Suite 3900
233 S. Wacker Drive
Chicago, IL 60606
(312) 234-7000

Trustmark
400 Field Drive
Lake Forest, IL 60045
(847) 615-1500

Union Health Service
1634 W. Polk St.
Chicago, IL 60612
(312) 829-4224

United HealthCare Corp. of Illinois
1 S. Wacker Drive
Chicago, IL 60606
(312) 424-4460

Universal Health Services
403 W. 14th St.
Chicago Heights, IL 60411
(708) 755-2462

University of Illinois HMO/Plan Trust
2023 W. Ogden, Room 205
Chicago, IL 60612
(312) 996-3553

Employers, Larger Hospitals:

NOTE: Today, many hospitals are part of large groups. We suggest consulting the Yellow Pages to see their affiliations.

Chicago Osteopathic Hospital
& Medical Center
5200 S. Ellis Ave.
Chicago, IL 60615-4314
(773) 947-3000

Chicago-Read Mental Health Center
4200 N. Oak Park Ave.
Chicago, IL 60634-1417
(773) 794-4000

Children's Memorial Medical Center
2300 Children's Plaza
Chicago, IL 60614-3394
(773) 880-4000

Christ Hospital & Medical Center
4440 W. 95th St.
Oak Lawn, IL 60453-2699
(708) 425-8000

Columbus Hospital
2520 N. Lakeview
Chicago, IL 60614-1804
(773) 883-7300

Cook County Hospital
1835 W. Harrison St.
Chicago, IL 60612-3701
(312) 633-6000

Edgewater Medical Center
5700 N. Ashland
Chicago, IL 60660-4087
(773) 878-6000

Evanston Hospital
2650 Ridge Ave.
Evanston, IL 60201-1718
(847) 570-2000

Gottlieb Memorial Hospital
701 W. North Ave.
Melrose Park, IL 60160
(708) 450-4933

Grant Hospital
550 W. Webster Ave.
Chicago, IL 60614-3787
(773) 883-3777

Highland Park Hospital
718 Glenview Ave.
Highland Park, IL 60035
(847) 432-8000

Hines, Edward, Jr., VA Medical Center
5th Ave. & Roosevelt Road
Hines, IL 60141
(708) 343-7200

Hinsdale Hospital
120 N. Oak St.
Hinsdale, IL 60521
(708) 856-9000

Holy Cross Hospital
2701 W. 68th St.
Chicago, IL 60629-1813
(773) 471-8000

Illinois Masonic Medical Center
836 W. Wellington Ave.
Chicago, IL 60657-5147
(773) 975-1600

Ingalls Memorial Hospital
1 Ingalls Drive
Harvey, IL 60426-3591
(708) 333-2300

Jackson Park Hospital & Medical Center
7531 Stony Island Ave.
Chicago, IL 60649-3913
(773) 947-7500

Little Company of Mary Hospital
2800 W. 95th St.
Evergreen Park, IL 60805
(708) 422-6200

Lutheran General Hospital
1775 Dempster St.
Park Ridge, IL 60068-1143
(847) 696-2210

MacNeal Memorial Hospital
3249 S. Oak Park Ave.
Berwyn, IL 60402-0715
(708) 795-9100

Madden, John J., Mental Health Center
1200 S. 1st Ave.
Hines, IL 60141-9999
(708) 338-7400

McGaw, Foster G., Hospital
Loyola University Medical Center
2160 S. 1st Ave.
Maywood, IL 60153-3304
(708) 216-9000

Mercy Hospital & Medical Center
Stevenson Expressway at King Drive
Chicago, IL 60616-2477
(312) 567-2000

Michael Reese Hospital & Medical Center
2929 S. Ellis St.
Chicago, IL 60616
(312) 791-3545

Mount Sinai Hospital-Medical Center
California Ave. at 15th St.
Chicago, IL 60608
(773) 542-2000

National Surgery Centers
35 E. Wacker Drive, Suite 2800
Chicago, IL 60601
(312) 553-4200
Owns freestanding surgery centers.

Northwestern Memorial Hospital
Superior St.& Fairbanks Court
Chicago, IL 60611
(312) 908-2000

Norwegian-American Hospital
1044 N. Francisco Ave.
Chicago, IL 60622-2743
(773) 292-8200

Oak Forest Hospital of Cook County
15900 S. Cicero Ave.
Oak Forest, IL 60452-4006
(708) 687-7200

Oak Park Hospital
520 S. Maple Ave.
Oak Park, IL 60304-1097
(708) 383-9300

Olympia Fields Osteopathic Hospital & Medical Center
20201 S. Crawford Ave.
Olympia Fields, IL 60461-1080
(708) 747-4000

Palos Community Hospital
12251 S. 80th Ave.
Palos Heights, IL 60463-1256
(708) 923-4000

Ravenswood Hospital Medical Center
4550 N. Winchester at Wilson
Chicago, IL 60640
(773) 878-4300

Rehabilitation Institute of Chicago
345 E. Superior St.
Chicago, IL 60611
(312) 908-6161

Resurrection Medical Center
7435 W. Talcott Ave.
Chicago, IL 60631-3702
(773) 774-8000

Riverside Medical Center
350 N. Wall St.
Kankakee, IL 60901-2959
(815) 933-1671

Rush-Presbyterian-St. Luke's Medical Center
1653 W. Congress Pkwy.
Chicago, IL 60612-3833
(312) 942-5000

Schwab Rehabilitation Institute
1401 S. California Ave.
Chicago, IL 60608
(773) 522-2010

South Suburban Hospital
17800 S. Kedzie Ave.
Hazel Crest, IL 60429-0989
(708) 799-8000

St. Elizabeth's Hospital
1431 N. Claremont Ave.
Chicago, IL 60622-1702
(773) 278-2000

St. Francis Hospital & Health Center
12935 S. Gregory St.
Blue Island, IL 60406-2470
(708) 597-2000

St. James Hospital & Health Centers
1423 Chicago Road
Chicago Heights, IL 60411-3483
(708) 756-1000

St. Joseph Health Center & Hospital
2900 N. Lake Shore Drive
Chicago, IL 60657-5640
(773) 665-3000

St. Mary of Nazareth Hospital Center
2233 W. Division St.
Chicago, IL 60622-3086
(312) 770-2000

Swedish Covenant Hospital
5145 N. California Ave.
Chicago, IL 60625-3642
(773) 878-8200

University of Chicago Hospitals
5841 S. Maryland
Chicago, IL 60637-1470
(773) 702-1000

University of Illinois at Chicago Medical Center
1740 W. Taylor St.
Chicago, IL 60612
(312) 996-3900

VA Lakeside Medical Center
333 E. Huron St.
Chicago, IL 60611-3004
(312) 943-6600

VA West Side Medical Center
820 S. Damen Ave.
Chicago, IL 60612-3740
(312) 666-6500

Weiss Memorial Hospital
4646 N. Marine Drive
Chicago, IL 60613
(773) 878-8700

West Suburban Hospital Medical Center
Erie at Austin
Oak Park, IL 60302
(708) 383-6200

Westlake Community Hospital
1225 Lake St.
Melrose Park, IL 60160-4000
(708) 681-3000

Hospitality: Hotels/Restaurants

WEB SITES:

http://www.hospitalitynet.nl/
is a central source for the hospitality
industry; includes a "virtual job exchange."

http://www.vnr.com/vnr/arch_ch.html
is the culinary and hospitality on-line
newsletter.

PROFESSIONAL ORGANIZATIONS:

For networking in the hospitality industry
and related fields, check out this local professional organization listed in Chapter 5:

Chicago Fine Dining Association

For more information, you can contact:

Chefs de Cuisine Association of America
155 E. 55th St., Suite 302B
New York, NY 10022
(212) 832-4939

**Hotel Sales & Marketing Association
International**
1300 L St., N.W., Suite 800
Washington, DC 20005
(202) 789-0089

National Restaurant Association
1200 17th St., N. W.
Washington, DC 20036
(202) 331-5900

PROFESSIONAL PUBLICATIONS:

Club Management
Food Management
Food and Wine
Hotel and Motel Management
Hotel and Resort Industry
Meetings and Conventions
Nation's Restaurant News
Restaurant Business
Restaurant Hospitality
Restaurants and Institutions

DIRECTORIES:

Directory of Hotel and Motel Companies
   (American Hotel Association Directory
   Corp., New York, NY)
Hotel and Motel Redbook (American Hotel
   and Motel Association, Washington,
   DC)
Meetings and Conventions Magazine,
   Directory Issue (Murdoch Magazines,
   New York, NY)
National Restaurant Association Directory
   (National Restaurant Association,
   Washington, DC)
Restaurant Hospitality, Hospitality 500
   Issue (Penton/IPC, Inc., Columbus, OH)
Restaurants Directory (American Business
   Directories, Omaha, NE)

Hotel management: more than "Puttin' on the Ritz"

With a little more than two years' experience in the hotel
business, Nancy Gordon landed a job as sales manager for
the Ritz-Carlton Hotel. We asked her for an overview of the
hospitality industry.

"If you want to move up quickly," says Nancy, "this
industry is the place to be. It's anything but a dead-end
business. Some people stay with the same organization for

most of their careers. But I'd say the average is probably around five years with any given company. People are constantly calling and making job offers.

"I studied hotel management and general business. Nevertheless, you can't just walk out of college and into a middle management position. I started as a receptionist at the Ritz-Carlton. Then I became a secretary. I don't know anyone who hasn't paid dues for a year or two. If you're interested in food or beverages, you might move up to dining room assistant. Essentially, you'd be doing the same thing as a secretary—typing up contracts or menus, that sort of thing. You really have to learn the business from the bottom up.

"In sales you move from secretarial work to a full-fledged sales position. I was a sales representative, then was promoted to sales manager. The next step might logically be director of sales or marketing, where I'd be responsible for advertising and marketing strategies, developing budgets and so on. An equivalent position would be director of food and beverages, the person who's responsible for all the food and drink served in the hotel, room service, all the dining rooms, special banquets, everything. After director of sales or of food and beverages, you go on to general manager.

"I'd say the competition is about average—not nearly as fierce as the advertising industry, for example. Earning potential is pretty good, too, depending, of course, on the size of the hotel, the city you're in, and what kind of company you're working for. You start pretty low, maybe around $23,000 a year. But each time you move up, you get a hefty raise, or ought to."

Employers, Hotels:

Allerton Hotel
701 N. Michigan Ave.
Chicago, IL 60611
(312) 440-1500

Bally Entertainment Corp.
8700 W. Bryn Mawr Ave.
Chicago, IL 60631
(773) 399-1300

Best Western Inn
162 E. Ohio St.
Chicago, IL 60611
(312) 787-3100

Bismarck Hotel
171 W. Randolph St.
Chicago, IL 60601
(312) 236-0123

Clarion Executive Plaza Hotel
71 E. Wacker Drive
Chicago, IL 60601
(312) 346-7100

Courtyard By Marriott
30 E. Hubbard St.
Chicago, IL 60611
(312) 329-2500

Days Inn
644 N. Lake Shore Drive
Chicago, IL 60611
(312) 943-9200

Doubletree Guest Suites
198 E. Delaware Place
Chicago, IL 60611
(312) 664-1100

Drake Hotel
140 E. Walton St.
Chicago, IL 60611
(312) 787-2200

Embassy Suites Hotel
600 N. State St.
Chicago, IL 60610
(312) 943-3800

Essex Inn
800 S. Michigan Ave.
Chicago, IL 60605
(312) 939-2800

Fairmont Hotel
200 N. Columbus Drive
Chicago, IL 60601
(312) 565-8000

Four Seasons Hotel Chicago
120 E. Delaware Place
Chicago, IL 60611
(312) 280-8800

Hickory Ridge Conference Center
1195 Summerhill Drive
Lisle, IL 60532
(630) 971-5000

Hilton, Chicago, & Towers
720 S. Michigan Ave.
Chicago, IL 60605
(312) 922-4400

Hilton, North Shore
9599 Skokie Blvd.
Skokie, IL 60077
(847) 679-7000

Hilton, O'Hare
P.O. Box 66414
Chicago, IL 60666
(773) 686-8000

Holiday Inn
350 N. Orleans St.
Chicago, IL 60654
(312) 836-5000

Hyatt Hotels Corporation
World Headquarters
200 W. Madison St.
Chicago, IL 60606
(312) 750-1234

Hyatt, Park
800 N. Michigan Ave.
Chicago, IL 60611
(312) 337-1234

Hyatt Regency
151 E. Wacker Drive
Chicago, IL 60601
(312) 565-1234

Hyatt Regency
1800 E. Golf Road
Schaumburg, IL 60173
(847) 605-1234

Hyatt Regency, Oak Brook
1909 Spring Road
Oak Brook, IL 60521
(630) 573-1234

Hyatt Regency, O'Hare
9300 Bryn Mawr Ave.
Rosemont, IL 60018
(847) 696-1234

Indian Lakes Resort
250 W. Schick Road
Bloomingdale, IL 60108
(630) 529-0200

Lodge, The
2815 Jorie Blvd.
Oak Brook, IL 60521
(630) 990-5800

Marriott, Chicago, Downtown
540 N. Michigan Ave.
Chicago, IL 60611
(312) 836-0100

Marriott, Lincolnshire
10 Marriott Drive
Lincolnshire, IL 60069
(847) 634-0100

Marriott, Oak Brook
1401 W. 22nd St.
Oak Brook, IL 60521
(630) 573-8555

Marriott, O'Hare
8535 W. Higgins Road
Chicago, IL 60631
(773) 693-4444

Marriott, Schaumburg
50 N. Martingale Road
Schaumburg, IL 60173
(847) 240-0100

Midland Hotel
172 W. Adams St.
Chicago, IL 60603
(312) 332-1200

Nikko Hotel Chicago
320 N. Dearborn St.
Chicago, IL 60610
(312) 744-1900

Nordic Hills Resort
Nordic Road
Itasca, IL 60143
(630) 773-2750

Oak Brook Hills Hotel & Resort
3500 Midwest Road
Hinsdale, IL 60522
(630) 850-5555

Omni Chicago Hotel
676 N. Michigan Ave.
Chicago, IL 60611
(312) 944-6664

Palmer House Hilton
17 E. Monroe St.
Chicago, IL 60603
(312) 726-7500

Pheasant Run Resort
4051 E. Main St.
St. Charles, IL 60174
(630) 584-6300

Quality Inn
6810 Mannheim Road
Rosemont, IL 60018
(847) 297-1234

Radisson Hotel
2111 Butterfield Road
Downers Grove, IL 60515
(630) 971-2000

Radisson Hotel Lincolnwood
4500 W. Touhy Ave.
Lincolnwood, IL 60646
(847) 724-9910

Radisson Suites
5500 N. River Road
Rosemont, IL 60018
(847) 678-4000

Ramada Congress Hotel
520 S. Michigan Ave.
Chicago, IL 60605
(312) 427-3800

Ramada Inn
6600 Mannheim Road
Rosemont, IL 60018
(847) 827-5131

Ritz Carlton Hotel
160 E. Pearson St.
Chicago, IL 60611
(312) 266-1000

Sheraton
6501 Mannheim Road
Rosemont, IL 60018
(847) 699-6300

Sheraton Chicago Hotel Towers
301 E. North Water St.
Chicago, IL 60611
(312) 464-1000

Sheraton Suites
933 Skokie Blvd.
Northbrook, IL 60062
(847) 498-6500

Sofitel Hotel Chicago
5550 N. River Road
Rosemont, IL 60018
(847) 678-4488

Summerfield Suites Hotel
166 E. Superior St.
Chicago, IL 60611
(312) 787-6000

Swissotel Chicago
323 E. Wacker Drive
Chicago, IL 60601
(312) 565-0565

Westin Hotel & Resorts
6100 N. River Road
Rosemont, IL 60018
(847) 698-6000

Westin Hotel & Resorts
909 N. Michigan Ave.
Chicago, IL 60611
(312) 943-7200

Wyndham Hamilton
400 Park Blvd.
Itasca, IL 60143
(630) 773-4000

Employers, Restaurant Chains:

Chicago is a great restaurant town. Chicagoland has more than 10,000 restaurants. Obviously, we can't list them all. Nor do we provide this list based on gourmet reports! This list represents the larger chains. Thousands of other possibilities abound. If you have access to the Internet, check out the many other Chicago restaurants on-line at:

http://www.city.net/

http://www.nwu.edu/ev-chi/restaurants.html

A la Carte Entertainment
6666 N. Oliphant Ave.
Chicago, IL 60631
(773) 774-9111
Number of units: 14

Amerihost Properties
2400 E. Devon, #208
Des Plaines, IL 60018
(847) 298-4500
Number of units: 44

AmeriKing
2215 Enterprise Drive
Westchester, IL 60154
(708) 947-2150
Owns 176 Burger King restaurants.

BAB Systems
8501 W. Higgins Road #320
Chicago, IL 60631
(773) 380-6100
Owns 58 Big Apple Bagels restaurants.

Boston Chicken
101 W. Ogden Ave.
Westmont, IL 60559
(630) 964-1600
Number of units: 1,023

Boz
14207 Chicago Road
Dolton, IL 60419
(708) 841-3747
Number of units: 32 hot doggeries.

Bravo Restaurants
205 W. Wacker Drive, Suite 1400
Chicago, IL 60606
(312) 345-8500
Number of units: 13, including Edwardo's Pizza and Gino's East.

Brown's Chicken and Pasta
Regional headquarters
2809 Butterfield Road, Suite 360
Oak Brook, IL 60521
(630) 571-5300
Number of units: 72

Burger King
National headquarters:
17777 Old Cutler Road
Miami, FL 33157
(305) 370-3000
Number of units: 8,400

International Double Drive-Thru
815 N. La Salle St.
Chicago, IL 60610
(312) 573-4000
Owns 15 Checkers restaurants.

Irving's for Red Hot Lovers
436 Frontage Road, Suite 2C
Northfield, IL 60093
(847) 446-2855
Number of units: 11

Junior's Hot Dogs
6335 W. 95th St.
Oak Lawn, IL 60453
(708) 424-0049
Number of units: 24

KFC Kentucky Fried Chicken
Regional office
1415 W. 22nd St.
Oak Brook, IL 60521
(708) 990-7888
Number of units: 40

Lettuce Entertain You Corp.
5419 N. Sheridan Road
Chicago, IL 60659
(773) 878-7340
Number of units: 40

Levy Restaurants
980 N. Michigan Ave., Suite 400
Chicago, IL 60611
(312) 664-8200
Owns 40 restaurants, including Spiaggia,
Blackhawk Lodge, and Bistro 110.

Lindy-Gertie Enterprises
8437 Park Ave.
Burr Ridge, IL 60521
(630) 323-8003
Number of units: 10 Lindy's Chili
restaurants.

McDonald's Corporation
World headquarters
1 McDonald's Plaza
Oak Brook, IL 60521
(630) 623-3000
Number of units: 12,000

Motorola Foodworks
1303 E. Algonquin Road
Schaumburg, IL 60196
(847) 576-5000
Number of units: 30

Pizza Hut
Regional office
4225 Naperville Road, Suite 300
Lisle, IL 60532
(630) 955-1938
Number of units: 7,900

Restaurant Development Group
412 N. Clark St.
Chicago, IL 60610
(312) 755-0990
Owns 12 restaurants, including The
Saloon, Kinzie Chophouse, Mambo Grill,
Grappa, and Bar Louie.

Rosati's Franchise Systems
33 W. Higgins Road #1010
Barrington, IL 60010
(847) 836-0400
Number of units: 62

Wendy's International
40 Sherman Blvd., Suite 130
Naperville, IL 60563
(630) 961-5800
Number of units: 4,993

Insurance

WEB SITES:

http://www.connectyou.com/talent/
an insurance career center with job
listings, corporate profiles, recruiter's
directory, and resume listing service.

For networking in insurance and related
fields, check out these professional
organizations listed in Chapter 5. Also see
"Health Care."

PROFESSIONAL ORGANIZATIONS:

Alliance of American Insurers
American Society of Safety Engineers
Healthcare Financial Management
Association
Million Dollar Round Table
National Association of Independent
Insurance Adjusters

For additional information, you can write
or call:

American Council of Life Insurance
1001 Pennsylvania Ave., N.W.
Washington, DC 20004
(202) 624-2000

American Insurance Association
1130 Connecticut Ave., N.W.
Washington, DC 20036
(202) 828-7100

National Association of Independent
Insurers
2600 River Road
Des Plaines, IL 60018
(847) 297-7800

National Association of Life
Underwriters
1922 F St., N.W.
Washington, DC 20006
(202) 331-6000

PROFESSIONAL PUBLICATIONS:

Best's Review
Business Insurance
Employee Benefit Plan Review
The Insurance Agent
Insurance Times
National Underwriter
NSACI News
Underwriter's Report

DIRECTORIES:

*Best's Directory of Recommended Insurance
Agencies* (A. M. Best Co., Oldwick, NY)
Insurance Almanac (Underwriter
Publishing Co., Englewood, NJ)
Who's Who in Insurance (Underwriter
Printing and Publishing Co.,
Englewood, NJ)

Employers:

Addison Farmers' Insurance Company
2500 Highland Ave., Suite 210
Lombard, IL 60148
(630) 932-7400
Underwriter of fire, marine, casualty,
property & casualty insurance.

Allstate Corp.
2775 Sanders Road
Northbrook, IL 60062
(847) 402-5199

American Country Financial Services
Corp.
222 N. LaSalle St.. Suite 1600
Chicago, IL 60601
(312) 346-3782
Fire, marine, and casualty insurance;
accident and health coverage.

Aon Risk Services
123 N. Wacker Drive
Chicago, IL 60606
(312) 701-3000
Accident, health, and disability insurance.

Associated Agencies
414 N. Orleans St.
Chicago, IL 60610
(312) 755-9444

Associated Aviation Underwriters
300 S. Riverside Plaza
Chicago, IL 60606
(312) 906-3200

Bankers Life & Casualty Company
222 Merchandise Mart Plaza
Chicago, IL 60654-2001
(312) 396-6000

Blue Cross & Blue Shield Association
676 N. St. Clair St.
Chicago, IL 60611
(312) 440-6000
Provides hospital, medical, and other
health services to subscribers.

Blue Cross & Blue Shield of Illinois
233 N. Michigan Ave.
Chicago, IL 60601
(312) 938-6000
Underwriter of insurance and reinsurance
policies for accident and health coverage.

Burns & Wilcox-Chicago Office
300 S. Wacker Drive, Suite 1150
Chicago, IL 60606
(312) 957-0510
Underwriter of fire, marine, and casualty
insurance.

Certified Life Insurance
222 Merchandise Mart Plaza
Chicago, IL 60654-2001
(312) 396-6000
Life, accident, health, and disability
insurance.

Chicago Title & Trust Co.
171 N. Clark St.-10CC
Chicago, IL 60601-3294
(312) 223-2000
Underwriter of title insurance.

**Cigna Excess & Surplus Insurance
Services**
525 W. Monroe, Suite 2220
Chicago, IL 60606
(312) 648-7580

Cigna Insurance Company of Illinois
8755 W. Higgins Road
Chicago, IL 60631
(773) 380-8100
Life, accident, health, disability, casualty &
property insurer.

CNA Insurance
CNA Plaza
Chicago, IL 60685
(312) 822-5000
Life, accident & health insurance. Fire,
marine, and casualty insurance. Disabil-
ity& property insurance.

**Combined Insurance Company of
America**
123 N. Wacker Drive
Chicago, IL 60606
(312) 701-3000

Crabtree Premium Finance
2500 Highland Ave., Suite 230
Lombard, IL 60148
(630) 932-7459
Underwriter of surety insurance.
Premium finance company.

Employers of Wausau
901 Warrenville Road
Lisle, IL 60532
(630) 719-9700

Illinois Banc One Insurance Services
800 Davis St.
Evanston, IL 60204
(847) 866-5462
Life, fire, marine, and casualty insurance.

Illinois Union Insurance Company
8755 W. Higgins Road
Chicago, IL 60631
(773) 380-8100
Accident, health, disability, fire, marine,
and casualty insurance.

Intercounty Title Co. of Illinois
120 W. Madison
Chicago, IL 60602
(312) 977-2600
Underwriter of title insurance.

Kemper National Insurance Companies
1 Kemper Drive
Long Grove, IL 60049
(847) 550-5500
Insurance underwriting services.

Marsh & McLennan
500 W. Monroe St.
Chicago, IL 60605
(312) 627-6000

**National-Ben Franklin Insurance Co.
of Illinois**
200 S. Wacker Drive
Chicago, IL 60606
(312) 876-5000
Life insurance carrier.

Old Republic Life Insurance Co.
307 N. Michigan Ave.
Chicago, IL 60601
(312) 346-8100
Life insurance & related products.

SAFECO Insurance Co.
2800 W. Higgins Road
Hoffman Estates, IL 60196
(847) 490-2900
Fire, marine, and casualty insurance.

St. Paul Insurance Co. of Illinois
500 W. Madison, 26th floor
Chicago, IL 60661
(312) 648-5000

Unitrin
1 E. Wacker Drive
Chicago, IL 60601
(312) 661-4500

Virginia Surety Co.
123 N. Wacker Drive
Chicago, IL 60606
(312) 701-3000

Washington National Insurance Co.
300 Tower Pkwy.
Lincolnshire, IL 60069-3665
(847) 793-3000
Life & health insurance & annuities.

Law Firms

WEB SITES:

http://www.gcwf.com/attylist.htm
contact information for attorneys
nationwide.

http://www.lawjobs.com/
a law employment center with job listings,
salary information, an index of top firms,
legal directories and bar exam information.

**http://www.law.indiana.edu/law/v-lib/
lawfirms.html**
a directory of law firms.

http://www.lawinfo.com/employment/
national job board.

http://www.legal.net/attorney.htm
discussion board for attorneys plus a
registry of firms by state and city.

PROFESSIONAL ORGANIZATIONS:

For networking in law and related fields,
check out the following professional
organizations listed in Chapter 5:
American Bar Association
Association of Legal Administrators
Chicago Bar Association
Chicago Council of Lawyers
Women's Bar Association of Illinois

For more information, you can write
or call:

American Bar Association
750 N. Lake Shore Drive
Chicago, IL 60611
(312) 988-5000

**National Bar Association
(Minority Attorneys)**
1225 11th St., N. W.
Washington, DC 20001
(202) 842-3900

National Paralegal Association
P.O. Box 406

Solebury, PA 18963
(215) 297-8333

PROFESSIONAL PUBLICATIONS:

ABA Journal
American Lawyer
The Bar News
CBA (Chicago Bar Association)
Chicago Lawyer
The Compleat Lawyer
Illinois Bar Lawyer
Illinois Legal Times
Lawyer's Weekly
The Paralegal
Student Lawyer

DIRECTORIES:

ABA Directory (American Bar Association,
   Chicago, IL)
Directory of Local Paralegal Clubs (National
   Paralegal Association, Solebury, PA)
Lawyer's List (Commercial Publishing Co.,
   Easton, MD)
Martindale-Hubble Law Directory
   (Martindale-Hubble, Summit, NJ)

Employers:

NOTE: Banks, title companies, and major
corporations all have legal staffs.

Altheimer & Gray
10 S. Wacker Drive
Chicago, IL 60606
(312) 715-4000
182 attorneys

Baker & McKenzie
130 E. Randolph Drive
Chicago, IL 60601
(312) 861-8000
158 attorneys

Bell Boyd & Lloyd
70 W. Madison St.
Chicago, IL 60602
(312) 372-1121
152 attorneys

Chapman & Cutler
111 W. Monroe St.
Chicago, IL 60603
(312) 845-3000
189 attorneys

Clausen Miller
10 S. La Salle St.
Chicago, IL 60603
(312) 855-1010
150 attorneys

D'Ancona & Pflaum
30 N. LaSalle St., Suite 2900
Chicago, IL 60602
(312) 580-2000

Gardner Carton & Douglas
321 N. Clark St.
Chicago, IL 60610
(312) 644-3000
178 attorneys

Hinshaw & Culbertson
222 N. La Salle St.
Chicago, IL 60601
(312) 704-3000
201 attorneys

Hopkins & Sutter
3 First National Plaza
Chicago, IL 60602
(312) 558-6600
141 attorneys

Jenner & Block
1 IBM Plaza
Chicago, IL 60611
(312) 222-9350
311 attorneys

Katten Muchin & Zavis
525 W. Monroe St.
Chicago, IL 60661
(312) 902-5200
253 attorneys

Keck Mahin & Cate
77 W. Wacker Drive
Chicago, IL 60601
(312) 634-7700
180 attorneys

Kirkland & Ellis
200 E. Randolph Drive
Chicago, IL 60601
(312) 861-2000
267 attorneys

Lord Bissell & Brook
115 S. La Salle St.
Chicago, IL 60603
(312) 443-0700
261 attorneys

Mayer Brown & Platt
190 S. La Salle St.
Chicago, IL 60603
(312) 782-0600
379 attorneys

McBride Baker & Coles
Northwestern Atrium
500 W. Madison, 40th floor
Chicago, IL 60603
(312) 715-5700

McDermott Will & Emery
227 W. Monroe St.
Chicago, IL 60606
(312) 372-2000
261 attorneys

Peterson & Ross
200 E. Randolph Drive, Suite 7300
Chicago, IL 60601
(312) 861-1400

Querrey & Harrow
180 N. Stetson Ave.
Chicago, IL 60601
(312) 540-7000
133 attorneys

Rooks Pitts & Poust
55 W. Monroe St., Suite 1500
Chicago, IL 60603
(312) 876-1700

Ross & Hardies
50 N. Michigan Ave.
Chicago, IL 60601
(312) 558-1000
143 attorneys

Rudnick & Wolfe
203 N. La Salle St.
Chicago, IL 60601
(312) 368-4000
189 attorneys

Schiff Hardin & Waite
233 S. Wacker Drive
Chicago, IL 60606
(312) 876-1000
201 attorneys

Seyfarth Shaw Fairweather Geraldson
55 E. Monroe St.
Chicago, IL 60603
(312) 346-8000
189 attorneys

Sidley & Austin
1 First National Plaza
Chicago, IL 60603
(312) 853-7000
351 attorneys

Skadden Arps Slate Meagher & Flom
333 W. Wacker Drive, 21st floor
Chicago, IL 60606

(312) 407-0700
98 attorneys

Sonnenschein Nath & Rosenthal
233 S. Wacker Drive
Chicago, IL 60606
(312) 876-8000
186 attorneys

Vedder Price Kaufman & Kammholz
222 N. La Salle St.
Chicago, IL 60601
(312) 609-7500
139 attorneys

Wildman Harrold Allen & Dixon
225 W. Wacker Drive
Chicago, IL 60606
(312) 201-2000
159 attorneys

Winston & Strawn
35 W. Wacker Drive
Chicago, IL 60601
(312) 558-5600
251 attorneys

Working in the non-profit world

We asked Tom Sanberg, once Director of Development for the Museum of Science and Industry, what it takes to make it in the non-profit world.

"Most of the people who enjoy non-profit work and are successful at it tend to be other-directed. They get satisfaction out of working for a so-called worthy cause. There are very few high–paying jobs in not-for-profit institutions. An executive-level job at the Museum, for example, probably pays about half what a job with similar responsibilities would pay in a profit-making company of the same size.

"One of the fastest-growing specialties within the non-profit world is fundraising management, probably because non-profit institutions rely so heavily on grants and contributions," Tom adds. He notes that Northwestern University's extension division offers a course in fundraising, and the local chapter of the National Society for Fund Raising Executives (listed in Chapter 5) conducts several seminars, workshops, and a certification program.

Museums/Theaters/Cultural Institutions/Fundraising

WEB SITES:

http://www.sirius.com/~robinson/musprof.html
is a resource for curators, researchers, and museum staff.

http://www.imagesite.com/muse/museylpgs.html
contains the museum and galleries Yellow Pages.

http://www.concourse.com/wwar/galleries.html
contains contact information for galleries.

PROFESSIONAL ORGANIZATIONS:

To help you learn more about employment with museums and other arts organizations, you can write or call the organizations below. Also, the Friday editions of local newspapers and the monthly *Chicago Magazine* carry extensive listings of cultural venues too numerous to mention here.

American Association of Museums
1225 I St., N.W.
Washington, DC 20005
(202) 289-1818

American Federation of Arts
41 E. 65th St.
New York, NY 10021
(212) 988-7700

Arts and Business Council
55 E. Monroe St.
Chicago, IL 60603
(312) 372-1876

Illinois Arts Council
100 W. Randolph St.
Chicago, IL 60601
(312) 814-6750

National Assembly of Local Art Agencies
1420 K St., N.W., Suite 204
Washington, DC 20005
(202) 371-2830

National Assembly of State Art Agencies
1010 Vermont Ave., N.W.
Washington, DC 20005
(202) 347-6352

PROFESSIONAL PUBLICATIONS

Art Business News
Art Newsletter, The
Art World
Avisco
Museum News
NASAA News

DIRECTORIES

American Art Directory (R. R. Bowker, New Providence, NJ)
Art Business News Guide (Brant Art Publications, New York, NY)
NASAA Directory (National Assembly of State Art Agencies, Washington, DC)
Official Museum Directory (American Association of Museums, Washington, DC)

Employers:

Adler Planetarium
1300 S. Lake Shore Drive
Chicago, IL 60605
(312) 322-0304
Museum of the stars, planets, galaxies, and beyond.

American City Bureau
1721 Moon Lake Blvd., Suite 201
Hoffman Estates, IL 60194
(847) 490-5858
Fundraising consultants.

Arie Crown Theater
McCormick Place
2300 S. Lake Shore Drive
Chicago, IL 60616
(312) 791-6000

Art Institute of Chicago, The
Michigan Ave. at Adams St.
Chicago, IL 60603
(312) 443-3600
Houses one of the world's richest
collections of Impressionist, modern,
oriental art and sculpture, and
decorative arts.

Auditorium Theater
50 E. Congress Pkwy.
Chicago, IL 60605
(312) 922-4046
Louis Sullivan-designed legitimate theater.

Balzekas Museum of Lithuanian Culture
6500 S. Pulaski Road
Chicago, IL 60629
(773) 582-6500
Permanent exhibition of cultural artifacts;
library; art gallery.

Brookfield Zoo
1st Ave. at 31st St.
Brookfield, IL 60513
(708) 485-2200
200-acre zoological park.

Candlelight Dinner Playhouse
5620 S. Harlem Ave.
Summit, IL 60501
(708) 496-3000
Dinner theater.

Chicago Academy of Sciences
2060 N. Clark St.
Chicago, IL 60614
(773) 549-0343
Nature museum; the earliest scientific
institution in Chicago.

Chicago Children's Museum
600 E. Grand Ave.
Chicago, IL 60611
(312) 527-1000

Chicago Cultural Center
78 E. Washington St.
Chicago, IL 60602
(312) 744-6630
Home to exhibits, programs, and the
Museum of Broadcast Communications.

Chicago Film Festival
415 N. Dearborn St.
Chicago, IL 60610
(312) 644-3400
Annual film festival.

Chicago Historical Society
North Ave. at Clark St.
Chicago, IL 60614
(312) 642-4600
The city's oldest cultural institution.

Chicago Horticultural Society
Lake Cook Road
Glencoe, IL 60022
(847) 835-5440
300-acre botanical garden.

Chicago Opera Theater
2501 N. Keeler Ave.
Chicago, IL 60647
(773) 292-7521
Professional opera company.

Chicago Public Library
400 S. State St.
Chicago, IL 60604
(312) 747-4999
Main library and headquarters of the 95-
branch system.

Chicago Symphony Chorus
220 S. Michigan Ave.
Chicago, IL 60604
(312) 294-3430

Chicago Symphony Orchestra
220 S. Michigan Ave.
Chicago, IL 60604
(312) 294-3000

Court Theater
5535 S. Ellis Ave.
Chicago, IL 60637
(773) 753-4472

Drury Lane Theater
2500 W. 95th St.
Evergreen Park, IL 60642
(708) 422-0404
Multiple theater locations.

DuSable Museum of African-American History
740 E. 56th Place
Chicago, IL 60637
(773) 947-0600
Museum houses a variety of permanent exhibitions dealing with African-American history and culture.

Field Museum of Natural History
Roosevelt Road at Lake Shore Drive
Chicago, IL 60605
(312) 922-9410
Natural history museum, specializing in the sciences of anthropology, botany, geology, and zoology and the composition and evolution of Earth and its near neighbors.

Flanagan & Associates
225 W. Ohio, Suite 250
Chicago, IL 60610
(312) 645-6010
Training in fundraising and development needs to non-profit organizations, institutions, and agencies.

Garfield Park Conservatory
300 N. Central Park Blvd.
Chicago, IL 60624
(312) 746-5100
Four and one-half acres of horticultural exhibitions.

Gartner & Associates
2 N. Riverside Plaza, Suite 2400
Chicago, IL 60606
(312) 454-0282
Fundraising consultation to non-profits.

Gonzer Gerber Tinker Stuhr
400 E. Diehl Road, Suite 380
Naperville, IL 60563
(630) 505-1433
Development consultation.

Goodman Theater
200 S. Columbus Drive
Chicago, IL 60603
(312) 443-3800

Grenzebach, John, & Associates
211 W. Wacker Drive, Suite 500
Chicago, IL 60606
(312) 372-4040
Philanthropic planning.

Holiday Star Theater
8001 Delaware St.
Merriville, IN 46410
(219) 769-6600
Las Vegas-style theater, booking nationally known acts.

League of Chicago Theaters
67 E. Madison St.
Chicago, IL 60603
(312) 977-1730
Association of local theaters.

Light Opera Works
927 Noyes
Evanston, IL 60202
(847) 869-6300
Professional opera company.

Lincoln Park Conservatory
2400 N. Stockton Drive
Chicago, IL 60614
(773) 742-7736
Indoor botanical garden.

Lincoln Park Zoo
2200 N. Cannon Drive
Chicago, IL 60614
(773) 742-2000
The city's zoological park.

Lyric Opera of Chicago
20 N. Wacker Drive
Chicago, IL 60606
(312) 332-2244
Chicago's resident opera company.

Marriott's Lincolnshire Theater
10 Marriott Drive
Lincolnshire, IL 60069
(847) 634-0200

Morton Arboretum
Route 53
Lisle, IL 60532
(630) 968-0074
Privately endowed 1,500-acre outdoor botanical garden.

Museum of Contemporary Art
220 E. Chicago Ave.
Chicago, IL 60601
(312) 280-2660
Dedicated to presenting the most
provocative developments in today's art.

Museum of Science & Industry
5700 S. Lake Shore Drive
Chicago, IL 60637
(773) 684-1414
The country's second most visited
museum. (Smithsonian is #1).

Newberry Library
60 W. Walton St.
Chicago, IL 60610
(312) 943-9090
Library for scholars.

Northlight Repertory Theater
817 Chicago Ave.
Evanston, IL 60201
(847) 869-7278

Oriental Institute
1155 E. 58th St.
Chicago, IL 60637
(773) 702-9520
University of Chicago's museum of Near
East archaeology.

Performing Arts Chicago
410 S. Michigan Ave., Suite 911
Chicago, IL 60605
(312) 663-1628
Presenter of performing arts at multiple
locations.

Ravinia Festival Association
400 Iris Lane
Highland Park, IL 60035
(773) 728-4642 Chicago number
Three-month summer festival; summer
home of Chicago Symphony Orchestra.

Sculpture Chicago
20 N. Michigan Ave.
Chicago, IL 60602
(312) 759-1690
Places sculpture in venues.

Shakespeare Repertory
820 N. Orleans St.
Chicago, IL 60610
(312) 642-8394
Acting company.

Shedd, John G., Aquarium
1200 S. Lake Shore Drive
Chicago, IL 60605
(312) 939-2426
One of the world's most advanced indoor
aquariums.

Shubert Theater
22 W. Monroe St.
Chicago, IL 60603
(312) 977-1710

Smart Museum of Art
5550 S. Greenwood Ave.
Chicago, IL 60637
(773) 702-0200
University of Chicago's art museum.

Spertus Museum of Judaica
618 S. Michigan Ave.
Chicago, IL 60605
(312) 922-9012
Memorabilia related to Jewish life and
history; mounts quarterly exhibitions.

Steppenwolf Theater
1650 N. Halsted St.
Chicago, IL 60657
(312) 335-1888

Terra Museum of Art
664 N. Michigan Ave.
Chicago, IL 60611
(312) 664-3939
Specializes in 19th and 20th century
American art.

Victory Gardens Theater
2257 N. Lincoln Ave.
Chicago, IL 60614
(773) 871-3000

Paper and Allied Products

WEB SITES:

http://www.tappi.org/
is the homepage of the Technical
Association of the Paper and Pulp
Industry.

**http://www.curbet.com/print/
merch.html**
links to paper merchants.

PROFESSIONAL ORGANIZATIONS:

For more information about the paper
industry, you can contact:

American Forest and Paper Association
1111 19th St., N. W., Suite 800
Washington, DC 20036
(202) 463-2700

American Paper Institute
260 Madison Ave.
New York, NY 10016
(212) 340-0600

National Paper Trade Association
c/o John J. Buckley
111 Great Neck Road
Great Neck, NY 11021
(516) 829-3070

Paper Industry Management Association
1699 Wall St., Suit. 212
Mount Prospect, IL 60056
(847) 956-0250

Sales Association of the Paper Industry
P.O. Box 21926
Columbus, OH 43221
(614) 326-3911

**Technical Association of the Paper and
Pulp Industry**
Technology Park, Box 105113
Atlanta, GA 30348
(770) 446-1400

PROFESSIONAL PUBLICATIONS:

Good Packaging Magazine
Packaging
Paper Age
Paper Sales
Pulp and Paper
Pulp and Paper Week
TAPPI Journal

DIRECTORIES:

American Papermaker, Mill and Personnel
   Issue (ASM Communications, Inc.,
   Atlanta, GA)
*Lockwood–Post's Directory of the Paper and
   Allied Trades* (Miller Freeman, New
   York, NY)
Paper Yearbook (Harcourt Brace
   Jovanovich, New York, NY)
Pulp and Paper, Buyer's Guide Issue
   (Miller Freeman, San Francisco, CA)
TAPPI Membership Directory (Technical
   Association of the Paper and Pulp
   Industry, Atlanta, GA)
*Walden's ABC Guide and Paper Production
   Yearbook* (Walden-Mott Corp., Ramsey,
   NJ)

Employers:

3M Co.
6850 S. Harlem Ave.
Summit, IL 60501
(708) 496-6500
Number of employees: 600

**American Envelope Co.-Chicago
Division**
3001 N. Rockwell St.
Chicago, IL 60618
(773) 267-3600
Number of employees: 290

Atlas Bag
7100 N. Ridgeway Ave.
Lincolnwood, IL 60645
(847) 679-0065
Number of employees: 200

Bagcraft Corp. of America
3900 W. 43rd St.
Chicago, IL 60632
(773) 254-8000
Number of employees: 600

Cameo Container Corp.
1415 W. 44th St.
Chicago, IL 60609
(773) 254-1030
Number of employees: 200

Crescent Cardboard Co.
100 W. Willow Road
Wheeling, IL 60090
(847) 537-3400
Number of employees: 220

CST Office Products
540 W. Allendale Drive
Wheeling, IL 60090
(847) 459-7600
Number of employees: 270

CTI Industries Corp.
22160 N. Pepper Road
Barrington, IL 60010
(847) 382-1000
Number of employees: 300

Fellowes' Manufacturing Co.
1789 Norwood Ave.
Itasca, IL 60143
(630) 893-1600
Number of employees: 500

Field Container Co.
1500 N. Nicholas Blvd.
Elk Grove Village, IL 60007
(847) 437-1700
Number of employees: 650

FSC Paper Co.
13101 S. Pulaski Road
Alsip, IL 60658
(708) 389-8520
Number of employees: 272

Glatfelter, P.H., Co.
1200 Harger Road., Suite 300
Oak Brook, IL 60521
(630) 574-4750

Jefferson Smurfit Corp.
400 E. North Ave.
Carol Stream, IL 60188
(630) 260-6500
Number of employees: 360

Mack Packaging Group
2445 S. Rockwell St.
Chicago, IL 60608
(773) 376-8100
Number of employees: 200

Mail-Well Envelope Co.
5445 N. Elston Ave.
Chicago, IL 60630
(773) 286-6400
Number of employees: 260

Mead Corp.
9540 S. Dorchester Ave.
Chicago, IL 60628
(773) 731-9500
Number of employees: 200

Nosco
651 S. Utica St.
Waukegan, IL 60085
(847) 336-4200
Number of employees: 260

Paper Group
2901 W. 36th Place
Chicago, IL 60632
(773) 376-8341
Number of employees: 210

Post-Pac Pocket Labels
500 N. Sacramento Blvd.
Chicago, IL 60612
(773) 638-1200
Number of employees: 200

Release International
915 Harger Road
Oak Brook, IL 60521
(630) 574-3400
Number of employees: 500

Riverwood International USA
288 W. S. Tec Drive
Kankakee, IL 60901
(815) 937-8600
Number of employees: 250

Solo Cup Co.
1501 E. 96th St.
Chicago, IL 60628
(773) 721-3600
Number of employees: 425

Stone Container Corp.
150 N. Michigan Ave.
Chicago, IL 60601
(312) 346-6600
Number of employees: 210

Sweetheart Cup Co.
7575 S. Kostner Ave.
Chicago, IL 60652
(773) 767-3300
Number of employees: 1,000

Transo Envelope Co.
3542 N. Kimball Ave.
Chicago, IL 60618
(773) 385-9200

Pharmaceuticals/Medical Products

WEB SITES:

**http://pharminfo.com/pharmmall/
pm_hp.html**
is the pharmaceutical information
network.

http://www.bio.com/
is BIO on-line, linking to biotechnology
resources and companies.

http://www.biospace.com/
is an educational forum for the biotechnology industry.

PROFESSIONAL ORGANIZATIONS:

For networking in the drug industry and
related fields, check out the following local
professional organizations listed in
Chapter 5:

American Hospital Association
American Medical Technologists
**Midwest Healthcare Marketing
    Association**

For additional information you can
contact:

**American Foundation for
Pharmaceutical Education**
1 Church St., Suite 202
Rockville, MD 20850
(301) 738-2160

American Pharmaceutical Association
2215 Constitution Ave., N.W.
Washington, DC 20037
(202) 628-4410

Biotechnology Industry Organization
1625 K St., N.W., Suite 1100
Washington, DC 20006
(202) 857-0244

**National Association of Pharmaceutical
Manufacturers**
320 Old Country Road
Garden City, NY 11530
(516) 741-3699

**Pharmaceutical Manufacturers
Association**
1100 15th St., N.W.
Washington, DC 20005
(202) 835-3400

PROFESSIONAL PUBLICATIONS:

American Druggist
Biotechnology Advances
Drug Topics
Health News Daily
*Journal of Pharmaceutical Marketing and
    Management*
PMA Newsletter
Pharmaceutical Executive

DIRECTORIES:

Biotechnology Directory (Stockton Press,
New York, NY)

Blue Book of American Druggists (Hearst Corp, New York, NY)

Drug Topics Red Book (Litton Publications, Oradell, NJ)

Genetic Engineering and Biotechnology Firms Worldwide Directory (Mega-Type Publishing, Princeton Junction, NJ)

Pharmaceutical Manufacturers of the U.S. (Noyes Data Corp., Park Ridge, NJ)

Pharmaceutical Marketers Directory (CPS Communications, Boca Raton, FL)

Employers:

Abbott Laboratories
1 Abbott Park Road
Abbott Park, IL 60064-3500
(847) 937-7000
Diversified manufacturer of health care products, including pharmaceuticals, hospital products, diagnostic products, chemicals, and nutritional products.

American Home Products
Ayerst Laboratories Division
745 N. Gary Ave.
Carol Stream, IL 60188
(630) 462-7200
Manufacturer of laboratory equipment and supplies.

Amersham Life Sciences
2636 S. Clearbrook Drive
Arlington Heights, IL 60005
(847) 593-6300
Specialty radioactive chemicals for the research, medical, and industrial fields.

Baxter Healthcare Corp.
1 Baxter Parkway
Deerfield, IL 60015
(847) 948-2000
Develops, manufactures, and distributes a diversified line of medical care products.

Baxter Healthcare Corp. / Renal Division
1620 Waukegan Road
McGaw Park, IL 60085
(847) 940-6296
Hemodialysis and peritoneal dialysis equipment.

Baxter Healthcare Corp. / Surgical Group
1500 Waukegan Road
McGaw Park, IL 60085
(847) 473-5000
Surgical and medical supplies including disposables hemostats, and clamps.

Beltone Electronics
4201 W. Victoria St.
Chicago, IL 60646
(773) 583-3600
Hearing aids and hearing test instruments.

Butler, John O., Co.
4635 W. Foster Ave.
Chicago, IL 60630
(773) 777-4000
Toothbrushes, dental floss, & dental care products.

Ciba-Geigy Corporation
900 Corporate Grove Drive
Buffalo Grove, IL 60089
(847) 520-7770
Manufacturer of pharmaceuticals and ethical drugs.

Dunlee Inc.
555 N. Commerce St.
Aurora, IL 60504
(630) 585-2000
Medical X-ray tubes.

Evron Industries
2159 W. Pershing Road
Chicago, IL 60609
(773) 847-1000
Pharmaceuticals manufacturer.

Fox Meyer McKesson Drug Co.
520 E. North Ave.
Carol Stream, IL 60188
(630) 462-6501
Wholesale distributer of ethical drugs and medical supplies.

Fujisawa USA
2020 N. Ruby St.
Melrose Park, IL 60160
(708) 345-6170
Manufacturer of pharmaceuticals.

General Drug Co.
200 N. Fairfield Ave.
Chicago, IL 60612
(773) 826-4242
Drug wholesaler.

Hipak Industries
1125 Carnegie St.
Rolling Meadows, IL 60008
(847) 506-1200
Medical packaging.

Hollister
2000 Hollister Drive
Libertyville, IL 60048
(847) 680-1000
Health care products.

Hu-Friedy Manufacturing Co.
3232 N. Rockwell St.
Chicago, IL 60618
(773) 975-6100
Dental & surgical hand instruments and
infection control systems.

Lab-Line Instruments
15th & Bloomingdale Ave.
Melrose Park, IL 60160
(708) 450-2600
Incubators, ovens, furnaces, orbital
shakers, and environmental chambers.

Landauer
2 Science Road
Glenwood, IL 60425
(708) 755-7000
Manufacturer of radon analyzers,
monitors, film, and neutron badges.

Lilly, Eli
8725 W. Higgins Road, Suite 810
Chicago, IL 60631
(773) 693-8740
Pharmaceuticals manufacturer.

Lindberg Corporation
6133 N. River Road, Suite 700
Rosemont, IL 60018
(847) 823-2021
Manufactures metal surgical products.

Medline Industries
1200 Townline Road
1 Medline Place
Mundelein, IL 60060
(847) 949-5500
Manufactures and distributes hospital
supplies.

Merck & Co.
2015 Spring Road, Suite 750
Oak Brook, IL 60521
(630) 575-2350
Pharmaceuticals manufacturer.

Morton International
100 N. Riverside Plaza
Chicago, IL 60606
(312) 807-2000
Manufacturer of salt, chemicals, and
Norwich-Eaton pharmaceuticals.

Pfizer
2400 W. Central Road
Hoffman Estates, IL 60196
(847) 413-4500
Pharmaceuticals manufacturer.

Pollenex
165 N. Canal St.
Chicago, IL 60606
(312) 454-5400
Manufactures health care appliances.

Precision Scientific
3737 W. Cortland St.
Chicago, IL 60647
(773) 227-2660
Scientific research & testing laboratory
equipment.

Searle, G. D., & Co.
5200 Old Orchard Road
Skokie, IL 60077
(847) 982-7000
Pharmaceutical and medical products;
prescription eyewear.

Siemens Medical Systems
2501 N. Barrington Road
Hoffman Estates, IL 60195
(847) 304-7700
Nuclear medical imaging cameras.

SoloPak Pharmaceuticals
1845 Tonne Road
Elk Grove Village, IL 60007
(847) 806-0080
Producer of generic injectable drugs.

Upjohn Pharmaceuticals
2001 Butterfield Road

Downers Grove, IL 60515
(630) 663-9300
Pharmaceuticals sales.

Wyeth/Ayerst Laboratories
745 N. Gary Ave.
Carol Stream, IL 60188
(630) 462-7200
Pharmaceuticals.

Printing

WEB SITES:

http://www.curbet.com/print/plink.html
links to commercial printers, paper
merchants, and printing associations.

PROFESSIONAL ORGANIZATIONS:

For information about printing and
related fields, check out these
organizations.

**National Association of Printers and
Lithographers**
780 Palisade Ave.
Teaneck, NJ 07666
(201) 342-0700

Printing Industries of America
100 Dangerfield Road
Alexandria, VA 22314
(703) 519-8100

**Technical Association of the
Graphic Arts**
68 Lomb Memorial Drive
Rochester, NY 14623
(716) 475-7470

PROFESSIONAL PUBLICATIONS:

American Printer
Graphic Arts Monthly
Printing Impressions
Printing News
Who's Printing What

DIRECTORIES:

Directory of Typographic Services (National
Composition Association, Arlington,
VA)
Graphic Arts Blue Book (A.F. Lewis & Co.,
New York, NY)
*Graphic Arts Monthly—Printing Industry
Sourcebook* (Cahners Magazines, New
York, NY)

Employers:

AGI
1950 Ruby St.
Melrose Park, IL 60160
(708) 344-9100

American International
9399 W. Higgins Road, Suite 900
Rosemont, IL 60018
(847) 292-0600

American Labelmark Co.
5724 N. Pulaski Road
Chicago, IL 60646
(773) 478-0900

Berlin Industries
175 Mercedes Drive
Carol Stream, IL 60188
(630) 682-0600

Bockman Printing & Services
950 S. 25th Ave.
Bellwood, IL 60104
(708) 544-4090

Bowne of Chicago
325 W. Ohio St.
Chicago, IL 60610
(312) 527-3080

Carqueville/TCR Graphics
2200 Estes Ave.
Elk Grove Village, IL 60007
(847) 439-8700

Celex group
919 Springer Drive
Lombard, IL 60148
(630) 953-8440

Circle Fine Art Corp.
303 E. Wacker Drive, Suite 830
Chicago, IL 60601
(312) 616-1300

Continental Web Press
1430 Industrial Drive
Itasca, IL 60143
(630) 773-1903

Donnelley, R. R.
77 W. Wacker Drive
Chicago, IL
(312) 326-8000

Duplex Products
1947 Bethany Road
Sycamore, IL 60178
(815) 895-2101

E & D Web
4633 W. 16th St.
Cicero, IL 60804
(708) 656-6600

Farm Progress Companies
191 S. Gary Ave.
Carol Stream, IL 60188
(630) 690-5600

Fort Dearborn Lithograph Co.
6035 W. Gross Point Road
Niles, IL 60714
(773) 774-4321

General Binding Corp.
1 GBC Plaza
Northbrook, IL 60062
(847) 272-3700

General Business Forms
7300 Niles Center Road
Skokie, IL 60077
(847) 677-1700

Johnson & Quin
7460 W. Lehigh Ave.
Niles, IL 60714
(847) 647-6900

Jordan Industries
1751 Lake Cook Road
Deerfield, IL 60015
(847) 945-5591

Kukla Press
855 Morse Ave.
Elk Grove Village, IL 60007
(708) 593-1090

Lehigh Press-Cadillac
25th & Lexington Ave.
Broadview, IL 60153
(708) 681-3612

Moore Business Forms & Systems
275 Field Drive
Lake Forest, IL 60045
(847) 615-6000

Moss Printing
4100 W. Victoria
Chicago, IL 60646
(773) 539-9800

Rand McNally
8255 Central Park Ave.
Skokie, IL 60076
(847) 329-8100

R.R.D. Direct
301 Alice
Wheeling, IL 60090
(847) 459-7000

Segerdahl Corp., The
1351 S. Wheeling Road
Wheeling, IL 60090
(847) 541-1080

Service Web Offset
2500 S. Dearborn
Chicago, IL 60616
(312) 567-7000

Sleepeck Printing Co.
815 25th Ave.
Bellwood, IL 60104
(708) 544-8900

Solar Communications
1120 Frontenac Road
Naperville, IL 60563
(630) 983-1400

Star Publications
1526 Otto Blvd.
Chicago Heights, IL 60411
(708) 755-6161

Strathmore Printing Co.
2000 Gary Lane
Geneva, IL 60134
(630) 232-9677

Wallace Computer Services
4600 W. Roosevelt Road
Hillside, IL 60162
(312) 626-2000

Publishing

WEB SITES:

http://www.library.vanderbilt.edu/law/
acqs/pubr.html#links
links to book publishers.

http://www.scescape.com/worldlibrary/
business/companies/publish.html
links to book publishers.

http://www.bocklabs.wisc.edu/ims/
agents.html
is a directory of literary agents.

PROFESSIONAL ORGANIZATIONS:

For networking in book publishing and
related fields, check out these local
professional organizations listed in
Chapter 5.

Agate Club of Chicago
American Library Association
American Medical Writers Association
Chicago Book Clinic
Chicago Headline Club
Chicago Women in Publishing

For additional information, you can
contact:

American Booksellers Association
828 S. Broadway
Tarrytown, NY 10591
(914) 591-2665

Association of American Publishers
71 5th Ave.
New York, NY 10003
(212) 255-0200

Book Industry Study Group
160 5th Ave.
New York, NY 10010
(212) 929-1393

**COSMEP, The International Association
of Independent Publishers**
P.O. Box 420703
San Franciso, CA 94142
(415) 922-9490

Magazine Publishers Association
919 3rd Ave.
New York, NY 10022
(212) 752-0055

National Newspaper Association
1101 17th St. N.W., Suite 1004
Washington, DC 20036
(202) 466-7200

Suburban Newspapers of America
401 N. Michigan Ave.
Chicago, IL 60611
(312) 644-6610

PROFESSIONAL PUBLICATIONS:

American Bookseller
Editor and Publisher
Innovative Publisher
Library Journal
Publishers Weekly
Publishing Trends and Trendsetters
Small Press

DIRECTORIES:

American Book-Trade Directory (R.R.
  Bowker, New Providence, NJ)
Guide to Chicago-area Publishers (Gabriel
  House, Chicago, IL)
Literary Agents of North America (Research
  Associates International, New York, NY)
Literary Market Place (R.R. Bowker, New
  Providence, NJ)
National Directory of Magazines (Oxbridge
  Communications, New York, NY)
Publisher's Directory (Gale Research,
  Detroit, MI)
Writer's Market (F&W Publications,
  Cincinnati, OH)

Employers:

Be sure to look at the extensive listing of
trade magazines in Chapter 4.

Academy Chicago Publishers
363 W. Erie, 7th floor east
Chicago, IL 60610

(312) 751-7300
Book publishing.

Baker & Taylor Co.
501 S. Gladiolus St.
Momence, IL 60954
(815) 472-2444
Book wholesaler.

Bonus Books
160 E. Illinois Ave.
Chicago, IL 60611
(312) 467-0580

Cahners' Publishing Co.
1350 E. Touhy Ave.
Des Plaines, IL 60018
(847) 635-8800

Carus Publishing Co.
332 S. Michigan Ave., Suite 2000
Chicago, IL 60604
(312) 939-1500
Book and magazine publishing.

Century Publishing Co.
990 Grove St.
Evanston, IL 60201
(847) 491-6440
Magazine publishing.

Chicago Defender
2400 S. Michigan Ave.
Chicago, IL 60610
(312) 225-2400
African-American newspaper.

Chicago Reader
11 E. Illinois St.
Chicago, IL 60611
(312) 828-8350
Weekly newspaper.

Chicago Review Press
814 N. Franklin St.
Chicago, IL 60610
(312) 337-0747
Book publishing.

Chicago Sun-Times
401 W. Wabash Ave.
Chicago, IL 60611
(312) 321-3000
Newspaper publishing.

Chicago Tribune, The
777 W. Chicago Ave.
Chicago, IL 60610
(312) 222-3232
Newspaper, book, encyclopedia publishing; owns TV and radio stations.

Commerce Clearing House
4025 W. Peterson Ave.
Chicago, IL 60646
(773) 583-8500
Tax & business law loose-leaf reports & books.

Commerce Clearing House
2700 Lake Cook Road
Riverwoods, IL 60015
(847) 267-7000
Law reports, information & knowledge products.

Contemporary Books
180 N. Stetson Court
Chicago, IL 60601
(312) 540-4500
Book publishing.

Cook Communications
850 N. Grove Ave.
Elgin, IL 60120
(847) 741-2400
Religious book publishing.

Crain Communications
740 W. Rush St.
Chicago, IL 60611
(312) 649-5200
Publishes *Crain's Chicago Business,*
Automotive News, and other trade magazines.

Dartnell Corporation
4660 N. Ravenswood Ave.
Chicago, IL 60640
(773) 561-4000
Business book publishing.

DBI Books
4092 Commercial Ave.
Northbrook, IL 60062
(847) 272-6310
Book publishing.

Dearborn Financial Publishing
155 N. Wacker Drive
Chicago, IL 60606
(312) 836-4400
Book publishing.

Des Plaines Publishing Co.
1000 Executive Way
Des Plaines, IL 60018
(847) 824-1111
Newspaper, catalogs, magazine directories, and circulars.

DonTech
205 N. Michigan Ave.
Boulevard Towers South
Chicago, IL 60601
(312) 861-3500
Yellow Pages publishing.

Dow Jones & Co.
340 Shuman Boulevard
Naperville, IL 60563
(630) 961-4666
Newspaper publishing.

Encyclopaedia Britannica
310 S. Michigan Ave.
Chicago, IL 60604
(312) 347-7000
Encyclopedia publishing.

Follett Corporation
2211 West St.
River Grove, IL 60171
(708) 583-3000
Book wholesaler.

Goodheart Willcox Publishing Co.
123 W. Taft Drive
South Holland, IL 60473
(708) 687-5000
Vocational textbook publisher.

Irwin McGraw-Hill
1333 Burr Ridge Parkway
Burr Ridge, IL 60521
(630) 789-4000
College, text & business trade book publishing.

Johnson Publishing Co.
820 S. Michigan Ave.
Chicago, IL 60605

(312) 322-9200
Publishers of *Ebony* and *Jet* magazines, books.

Lerner Newspapers
7331 N. Lincoln
Lincolnwood, IL 60646
(847) 829-2000
Newspaper publishing.

Levy, Chas., Circulating Co.
1200 N. North Branch St.
Chicago, IL 60622
(312) 440-4400
Book and periodical distributor.

Levy Home Entertainment
4201 Raymond Drive
Hillside, IL 60162
(708) 547-4400
Book and video distributor.

Loyola University Press
3441 N. Ashland Ave.
Chicago, IL 60657
(773) 281-1818
Book publisher.

Manufacturers' News
1633 Central St.
Evanston, IL 60201
(847) 864-7000
State industrial directories, diskettes, mailing lists.

McDougall Littel/Houghton-Mifflin
1560 Sherman Ave.
Evanston, IL 60201
(847) 869-2300
Educational publishing.

Mosby Medical Publishing
200 N. LaSalle
Chicago, IL 60601
(312) 726-9733
Book and yearbook publishing.

NTC Publishing Co.
4255 W. Touhy Ave.
Lincolnwood, IL 60646
(847) 679-4210
Educational and trade book publishing.

Nelson-Hall Publishers
111 N. Canal St.
Chicago, IL 60606
(312) 930-9446
Book publishing.

News-Sun, The
100 Madison St.
Waukegan, IL 60085
(847) 336-7000
Newspaper publishing.

Northwest Newspapers
1 Herald Square
Crystal Lake, IL 60014
(815) 459-4040
Newspaper publishing.

Nystrom
3333 W. Elston Ave.
Chicago, IL 60618
(773) 463-1144
Maps, globes, charts, models & multimedia kits.

Official Airline Guides
2000 Clearwater Drive
Oak Brook, IL 60521
(630) 574-6000
Directory publishing.

Paddock Publications
217 W. Campbell St.
Arlington Heights, IL 60005
(847) 870-3600
Newspaper publishing, including *Daily Herald.*

Pioneer Press Newspaper
130 S. Prospect Ave.
Park Ridge, IL 60068
(847) 696-3133
Newspaper publishing.

Playboy Enterprises
680 N. Lake Shore Drive
Chicago, IL 60611
(312) 751-8000
Magazine and video publishing.

Publications International
7373 N. Cicero Ave.
Lincolnwood, IL 60646

(847) 676-3470
Book and periodical publishing.

Quality Books
1003 W. Pines Road
Oregon, IL 61061
(815) 732-4450
Book distributor.

Rand McNally & Co.
8255 N. Central Park Ave.
Skokie, IL 60076
(847) 673-9100
Book and map publishing.

Scott Foresman & Co.
1900 E. Lake Ave.
Glenview, IL 60025
(847) 729-3000
Textbooks & learning materials.

Southtown Economist
5959 S. Harlem Ave.
Chicago, IL 60638
(773) 586-8800
Newspaper publishing.

Standard Rate & Data Co.
3004 Glenview Road
Wilmette, IL 60091
(847) 256-6067
Directory publishing.

Surrey Books
230 E. Ohio, Suite 120
Chicago, IL 60611
(312) 751-7330
Book publishing.

University of Chicago Press
5801 S. Ellis Ave.
Chicago, IL 60637
(773) 702-8878
Book and periodical publishing.

Vance Publishing Corporation
400 Knightsbridge Parkway
Lincolnshire, IL 60069
(847) 634-2600

World Book Publishing
525 W. Monroe St., 20th floor
Chicago, IL 60606
(312) 258-3700
Encyclopedia publishing.

Real Estate

PROFESSIONAL ORGANIZATIONS:

To learn more about the real estate
industry, you can contact the following
local professional organizations listed in
Chapter 5:

Appraisal Institute
Building Owners and Managers
   Association of Chicago
Chicago Board of Realtors
Commercial-Investment Real Estate
   Institute
Institute of Real Estate Management
Million Dollar Round Table
National Association of Realtors

For more information, you can contact:

Counselors of Real Estate
430 N. Michigan Ave.
Chicago, IL 60611
(312) 329-8427

International Real Estate Institute
8383 E. Evans Road
Scottsdale, AZ 85260
(602) 998-8267

National Association of Realtors
430 N. Michigan Ave.
Chicago, IL 60611
(312) 329-8200

PROFESSIONAL PUBLICATIONS:

Journal of Property Management
National Real Estate Investor
Real Estate Issues
Real Estate News
Real Estate Review
Realty and Building

DIRECTORIES:

American Real Estate Guide (LL&IL
   Publishing, Marhasset, NY)
*American Society of Real Estate Counselors
   Directory* (ASREC, Chicago, IL)
Directory of Certified Residential Brokers
   (Retail National Marketing Institute,
   Chicago, IL)
National Real Estate Directory (Real Estate
   Publications, Tampa FL)
National Roster of Realtors (Stamats
   Communications, Cedar Rapids, IA)

Location, location, location

Bob Kramer is a partner in a firm that leases office space in
downtown Chicago. We talked with him recently about
getting started in commercial real estate. "Leasing commercial real estate in Chicago is a very tough business," says
Kramer. "You don't make any money during your first year
or two in the business. There's a very high attrition rate.

"But if you stick with it, you can make more money than
your peers in other fields ever dreamed of. Six-figure
incomes are not uncommon among people who have been
in the business only five years.

"At our firm, we don't hire people right out of school; we look for people with some experience in the business world and in real estate. But many of the larger firms will hire recent grads and train them. In fact, some large firms have formal training programs.

"If you're a young person just starting out, I'd suggest getting a job with a bigger firm. Then be like a blotter—soak up everything they can teach you. After a few years, reevaluate your position with the company. The problem with the bigger firms is that they sometimes tend to ignore you once they've trained you. In a smaller firm, the senior people see more of a relationship between your success and the overall success of the company. Also, there's a lot of competition within a large firm. It's easy to get lost in the shuffle."

We asked Kramer what qualifications are needed to succeed in commercial real estate. "You have to be tough because you'll face a certain amount of rejection. You have to be hungry because this is an extremely competitive business. A college degree is helpful, but it isn't required. This business is basically sales—getting out and seeing people, convincing them that your skills and knowledge are up to snuff. When you're just starting out, it's also very important to have a mentor in the company—someone to help you and look out for you."

Employers:

Amli Residential Properties Trust
125 S. Wacker Drive, Suite 3100
Chicago, IL 60606
(312) 443-1477

Amoco Realty & Development Corp.
200 E. Randolph Drive
Chicago, IL 60601
(312) 856-6111

Baird & Warner
200 W. Madison St.
Chicago, IL 60606
(312) 368-1855

Ben Franklin Realty Corp.
500 E. North Ave.
Carol Stream, IL 60188
(630) 462-6100

Binswanger Realty Group-Midwest
233 S. Wacker Drive, Suite 5510
Chicago, IL 60606
(312) 655-9500

Buck, John, Co.
200 S. Wacker Drive, Suite 400
Chicago, IL 60606
(312) 993-9800

Capital Agricultural Property Services
801 Warrenville Road, Suite 150
Lisle, IL 60532
(630) 434-9150

CB Commercial Real Estate
6133 N. River Road, Suite 500
Rosemont, IL 60018
(847) 518-2430

CC Industries
222 N. LaSalle St.
Chicago, IL 60601
(312) 855-4000

Centerpoint Properties Corp.
401 N. Michigan Ave., Suite 3000
Chicago, IL 60611
(312) 346-5600

Century 21 Real Estate
Check phone book for many individual
offices.

Compass Management & Leasing
455 N. Cityfront Plaza Drive
Chicago, IL 60611
(312) 527-9494

Continental Materials Corp.
225 W. Wacker Drive, Suite 1800
Chicago, IL 60606
(312) 541-7200

Cushman & Wakefield of Illinois
150 S. Wacker Drive, Suite 3100
Chicago, IL 60606
(312) 853-0030

Draper & Kramer
33 W. Monroe St.
Chicago, IL 60603
(312) 346-8600

Edison Development Canada
1 First National Plaza
Chicago, IL 60603
(312) 294-4321

First Capital Financial Corp.
2 N. Riverside Plaza, Suite 2121
Chicago, IL 60606
(312) 207-0020

First Industrial Realty Trust
150 N. Wacker Drive, Suite 150
Chicago, IL 60606
(312) 704-9000

Frain Camins & Swartchild
300 W. Washington St.
Chicago, IL 60606
(312) 444-9797

Golub & Co.
625 N. Michigan Ave., Suite 2000
Chicago, IL 60611
(312) 440-8800

Good, Sheldon, & Co.
333 W. Wacker Drive, Suite 450
Chicago, IL 60606
(312) 346-1500

Heitman Properties
180 N. La Salle St., Suite 360
Chicago, IL 60601
(312) 855-5700

Hiffman Shaffer Associates
180 N. Wacker Drive, Suite 500
Chicago, IL 60606
(312) 332-3555

Homart Development Co.
Sub. of Sears, Roebuck
55 W. Monroe, Suite 3000
Chicago, IL 60603
(312) 551-5000

Hostmark Management Group
1600 Golf Road, Suite 800
Rolling Meadows, IL 60008
(847) 439-8500

Hyatt Corp.
200 W. Madison St.
Chicago, IL 60606
(312) 750-1234
Hotel holding company.

Inland Group
2901 Butterfield Road
Oak Brook, IL 60521
(630) 218-8000

James Building Corp.
1535 Lake Cook Road, Suite 302
Northbrook, IL 60062
(847) 564-7720

JMB Realty Corp.
900 N. Michigan Ave.
Chicago, IL 60611
(312) 440-4800

Jupiter Industries
919 N. Michigan Ave., Suite 1500
Chicago, IL 60611
(312) 642-6000

Kahn Realty
875 N. Michigan Ave.
Chicago, IL 60611
(312) 751-9100

Koll
10 S. La Salle St., Suite 2600
Chicago, IL 60603
(312) 984-1010

Landau & Heyman
180 N. LaSalle, Suite 1420
Chicago, IL 60601
(312) 372-3133

LaSalle Partners
11 S. LaSalle St.
Chicago, IL 60603
(312) 782-5800

Levy Real Estate Partners
980 N. Michigan Ave., Suite 400
Chicago, IL 60611
(312) 664-8200

Miglin-Beitler Management
181 W. Madison St., Suite 3900
Chicago, IL 60602
(312) 726-1700

Milwaukee Land Co.
547 W. Jackson Blvd.
Chicago, IL 60661
(312) 294-0497

MS Management Services
111 E. Wacker Drive, Suite 1200
Chicago, IL 60601
(312) 938-2610

Orix Real Estate Equities
100 N. Riverside Plaza, Suite 1400
Chicago, IL 60606
(312) 669-6400

Pittway Corp.
200 S. Wacker Drive, Suite 700
Chicago, IL 60606-5802
(312) 831-1070

PM Realty Group
919 N. Michigan Ave.
Chicago, IL 60611
(312) 944-2800

Premisys Real Estate Services
222 S. Riverside Plaza, Suite 2110
Chicago, IL 60606
(312) 551-6600

Prime Group
77 W. Wacker Drive
Chicago, IL 60601
(312) 917-1500

Property & Facility Management Group
20 N. Michigan Ave., Suite 400
Chicago, IL 60602
(312) 456-7040

Randhurst Shopping Center
999 Elmhurst Road
Mount Prospect, IL 60056
(847) 392-2287

Real Estate Auctions
333 W. Wacker Drive, Suite 450
Chicago, IL 60606
(312) 630-0915

Real Estate Research Corporation
2 N. LaSalle, Suite 400
Chicago, IL 60602
(312) 346-5885
Appraisal, investment analysis, environmental assessment, and development
advice by a multi-disciplinary team of
economists, real estate and financial
experts, appraisers, and planners.

Rreef Management Co.
645 N. Michigan Ave.
Chicago, IL 60611
(312) 943-4534

Rubloff Realtors
980 N. Michigan Ave.
Chicago, IL 60611
(312) 368-5300

Stein & Co.
227 W. Monroe St., Suite 3400
Chicago, IL 60606
(312) 372-4240

Sudler-Nagy Inc.
875 N. Michigan Ave.
Chicago, IL 60611
(312) 751-1717

Tishman-Speyer Properties
55 E. Monroe St.
Chicago, IL 60603
(312) 855-0055

Tribune Properties
435 N. Michigan Ave.
Chicago, IL 60611
(312) 222-3994
Owns & manages real property.

U.S. Equities Realty
20 N. Michigan Ave., Suite 400
Chicago, IL 60602
(312) 456-7000

Urban Retail Properties
900 N. Michigan Ave., Suite 1500
Chicago, IL 60611
(312) 915-2000

Wirtz Corp.
680 N. Lakeshore Drive
Chicago, IL 60611
(312) 943-7000

Retailers/Wholesalers

WEB SITES:

http://www.pncl.co.uk/subs/james/vl/
vretail.html
is the WWW virtual library homepage for
retailing.

http://www.retail-experts.com/
provides education and resources to
retailers.

http://www.inetbiz.com/market/
is a worldwide marketplace of wholesalers.

PROFESSIONAL ORGANIZATIONS:

For networking in retailing and wholesal-
ing, check out these professional organizations listed in Chapter 5:

**Chicago Association of Women Business
Owners
International Hardware Distributors
Association
National Sporting Goods Association**

For more information, you can contact:

**National Association of Convenience
Stores**
1605 King St.
Alexandria, VA 22314
(703) 684-3600

**National Association of Wholesale
Distributors**
1725 K St., N.W., 3rd floor
Washington, DC 20006
(202) 872-0885

National Retail Federation
325 7th St., N.W., Suite 1000
Washington, DC 20004
(202) 783-7971

PROFESSIONAL PUBLICATIONS:

Chain Store Age
Inside Retailing

Journal of Retailing
Merchandising
Store Planning
Stores
Women's Wear Daily

DIRECTORIES:

American Manufacturers Directory
 (American Business Information,
 Omaha, NE)
American Wholesalers and Distributors
 Directory (Gale Research, Inc., Detroit,
 MI)
Convenience Stores Membership Directory
 (National Association of Convenience
 Stores, Alexandria, VA)
Fairchild's Financial Manual of Retail
 Stores (Fairchild Books, New York, NY)
Sheldon's Retail Directory of the U.S. and
 Canada (PS & H, Inc., New York, NY)

Employers:

Ace Hardware Corp.
2200 Kensington Court
Oak Brook, IL 60521
(630) 990-6600
National chain of retail hardware stores.

American Drug Stores
1818 Swift Drive
Oak Brook, IL 60521
(630) 572-5000
Chain of retail drug stores, owned by
Osco.

Amlings Flowerland
540 W. Ogden Ave.
Hindsdale, IL 60521
(630) 654-8820
Floral, garden, and gift center.

Arvey Paper & Office Products Corp.
Division Office
3351 W. Addison St.
Chicago, IL 60618
(773) 463-6423

Baby's Room/USA Baby
857 Larch
Elmhurst, IL 60126
(630) 832-9880
National chain of home furnishings stores.

Baker & Taylor Entertainment
8140 N. Lehigh Ave.
Morton Grove, IL 60053
(847) 965-8060
Computer and software distributor.

Baker & Taylor Co.
501 S. Gladiolus St.
Momence, IL 60954
(815) 472-2444
Large national book distributor.

Barnes & Noble
District Headquarters
351 Town Square
Wheaton, IL 60187
(630) 653-2122
Large national bookstore chain, with
several "superstores" in the Chicago area.

Baskin, Al, Co.
161 Tower Drive, Unit 6
Burr Ridge, IL 60521
(630) 472-3020
Owns Mark Shale, multi-location upscale
clothing stores.

Bigsby and Kruthers
57 W. Grand Ave.
Chicago, IL 60610
(312) 440-1700
Upscale retail clothing stores.

Blockbuster Video
District Manager
2577 N. Clark St.
Chicago, IL 60614
(773) 880-0968
National retail chain of video stores.

Ben Franklin Retail Stores
500 E. North Ave.
Carol Stream, IL 60188
(630) 462-6100
General merchandise stores.

Best Buy
District Office
1432 Butterfield Road
Downers Grove, IL 60515
(708) 495-5380
Electronics, appliances.

Bloch Lumber Co.
2 N. Riverside Plaza
Chicago, IL 60606
(312) 466-4500

Bloomingdale's
900 N. Michigan Ave.
Chicago, IL 60611
(312) 787-5511
Specialty department store.

Border's Books and Music
District Office
2817 N. Clark St.
Chicago, IL 60657
(773) 935-8527

Bradford Exchange
9333 N. Milwaukee Ave
Niles, IL 60648
(847) 966-2770
Retail and catalog sales of unusual
products.

Carson Pirie Scott & Co.
1 S. State St.
Chicago, IL 60603
(312) 641-7000
Retail department stores in city and
suburbs; owns resorts, shopping centers,
restaurants.

CDW Computer Centers
2840 Maria Ave.
Northbrook, IL 60062
(847) 564-4900
Direct-market retail computer stores.

Chernin's Shoes
1001 S. Clinton St.
Chicago, IL 60607
(312) 922-5900
Local shoe store chain.

Circuit City
Apply to individual stores or contact
headquarters:
9950 Mayland Drive
Richmond, VA. 23233
(800) 627-2274
Appliances and electronics chain.

COMPUSA
3000 Finley Road
Downer's Grove, IL 60515
(630) 241-1144
National chain of computer stores.

Computer City
352 W. Grand Ave.
Chicago, IL 60610
(312) 840-5900
National chain of computer stores.

Cotter & Co.
8600 W. Bryn Mawr
Chicago, IL 60631
(773) 695-5000
Cooperative, distributing to Tru-Value
hardware stores.

Crate & Barrel
725 Landwehr Road
Northbrook, IL 60062
(847) 272-2888
National chain of upscale housewares
stores.

Crown Books
1250-C Greenbriar Drive
Addison, IL 60101
(630) 268-2700
Regional headquarters of national
discount bookstore chain.

Dalton, B., Bookseller
129 N. Wabash Ave.
Chicago, IL 60602
(312) 236-7615
National chain of bookstores, owned by
Barnes & Noble.

Distribution America
2700 River Road #300
Des Plaines, IL 60018
(847) 296-7000
Hardgoods/equipment/supplies
distributor.

Dominick's Finer Foods
505 Railroad Ave.
Northlake, IL 60164
(708) 562-1000
Grocery and drug retailers.

Eddie Bauer
123 N. Wabash Ave.
Chicago, IL 60602
(312) 263-6005
National sportswear and catalog operation
with several stores in the Chicago area.

Elek-Tek
7350 N. Linden Ave.
Skokie, IL 60077
(847) 667-7660
Computers, software, and office equipment.

Evans Inc.
36 S. State St.
Chicago, IL 60603
(312) 855-2000
Women's apparel and furs; operates leased
departments in 90 department stores.

FAO Schwartz
840 N. Michigan Ave.
(312) 587-5000
National chain of upscale toy stores.

Filene's Basement
1 N. State St.
Chicago, IL 60606
(312) 553-1055
Off-price retail clothing.

Fitness Warehouse
158 S. Waukegan Road
Deerfield, IL 60015
(847) 509-9300
Chain of sporting goods.

Florsheim Shoe Shops
130 S. Canal St.
Chicago, IL 60606
(312) 559-2500

Follett College Stores
400 W. Grand Ave.
Elmhurst, IL 60126
(630) 279-2330
Operates book stores on 60 college
campuses.

Frank Consolidated Enterprises
666 Garland Place.
Des Plains, IL 60016
(847) 699-7000
Large auto retailer and car leasing
organization.

Gap, The
679 N. Michigan Ave. and other locations
Chicago, IL 60611
(312) 335-1896
National retailer of casual and children's
clothing.

Hammacher Schlemmmer
212 W. Superior St.
Chicago, IL 60601
(312) 664-8170
Specialty retail and mail order.

Heinemann's Bakeries
3925 W. 43rd St.
Chicago, IL 60632
(773) 523-5000
Chain of bakeries.

Home Depot
1101 Perimeter Drive, Suite 300
Schaumburg, IL 60173
(847) 413-8060

Jewel Osco
1955 W. North Ave.
Melrose Park, IL 60160
(708) 531-6000
Major chain of supermarkets and drug
stores.

J.G. Industries
5630 W. Belmont Ave.
Chicago, IL 60634
(312) 481-5400
Operates 14 Goldblatt's department
stores.

Kaehler Luggage
1421 Sherman Ave.
Evanston, IL 60201
(847) 328-0744
Leather/luggage stores

K-Mart Corporation
Regional headquarters
537 N. Hicks Road
Palatine, IL 60067
(847) 358-8181
National chain of discount department
stores.

Lord & Taylor
835 S. Michigan Ave.
Chicago, IL 60611
(312) 787-7400
Specialty department store, with branches
in Chicago and suburbs.

Marks Brokers
155 N. Wacker Drive
Chicago, IL 60606
(312) 782-6800
Jewelry stores, including Whitehall.

Marshall Field & Co.
111 N. State St.
Chicago, IL 60690
(312) 781-1000
Now owned by Dayton Hudson Corp.,
Chicago's flagship retailer operates
department stores in the Midwest, South,
and West; invests in shopping center
development.

McKesson Drug Company
1355 Enterprise Drive
Romeoville, IL 60441
(708) 759-2411
Retail drug store chain.

Michael's Creative Crafts
1200 St. Charles St.
Elgin, IL 60120
(847) 888-5800
Retail arts, crafts, framing, and floral
stores.

Montgomery Ward & Co.
619 W. Chicago Ave.
Chicago, IL 60671
(312) 467-2000
Retail department stores.

Neiman-Marcus
737 N. Michigan Ave.
Chicago, IL 60611
(312) 642-5900
Specialty retailer.

NikeTown Chicago
669 Michigan Ave.
Chicago, IL 60611
(312) 642-6363

Nordstrom Inc.
10 Oak Brook Center Mall
Oak Brook, IL 60521
(708) 571-2121
Specialty retailer.

Northbrook Court Shopping Center
2171 Northbrook Court
Northbrook, IL 60062
(847) 498-5144
Retail shopping center, serving North
Shore suburbs.

Oak Brook Center
JMB Realty Co.
100 Oak Brook Center
Oak Brook, IL 60521
(630) 573-0700
Retail shopping center, serving the
western suburbs.

Office Depot - Zone Office
400 Skokie Blvd.
Northbrook, IL 60062
(847) 509-1606
Office supply stores.

Office Max - Regional Offices
368 W. Army Trail Road
Bloomingdale, IL 60108
(630) 307-6400
Office supply stores.

Old Orchard Shopping Center
Skokie Blvd. at Old Orchard Road
Skokie, IL 60077
(847) 673-6800
Retail shopping center, serving the North
Shore suburbs.

Penney, J. C., Co.
Regional headquarters
1901 N. Roselle Road.
Schaumburg, IL 60195
(847) 884-4600
National retail merchandiser.

Pier 1 Imports
170 N. Barrington Road
Schaumburg, IL 60194
(847) 798-1239
National retail merchandiser.

Quill Corp.
100 Schelter Road
Lincolnshire, IL 60069-3621
(847) 634-4800
Mail order office supply firm.

Radio Shack
Regional headquarters
14048 Pertonella Drive, Suite 201A
Libertyville, IL 60048
(847) 680-1800
National retailer of electronic equipment
and computers.

Rogers Enterprises
5 Centre
Park Forest, IL 60466
(708) 748-6400
Chain of jewelry stores.

Saks Fifth Avenue
700 N. Michigan Ave.
Chicago, IL 60611
(312) 944-6500
Specialty retailer.

Sears, Roebuck & Co.
3333 Beverly Road
Hoffman Estates, IL 60179
(847) 286-2500
Headquarters of world's largest retailer.

Seigle's Home & Building Centers
1331 Davis Road
Elgin, IL 60123
(847) 742-2000
Retailer of gardening and building
materials.

Smyth, John M., Homemakers
1013 Butterfield Road
Downers Grove, IL 60515
(630) 960-4100
Retail furniture stores located in Chicago
and suburbs.

Spiegel
3580 Lacey Road
Downers Grove, IL 60515
(630) 986-7500
National catalog merchandiser.

Sportmart
1400 S. Wolf Road, Suite 200
Wheeling, IL 60090
(847) 520-0100
Owns and operates discount sporting
goods stores.

Strictly Golf
29 W. 221 N. Aurora Road
Naperville, IL 60563
(630) 355-5353
Chain of sporting goods stores.

Target Stores
2621 W. Schaumburg Road
Schaumburg, IL 60194
(708) 289-1033
National discount chain.

Uhlemann Optical
3340 W. Main St.
Skokie, IL 60076
(847) 677-0116
Optical stores.

Ultimo, Ltd.
48 E. Oak St.
Chicago, IL 60611
(312) 787-0906

United Stationers
2200 E. Golf Road
Des Plaines, IL 60016
(847) 699-5000
Office products wholesalers.

Venture Stores
17 W. 734 22nd St.
Oakbrook Terrace, IL 60181
(630) 627-9750
National discount retailer.

Video Outlet, Ltd.
7123 Clinton Road
Loves Park, IL 61111
(815) 877-0267
Video and software rental stores.

Vision Tek
1175 Lakeside Drive
Gurnee, IL 60031
(847) 360-7500
Computer and software distributor.

Waldenbooks
Regional office
251 Golfmill Shopping Center
Niles, IL 60648
(847) 824-2218
National chain of retail bookstores.

Walgreen Co.
200 Wilmot Road
Deerfield, IL 60015
(847) 940-2500
International chain of drug stores.

Walmart
702 S. W. 8th St.
Bentonville, AR 72716
(501) 273-4000
National chain of discount stores. All
hiring for Chicago-area stores is done
from this office. Call first.

Water Tower Place
845 N. Michigan Ave.
Chicago, IL 60611
(312) 440-3165
Retail shopping center and condominium
development.

White Hen Pantry
660 Industrial Drive
Elmhurst, IL 60126
(630) 833-3100
Convenience stores.

Whitney, J.C., Co.
1104 S. Wabash Ave.
Chicago, IL 60605
(312) 431-6000
Auto parts retailer.

Wickes Furniture Co.
351 W. Dundee Road
Wheeling, IL 60090
(847) 541-0100
Home furnishings stores.

Wickes Lumber Co.
706 Deerpath Drive
Vernon Hills, IL 60061
(847) 367-6540
Retailer of lumber and building materials.

Woodfield Shopping Center
5 Woodfield Mall
Schaumburg, IL 60173
(847) 330-1537
Shopping center serving the northwest
suburbs.

Woolworth, F. W., Co.
Regional headquarters
915 Lee St.
Des Plaines, IL 60016
(847) 827-7731
National chain of retail variety and
discount department stores.

Yorktown Shopping Center
203 Yorktown Center
Lombard, IL 60148
(630) 629-7330
Retail shopping center, serving the
western suburbs.

Social Services

WEB SITES:

**http://lib4.fisher.su.oz.au/Social_Work/
socwkls.html**
links to journals, newsgroups, and
listserves.

**http://caster.ssw.upenn.edu/cont-ed/
index.html**
offers social work courses via the Internet.

**http://http.bsd.uchicago.edu/~r-tell/
socwork.html**
provides comprehensive links to social
work sites.

PROFESSIONAL ORGANIZATIONS:

For information on human services and
related fields, contact the following
professional organizations. Also see
"Health Care."

Center for Human Services
7200 Wisconsin Ave., Suite 600
Chevy Chase, MD 20814
(301) 654-8338

National Association of Social Workers
750 1st St., N.E.
Washington, DC 20002
(202) 408-8600

PROFESSIONAL PUBLICATIONS:

Children and Youth Services Review
Community Jobs
Journal of Social Welfare
The Nonprofit Times

DIRECTORIES:

Directory of Agencies (National Association
 of Social Workers, Washington, DC)
*National Directory of Children and Youth
 Services* (Marion Peterson Longmont,
 CO)
*National Directory of Private Social
 Agencies* (Croner Publications, Queens
 Village, NY)
Public Welfare Directory (American Public
 Welfare Association, Washington, DC)

Employers:

Abraham Lincoln Center
3858 S. Cottage Grove Ave.
Chicago, IL 60653
(773) 373-6600
Comprehensive social services agency.

American Cancer Society
77 E. Monroe, 13th floor
Chicago, IL 60603
(312) 641-6150
Education, research, and special services.

American Heart Association of Chicago
208 S. LaSalle St., Suite 900
Chicago, IL 60604
(312) 731-7277

American Red Cross
43 E. Ohio St.
Chicago, IL 60611
(312) 440-2000
Social and disaster services.

Arthritis Foundation
111 E. Wacker Drive, #1928
Chicago, IL 60601
(312) 616-3470

Aspera of Illinois
1567 N. Milwaukee, 2nd floor
Chicago, IL 60622
(773) 252-0970
Youth education and motivation
programs.

Association House of Chicago
2150 W. North Ave.
Chicago, IL 60647
(773) 276-0084
Comprehensive social services.

Big Brothers/Big Sisters Metro Chicago
542 S. Dearborn St., #650
Chicago, IL 60605
(312) 427-0637

Boy Scouts Chicago Area Council
1218 W. Adams St.
Chicago, IL 60607
(312) 421-8800

Boys and Girls Club of Chicago
625 W. Jackson, Suite 300
Chicago, IL 60661
(312) 627-2700

Brass Foundation
8659 S. Ingleside Ave.
Chicago, IL 60019
(773) 488-6600
Treatment programs and services.

Catholic Charities of Chicago
128 N. Des Plaines St.
Chicago, IL 60661
(312) 655-7000
Major social service agency.

Chicago Association for Retarded Citizens
8 S. Michigan Ave., Suite 1700
Chicago, IL 60603
(312) 346-6230

Chicago Child Care Society
5467 S. University Ave.
Chicago, IL 60637
(773) 643-0452
Social service agency.

Chicago Commons
915 N. Walked Ave.
Chicago, IL 60622
(773) 342-5330
Family and community services.

Chicago Community Trust
222 N. LaSalle St.
Chicago, IL 60601
(312) 372-3356
Foundation.

Chicago Department of Human Services
510 N. Peshtigo Court
Chicago, IL 60611
(312) 744-8111

Chicago Lighthouse
1850 W. Roosevelt Road

Chicago, IL 60608
(312) 666-1331
Services for the visually impaired.

Chicago Urban League
4510 S. Michigan Ave.
Chicago, IL 60653
(773) 285-5800

Chicago Youth Centers
231 S. Jefferson St. 6th floor
Chicago, IL 60661
(312) 648-1550
Large network of youth agencies.

ChildServ
8765 W. Higgins Road, Suite 450
Chicago, IL 60631
(773) 693-0300
Day care, foster home, and family services.

Council for Jewish Elderly
3003 W. Touhy Ave.
Chicago, IL 60645
(773) 508-1000
Services and care for the elderly.

Easter Seal Society of Metropolitan Chicago
220 S. State St.
Chicago, IL 60604
(312) 939-5115

Family Care Services
234 S. Wabash
Chicago, IL 60604
(312) 427-8790

Gateway Foundation
819 S. Wabash, Suite 300
Chicago, Il 60605
(312) 663-1130
Substance abuse services.

Girl Scouts
222 S. Riverside Plaza
Chicago, Il 60606
(312) 416-2500

Glenkirk
3504 Commercial Ave.
Northbrook, Il 60062
(847) 272-5111
Services for persons with disabilities.

Goodwill Industries of Metro Chicago
601 W. Polk Ave.
Chicago, IL 60607
(312) 939-0040

Heartland Society for Travelers Aid
208 S. LaSalle St., Suite 1818
Chicago, IL 60604
(312) 629-4500

Hull House Association
10 S. Riverside Drive, Suite 1720
Chicago, IL 60606
(312) 906-8600
Social and community services at multiple
locations.

**Illinois Department of Children and
Family Services**
100 W. Randolph, 6th floor
Chicago, IL 60601
(312) 814-4650

Interventions
1234 S. Michigan Ave., Room 200
Chicago, IL 60605
(312) 663-0817
Substance abuse services.

**Jewish Federation of Metropolitan
Chicago**
1 S. Franklin St.
Chicago, IL 60429
(312) 346-6700
Large network of comprehensive services.

Little Friends
140 N. Wright St.
Naperville, IL 60540
(708) 355-6533
Developmental services for youth.

Lutheran Social Services of Illinois
1001 W. Touhy Ave., Suite 150
Des Plaines, IL 60018
(847) 635-4600

McKinley, Ada. S., Community Services
725 S. Wells
Chicago, IL 60607
(312) 554-0600
Therapeutic and educational services.

Metropolitan Family Services
14 E. Jackson Blvd.
Chicago, IL 60604
(312) 986-4000
Provides social services at multiple
locations.

Neumann, Victor C., Assn.
2354 N. Milwaukee Ave.
Chicago, IL 60622
(773) 278-1124
Social service agency with multiple
locations.

Operation Able
180 N. Wabash, #802
Chicago, IL 60601
(312) 782-3335
Services for older and displaced workers.

Salvation Army
5040 N. Pulaski Road
Chicago, Il 60630
(773) 725-1100

United Way
560 W. Lake St.
Chicago, IL 60661
(312) 876-1808

YMCA of Metropolitan Chicago
755 W. North Ave.
Chicago, IL 60610
(312) 280-3400
Provides a wide range of social, educational, and recreational services at
multiple locations.

YWCA of Metropolitan Chicago
180 N. Wabash, Suite 301
Chicago, IL 60601
(312) 372-6600
Operates recreational, educational, and
social programs primarily for women and
girls at multiple locations.

Turning volunteer work into a job

After spending many years working as a volunteer for various organizations, Marion Simon's daughters advised her to "stop giving it away." She decided to look for paid employment. But because she had never had a paid job, Simon was not sure how to begin her job search.

"As a woman in my middle years, I wondered where in the world I would go," says Marion. "I had a good education and a great deal of volunteer experience. I had planned and orchestrated large benefits and had done an inordinate amount of fundraising over the years. I also had done community work in the inner city.

"I talked to some career counselors at a local college and they helped me put together a resume. Then I began to talk to people I knew. They offered me various jobs, none of which thrilled me.

"Then I happened to mention my job search to the president of a hospital where I had done a great deal of volunteer work," says Marion. "He asked me not to take a job until I had talked to him. Later, he hired me as his special assistant, with the charge to 'humanize the hospital.' Over a period of time, I developed a patient representative department.

"When I began the job 11 years ago, I was a one-person operation. As time went on, I added staff. I currently supervise a staff of 9, plus about 25 volunteers. The job of patient representative is now a full-fledged profession. Many women in the field began as volunteers. They knew a lot about the hospital where they were volunteering and thus made the transition into a paid position more easily."

We asked Simon what advice she has for volunteers who want to move into the paid workforce. "Go to the career counseling departments of some small colleges. If they suggest that you need additional training, get it. Nevertheless, before you go back to school, investigate the kinds of jobs available in your chosen field. Think about how you can use your volunteer experience in a paid position. Take what you've done and build from it."

Sports/Recreation

WEB SITES:

**http://www.sportsite.com/mac/allshop/
sgma/html/sgma_hp.html**
is the SportsLink page, listing companies,
publications, industry news, and jobs.

**http://www.onlinesports.com/pages/
CareerCenter.html**
is the on-line Sports Career Center, with
career opportunities and a resume bank.

http://www.fitnessworld.com/
is the homepage of *Fitness World.*

http://www.fitnessworld.com/
links to fitness Web sites.

PROFESSIONAL ORGANIZATIONS:

For networking in the sports and
recreation fields, check out this professional organization listed in Chapter 5.

**Amusement and Music Operators
   Association**

For more information, you can contact:

**Aerobics and Fitness Association of
America**
15250 Ventura Blvd.
Sherman Oaks, CA 91403
(818) 905-0040

**American Association for Leisure and
Recreation**
1900 Association Drive
Reston, VA 22091
(703) 476-3472

**IDEA: The International Association of
Fitness Professionals**
6190 Cornerstone Court E., Suite 204
San Diego, CA 92121
(800) 999-4332

National Recreation & Parks Association
2775 S. Quincy St., Suite 300
Arlington, VA 22206
(703) 820-4940

National Sporting Goods Association
1699 Wall St.
Mt. Prospect, IL 60056
(847) 439-4000

Society of Recreation Executives
P.O. Drawer 17148
Pensacola, FL 35222
(904) 477-7992

PROFESSIONAL PUBLICATIONS:

American Fitness
Athletic Business
Athletic Management
Fitness Management
Parks and Recreation
Sporting Goods Market
Sports Industry News

DIRECTORIES:

American Fitness Association Directory
   (American Fitness Association, Long
   Beach, CA)
Athletic Business, Professional Directory
   Section (Athletic Business Publications,
   Madison, WI)
Fitness Management Source Book (Leisure
   Publications, Los Angeles, CA)
Health Clubs Directory (American
   Business Directories, Omaha, NE)
Information Sources in Sports and Leisure
   (K.G. Saur, New Providence, NJ)
*New American Guide to Athletics, Sports,
   and Recreation* (New American Library,
   New York, NY)
Recreation Centers Directory (American
   Business Directories, Omaha, NE)
Sports Administration Guide and Directory
   (National Sports Marketing Bureau,
   New York, NY)
Sports Market Place (Sports Guide,
   Phoenix, AZ)
Who's Who in Recreation (Society of
   Recreation Executives, Pensacola, FL)
Who's Who in Sports and Fitness (American
   Fitness Association, Long Beach, CA)

Employers:

Arlington International Racecourse
P.O. Box 7
Arlington Heights, IL 60006
(847) 255-4300
Horse race track.

Bally Manufacturing Co.
8700 W. Bryn Mawr
Chicago, IL 60631
(773) 399-1300
Manufacturer of games and slot machines;
owns hotels, casinos, and Chicago Health
Clubs.

Brunswick Corporation
1 N. Field Court
Lake Forest, IL 60045
(847) 735-4700
Manufacturer of sports equipment;
operates bowling centers.

Chicago Bears
Halas Hall
250 N. Washington Road
Lake Forest, IL 60045
(847) 295-6600
NFL football team.

Chicago Blackhawks
1901 W. Madison
Chicago, IL 60612
(312) 455-7000
NHL hockey team.

Chicago Bulls
1901 W. Madison St.
Chicago, IL 60612-2459
(312) 455-4000
NBA basketball team.

Chicago Cubs
1060 W. Addison St.
Chicago, IL 60613
(773) 404-2827
National league baseball team.

Chicago Health Clubs
A Division of Bally Manufacturing Co.
8700 W. Bryn Mawr
Chicago, IL 60631
(773) 399-7600

Chicago Park District
425 E. McFetridge Drive
Chicago, IL 60605
(312) 747-0946
Owns and operates Chicago's 550 parks
and beaches.

Chicago White Sox
333 W. 35th St.
Chicago, IL 60616
(773) 924-1000
American league baseball team.

Chicago Wolves
10550 Lunt Ave.
Rosemont, IL 60018
(847) 390-0404
Professional hockey team.

Chicago Yacht Club
East Monroe at Lakefront
Chicago, IL 60602
(312) 861-7777

East Bank Club
500 N. Kingsbury St.
Chicago, IL 60614
(312) 527-5800
Fitness club.

Evanston Recreation Dept.
2100 Ridge Ave.
Evanston, IL 60204
(847) 328-2100

Forest Preserve District of Cook County
536 N. Harlem Ave.
River Forest, IL 60305
(708) 366-9420
Responsible for maintenance and
preservation of Cook County forest
preserves.

**Forest Preserve District of DuPage
County**
P.O. Box 2339
Glen Ellyn, IL 60138
(630) 790-4900
Responsible for maintenance and
preservation of DuPage County forest
preserves.

Gold's Gym & Fitness Center
820 N. Orleans
Chicago, IL 60601
(312) 664-6537
Chain of exercise facilities.

Hawthorne Race Course
3501 S. Laramie Ave.
Cicero/Stickney, IL 60650
(708) 780-3700
Horse race track.

Homewood-Flossmoor Park District
18350 Harwood Ave.
Homewood, IL 60430
(708) 957-0300
Provides wide range of leisure, recreational, and educational activities to the community.

Hyde Park Neighborhood Club
5480 S. Kenwood Ave.
Chicago, IL 60615
(773) 643-4062
Provides recreational and educational services to the community.

Jewish Community Centers of Chicago
1 S. Franklin St.
Chicago, IL 60606
(312) 346-6700
Provides recreational, educational, and social services to all ages through numerous neighborhood centers.

Lake County Forest Preserve District
2000 N. Milwaukee Ave.
Libertyville, IL 60048
(847) 367-6640
Responsible for the maintenance and preservation of forest preserves in Lake County.

Lakeshore Athletic Club
1320 W. Fullerton Pkwy.
Chicago, IL 60614
(773) 477-9888
Fitness club.

Maywood Park
8600 W. North Ave.
Maywood, IL 60153
(708) 343-4800
Horse race track.

Midtown Tennis Club
2020 W. Fullerton Pkwy.
Chicago, IL 60657
(773) 235-2300

National Sporting Goods Assn.
1699 Wall St.

Mount Prospect, IL 60056-5780
(847) 439-4000

Outboard Marine
100 Seahorse Drive
Waukegan, IL 60085
(847) 689-6200
Manufacturer of boats and marine equipment.

United Center
1901 W. Madison St.
Chicago, IL 60612
(312) 455-4500
Athletic facility.

Wilmette Park District
1200 Wilmette Ave.
Wilmette, IL 60091
(847) 256-6100
Conducts athletic and sports events, recreational programs for the community.

Winnetka Community House
620 Lincoln Ave.
Winnetka, IL 60093
(847) 446-0537
Provides recreational programs for children of all ages.

Women's Workout World
1031 N. Clark St.
Chicago, IL 60602
(312) 664-2106
Chain of fitness clubs.

YMCA National Health & Physical Education Department
101 N. Wacker Drive
Chicago, IL 60606
(312) 977-0031
Athletic and community services at numerous locations.

Young Men's Jewish Council
25 E. Washington St.
Chicago, IL 60602
(312) 726-8891
Operates non-profit day camps and overnight camp.

YWCA
180 N. Wabash Ave.
Chicago, IL 60601
(312) 372-6600
Athletic and community services at numerous locations.

Stock Brokers/Financial Services

WEB SITES:

http://bank.net/home.rich.html
links to investment industry sites and
directories.

http://www.io.org/~invest/places.htm
links to finance-related groups, newsletters, and corporate information.

**http://www.nextnet.com/iwctr/
iwctr.html**
is the homepage of *Securities Industry
Daily;* links to employment opportunities.

PROFESSIONAL ORGANIZATIONS:

For networking in finance and related
fields, check out these professional
organizations listed in Chapter 5. Also see
"Banks."

**Chicago Association of Business
   Economists**
Chicago Bond Club
Chicago Finance Exchange
Chicago Stock Exchange

For more information, you can contact:

**Association for Investment Management
and Research**
5 Boar's Head Lane
Charlottesville, VA 22903
(804) 977-6600

Financial Executives Institute
10 Madison Ave.
Morristown, NJ 07960
(201) 898-4600

**International Association of Financial
Planning**
2 Concourse Parkway, Suite 800
Atlanta, GA 30328
(404) 845-0011

**National Association of Personal
Financial Advisors**
1130 Lake Cook Road, Suite 105

Buffalo Grove, IL 60089
(847) 537-7722

**National Association of Securities
Dealers (NASD)**
1735 K St., N. W.
Washington, DC 20006
(202) 728-8000

National Venture Capital Association
1655 N. Fort Meyer Drive
Arlington, VA 22209
(703) 351-5269

Securities Industry Association
635 Slaters Lane, Suite 110
Alexandria, VA 22314
(703) 683-2075

PROFESSIONAL PUBLICATIONS:

*Barron's National Business and
   Financial Weekly*
CFO
D & B Reports
Commodity Journal
Corporate Finance Letter
Dun's Business Month
Financial Executive
Financial World
Institutional Investor
Investment Dealer's Digest
Journal of Finance
Morningstar
Securities Week
Stock Market Magazine
Traders Magazine
Wall Street Letter

DIRECTORIES:

Corporate Finance Sourcebook (National
   Register Publishing, New Providence,
   NJ)
CUSIP Master Directory (Standard &
   Poor's, New York, NY)
Financial Yellow Book (Monitor Publishing
   Co., New York, NY)

Handbook of Financial Markets and Institutions (John Wiley and Sons, New York, NY)

Investment & Securities Directory (American Business Directories, Omaha, NE)

Securities Industry Yearbook (Securities Industry Association, New York, NY)

Security Dealers of North America (Standard and Poor's, New York, NY)

STA Traders Annual (Security Traders Association, New York, NY)

Who's Who in Finance and Industry (Reed Reference Publishing, New Providence, NJ)

Employers, Stock Brokers/Investment Bankers:

ABN AMRO NA
135 S. La Salle St.
Chicago, IL 60603
(312) 443-2000
Investment bankers.

AVM Financial Group
150 N. Wacker Drive, Suite 2360
Chicago, IL 60606
(312) 236-7977

BA Futures
200 W. Adams St., Suite 2700
Chicago, IL 60606
(312) 269-4555
Commodity contract broker and dealer.

BA Securities
231 S. La Salle St.
Chicago, IL 60697
(312) 828-2345
Investment bankers.

Bacon Whipple Division (of Stifel Nicolaus)
135 S. LaSalle St., Suite 2323
Chicago, IL 60603
(312) 704-7000
Investment bankers.

Baird, Robert W., & Co.
135 S. La Salle St., Suite 2610
Chicago, IL 60603
(312) 609-4999
Investment bankers.

Baker, Fentress & Co.
200 W. Madison St., Suite 3510
Chicago, IL 60606
(312) 236-9190
Investment bankers.

Banker's Trust Co.
8400 Sears Tower
Chicago, IL 60606
(312) 993-8000
Investment bankers.

Bear, Stearns & Co.
3 First National Plaza
Chicago, IL 60602
(312) 580-4000
Brokers.

Blair, William, & Co.
222 W. Adams St
Chicago, IL 60606
(312) 236-1600
Major Chicago-based investment banking firm.

Blunt, Ellis & Loewi
111 W. Monroe St., Suite 1700E
Chicago, IL 60603
(312) 454-3220
Brokers.

Brinson Partners
70 W. Madison
Chicago, IL 60602-4298
(312) 220-7100
Brokers.

Cargill Investor Services
233 S. Wacker Drive, Suite 2300
Chicago, IL 60606
(312) 460-4000
Commodity contract brokers..

Chase Futures & Options
10 S. LaSalle St.
Chicago, IL 60603
(312) 726-9250
Commodity contract broker.

Chase Securities
10 S. La Salle St., 23rd floor
Chicago, IL 60603
(312) 807-4000
Brokers.

Chemical Securities
10 S. La Salle St.
Chicago, IL 60603
(312) 807-4007
Investment bankers.

Chicago Corporation
208 S. La Salle St.
Chicago, IL 60604
(312) 855-7600
Major Chicago-based investment banking firm.

Citicorp Securities
200 S. Wacker Drive
Chicago, IL 60614
(312) 993-3000
Investment bankers.

Clayton Brown & Associates
500 W. Madison
Chicago, IL 60606
(312) 559-3000
Brokers.

CS First Boston
227 W. Monroe St.
Chicago, IL 60606
(312) 750-3000
Investment bankers.

Dean Witter Reynolds
6000 Sears Tower
Chicago, IL 60606
(312) 984-4321
Investment bankers.

Donaldson Lufkin & Jenrette Securities
200 W. Madison St., Suite 1700
Chicago, IL 60606
(312) 345-6100
Investment bankers.

Edwards, A. G., and Sons
222 S. Riverside Plaza
Chicago, IL 60606
(312) 648-5200
Brokers.

Ernst & Young
233 S. Wacker Drive
Chicago, IL 60606
(312) 879-2000
Investment bankers.

Everen Securities
77 W. Wacker Drive
Chicago, IL 60601
(312) 574-6000
Brokers.

Fiduciary Management Associates
55 W. Monroe St., Suite 2550
Chicago, IL 60603
(312) 930-6850

First Analysis Corp.
9600 Sears Tower
Chicago, IL 60606
(312) 258-1400

First Boston Corporation
227 W. Monroe St.
Chicago, IL 60606
(312) 750-3000
Brokers.

First Chicago Capital Markets
1 First National Plaza
Chicago, IL 60670
(312) 732-7046
Investment bankers.

First Chicago Futures
1 First National Plaza
Chicago, IL 60670
(312) 368-1556
Commodity contract broker and dealer.

Freehling & Co.
190 S. LaSalle St., 22nd floor
Chicago, IL 60603
(312) 704-7400
Chicago-based investment banker.

Geneva Companies
125 S. Wacker Drive, Suite 2100
Chicago, IL 60606
(312)782-8900
Investment bankers.

Goldman Sachs & Co.
4900 Sears Tower
Chicago, IL 60606
(312) 655-4600
Investment bankers.

Gruntal & Co.
135 S. LaSalle St.
Chicago, IL 60603
(312) 269-0380
Brokers.

Harris Associates
2 N. LaSalle St., Suite 500
Chicago, IL 60602
(312) 621-06Ω0
Brokers.

Heitman/JMB Advisory Corp.
180 N. LaSalle St.
Chicago, IL 60601-2886
(312) 855-5700
Brokers.

Howe Barnes Investments
135 S. LaSalle St., Suite 1500
Chicago, IL 60603
(312) 655-3000
Brokers.

Hummer, Wayne, & Co.
175 W. Jackson Blvd., Suite 1700
Chicago, IL 60604
(312) 431-1700
Brokers.

Institutional Capital Corporation
303 W. Madison, Suite 1800
Chicago, IL 60606
(312) 424-9100
Brokers.

Kemper Financial Services
120 S. La Salle St.
Chicago, IL 60603
(312) 781-1121
Brokers.

LaSalle Street Capital Management Ltd.
10 S. LaSalle St.
Chicago, IL 60603
(312) 220-7550
Investment bankers.

Lazard Freres & Co.
200 W. Madison St., Suite 2200
Chicago, IL 60601
(312) 407-6600
Investment bankers.

Lehman Bros.
190 S. La Salle St., Suite 2500
Chicago, IL 60603
(312) 609-8000
Investment bankers.

Lincoln Capital Management
200 S. Wacker Drive
Chicago, IL 60606
(312) 559-2880
Brokers.

LIT America
30 S. Wacker, Suite 1120
Chicago, IL 60606
(312) 906-7100
Commodity contract broker and dealer.

Loomis Sayles & Co.
3 First National Plaza, Suite 5450
Chicago, IL 60602
(312) 346-9750
Brokers.

Merrill Lynch & Co.
5500 Sears Tower
Chicago, IL 60606
(312) 906-6200
Investment bankers and brokers.

Mesirow Financial
350 N. Clark St.
Chicago, IL 60610
(312) 670-6000

Mid-America Commodity Exchange
141 W. Jackson Blvd.
Chicago, IL 60604
(312) 341-3000
Trading in commodity futures.

Morgan, J. P., & Co.
227 W. Monroe St., Suite 2800
Chicago, IL 60606
(312) 541-3300
Investment bankers.

Morgan Stanley & Co.
440 S. La Salle St., Suite 3700
Chicago, IL 60605
(312) 706-4000
Investment bankers.

Nesbitt Burns Securities
111 W. Monroe St.
Chicago, IL 60603
(312) 461-7219
Investment bankers.

Northern Futures Corp.
50 S. LaSalle St.
Chicago, IL 60675
(312) 444-5460
Investment banker associated with
Northern Trust.

Noyes, David A., & Co.
208 S. LaSalle St.
Chicago, IL 60604
(312) 782-0400
Brokers.

Nuveen, John, & Co.
333 W. Wacker Dr.
Chicago, IL 60606
(312) 917-7700
Chicago-based leader in municipal bond
funds.

Oppenheimer & Co.
311 S. Wacker Drive
Chicago, IL 60606
(312) 360-5500
Brokers.

Paine Webber
181 W. Madison St.
Chicago, IL 60602
(312) 683-6000
Brokers.

Principal Financial Securities
2 N. LaSalle St.
Chicago, IL 60602
(312) 444-2100
Brokers.

Prudential-Bache Securities
1 S. Wacker Drive, Suite 2900
Chicago, IL 60606
(312) 630-7000
Brokers.

Refco Group, Ltd.
111 W. Jackson Blvd., Suite 1700
Chicago, IL 60604
(312) 930-6500
Commodity contract broker.

Rodman & Renshaw Capital Group
233 S. Wacker Drive
Chicago, IL 60606
(312) 526-2000
Brokers.

Rothschild Securities Co.
181 W. Madison, Suite 4800
Chicago, IL 60602
(312) 781-8900
Brokers.

Salomon Bros.
8700 Sears Tower
Chicago, IL 60606
(312) 876-8700
Investment bankers.

Schwab, Charles A., & Co.
500 N. Michigan Ave.
Chicago, IL 60611
(312) 467-9250
Discount broker.

Smith Barney, Harris Upham
3 First National Plaza, Suite 5200
Chicago, IL 60603
(312) 419-3600
Brokers.

Tucker Anthony
1 S. Wacker Drive
Chicago, IL 60606
(312) 853-6900
Brokers.

Vector Securities International
1751 Lake-Cook Road, Suite 350
Deerfield, IL 60015
(847) 940-1970
Investment bankers.

Wasserstein Perella & Co.
3 First National Plaza, Suite 5700
Chicago, IL 60602
(312) 263-2020
Brokers.

Ziegler Securities
1 S. Wacker Drive, Stuite 3080
Chicago, IL 60606
(312) 263-0110
Leader in church and hospital financing.

Employers, Investment Advisors:

Ameritech Pension Fund
30 S. Wacker Drive
Chicago, IL 60606
(312) 750-5000

Amoco Corporation Pension Fund
P.O. Box 87703
Chicago, IL 60680-0703
(312) 856-6111

Chicago Asset Management Company
70 W. Madison St., 56th floor
Chicago, IL 60602
(312) 372-2800
Investment advisors.

Dimensional Fund Advisors
10 S. Wacker Drive
Chicago, IL 60606
(312) 382-5376

Duff and Phelps Investment Management
55 E. Monroe St., Suite 3600
Chicago, IL 60603
(312) 263-2610
investment advisors.

Gofen & Glossberg
455 Cityfront Plaza, Suite 3000
Chicago, IL 60611
(312) 828-1100
Investment advisors.

Heller Financial
500 W. Monroe
Chicago, IL 60661
(312) 441-7000
Commercial finance company.

Municipal Retirement Fund
City of Chicago
100 S. Wacker Drive, 10th floor
Chicago, IL 60606
(312) 236-4700

Public School Teachers' Pension and Retirement Fund of Chicago
205 W. Wacker Drive, Room 820
Chicago, IL 60606
(312) 641-4464

Scudder, Stevens & Clark
111 E. Wacker Drive, Suite 2200
Chicago, IL 60601
(312) 861-2700
Investment advisor.

Sears, Roebuck and Co. Pension Fund
55 W. Monroe St.
Chicago, IL 60603
(312) 875-0450

Stein Roe & Farnham
1 S. Wacker Drive
Chicago, IL 60606
(312) 368-7700
Investment advisors.

Employers, Financial Exchanges:

Chicago Board Options Exchange
400 S. LaSalle St.
Chicago, IL 60605
(312) 786-5600
Trading in stock options.

Chicago Board of Trade
141 W. Jackson Blvd.
Chicago, IL 60604
(312) 435-3500
Trading in grain and financial futures.

Chicago Mercantile Exchange
30 S. Wacker Drive
Chicago, IL 60606
(312) 930-1000
Trading in commodities.

Midwest Stock Exchange
440 S. LaSalle St.
Chicago, IL 60605
(312) 663-2222
Trading in securities.

How to be a player on LaSalle Street

Lisa Marini, a stock broker with Merrill Lynch, gave us this rundown on Chicago's trading scene.

"The Chicago Board Options Exchange is the auction market capital of the world. On the trading floor, what you see is the most naked form of supply and demand in action. It's a public outcry market. Floor traders literally shout out their bids.

"There are two classes of people in the auction—the traders and everybody else. You start out as a runner, running orders to the floor traders, who are the only ones who can actually bid. Next you become a phone clerk; they're the people who answer the phones and give the orders to the runners. From phone clerk you move up to crowd assistant or market-maker clerk. A crowd assistant helps the broker or trader execute the orders. A market-maker clerk monitors a trader's position and risk in the market.

"Some phone clerks earn upward of $60,000 a year. I know one market-maker clerk who made $160,000 one year. But you'll never be promoted to floor trader just by working hard. You have to take a national standardized test, which gives you a license to trade. It's called the R.O.P.—the Registered Options Principal test.

"Once you pass the test, you may bid on a seat. In 1974, CBOE seats were around $10,000. In 1976 they went to $135,000. At the tail end of '77 they were down to $20,000. Now I think they go for $270,000.

"The major exchanges are the Midwest Stock Exchange for stocks. Options are traded at the Chicago Board Options Exchange. At the Chicago Board of Trade, the trading is in grains, beans, metals, and financial futures. The Chicago Mercantile Exchange handles gold, currencies, and meats. The Mid-America Commodity Exchange is just like the Board of Trade but they deal in smaller amounts.

"About half the people on the floor work for big companies, and the others for small outfits, usually less than five people. The floor is treated as a completely separate hiring center. To be a Merrill Lynch floor clerk you go to the floor, not Merrill Lynch.

"The way to get a job on the floor is to know someone. Network through the various professional associations or even try the bars where brokers and traders congregate after hours."

Travel/Shipping/Transportation

WEB SITES:

http://www.earthlink.net/
~hotelanywhere/
links to travel-related industry sites.

http://www.slip.net/~jwithers/
tawww.html
is a site for professional travel agents.

http://www.yahoo.com/
Business_and_Economy/Companies/
Shipping
lists shipping companies on the Net.

http://iti.acns.nwu.edu/tran_res.html
links to transportation sites and news
groups.

http://www.itsonline.com/
is the Independent Forum for Intelligent
Transportation Systems.

PROFESSIONAL ORGANIZATIONS:

To learn more about the travel, shipping,
and transportation industries, you can
contact the following local professional
organizations listed in Chapter 5:

Airline Employees Association
Air Transport Association of Chicago
Chicago Transportation Club

For more information, you can contact:

American Public Transit Association
1201 New York Ave., N.W., Suite 400
Washington, DC 20005
(202) 898-4000

American Society of Travel Agents
1101 King St.
Alexandria, VA 22314
(703) 739-2782

American Trucking Association
200 Mill Road
Alexandria, VA 22314
(703) 838-1700

Institute for Transportation and
Development Policy
611 Broadway, Rm. 616
New York, NY 10012
(212) 260-8144

Institute of Transportation Engineers
525 School St., S. W.
Washington, DC 20024
(202) 554-8050

Travel Industry Association of America
1133 21st St., N. W.
Washington, DC 20036
(202) 408-8422

United States Tour Operators
Association (USTA)
211 E. 51st St., Suite 12B
New York, NY 10022
(212) 750-7371

PROFESSIONAL PUBLICATIONS:

Air Travel Journal
ASTA Travel News
Aviation Week and Space Technology
Business and Commercial Aviation
Daily Traffic World
Mass Transit
Passenger Transport
Tours and Resorts
Travel Agent
Travel Trade: The Business Paper of the
  Travel Industry
Travel Weekly
Urban Transport News

DIRECTORIES:

Aviation Directory (E.A. Brennan Co., Garden Grove, CA)

Mass Transit: Consultants (PTN Publishing Corp., Melville, NY)

Moody's Transportation Manual (Moody's Travel Service, New York, NY)

Official Directory of Industrial and Commercial Traffic Executives (K-III Information Co., New York, NY)

Travel Weekly's World Travel Directory (Reed Travel Group, Secaucus, NJ)

Worldwide Travel Information Contact Book (Gale Research, Detroit, MI)

Employers:

Air Express Int'l. Corp.
220 Thorndale Ave.
Bensenville, IL 60106
(630) 766-3380

Alitalia Airlines
618 S. Access Road
Chicago, IL 60666
(773) 686-5938

America West Airlines
618 S. Access Road
Chicago, IL 60666
(773) 686-0782

American Express Travel Services
1701 Golf Road, Suite 1107
Rolling Meadows, IL 60008
(847) 437-9285
Travel agency with 40 local offices.

American Freightways Corp.
4300 W. 72nd St.
Chicago, IL 60629
(773) 582-8855

Amtrak
210 S. Canal St.
Chicago, IL 60607
(312) 558-1075

Arrington Travel Center
55 W. Monroe St., Suite 3800
Chicago, IL 60603
(312) 726-4900
Travel agency with 46 local offices.

Avis Rent-A-Car System
214 N. Clark St.
Chicago, IL 60601
(312) 782-6827

Belt Railway Co.-Chicago
6900 S. Central Ave.
Chicago, IL 60638
(708) 496-4000

Best/Easy Travel
8600 W. Bryn Mawr Ave.
Chicago, IL 60631
(773) 380-0150
Travel agency with 19 local offices.

BTI Americas
400 Skokie Blvd.
Northbrook, IL 60062
(847) 480-8400
Travel agency with 51 local offices.

Budget Rent-a-Car
4225 Naperville Road
Lisle, Il 60532
(630) 955-1900

Burlington Air Express
P.O. Box 66522
Chicago, IL 60666
(773) 601-2900

Burlington Northern Santa Fe Corp.
1700 E. Golf Road
Schaumburg, IL 60173
(847) 995-6000

Caravelle Travel Management
1900 E. Golf Road, Suite 1100
Schaumburg, IL 60173
(847) 619-8323
Travel agency .

Carlson Wagonlit Travel
3601 Algonquin Road
Rolling Meadows, IL 60008
(847) 818-3242
Travel agency with 58 local offices.

Chicago O'Hare International Airport
P.O. Box 66142
Chicago, IL 60666
(773) 686-2200

Chicago Motor Club/AAA
999 E. Touhy Ave.
Des Plaines, IL 60018
(847) 390-9000

Chicago Transit Authority
Merchandise Mart Plaza
P. O. Box 3555
Chicago, IL 60654
(312) 664-7200

CMS Air Express
1600 S. Ashland Ave.
Chicago, IL 60608
(312) 666-3400

Corporate Travel Consultants
455 E. Illinois St., Suite 460A
Chicago, IL 60611
(630) 691-9100
Travel agency with 8 local offices.

Delta Airlines
District Sales Office
999 Plaza Dive, Suite 800
Schaumburg, IL 60173
(847) 330-9333

DHL Worldwide Express
1794 Sherwin Ave.
Des Plaines, IL 60018
(847) 298-9060

Direct Travel of Chicago
303 W. Madison St., Suite 950
Chicago, IL 60606
(312) 606-0800
Travel agency with 4 local offices.

Federal Express Corporation
203 N. LaSalle
Chicago, IL 60601
(800) 463-3339

Getz International Travel
225 W. Washington Blvd., 18th floor
Chicago, IL 60606
(312) 551-5814
Travel agency with 4 local offices.

Greyhound-Trailways Bus System
630 W. Harrison St.
Chicago, Il 60607
(312) 408-5970

Hertz Corporation
O'Hare International Airport
P. O. Box 6609
Chicago, IL 60666
(773) 686-7272

Illinois Central Corp.
455 N. Cityfront Plaza Drive
Chicago, IL 60611
(312) 755-7500

Itel Corporation
2 N. Riverside Plaza
Chicago, IL 60606
(312) 902-1515
Leases cargo containers.

ITS
108 Wilmot Road
Deerfield, IL 60015
(847) 940-2100
Travel agency with 5 local offices.

Keeshin Charter Service
615 W. 41st St.
Chicago, IL 60609
(773) 254-6400
Chartered bus transportation.

KLM Royal Dutch Airlines
P.O. Box 66357
Chicago, IL 60666
(773) 686-6080

Maritz Travel Co.
10 S. Riverside Plaza, Suite 1470
Chicago, IL 60606
(312) 466-2700
Travel agency with 8 local offices.

McCord Travel Management
321 N. Clark St.
Chicago, IL 60610
(312) 527-1500
Travel agency with 34 local offices.

Metra Metropolitan Rail
547 W. Jackson Blvd.
Chicago, IL 60661
(312) 322-6777
All commuter railroads in Chicagoland.

Monarch Air Service
5923 S. Central Ave.
Chicago, IL 60638
(773) 471-4530

Nippon Express Travel USA
1000 Tower Lane, Suite 135
Bensenville, IL 60106
(630) 350-0210
Travel agency with 4 local offices.

Northeast Illinois Railroad
547 W. Jackson Blvd.
Chicago, IL 60661
(312) 939-2929

Northwest Airlines
P.O. Box 66044
Chicago, IL 60666
(773) 686-5520

Qantas Airways
618 S. Access Road
Chicago, IL 60666
(773) 686-7942

Roadway Express
3434 W. 51st St
Chicago, IL 60657
(773) 436-9400
Large freight transport system.

Rosenbluth International
455 N. Cityfront Plaza Drive, Suite 2500
Chicago, IL 60611
(312) 755-4300
Travel agency with 9 local offices.

Seko-Air Freight
790 Busse Road
Elk Grove Village, IL 60007
(847) 806-4800

Signature Flight Support
521 Bessie Coleman Drive
Chicago, IL 60666
(773) 686-7000

Southwest Airlines Co.
5700 S. Cicero Ave.
Chicago, IL 60638
(773) 471-3457

Super Cartage Co.
3800 W. 41st St.
Chicago, IL 60632
(773) 579-1300

Swissair
150 N. Michigan Ave., Suite 2900
Chicago, IL 60601
(312) 630-5800

Tower Travel Management
401 N. Michigan Ave.
Chicago, IL 60611
(312) 397-9000
Travel agency with 7 local offices.

Travel Desk
1450 E. American Lane, Suite 1400
Schaumburg, IL 60173
(847) 330-4441
Travel agency with 6 local offices.

Travelmasters
450 W. Algonquin Road
Arlington Heights, IL 60005
(847) 439-8800
Travel agency with 5 local offices.

Travel-Rite International
1211 W. 22nd St.
Oak Brook, IL 60521
(630) 571-8000
Travel agency with 6 local offices.

Travel & Transport
4343 Commerce Court, Suite 207
Lisle, IL 60532
(630) 505-1212
Travel agency with 18 local offices.

UAL Corp.
P. O. Box 66919
Chicago, IL 60666
(847) 700-4000
Parent company of United Airlines.

U-Haul Co.
1200 W. Fullerton Ave.
Chicago, IL 60647
(773) 935-0620

Uniglobe Travel (Midwest)
377 E. Butterfield Road, Suite 390
Lombard, IL 60148
(630) 241-2300
Travel agency with 37 local offices.

Unistar Air Cargo
500 Thorndale Ave., #F
Wood Dale, IL 60191
(630) 616-8030

United Van Lines
2100 Ogden Ave.
Lisle, IL 60532
(630) 971-1000

U. S. Auto Leasing Co.
1800 N. Ashland Ave.
Chicago, IL 60622
(773) 278-4200

Willett Laidlaw Co.
4552 W. Patterson Ave.
Chicago, IL 60641
(773) 283-7860
Charter bus service.

Wisconsin Central Transportation Corp.
6250 N. River Road
Des Plaines, IL 60017
(847) 318-4600
Midwest freight railroad.

Yellow Freight System
10301 Harlem Ave.
Chicago Ridge, IL 60415
(708) 423-8153
Major freight carrier.

Yellow Cab Company
1730 S. Indiana Ave.
Chicago, IL 60616
(312) 225-7440

Utilities

WEB SITES:

http://www.webfeats.com/preecs/mive/resource.html
is a comprehensive list of utility resources on the Net; includes employment opportunities.

http://www.energynet.com/
is a homepage for the public utilities sector.

http://home.ptd.net/~srjubin/pubutil.html
links to electric, natural gas, and water utility sites.

PROFESSIONAL ORGANIZATIONS:

For information about the utilities industry, contact the following organizations. Also see **"Electronics/Telecommunications"** for major phone and cellular companies.

American Gas Association
1515 Wilson Blvd.
Arlington, VA 22209
(703) 841-8400

American Public Gas Association
11094 "D" Lee Highway
Fairfax, VA 22030
(703) 352-3890

American Public Power Association
2301 M St., N.W.
Washington, DC 20037
(202) 467-2900

Institute of Public Utilities
Michigan State University
410 Eppley Center
East Lansing, MI 48824
(517) 355-1876

United States Telephone Association
1401 H St., N.W., Suite 600
Washington, DC 20005
(202) 326-7300

PROFESSIONAL PUBLICATIONS:

Electric Light and Power
Public Power
Public Utilities
Public Utility Fortnightly
Telephone Engineering and Management
Telephony

DIRECTORIES:

APGA Directory of Municipal Gas Systems (American Public Gas Assoc., Fairfax, VA)
Brown's Directories of North American Gas Companies (Edgel Communications, Cleveland, OH)
Electrical World Directory of Electrical Utilities (McGraw-Hill, New York, NY)
Moody's Public Utility Manual (Moody's Investors Service, New York, NY)

Employers:

Chicago Natural Gas
444. N. Orleans St., Suite 200
Chicago, IL 60610
(312) 527-4100

Commonwealth Edison Co.
10 S. Dearborn St., floor 37
Chicago, IL 60690
(800) 334-7661
Electric company.

Indeck Energy Services
1130 Lake Cook Road, Suite 300
Buffalo Grove, IL 60089
(847) 520-3212
Operates co-generation plants.

**Metropolitan Water Reclamation
District of Greater Chicago**
100 E. Erie St.
Chicago, IL 60611
(312) 751-5600
Operates the city's water purification
system.

Mid Congregation Corp.
701 E. 22nd St.
Lombard, IL 60148
(630) 691-2500
Natural gas transmission & distribution.

Nicor
1844 W. Ferry Road
Naperville, IL 60566
(630) 305-9500
Natural gas transmission & distribution.

North Shore Gas Co.
3001 Grand Ave.
Waukegan, IL 60085
(847) 336-7400
Natural gas transmission & distribution.

Peoples Energy Corp.
130 E. Randolph Ave.
Chicago, IL 60601
(312) 240-4000
Parent company of People's Gas.

Employers Index

General Index   Boldface indicates employer listings